SOUTHEAST ASIAN AFFAIRS 2009

The **Institute of Southeast Asian Studies (ISEAS)** was established as an autonomous organization in 1968. It is a regional centre dedicated to the study of socio-political, security and economic trends and developments in Southeast Asia and its wider geostrategic and economic environment. The Institute's research programmes are the Regional Economic Studies (RES, including ASEAN and APEC), Regional Strategic and Political Studies (RSPS), and Regional Social and Cultural Studies (RSCS).

ISEAS Publications, an established academic press, has issued almost 2,000 books and journals. It is the largest scholarly publisher of research about Southeast Asia from within the region. ISEAS Publications works with many other academic and trade publishers and distributors to disseminate important research and analyses from and about Southeast Asia to the rest of the world.

SOUTHEAST ASIAN AFFAIRS 2009

Edited by
Daljit Singh

LSEAS
INSTITUTE OF SOUTHEAST ASIAN STUDIES
Singapore

First published in Singapore in 2009 by
ISEAS Publications
Institute of Southeast Asian Studies
30 Heng Mui Keng Terrace
Pasir Panjang
Singapore 119614
E-mail: publish@iseas.edu.sg
Website: http://bookshop.iseas.edu.sg

The responsibility for facts and opinions in this publication rests exclusively with the authors and their interpretations do not necessarily reflect the views or the policy of the publisher or its supporters.

ISEAS Library Cataloguing-in-Publication Data

Southeast Asian affairs.
1974–
Annual
1. Southeast Asia — Periodicals.
I. Institute of Southeast Asian Studies.
DS501 S72A

ISSN 0377-5437
ISBN 978-981-230-946-4 (soft cover)
ISBN 978-981-230-948-8 (hard cover)
ISBN 978-981-230-947-1 (PDF)

Typeset by International Typesetters Pte Ltd
Printed in Singapore by Utopia Press Pte Ltd

Contents

Foreword   vii
K. Kesavapany

Introduction   ix
Daljit Singh

THE REGION
Southeast Asia in 2008: Challenges Within and Without   3
Catharin Dalpino

ASEAN Economies: Challenges and Responses Amid the Crisis   17
Aladdin D. Rillo

Managing Armed Conflict in Southeast Asia: The Role of Mediation   28
Michael Vatikiotis

Maritime Security in Southeast Asia: Two Cheers for Regional Cooperation   36
Ian Storey

BRUNEI DARUSSALAM
Brunei Darussalam: Cautious on Political Reform, Comfortable in ASEAN,   61
Pushing for Economic Diversification
Christopher Roberts and Lee Poh Onn

CAMBODIA
Cambodia: The Cambodian People's Party Consolidates Power   85
Carlyle A. Thayer

INDONESIA
Indonesia in 2008: Democratic Consolidation in Soeharto's Shadow   105
Marcus Mietzner

Legacies of History, Present Challenges, and the Future   124
Jusuf Wanandi

LAOS
Laos: The Chinese Connection   141
Martin Stuart-Fox

MALAYSIA

Malaysia: Political Transformation and Intrigue in an Election Year   173
Johan Saravanamuttu

MYANMAR

Myanmar in 2008: Weathering the Storm   195
Tin Maung Maung Than

The War on Drugs   223
Paul Sarno

THE PHILIPPINES

Philippines in 2008: A Decoupling of Economics and Politics?   245
Melanie S. Milo

Philippine Economic Development: A Turning Point?   267
Kelly Bird and Hal Hill

SINGAPORE

Singapore in 2008: Negotiating Domestic Issues, Confrontations and Global   289
Challenges
Terence Chong

The Singapore of My Dreams   305
Tommy Koh

THAILAND

Thailand in 2008: Democracy and Street Politics   315
James Ockey

Thailand's Crisis Overload   334
Peter Warr

TIMOR LESTE

East Timor in 2008: Year of Reconstruction   357
Damien Kingsbury

VIETNAM

Vietnam in 2008: Foreign Policy Successes but Daunting Domestic Problems   373
Joern Dosch

Vietnam's Economic Crisis: Policy Follies and the Role of State-Owned   389
Conglomerates
Vu Quang Viet

Foreword

The year 2008 will be remembered for the tragedy of Cyclone Nargis, which devastated the Ayeyarwady delta region of Myanmar, resulting in the loss of more than 140,000 lives. More broadly, it will also be remembered for the onset of the global financial crisis which clouded the performance of Southeast Asian economies and led to a downturn in the later part of the year. Growth rates were starting to plummet, especially in the more export-dependent economies, accompanied by the spectre of rising unemployment into 2009.

Politics in both Malaysia and Thailand were more tumultuous. In Malaysia, pressures for change led the ruling UMNO-dominated coalition to lose its two-thirds majority in Parliament in the general election in March 2008, ushering in a period of uncertainty and forcing incumbent Prime Minister Abdullah Badawi to agree to step down in March 2009 in favour of his deputy, Najib Razak. Thailand was increasingly polarized between anti- and pro-Thaksin political forces. The former seemed to triumph when, through unprecedented street protests and siege of government buildings and airports, they succeeded in forcing two governments, perceived as pro-Thaksin, to resign. Defections by parliamentarians from the ruling party then enabled the Democrat Party to form the government. However, the risk remained that the same destabilizing tactics might be used against the new government by pro-Thaksin forces.

Elsewhere in Southeast Asia, there was more political continuity than change. In Myanmar, Nargis resulted in greater interaction between the international community and the ruling junta but there was no deviation from the regime's plans to have a new constitutional order dominated by the military, as it successfully conducted a referendum on its draft constitution to achieve this end. Indonesia, the largest country in the region, impressed through its stability and progress, though the clouds of the global economic downturn raised questions about how it would weather the crisis.

Meanwhile, the Association of Southeast Asian Nations (ASEAN) continued its evolution towards a more rules-based organization with the coming into effect of the ASEAN Charter, which provides a legal identity to the grouping and establishes normative and institutional goals for its development.

Southeast Asian Affairs 2009, like the previous 35 editions of this flagship publication of ISEAS, provides an informed and readable analysis of developments in the region. I am confident that it will continue to be of interest to scholars, policy-makers, diplomats, students and the media. I wish to thank the editor and the contributors for the work they have put in to bring out this volume.

K. Kesavapany
Director
Institute of Southeast Asian Studies

April 2009

Introduction

It is not possible to pull together into this introductory essay the many rich themes and insights contained in this volume. Instead I have selected eight points which, in my view, deserve the reader's attention when looking at Southeast Asia in the year 2008.

A Region Mostly At Peace

First, Southeast Asia enjoyed a relatively peaceful year. While it is true that Thailand and Cambodia fired at each other in anger, the fighting was quickly ended. As Michael Vatikiotis says in his chapter in this volume, "the instinctive avoidance of conflict which is rooted deep in the region's cultural DNA" helped to defuse a potential crisis. Southeast Asia has also been fortunate that relations between the major powers in its broader Asian and Pacific environment, especially U.S.-China relations, have remained generally stable, which is crucial for the region's peace and tranquility. Further, several internal conflicts within Southeast Asian states have been settled or mitigated in recent years, mostly within Indonesia. Al Qaeda-linked terrorism has continued to suffer setbacks (see below).

The principal blots on this generally peaceful scene have been the conflicts in the southern Philippines and southern Thailand. The unfortunate breakdown of the Malaysian-brokered peace negotiations between the Philippines government and the Moro Islamic Liberation Front (MILF), the main armed Muslim group confronting the government in the south of the country, was a significant setback, while the insurgency in the southern provinces of Thailand continued to rage as before with no prospect of an early end.

Given the virtual absence of interstate conflict and relative freedom from big power tensions and conflicts, at this moment in history, the security threats to Southeast Asia are largely of the 'non-traditional' type — like violence or tensions associated with ethnic, religious or separatist conflict; terrorism; illegal migrations; and pandemic diseases.

ASEAN's Progress

Second, ASEAN's institutional evolution advanced a few more steps. The ASEAN Charter came into force on 15 December, giving a legal identity to the organization and setting institutional and normative benchmarks towards which it must move if it is to achieve its goal of becoming a more cohesive rules-based organization that also respects human rights and democratic values. Member countries now have Permanent Representatives to ASEAN based in Jakarta, while some ASEAN Dialogue Partners have Ambassadors accredited to ASEAN. A high-level task force has been appointed to recommend the responsibilities and powers of the human rights body provided for in the Charter. During the year, past agreements on trade in goods and services were consolidated into one agreement, while the two investment–related agreements were likewise consolidated into one. A free trade agreement was signed with Australia and New Zealand, but one with India unexpectedly did not materialize because of technical and legal problems. There was also progress in moving the Chiangmai Initiative, under the ASEAN Plus Three framework, beyond a network of bilateral swops towards in effect a central pool of funds which a country in crisis could draw from.

However, the challenges facing the Association as it seeks to move towards its proclaimed goals were also significant, as Catharin Dalpino points out in the first chapter of this volume. Basically, they revolve around implementation, given ASEAN's tendency to agree on principles and goals first and leave the practical steps of implementation to be worked out later. For instance, how will ASEAN implement the norms adopted in the Charter about the internal behaviour of states in relation to matters like good governance and respect for human rights? Likewise, while it is laudable to set the goal of achieving economic integration by 2015, how will ASEAN take the practical steps to achieve this?

Still, whatever its challenges and shortcomings, ASEAN continues to provide Southeast Asia with a certain common identity and an invaluable cooperative framework. Without it, the region would be more fragmented, and pulling in different directions. ASEAN also remains the anchor of wider Asian regional cooperation involving the major powers through which ASEAN seeks to nurture friendly and cooperative relations between the major powers, between them and ASEAN, and an equilibrium in their influence in the region.

ASEAN is not Southeast Asia

Third, it is worth bearing in mind that ASEAN, the regional organization, with ten countries as members, is not the same as Southeast Asia the geographical region, which now, with Timor Leste, embraces eleven countries (a fact that *Southeast Asian Affairs* has recognized since 2003 by including an annual review of the region's newest sovereign state in this series). More happens in geographical Southeast Asia with perhaps greater consequence for the region than it does in ASEAN. The eleven countries have different systems of government, ranging from authoritarian and non-democratic to new democracies. With a long history of pre-colonial kingdoms under absolute rulers and then authoritarian Western colonial rule , political systems in the region remain works in progress that will evolve only slowly in response to internal political and cultural dynamics, though the overall trend in most countries is towards greater openness and better governance.

The foreign policies of the eleven countries are naturally driven primarily by their own national interests and motivations. They can either facilitate ASEAN's desire to better integrate the region or they can hinder, even undermine it. This could be particularly relevant in the sphere of alignments with external powers. This volume does not have a chapter on major power interactions with Southeast Asian states. However, developments in recent years suggest increased competition among them for influence, including a more assertive Chinese posture. In this volume, the expansion of Chinese presence in Laos is dealt with in Martin Stuart-Fox's chapter on Laos, entitled "The Chinese Connection" while Carl Thayer in his chapter on Cambodia also notes the rise of Chinese influence in Cambodia.

Successes Against Al Qaeda-linked Terrorism

Fourth, Southeast Asia has had significant successes in the fight against Al Qaeda-linked jihadi terrorism. This achievement tends to get overlooked in the international media. The networks of the main terrorist organization in Southeast Asia, the Jemaah Islamiyah (JI), have been virtually destroyed in Singapore and Malaysia. JI and related jihadi groups still have their network in Indonesia, their main base, but they are much weaker than they were in 2002 at the time of the first Bali bombing. Meanwhile the Philippines security forces, assisted by the U.S., have contained the threat from the terrorist-cum-bandit Abu Sayyaf Group (ASG).

A number of factors account for these successes. All Southeast Asian countries affected by terrorism have the will and the resolve to fight it. Their security services have, on the whole, been effective. In view of the importance of Indonesia in the fight against the JI, it is noteworthy that the Indonesian national police have made big strides in effectiveness and professionalism in its counter-terrorism work in recent years. The intelligence services of these countries have cooperated well with one another and with the services of friendly outside powers in the fight against terrorism. The cooperation with the latter has gone beyond mere exchange of information: for example, the Australian Federal Police has worked closely with the Indonesian national police in investigations into terrorist attacks, while in the Philippines, U.S. forces have worked on the ground with the Philippines armed forces to provide technical intelligence and operational advice in the fight against the ASG. Such assistance, together with capacity building, has made a difference — without leaving a large Western footprint.

Politics: Turbulence in Malaysia and Thailand, Continuity Elsewhere

Fifth, the year 2008 will be remembered for the political tumult and drama in Malaysia and Thailand which could be symptomatic of deeper processes of political change, though it was not clear what the denouement would be. The developments in Malaysia are covered by Johan Saravanamuttu, while James Ockey and Peter Warr in their respective chapters provide analyse of Thai politics and economy. Elsewhere in the region, there was generally more political continuity than change.

In Malaysia, the UMNO-dominated ruling coalition's biggest ever election setback saw it lose its two-thirds majority in Parliament. The political pressures generated by the election blow forced Prime Minister Abdullah Badawi to agree to step down in March 2009 in favour of his deputy Najib Razak. While some may find comfort in the apparent emergence of a de facto two-party political system in the aftermath of the elections, with the opposition coalition under former Deputy Prime Minister Anwar Ibrahim commanding a significant presence in Parliament and running four state governments, to many Malaysians the future was marked with uncertainty, even unease, given the racial undertones of Malaysian politics As Saravanamuttu puts it: "Both the leaders of the government and the opposition will have unpredictable political trajectories in 2009 and beyond. Who will navigate through the political minefields and emerge as victor? As Malaysians edged gingerly into 2009, a still fluid and uncertain political scenario awaits them." However, he is optimistic on one score: one thing that has changed for good in Malaysia, in his view, is the emergence of "new politics" in which "a political society resists the worst attempts by extremist elements to tilt the political balance in the direction of violence" by playing the racial card, which some in UMNO were still doing.

In Thailand, the protracted struggle between anti-Thaksin and pro-Thaksin forces continued to polarize Thai politics and society. Two governments, perceived as pro-Thaksin, were forced to resign through unprecedented street protests and siege of government buildings and airports (with some additional help from activist courts). The danger was that the same tactics may be used by supporters of pro-Thaksin forces against the Abhisit government which was formed around the minority Democrat Party at the end of the year. No democrat himself, Thaksin Shinawatra, during his six years as Prime Minster, had used the one-man-one-vote system and populist policies to mobilize the rural masses of north and northeast Thailand behind him, in the process threatening the interests of the traditional ruling elite comprising the civil service, the military and the aristocracy, products mostly of the educated Bangkok middle class. The traditional elite used a military coup in 2006 to remove Thaksin from power and convicted him on corruption charges but failed to exorcise his perceived malign influence from the Thai body politic, since even with Thaksin in exile, his supporters returned to power again through new elections in December 2007 and, according to most observers of the Thai scene, could do so again in a future election. Hence a desire among the traditional elite for a more restrictive form of democracy which can prevent Thaksin or his supporters from making a comeback through the ballot box. But such a course, if taken, will carry its own risks, as the genie of the politically aroused rural masses who see Thaksin as their hero will be difficult to put back into the bottle. As Peter Warr puts it in his chapter: "Thailand is groping, sometimes stumbling, towards a form of democracy that suits its own circumstances. The underlying conflict is deep and will not be resolved easily."

Myanmar: Movement Without Change?

Sixth, the special case of Myanmar deserves attention. There was some political movement, if not change, in the country, though the year may be remembered less for this than for Cyclone Nargis, which devastated the Ayeyarwady delta region. Unlike the Aceh tsunami of December 2004 which facilitated a breakthrough in resolving the long running conflict between the Free Aceh Movement (GAM) and the Indonesian government, Cyclone Nargis, coming less than a year after the violent suppression of the uprising of the Buddhist clergy in 2007, caused no change in the two-decade long political deadlock between the National League for Democracy led by Aung San Suu Kyi and the ruling junta. However it did result in at least better interactions between the Myanmar regime and the international community on disaster relief, with the junta eventually accepting an international assistance effort under the aegis of ASEAN and the United Nations and even allowing foreign military planes to deliver relief supplies to Yangon. Further, as Tin Maung Maung Than opines in his chapter, the disaster "seemed to have opened some space for the nascent civil society" that came to the fore during the relief and rehabilitation effort, but, as the International Crisis Group has argued, the opportunity provided by this small opening to engage positively with the military regime was not followed up by the West.

On domestic political evolution, the regime, as expected, marched to its own familiar tune. The draft constitution was at last completed and also put to a referendum in which it obtained overwhelming approval. While allowing for multiparty elections, the constitution ensures continued military control of the government. This was of course long expected, including by opposition groups, and Western governments and NGOs who protested loudly. Still, it was a step forward, however small, towards a new constitutional order.

There were also some signs of possible review of Myanmar policy in certain quarters in the West. The existing policy, driven by ideology, Myanmar opposition circles, and special interest groups in the West, has not worked in bringing change to the country. The issue is not whether the Myanmar regime is undemocratic and oppressive. It certainly is, though arguably less so than the North Korean regime which the U.S. government has been engaging for years in the six-party talks. The issue is how to bring change in Myanmar. A more pragmatic policy based on engagement would be better placed to help Myanmar gradually move towards more openness and better governance. ASEAN alone cannot achieve this if the junta constantly feels a sense of threat from the West, and especially the U.S. It is perhaps also time for the U.S. to appreciate the strategic importance of Myanmar and of its stability to America's friends and allies in Southeast Asia.

Indonesia

Seventh, the largest country of Southeast Asia, Indonesia, has been making quiet progress in recent years which cumulatively has been quite remarkable at least in terms of self-confidence and perceptions among outsiders. Ten years ago, at the time of the Asian financial crisis, Indonesia's economy had virtually collapsed.

There was communal and separatist violence, and terrorism was on the upsurge. Many believed the country would break up. Today, as Marcus Mietzner says in his review of the country, it is largely peaceful and stable with a remarkable absence of large-scale political and communal violence and with its unity taken for granted. No major terrorist attack has taken place during the past few years. Democratic consolidation has continued. The Indonesian military has gone back "to the barracks" after a high profile role for decades in the politics and governance of the country, apparently with scarcely any ripples in the body politic. Compared to the Soeharto years, ethnic minorities like the Indonesian Chinese feel that they are more accepted as equals. Notwithstanding a minority of vocal extremist Muslim groups, most important Muslim organisations and political parties are willing to accept Pancasila as the state ideology.

No doubt many challenges remain. As Jusuf Wanandi explains in his chapter, history has severely handicapped Indonesia. So, despite the progress over the past decade, the country starts off from a low base. The critical challenges for some time will be better economic performance; fighting corruption; building sound institutions, including the proper rule of law and more effective central and regional governments; higher standards of education; and better infrastructure. Even before the current global crisis the economy had not attained the 7 per cent growth last seen in the Soeharto years, a rate of growth necessary to absorb the two million plus new entrants to the labour force each year. Indonesia will be tested by the global economic crisis and the fight against poverty and unemployment could suffer serious setbacks.

The Impact of the Global Economic Crisis

The eighth and last point I want to bring up may potentially turn out to be the most consequential. The year 2008 will be remembered for the onset of the global financial and economic crisis. The economies of Southeast Asia, especially those that are more export-dependent, showed a rapid decline towards the end of the year as the global downturn began to bite in earnest. The prognosis for 2009 was either outright negative growth, as in the case of Singapore, or significantly lower growth even in the larger economies that are less export-reliant. It was not clear at the end of 2008 how long the global recession would last. With lower growth comes the spectre of higher unemployment and, given the absence of significant social safety nets, social stresses and possible upheavals. The global crisis could also have geopolitical implications affecting the posture of the major powers to Southeast Asia. Could the challenge of the crisis also drive ASEAN to greater cohesiveness, as has happened before in the organization's history? That too was left to be seen.

* * *

Apart from the eleven country reviews, this volume of *Southeast Asian Affairs* has four regional chapters and six country-specific thematic chapters. The regional chapters include the annual political and economic overviews of Southeast Asia by Catharin Dalpino and Aladdin Rillo respectively; an essay by Michael Vatikiotis on the role of mediation in managing armed conflict in Southeast Asia; and an examination by Ian Storey of the role of regional cooperation, assisted by capacity building assistance from outside powers, especially the United States, in helping to improve maritime security in Southeast Asia.

The six country-specific thematic chapters cover a range of subjects. Jusuf Wanandi examines how the legacies of former presidents Sukarno and Soeharto have shaped present-day Indonesia, the trends and achievements in the country since Soeharto's fall, and what more needs doing. In "The Singapore of My Dreams" Tommy Koh gives his personal perspective on the many things that he had wished for Singapore which have come true and some which have not, in the process highlighting the achievements of Singapore and also some of its warts. The other chapters include a survey of the efforts of the Myanmar regime to eradicate the drug menace in the country, with a suggestion by the author, Paul Sarno, for a change in the U.S. government's narcotics policy to Myanmar in response to the Yangon government's performance; an analysis by Kelly Bird and Hal Hill of how the implementation of certain reforms has contributed importantly to the better performance of the Philippine economy in recent years; and an assessment by Peter Warr of the effects of the twin crises — the domestic political one and the global economic crisis — on Thailand's economy. Finally, in the last chapter of the volume, Vu Quang Viet dwells on the policy follies that contributed to Vietnam's economic crisis in the first half of 2008 when inflation sky-rocketed, the stock market crashed and the country was threatened with an imminent balance of payments crisis. In the process the author also provides valuable insights into the workings of Vietnam's state-owned enterprises.

I would like to thank all the contributors for making this volume possible. *Southeast Asian Affairs* seeks to accommodate a variety of views and opinions, both Southeast Asian and others, for which the contributors alone are responsible.

I thank my colleagues Tin Maung Maung Than, Rod Severino, Asad Latif and Melanie Milo for graciously allowing me to consult them on specific matters relating to the preparation of this volume. Tin also assisted by editing the chapter on the War on Drugs in Myanmar. Special thanks must go to Pushpa Thambipillai of the University of Brunei Darussalam, an old friend of ISEAS, for her invaluable advice and comment relating to the Brunei chapter; to Christopher Roberts and Lee Poh Onn who agreed to do the Brunei chapter on very short notice, and Professor Carlyle Thayer of the Australian Defence Academy for approaching Christopher Roberts in my hour of need. I also thank Ms Sheryl Sin for her copyediting and patience in accommodating the many amendments and Ms Betty Kwan who, while serving as secretary to several other projects, did a splendid job as secretary to the *Southeast Asian Affairs 2009* project.

Daljit Singh
Editor
Southeast Asian Affairs 2009

The Region

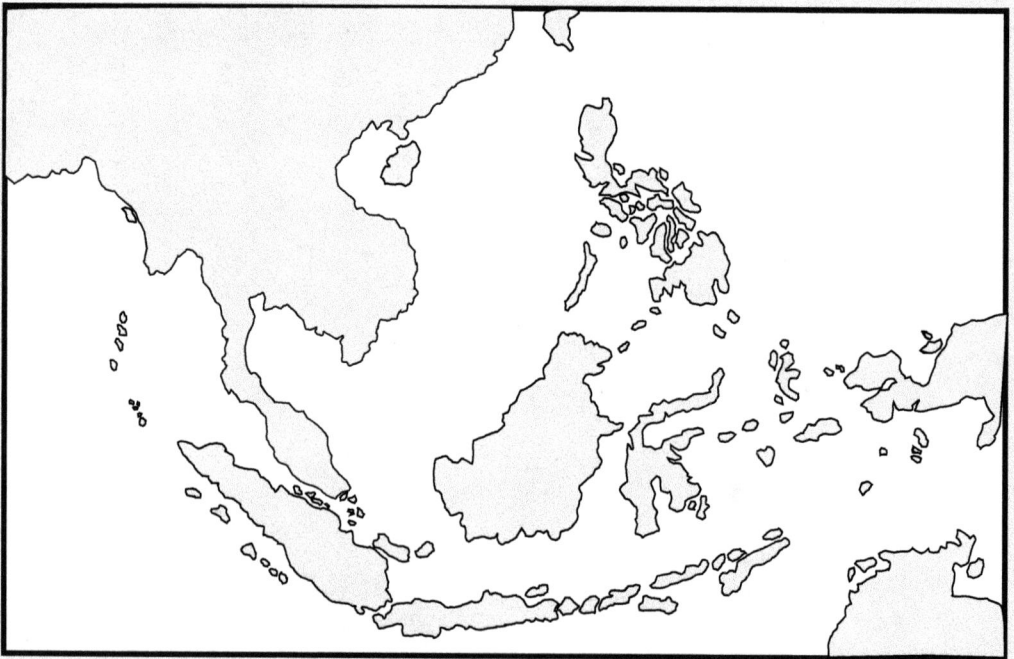

SOUTHEAST ASIA IN 2008
Challenges Within and Without

Catharin Dalpino

In 2008 ASEAN intensified its longstanding search for identity. In the final quarter of the year the Association was transformed from a consultative group into a legal entity when the Philippines, Indonesia and Thailand became the last member states to ratify the ASEAN Charter.[1] However, the translation of the group's new status into policies remains an open question. ASEAN continues to be the bedrock of Asian regional architecture, but signs are emerging that the Northeast Asia members of the ASEAN+3 may not need Southeast Asian training wheels much longer. At the same time, ASEAN was pulled closer into Northeast Asian conundrums — and potential conflicts — with new overtures from North Korea and Taiwan.

However, more tangible challenges to Southeast Asian unity in 2008 came from developments within and between the member states themselves. The protracted multi-party process to forge a peace agreement between the Moro Islamic Liberation Front (MILF) and the Philippine government failed, assuring continued instability in Mindanao and calling into question the efficacy of ad hoc regional diplomacy. A dispute over an historic border temple sparked a brief military clash between Thailand and Cambodia, with each side accusing the other of provoking conflict for domestic political gain. At the end of the year international attention was drawn to Thailand's complicated political crisis when anti-government protestors seized the international airport in Bangkok, disrupting regional air routes and forcing Bangkok to postpone the annual ASEAN Summit.

But arguably the greatest challenge to ASEAN coherence posed by a member state in 2008 was the response — or lack of — by the government of Myanmar to Cyclone Nargis and to offers of humanitarian relief from the international

CATHARIN DALPINO is Visiting Associate Professor of Southeast Asian Studies at the Edmund A. Walsh School of Foreign Service at Georgetown University.

community. Less than a year after the government's crackdown of the "Saffron Revolution", the disaster became a diagnostic for Myanmar's regional relations. ASEAN emerged as the interlocutor of choice, but the limits of the Association's influence on its isolated and isolationist member were obvious.

ASEAN Charter: Back-and-Fill Institutional Development?

The birth of ASEAN as a legal entity was marked at a special meeting of the Association's Foreign Ministers in Jakarta on 15 December 2008.[2] The ASEAN Charter was signed the year before in a game of brinksmanship with a handful of member governments that believed the Charter lacked sufficient mechanisms to handle the difficulties presented by Myanmar's membership in the Association.[3] Although doubts on this score continued into 2008 and made for a ragged ratification schedule, there was little sign of that drama at the Jakarta meeting.

The Charter institutionalizes the ASEAN meeting process by moving from a schedule of meetings to a structure of ministerial-level permanent councils, one for each of the three areas of ASEAN community building: economic; political-security, and sociocultural. The Charter also enables ASEAN members to post permanent representatives to the Association, and allows ASEAN's external partners to do the same. The first such country to do so in 2008 was the United States, with several countries following in rapid fashion. Some external partners have based the ASEAN Ambassador position in their own capitals, while others have representatives in Jakarta. The Charter also provides for measures to strengthen the ASEAN Secretariat.

To date, the most developed of the ASEAN communities is the economic one. The Charter stipulates that the original six ASEAN members — Thailand, Indonesia, the Philippines, Malaysia, Singapore and Brunei — will reduce tariffs on intra-regional trade by 2010, while the four newer members — Vietnam, Laos, Cambodia and Myanmar — will complete that process by 2015. Some analysts attribute the momentum toward economic integration to a desire on ASEAN's part to present a solid bloc in negotiations with China.[4] Others trace the origins of the ASEAN Economic Community to the early 1990s, and view it as a defense against the perceived division of the international market into trade blocs, with the rise of the European Union and the establishment of the North American Free Trade Agreement.

Although the reorganization of ASEAN under the Charter provides for more permanent structures, it is not clear if it provides a sufficient foundation to make ASEAN truly a rules-based entity. This issue is likely to surface increasingly as

ASEAN moves closer to the 2010 and 2015 target dates for the ASEAN Economic Community. Liberalization does not prevent trade disputes; on the contrary, it often invites them. Over time, a permanent economic community will require that ASEAN develop a body of trade law and a central authority to hear and settle trade disputes. How far the ASEAN Economic Community can progress without attention to these tasks is a key question.

When the ASEAN Charter was signed, international attention was drawn to the Charter's mission to promote the definition and development of regional norms. In particular, the stated intention to create a human rights body was regarded with interest in the United States and Europe. The precise form and function of this body remains undefined but the ASEAN process of consensus, which gives weight to the least common denominator, is likely to ensure that the body will remain consultative at best. This has disappointed some Western policy-makers, who had hoped the new human rights mechanism would include provisions to sanction members that violate regional norms — clearly they had Myanmar in mind. Some Southeast Asian analysts view this as putting the cart before the horse, and point out that ASEAN must first define regional norms before it can develop mechanisms to safeguard them.

However, the member states continue to disagree on the way forward to develop the human rights body, and some Southeast Asian analysts fear that the ASEAN principle of non-interference ensures that it will lack traction. In November Djoko Susilo, Indonesian Member of Parliament and Chair of the Parliament's Myanmar Caucus, complained that "The human rights mechanism in the Charter … gives a warm blanket to the (Myanmar) military junta."[5] Critics of the Charter, both within and outside Southeast Asia, are often reminded that the Charter contains a provision for amendment after the first five years, and that it should be considered a work in progress.

ASEAN's Extra-Regional Stretch

Despite perennial grumbling from some Western diplomats that ASEAN is primarily a "talk shop", over the past two decades the Association has demonstrated that it is valued-added in building Asian regional institutions. ASEAN is the convening agent for the region's most active security dialogue — the ASEAN Regional Forum (ARF) — and underpins major new groupings such as the ASEAN+3. ASEAN's role as a regional fulcrum may be due not only to its own institutional structure but also to its promulgation of the "ASEAN Way" in the broader Asia-Pacific region. The traditional ASEAN principles of decision by consensus and non-interference in the domestic affairs of member states have enabled disparate actors in the region to come together in consultative groups such as the East Asia Summit.

The non-interference principle has come under fire within ASEAN in the past decade. The Association has occasionally, if tacitly, set that rule aside to pursue a policy of ad hoc "flexible engagement", such as in 1998 when ASEAN was instrumental in persuading Indonesia to accept international peacekeeping assistance in East Timor. There is little possibility that ASEAN will officially abandon these two founding tenets — a draft of the Charter that sought to remove them was ultimately rejected — but they will be quietly modified as ASEAN develops further as a legal entity. Ironically, the "ASEAN Way" may be kept alive in the broader Asia-Pacific region long after it has lost its luster in ASEAN itself.

For the time being, however, the entry ticket for new Asia-Pacific regional organizations remains accession to the ASEAN Treaty of Amity and Cooperation. The creation of the East Asia Summit, which required all members to be signatories to the TAC, sparked a flurry of activity from ASEAN's external partners in that regard. To date fifteen countries have signed the TAC: China, Japan, Republic of Korea, Russia, France, Australia, India, Pakistan, East Timor, Papua New Guinea, New Zealand, Mongolia, Bangladesh, Sri Lanka and, in July 2008, the Democratic People's Republic of Korea (North Korea).[6] In September the European Union indicated that it intended to sign the TAC in July 2009 at the ASEAN-EU Ministerial Meeting in Phnom Penh. The EU will thus become the first group of nations to sign the TAC, and intends to use that as the foundation for negotiation of an ASEAN-EU Free Trade Agreement.[7]

Among ASEAN's external partners, the notable holdout in signing the TAC is the United States. Objections in Washington to taking this action have traditionally been two-fold. First, the U.S. defense sector feared that provisions in the TAC on non-interference and renunciation of the use of force would disadvantage the United States as the sole superpower in the region. Security analysts also believed that ASEAN's policy of promoting a nuclear free zone, which is not an explicit feature of the TAC but nevertheless figures into the ASEAN profile, would hamper the ability to deploy nuclear weapons on U.S. aircraft and ships in the region.[8] A second and more general constraint was the belief that if the executive branch signed the TAC, the U.S. Senate would not ratify it. Some believe the latter reservation is based in the TAC's broad language that suggested a non-aggression pact, while others perceive a more pointed objection to a treaty that includes Burma as a party. Both of these sets of objections are believed to have dissipated in recent months. Although the administration has not made a decision with regard to signing the TAC, the perception in the Washington policy community is that doing so would be less controversial now than in the past.

Drawing all of the Asia-Pacific powers into the regional tent may bode well for the long term, but there are potential short-term downsides. Asian policy-makers have expressed informal reservations about admitting both Russia and the United States into the East Asia Summit, should the U.S. sign the TAC and seek entry into the EAS. They fear that the two countries could import their recent bilateral flare-ups into the EAS; for the time being, they are holding both at bay with respect to EAS entry.

North Korea's accession to the TAC points out both the advantages and disadvantages of the big tent approach. The DPRK has been a member of the ASEAN Regional Forum since 2000. In recent years, Asian policy-makers have expressed quiet hopes that engagement with North Korea could reinforce attempts by the Six Party Process and other diplomatic initiatives to persuade Pyongyang to abandon its nuclear programme. Others, particularly some analysts in the United States, are doubtful that North Korea's accession to the TAC and its possible entry into the EAS as a result will have an appreciable impact. However, the value of additional dialogue channels with Pyongyang over the long-run is self-evident.

In the coming year ASEAN could face a more delicate issue as Taiwan proclaimed its desire to join the ASEAN Regional Forum. When President Ma Ying-jeou was inaugurated in May, he announced a new turn in Taipei's external relations, which he described as seeking a "diplomatic truce" with Beijing.[9] Under this new policy, Taiwan would abandon its quest for diplomatic recognition in the international community and expand its participation in trade, cultural and regional organizations. Taiwan is a member of the World Trade Organization and APEC in its capacity as an "economy" rather than a state, and has long sought to be given observer status at the World Health Assembly, the decision-making body of the World Health Organization, a move that Beijing has heretofore blocked. Taipei's entry into ARF may be interpreted as trying to cross political red lines. Taiwan figures prominently in Southeast Asia's investment sector, but ASEAN will need to tread lightly to avoid being caught between Beijing and Taipei on this issue.

As ASEAN's role in the Asia-Pacific region changes, it will appear at times to contract and at others to expand. On 13 December the leaders of China, Japan and South Korea met in Fukuoka, Japan for the first-ever trilateral summit of the three countries. The trio had met eight times as a tripartite group on the margins of ASEAN+3 meetings, but the December meeting marked its first solo flight.[10] The event was a quiet triumph for the three Northeast Asian countries but also for ASEAN, which had provided the basis for informal diplomatic dialogue among the three powers for a decade.

In 2008 ASEAN, collectively and through bilateral relations, deepened its engagement with key rising powers in the reason. The year held a number of first-ever developments with China. Beijing was active on the defense front early in the year: in January it signed a defense exchange and security cooperation pact with Singapore, formalizing the basket of visits, courses and port calls that had been developed in recent years. Soon after China signed an agreement with Indonesia to work together on military training and military vehicle production.[11] In September Singapore and China concluded a free trade agreement, the first such bilateral FTA between China and an ASEAN nation.[12]

But the year was also marked by heightened tensions between China and an ASEAN member state, Vietnam, over oil exploration and other issues in the South China Sea. Although Chinese-Vietnamese relations in this area have been on the edge since competition for the Spratly Islands intensified in the 1990s, tensions were ratcheted up when China warned ExxonMobil against working with PetroVietnam, the Vietnamese state oil firm, to explore areas in the South China Sea off the south and central coasts of Vietnam.[13] In the ensuing media war, Beijing issued statements claiming sovereignty over the South China Sea, in which it managed to reiterate its threats against ExxonMobil.[14] The deteriorating situation was enough to persuade officials in Beijing and Hanoi to introduce a hotline for communication between state leaders. Some analysts attributed the clash simply to rising energy prices but to Vietnamese officials, Beijing's actions were part of a larger piece.

The hotline presumably saw use in September when a Chinese website published "invasion plans" for a Chinese military conquest of Vietnam. The unsourced material described five days of missile strikes from land, sea and air; a blockade of Hanoi; and a 300,000 troop force that would sweep into Vietnam from three points: Yunnan Province, Guangxi Province and the South China Sea.[15] In response to Hanoi's predictable protests, the Chinese government disavowed the website. Perhaps to draw attention away from maritime friction, China and Vietnam settled a land border dispute on the last day of the year. The land issue derived from the 1979 China-Vietnam border war and resolving it had both political and symbolic importance, but Vietnam continues to cast a wary eye on the South China Sea and its northern neighbour.

Conflict Restarts in Mindanao, Flares Up on the Thai-Cambodian Border

2008 saw the unhappy end — for the time being — of a longstanding attempt to forge a peace agreement between the Moro Islamic Liberation Front (MILF) and the government of the Philippines. The talks foundered in August when the draft Memorandum of Agreement on Ancestral Domain was blocked by the Philippines Supreme Court, which eventually killed it altogether.[16] The return of some ancestral lands lost by Mindanao's Muslims in the transmigration of Christians into the southern province after Philippine independence was an economic and political issue, as well as a potent symbol. The Court ruled that granting territory to the MILF under the agreement could be in violation of Philippine sovereignty, although land had been granted to form an Autonomous Region of Muslim Mindanao under a previous agreement with the Moro National Liberation Front (MNLF), a predecessor of the MILF. Some analysts attribute the agreement's collapse to a failure on Manila's part to consult adequately with Christian groups before agreeing to cede land to Philippine Muslims. After it was clear that the agreement had failed, both sides moved rapidly to hardline positions. Splinter MILF groups resumed attacks on the Armed Forces of the Philippines (AFP) as well as civilians, while Manila demanded that the MILF disarm and demobilize before peace negotiations could resume. The possibility of restarting the talks in the near term appears remote.

The negotiation process had endured for nearly five years and was a regional as well as an internal effort. Malaysia had served as the mediator, in a role it has cultivated over several years as a sponsor of negotiations to resolve issues between Muslim and non-Muslim groups in the region. (Libya had played a similar role in Manila's negotiations with the MNLF two decades prior.) Beyond its negotiating services, the Malaysian government had also encouraged Malaysian businesses to invest in Mindanao. Kuala Lumpur's chagrin over the collapse of the process was palpable, not least because the Memorandum on the Ancestral Domains was scheduled to be signed in Kuala Lumpur just before the Supreme Court intervened.[17]

So does the failure of the Manila-MILF process affect one of the Philippines' most important external bilateral relations, with the United States? The joint U.S.-Philippine Balikatan exercises were designed in part to enable U.S. forces to train their Philippine counterparts in counter-insurgency. The United States has a particular interest in checking the violent fundamentalist Abu Sayyaf Group, but a key element to stabilizing Mindanao was a successful agreement with the

MILF. For several years the U.S. Congress had earmarked several million dollars for assistance to reintegrate MILF insurgents into Mindanao society with training and other support for demobilization. With violence in Mindanao now more likely in the short term, Washington and Manila are under new pressure to assess their cooperation and the nature of the bilateral military-to-military relationship.

But if conflict returned to Mindanao after a wearying effort to end it, it made a surprise appearance on the Thai-Cambodian border in 2008. In June Thailand and Cambodia renewed their dispute over the historic Preah Vihear temple, one of the landmarks of the ancient Khmer Empire. The temple sits atop a mountain in northern Cambodia close to the border with Thailand, but the primary access roads to it lie in Thai territory, a fact that is not insignificant at a time when tourism revenue is important to both Cambodia and Thailand. The territorial arrangement originated in an attempt in 1904 between Thailand (then Siam) and French colonial authorities in Cambodia, the results of which were ambiguous enough to restart the conflict at regular intervals in the century that followed. In 1962 the International Court of Justice awarded Preah Vihear to Cambodia, while much of the territory surrounding it remained in Thailand.

The conflict restarted with Cambodia's application to have Preah Vihear declared a UNESCO World Heritage Site. Although Thailand originally had not objected, it began to fear that the designation, which UNESCO duly made, would endanger Thai sovereignty over the access roads and related territory. Such disputes are common on mainland Southeast Asia, where clear and uncontested border demarcations are a rarity. What is more unusual is that the conflict escalated rapidly through summer and into fall. In July Cambodia arrested Thai protestors at the site and in short order a combined 1,000 troops from both countries were positioned on the border. Small arms fire and exchanges with rocket-launched grenades resulted in injuries on both sides and a handful of casualties.[18]

Although the historical dispute was doubtless a major factor in the conflict, analysts also suggested it served a short-term political purpose for both governments. Cambodian Prime Minister Hun Sen's was facing re-election in July, which his party won with a larger-than-expected margin. Polls preceding the election indicated that the border conflict had raised nationalist hackles in Cambodia and placed Hun Sen in a more favourable light. In 2008 Thailand endured a revolving door of governments — three in the space of the year — each of them with a tenuous hold on power. Paradoxically, the conflict was a benefit to both the beleaguered People's Power Party, as it distracted the public momentarily from the large-scale protests in Bangkok, and the anti-PPP (and anti-Thaksin) protesters themselves, since the border hostilities put additional pressure on the government.

The conflict dissipated gradually through bilateral talks and resulted in joint border patrols to help prevent future flare-ups. However, its more lasting impact is likely to be a renewal of debate over ASEAN's role — or lack of — in helping to settle conflicts between member states. Proposals were mooted to have ASEAN mediate the conflict, but the ASEAN chair had passed to Bangkok over the summer, and the Thai government was resolute that the conflict would need to be addressed through bilateral dialogue. Suggestions that the United Nations or the ICJ attempt to mediate were similarly, and firmly, rejected. Hints that Indonesia, as the largest ASEAN state, might play a special role in helping to resolve the conflict proved to be equally unpopular in Bangkok and Phnom Penh.[19] This proposal, which oddly came after the conflict had essentially subsided, was probably aimed more for domestic Indonesian consumption, harking back to the Soeharto era when Indonesia and its legendary Foreign Minister, Ali Alatas, were considered unofficial leaders in ASEAN. The fact that Alatas had died in early December strengthens the likelihood that the suggestion to intervene was probably intended in part to honour him.

But in terms of ASEAN's institutional development, the conflict could not have been more unfortunately timed, just months before ratification of the ASEAN Charter was complete. Another ironic juxtaposition was a decision by the International Court of Justice (ICJ) on disputes between Singapore and Malaysia over three maritime features in the Singapore Straits. In May the ICJ awarded sovereignty of Pedra Branca/Pulau Batu Puteh to Singapore; of Middle Rock to Malaysia; and of the South Ledge to both countries, according to their territorial waters.[20] Although the acceptance of the ICJ decision by both parties was encouraging, the fact that they were forced to turn to an extra-regional body to settle the dispute was taken by some as an inherent criticism of ASEAN. This is a periodic complaint, both within ASEAN and in the international community, when conflicts erupt between or among member states.

ASEAN's defenders in debates over the conflict resolution deficit point out that the Association has been successful at times in mediating conflicts outside its membership. In 1997 the ASEAN Troika helped to settle the violent conflict within the Cambodian ruling coalition, but Cambodia was not at that time a member of ASEAN. Some also insist that ASEAN's consultative nature and its consensus process may have prevented or minimized numerous conflicts among members. However, proving a negative is difficult if not impossible, and attention is inevitably focused on ASEAN's perceived failures in this regard, with accusatory fingers usually pointing to the principle of non-interference. Thus far, angry and even violent flare-ups between members have been short-lived and are often settled between the concerned governments before ASEAN is able to mobilize for even a group discussion. However, as the Association moves more closely toward regional integration there is no assurance that conflicts of this nature can be so easily contained, and debate over ASEAN's ability and responsibility to resolve disputes between member states is only likely to increase in the coming years.

Myanmar and ASEAN Humanitarian Response

The 2004 tsunami in the Indian Ocean was a tragedy of epic proportions but also a model of international cooperation for disaster relief. Moreover, the Indonesian government's decision to open the troubled province of Aceh, which was heavily stricken by the tsunami, to the international relief effort helped to set the stage for a peace process in the province that would fare better than earlier attempts.

With this paradigm in mind, the international community was prepared to come to Myanmar's assistance when Cyclone Nargis hit the Irawaddy Delta on 3 May. Although as many as 1.5 million Burmese were believed to be affected[21], directly or indirectly, the Myanmar government refused access to U.S. and European military in the region that had offered ships, helicopters and landing craft to ferry aid, and then denied entry to international aid workers. Analysts theorized that the junta feared that granting access to the international community — and particularly to Western militaries — was tantamount to inviting an invasion. This impression may have been reinforced when U.S. First Lady Laura Bush called for the regime to step aside on 5 May.

The Myanmar government's reaction caused Washington and some European capitals to consider requesting UN authorization to enter Myanmar without the government's permission to distribute aid, but China made clear it would block any such action in the Security Council. At the May Shangri-la Dialogue of Asia-Pacific Defense Ministers in Singapore, U.S. Secretary of Defense Robert Gates charged the Myanmar government with "criminal neglect" for refusing to permit large-scale international aid in the country, but he allowed that it would be impossible to deliver aid without their cooperation.[22]

Ultimately, the government of Myanmar permitted ASEAN to distribute limited aid on a case-by-case basis, in collaboration with the United Nations. These missions were assisted by military transportation from the United States and other countries, but the ASEAN/UN lead was clearly critical for the government. In recent years the West has tended to focus on China's growing influence with Myanmar and India's new relationship with it and has been inclined to underestimate ASEAN's influence. Although Beijing may still be Myanmar's most important external partner, the Nargis crisis suggests that ASEAN's leverage is greater than the West may have estimated. Several Southeast Asians were outspoken in their criticism of the military regime following the cyclone — in July Institute of Southeast Asian Studies (ISEAS) Director Ambassador K. Kesavapany wrote that its handling of the crisis was "breathtaking in its callousness"[23] but ASEAN will likely retain an edge in relations with Myanmar for the foreseeable future.

One immediate response from ASEAN to the crisis, beyond its actions toward Myanmar, was to strengthen its disaster response capability. In August the ASEAN Committee on Disaster Management conducted a joint humanitarian response simulation, hypothesizing that a major typhoon had struck the industrial and coastal province of Rayong, Thailand. Building on the affected state's national response and working through the ASEAN Coordinating Center for Humanitarian Assistance, the other participating states (Brunei, Cambodia, Malaysia, Philippines and Singapore) mobilized their own fire-fighting and search and rescue teams to supplement the Thai response.[24] Thailand will again be the site of a joint humanitarian exercise in 2009, this time when the ARF conducts its first joint disaster response exercise. This innovation had been suggested by the United States in March, two months before Cyclone Nargis struck Burma, and quickly proved to be all too timely. Increasing piracy around the world in 2008 underscored the need for stronger maritime cooperation, particularly when heavily armed pirates attacked a Thai oil tanker in Malaysian waters in April.[25]

The Coming Economic Crisis

In the last quarter of 2008 Southeast Asia was pulled away from its regional and domestic problems to consider the economic crisis that began in the United States and quickly spread to Europe. The initial impact was muted in Asia, and Asian analysts expressed optimism that China would be able to sustain stable growth apart from financial turmoil in the West. If it can, Southeast Asia might be able to escape significant fallout from the crisis by virtue of its growing economic interdependence with China. That scenario may underestimate the degree to which Southeast Asia is still tied to trade with the West, and it assumes that China's efforts to protect its own export sector — particularly in fiscal policy — would not disadvantage Southeast Asia. Toward the end of the year, Asian policy-makers and economists expressed some doubt that either of these assumptions will hold.[26]

Even if Southeast Asia is able to escape major economic damage in the short term, the crisis is sure to have an impact on relations with the United States and the European Union, and most likely with China as well. Apart from the obvious and monumental task of applying a tourniquet to the hemorrhaging American economy, the Obama administration will first need to address a backlog of free trade agreements — including the critical U.S.-Korea FTA — before turning to Southeast Asian agreements still under negotiation. It is unclear as a result whether negotiations on the U.S.-Malaysia and U.S.-Thailand FTAs will resume in 2009. Indeed, economic liberalization schemes with ASEAN's other external trading partners may also be affected by the crisis, and it may slow ASEAN's own plans to forge an economic free trade area of its own. Nor are the ASEAN member governments likely to avoid political pressure from their domestic populations as export sectors, particularly those dependent upon trade with the West, begin to lag. A severe economic downturn could affect the tenor, if not the outcome, of political transitions in Malaysia and Indonesia in 2009, and even in the Philippines in 2010.

Although it is impossible to know at this time how the current global economic crisis will end or how severely it will affect Southeast Asia, it clearly presents a significant challenge to the member states of ASEAN and ASEAN's efforts to strengthen itself as an institution in the coming year. To some, however, the crisis could act as a spur to regional integration. At the ASEAN ratification ceremony in December, ASEAN Secretary General Surin Pitsuwan put this problem in a hopeful context, by asserting that the ratification could not be better timed, because tighter ASEAN economic integration is the best hedge against a global economic crisis.[27] While this may make theoretical sense, the crisis has created a more difficult environment in which to pursue implementation.

Notes

[1]   "ASEAN Charter Enters Into Force Next Month, 15 November 2008", ASEAN Secretariat Press Release <http://aseansec.org/22072.htm>.

[2]   "Press Statement by the Chairman of ASEAN at the Special ASEAN Foreign Ministers Meeting, ASEAN Secretariat, 15 December 2008", ASEAN Secretariat Press Release <http://www/aseansec.org/22114.htm>.

[3]   For a more extensive review of the ASEAN Charter and ASEAN's institutional development, see Rodolfo Severino, "ASEAN At Forty: A Balance Sheet" and Mely Caballero-Anthony, "The ASEAN Charter: An Opportunity Missed or One that Cannot Be Missed?", in *Southeast Asian Affairs 2008*, edited by Daljit Singh and Tin Maung Maung Than (Singapore: Institute of Southeast Asian Studies, 2008).

[4]   See, for example, Brian McCartan, "ASEAN Tightens Up to Ride China's Rise", *Asia Times Online*, 17 December 2008 <http://www.atimes.com/atimes/Southeast_Asia/JL17Ae01.html>.

5   Djoko Susilo, "Myanmar (Burma), The Pebble in ASEAN's Shoe", *Southeast Asia Bulletin*, Center for Strategic and International Affairs, November 2008 <http://www.csis.org/,kedia/csis/pubs/08113_sea_bulletin_november.pdf>.

6   "DPRK Signs ASEAN TAC", 24 July 2008 <http://www.allheadlinnews.com/articles/701171310>.

7   "EU to Sign ASEAN Amity, Cooperation", *The Nation*, 13 September 2008.

8   Matthew Daley, "Why We Should Sign the TAC", *Southeast Asia Bulletin*, Center for Strategic and International Studies, April 2008 <http://www.csis.org/media/csis/pubs/080414_southeast_asia_bulletin.pdf>.

9   "Foreign Relations", *Republic of China Yearbook 2008*, Chapter 6 <http://www.gio.gov/tw/taiwan-website/5-gp/yearbook/ch6,html>.

10 "Trilateral Meeting of Leaders of China, Japan, South Korea", *China View*, 13 December 2008 <http://news.xinhuanet.com/english/2008-12/13/content_10498196.htm>.

11 *Southeast Asia Bulletin*, Center for Strategic and International Studies, February 2008 <http://www.csis.org/media/csis//pubs/080201_southeastasia_bulletin.pdf>.

12 *Southeast Asia Bulletin*, Center for Strategic and International Studies, October 2008 <http://www.csis.org/media/csis/pubs/081014_sea_bulletin_october.pdf>.

13 *South China Morning Post*, 20 June 2008.

14 R. Sutter and Huang Chin-Hao, "Small Advances, Trouble with Vietnam", *Comparative Connections*, October 2008 <http://www.csis.org/media/csis/pubs/0803qchina_seasia.pdf>.

15 *Southeast Asia Bulletin*, October 2008.

16 Sheldon W. Simon, "U.S. Responds to Southeast Asian Political Turmoil", *Comparative Connections*, October 2008 <http://www.csis.org/media/csis/pubs/0803qus_seasia.pdf>.

17 Ibid.

18 "Gunfire on Thai-Cambodian Border", *BBC News*, 15 October 2008 <http://news.bbc.co.uk/2/asia-pacific/7668657.stm>.

19 "Thailand-Cambodia Dispute: Indonesia Sees a Role to Help Resolve Conflict", *ASEAN Affairs*, 22 December 2008 <http://www.aseanaffairs.com/indonesia_sees_a_role_to_help_resolve_conflict>.

20 International Court of Justice Press Release, 23 May 2008 <http://www.icj-cij.org/docket/files/130/14490.pdf>.

21 Sheldon W. Simon, "U.S. Frustrated as Burma Obstructs Cyclone Relief", *Comparative Connections*, July 2008 <http://www.csis.org/media/csis/pubs/0802qus_seasia.pdf>.

22 Ibid.

23 K. Kesavapany, "Myanmar, ASEAN's Albratross", *Southeast Asia Bulletin*, Center for Strategic and International Studies, July 2008 <http://www.csis.org/media/csis/pubs/0807011_se_asia_bulletin.pdf>.

24   "ASEAN's Regional Emergency Response and Humanitarian Assistance Capability Put to the Test in Simulated Typhoon Disaster Scenario", Announcement by ASEAN Committee on Disaster Management, 22 August 2008 <http://acdm-online.net>.

25   MIMA Newsflash, 15 April 2008 <http://www.mima.gov/my/mima/htmls/mimere/news/newsflash_files/news_cit/apri08.htm>.

26   R. Sutter and Huang Chin-Hao, "Economic Concerns Begin to Hit Home", *Comparative Connections*, January 2009 <http://www'csis.org/media/csis/pubs/0804qchina_seasia.pdf>.

27   McCartan, *Asia Times Online*.

ASEAN ECONOMIES
Challenges and Responses
Amid the Crisis

Aladdin D. Rillo

What began as credit turmoil in the United States has intensified into a global financial crisis, leading to protracted slowdown and severe financial deleveraging in many countries. Like other regions in the world, ASEAN is not immune from this downturn. Since the crisis further deepened in September 2008, the region has been confronted with many challenges arising from slowing growth, tighter external financing conditions, volatile capital flows, and increased vulnerabilities. In response to the deepening crisis, many countries in the region have put in place various policy measures to recapitalize and inject liquidity into financial institutions, in addition to huge stimulus packages being implemented in some economies to firm up domestic demand.

ASEAN Has Not Decoupled from the Global Downturn ...

Faced by increasingly difficult external conditions, the economies of ASEAN have slowed in 2008 (see Figure 1). Preliminary figures for the first three quarters of 2008 suggest that the region grew by 5.5 per cent, down from 6.2 per cent registered in 2007.[1] Two factors account for this downward shift in regional growth. First is the deeper-than-expected financial crisis and second is the severe recession in advanced economies. Together, these headwinds moderated growth in global economy last year (estimated at 3.4 per cent by the IMF versus 5.2 per cent in 2007), and exerted significant spill over to the region, in terms of sharp decline in export growth and tighter financial conditions.

ALADDIN D. RILLO is Head of Finance and Macroeconomic Surveillance Unit at the ASEAN Secretariat in Jakarta. The views expressed in this paper are the views of the author and do not necessarily reflect the views of the ASEAN Secretariat or the Member States it represents.

Although the impact of the crisis on the real economy of ASEAN was not so severe, available growth indicators point to deceleration in economic activity particularly in the Philippines and Singapore where growth rates fell markedly from a year ago. After growing by an average of 8.5 per cent in the first three quarters of 2007, Singapore managed to grow by 3.1 per cent during the same period in 2008. In the third quarter alone, output did not grow at all, as output of manufacturing, construction and services sectors plunged. In the Philippines, growth also slowed significantly to 4.7 per cent for the first nine months, from 7.5 per cent during the same period in 2007, on weak consumption and exports. In Indonesia, Malaysia and Thailand, growth continued but at a decelerated pace and signs of further slowdown have become more evident recently.

Net exports have been quite resilient, certainly by past performance, despite the turmoil in global credit markets and threat of global recession. Growth in net exports increased to 4.8 per cent after contracting a year ago. Developments across countries, however, varied. Net exports turned around strongly in Malaysia and the Philippines, moderated in Indonesia and Thailand, but contracted sharply in Singapore. But in terms of contribution to growth, net exports performed poorly and contributed negatively (–0.1 per cent) to overall GDP growth rate of ASEAN as at end-September 2008.

Nonetheless, domestic demand, particularly private consumption, remained a key driver and an important source of growth, contributing 5.6 per cent to the region's overall growth. Over the last ten years, private consumption contributed on the average between 2 per cent and 4 per cent to output growth in Indonesia, Malaysia and the Philippines. In 2008, despite the weakening economic prospects, it added between 3 per cent and 5 per cent to growth in GDP in these countries, with the highest contribution in Malaysia (4.8 per cent). In Thailand, however, the contribution of private consumption to growth (1.4 per cent) remained below its average over the last eight years (4.6 per cent) as political uncertainty continued to weigh on consumer confidence; while it rose slightly in Singapore at 1.8 per cent. With rising unemployment and falling incomes, the contribution of private consumption is expected to diminish in the coming months.

Private investment has held up steadily, contributing to around 2.2 per cent of the region's domestic output growth, with notable performance in Singapore (where fixed investment accounted for 5.6 per cent of GDP growth) and in Indonesia (contributing 3 per cent). But with increasing risk aversion among investors, and the consistently slow recovery of private investment in ASEAN over the last ten years, sustaining the growth of private investment in a current weak economic environment is a challenge. As a per cent of GDP (23.2 per cent), gross fixed

FIGURE 1
ASEAN Economies Are Not Immune to the Global Financial Crisis

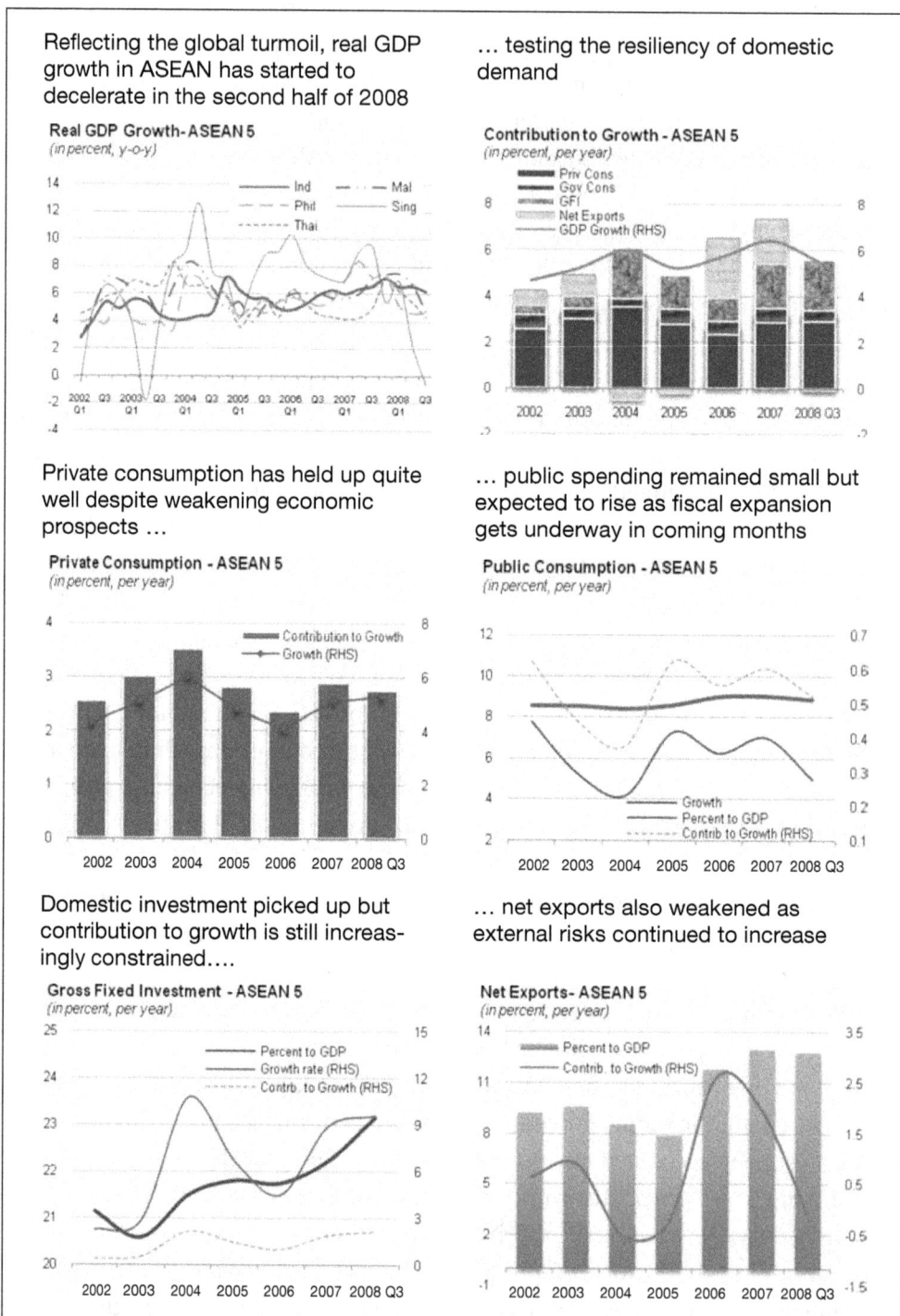

Reflecting the global turmoil, real GDP growth in ASEAN has started to decelerate in the second half of 2008

Real GDP Growth-ASEAN 5
(in percent, y-o-y)

... testing the resiliency of domestic demand

Contribution to Growth - ASEAN 5
(in percent, per year)

Private consumption has held up quite well despite weakening economic prospects ...

Private Consumption - ASEAN 5
(in percent, per year)

... public spending remained small but expected to rise as fiscal expansion gets underway in coming months

Public Consumption - ASEAN 5
(in percent, per year)

Domestic investment picked up but contribution to growth is still increasingly constrained....

Gross Fixed Investment - ASEAN 5
(in percent, per year)

... net exports also weakened as external risks continued to increase

Net Exports- ASEAN 5
(in percent, per year)

Source: ASEAN Secretariat, country websites, Economist Intelligence Unit.

investment has been declining and remains below the pre-crisis levels (34.9 per cent) in ASEAN. Its average contribution to growth in the region over the last ten years has been very low (0.2 per cent) and growth has been stagnant in real terms.

In the smaller economies of ASEAN,[2] economic activity has also been decelerating, as weak external demand weighed on exports and investment. In Brunei Darussalam, real GDP growth slowed to 0.4 per cent due to weak output and exports in the energy sector. After expanding by an average of 10.6 per cent over the last five years, growth in Cambodia moderated to 6.8 per cent in 2008 due to slowdown in garment, tourism and construction sectors. In Vietnam, the declining investor risk appetite caused the demand boom generated by capital inflows to unwind, resulting in real GDP growth to 6.5 per cent in the first three quarters. Meanwhile, domestic expansion in Lao PDR and Myanmar remained relatively robust and steady, perhaps reflecting the limited trade and financial linkages of their economies with the global markets. In Lao PDR the economy grew by 7.9 per cent on the back of growth in newly emerging processing industries, agriculture and new construction of hydropower projects, while official projections in Myanmar put overall GDP growth at 11.9 per cent with growth evident across key sectors (agriculture, industry and services).

... As Asean Financial Conditions Tightened and Came Under Stress

By end-September 2008, it was evident that the mortgage crisis that started in the United States had spread quickly and created extraordinary financial stresses in emerging markets like ASEAN (see Figure 2). Reflecting the deepening crisis and rising risk aversion, equity prices in the region have fallen sharply, declining on average by 28.6 per cent from end-September 2007 to end-September 2008. During this period net equity outflows increased as net heavy selling, primarily by foreign investors, intensified during the last quarter of the year. New issuance of bonds, equity and syndicated loans also declined significantly. After posting a high US$51.2 billion in 2007, new issues declined to US$45.2 billion as at end-June 2008, most of which were in debt markets. Spreads on both sovereign and corporate paper have widened markedly as well with Indonesia as the hardest hit. As banks started to scramble for dollars, liquidity shortage also spread and access to U.S. dollar funding became limited for some countries such as Indonesia and Vietnam.

Despite the tight financial conditions, private credit remained relatively stable by end-September, as most countries (except Malaysia) registered double-digit

FIGURE 2
Financial Stresses Have Led to Tighter Liquidity Conditions

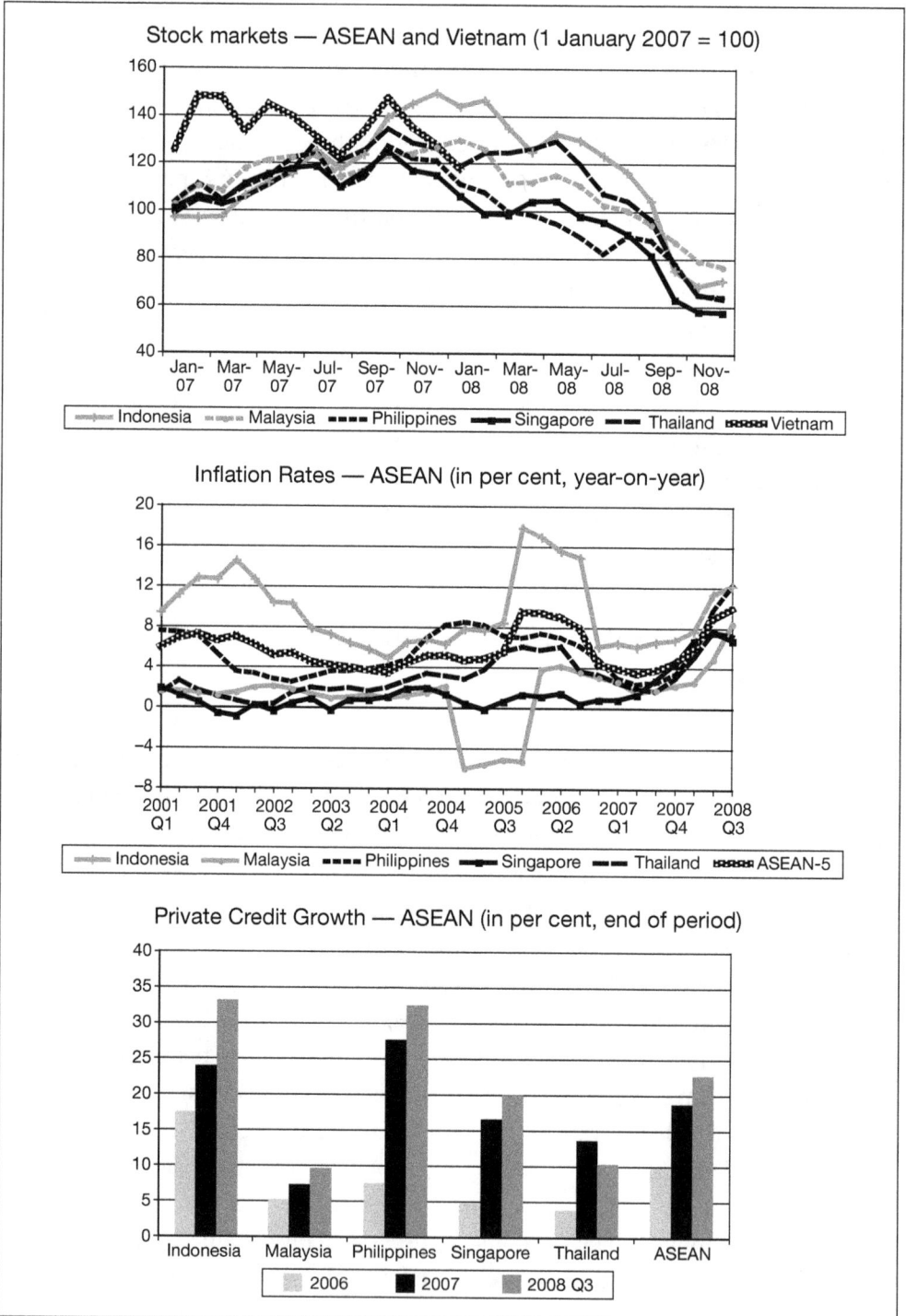

Stock markets — ASEAN and Vietnam (1 January 2007 = 100)

Inflation Rates — ASEAN (in per cent, year-on-year)

Private Credit Growth — ASEAN (in per cent, end of period)

Source: ASEAN Secretariat, country websites, Economist Intelligence Unit.

growth rates in their credit expansion. With the underlying strength of credit in ASEAN still intact, it appears that the turmoil in global financial markets in mid-September has had limited impact so far, although the spill over from the deepening crisis cannot be totally ignored. In Vietnam efforts by the authorities to contain inflation led to moderation in credit growth to around 18.6 per cent from 53.9 per cent at end-2007, while in Cambodia, the rapid expansion in private credit (53.2 per cent year-to-year growth) was reinforced by the government's centralization policy of commercial banks in the country.

A key issue in the region in 2008 was the resurgence of headline inflation, pushed by soaring food and energy prices and cyclical expansion in a few countries. In Indonesia, rising prices of food stuffs (which account for 25 per cent of goods in the CPI basket) and fuel adjustment (removal of fuel subsidy) forced inflation rate to surge to 12.2 per cent in September. Volatile food prices also caused inflation rates in the Philippines, Singapore and Vietnam to hit new highs. In Vietnam, the rate surged to 28.3 per cent in August, the highest since the peak in 1995; while it rose to 7.5 per cent in Singapore in April, the highest rate in more than two decades. In the Philippines, inflation rose sharply to 12.4 per cent in August and turned into double-digit rate for the first time in nine years.

Heightened concerns over inflation, particularly during the beginning of the year, have kept monetary conditions largely under control. By end-September, broad money grew slowly by 15.5 per cent as a result of slower increases in net foreign assets (NFA). In fact, the contribution of NFA to monetary growth in the region declined substantially to 3.7 per cent during the first three quarters compared to 10.5 per cent a year before. Except for an increase in Indonesia and Malaysia, monetary expansion in all countries moderated, with declining contribution of NFA evident in all countries. In contrast, the contribution of domestic credit to money supply remained steady at 12.5 per cent despite the increasing financial strains. Among the small ASEAN countries, monetary expansion continued to be high, albeit declining, particularly in Lao PDR and Vietnam.

Responding to rising inflation, policy-makers in the region implemented a number of measures, ranging from interest rate hikes (Indonesia, Philippines and Thailand) to credit tightening (Cambodia and Vietnam). However, some of these measures were reversed toward the end of the year as the liquidity strains related to financial turmoil intensified. Since then inflation rates in most countries have started to decline, especially during the fourth quarter, on the back of weakening global demand and easing commodity prices.

External Challenges Have Mounted and Are Likely to Continue for the Time Being

Despite global uncertainties, exports held up well through the third quarter, growing by 23.3 per cent by end-September from 10.9 per cent during the same period in 2007. Except the Philippines, all countries registered double-digit growth in their exports, particularly Indonesia (28 per cent) and Thailand (27.1 per cent). Reflecting higher commodity prices, imports also increased strongly and even outpaced growth in exports in most countries, thus resulting in smaller trade surplus (6.6 per cent of GDP) among the ASEAN-5, and further deterioration in trade deficits in Cambodia (17.1 per cent of GDP), Lao PDR (4.3 per cent) and Vietnam (1.8 per cent). As of this writing full-year trade data are not available, but anecdotal evidence suggests further decline in the region's trade surplus ahead as exports in some ASEAN countries have already slowed in the fourth quarter.

Amid increased risk aversion and poor investor sentiments, capital flows have also become more volatile. Portfolio outflows from the region amounted to 3.1 per cent of GDP, reversing the positive net inflows (1.7 per cent of GDP) registered in 2007. Direct investments also slowed to 1.1 per cent of GDP from 2.5 per cent of GDP a year before. Thus, by the end of third quarter, ASEAN's capital and financial account remained in negative territory (i.e., indicating net outflows) and is expected to remain so for the time being as global deleveraging intensifies. Obviously the reversal of capital flows will not only put further pressure on liquidity conditions in the region, but will likewise pose more difficulties for countries that have relied on external financing to fund domestic credit needs and current account deficits (e.g., Cambodia and Lao PDR).

In 2008 (from end-January to end-October) all ASEAN currencies depreciated against the U.S. dollar as investors tried to hold on their investments to safety and as export earnings dwindled. The Philippine peso depreciated most (19.9 per cent) on the back of significant foreign portfolio deleveraging, followed by Indonesian rupiah (18.3 per cent) and Malaysian ringgit (8.5 per cent), thus prompting the monetary authorities in these countries to intervene in support. Meanwhile, currency developments have varied in the smaller ASEAN countries, with appreciations in Brunei Darussalam, Lao PDR and Myanmar, and slight depreciations in Cambodia and Vietnam. In this environment, regional currencies are expected to further weaken particularly if global sentiments deteriorate further.

There is no doubt that the worsening terms of trade and volatile capital flows have increased external risks and rendered the region more vulnerable to the global downturn (see Figure 3). Nevertheless, foreign reserves accumulation

FIGURE 3
External Positions Are Generally Robust but the Deepening Turmoil May Diminish the Cushions

Current account balances have come under pressure...

External Balances - ASEAN 5
(in percent, end of period)

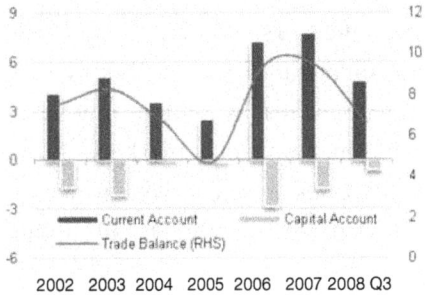

Current Account   Capital Account
Trade Balance (RHS)

2002 2003 2004 2005 2006 2007 2008 Q3

... from rising import bills for commodities and slowing export growth

Exports and Imports Growth - ASEAN 5
(in percent, end of period)

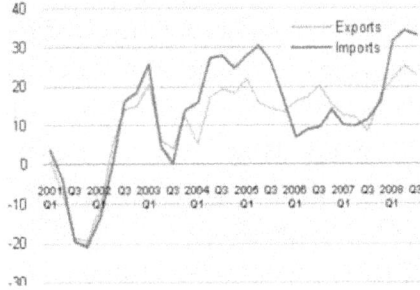

Exports
Imports

... making more difficult for smaller countries that have relied on external financing over the years

External Balances - Cambodia, Lao PDR and Vietnam
(in percent, end of period)

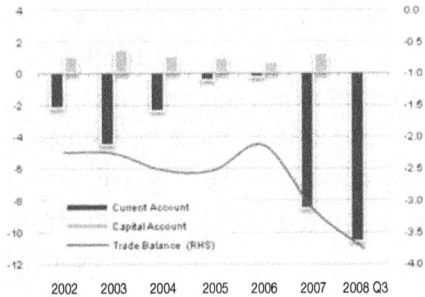

Current Account
Capital Account
Trade Balance (RHS)

2002 2003 2004 2005 2006 2007 2008 Q3

Capital flows are likely to remain volatile especially portfolio flows

Composition of Net Capital Outflows
2008 Q3 - ASEAN 5
(in percent, end of period)

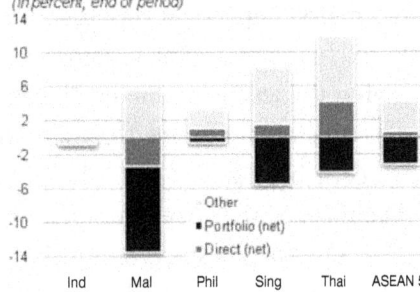

Other
Portfolio (net)
Direct (net)

Ind   Mal   Phil   Sing   Thai   ASEAN 5

... weakening regional currencies

Currencies
(year-to-date, % change, latest closing as of 31 Oct 2008, negative figures indicate depreciation)

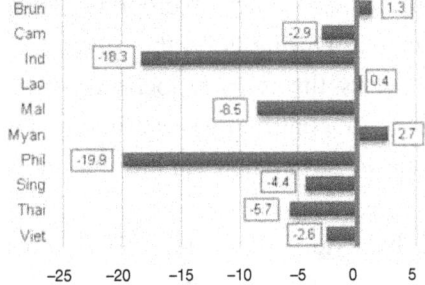

Brun   1.3
Cam   -2.9
Ind   -18.3
Lao   0.4
Mal   -8.5
Myan   2.7
Phil   -19.9
Sing   -4.4
Thai   -5.7
Viet   -2.6

-25   -20   -15   -10   -5   0   5

Putting further pressure in reserve positions

Official Reserves - ASEAN 5
(US$ billion)

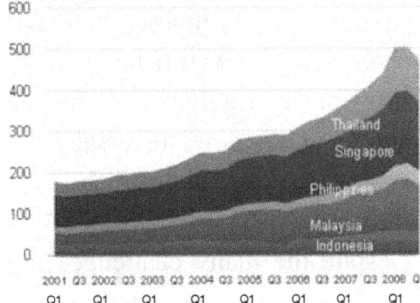

Thailand
Singapore
Philippines
Malaysia
Indonesia

Source: ASEAN Secretariat, country websites, Economist Intelligence Unit, Bloomberg.

has remained resilient across all countries, such that by end-September, total official reserves in ASEAN stood at US$474 billion, up from US$415 billion a year ago. The higher official reserves and greater exchange rate flexibility have provided some countries enough room to deal with the crisis.

Issues and Challenges of Global Financial Crisis

Against an environment of increased macroeconomic risks, a major policy challenge for the region is how to respond to the global financial crisis. In 2008 the region saw how these risks have played out in various countries, as evident in weakening growth prospects and growing strains in individual financial markets. Although there were notable differences in country responses to the crisis, it was clear that policy priorities in each country have shifted considerably to strengthening domestic demand and reforming financial systems.

- One key issue is how to sustain the growth in domestic demand so as to make the region resilient, in particular by increasing reliance on private investment as a key source of growth. Although ASEAN has recovered from the last financial crisis since 1999, the export-driven nature of the recovery has made the region dependent on global growth, and as a result, renders it vulnerable to fluctuations in global demand. Amid the current global financial crisis, the region is faced with the challenge again of implementing policies that create a domestically sourced growth such as investment. Weak investment is a concern because it limits the productive capacity of the regional economy.

- The risks of spill over from the financial crisis have increased from 2008, and it is against this uncertainty that financial sector vulnerabilities need closer attention. So far authorities in the region have recognized the importance of increased financial sector surveillance to ensure that vulnerabilities do not build up to more systemic levels.

- Managing capital flows in an environment of increased market volatility is crucial. Capital flows, while beneficial to economic development, can be challenging as well if not properly managed. During 2008 the increased risk aversion by foreign investors clearly shows the risks associated with any sharp capital flows reversals. In the face of continuing volatility in global capital markets, policies should continue to strengthen capital management measures.

- Despite the many challenges imposed by external factors, ASEAN should not lose sight of the ongoing economic restructuring efforts, both nationally and regionally. At the national level, key concern is the lack of momentum that might derail the implementation of key reforms that have been the focus of economic policies in previous years. Within the region, it is imperative that ASEAN as a region takes advantage of the increasing momentum on regional economic integration.

ASEAN Rising — How Can ASEAN Respond to the Crisis?

Given the challenges imposed in 2008 by the global financial crisis, it is only appropriate that ASEAN responds well to the crisis.

One important policy action for ASEAN is to keep the momentum of growth on track. With weak external demand, one saving grace for ASEAN is to reorient its growth strategy toward domestic driven growth. This is important in view of a potential threat of increased protectionism from advanced countries as they try to resort to more inward-oriented policies to protect their individual economies. In this case, ASEAN must be ready to implement vigorous measures that promote domestically sourced growth. A new business model is needed that emphasizes strong commitment to develop local demand, particularly domestic investment. Exports are important as well but as long as they enhance investment potentials of local industries with significant linkages to domestic industries.

Coordinated monetary and fiscal policies must be undertaken to ensure maximum impact for the region's economies. This coordination entails deliberate efforts on the part of authorities across the region to design the timing and magnitude of their interventions. For example, countries can announce common targets for their fiscal stimulus packages and the proper timing for undertaking them. Monetary policy stance can also be coordinated in such a way that authorities can collectively announce movements in their policy rates.

Finally, given that the current crisis is all about the failure of global governance to detect the problems in global financial systems, it is about time for ASEAN to really focus on establishing a credible regional financial architecture. Since the crisis in 1997/98, calls for reforms of global financial architecture have been made, but the outcomes are still quite disappointing. ASEAN can take this opportunity to heed on those calls by undertaking significant reforms in regional financial institutions, including reforms that focus on: (i) enhanced financial regulation and supervision; (ii) better early warning systems; (iii) enhanced regulatory cooperation and coordination; and (iv) effective crisis management.

Final Thoughts: ASEAN and the Opportunity to Contribute to Global Recovery

The financial crisis that now confronts ASEAN is a clear reminder that greater cooperation at regional and global levels is more important than ever to address economic issues that have become closely interrelated over the years. It has also exposed the decade-long problem of anchoring global growth on a single region/country (e.g. the United States) and the failure to achieve a balanced growth in world economy.

One key issue to ponder is that ASEAN should start to respond and rise to the expectations of the world and play a more significant role in reducing global imbalances and financial stresses. Amid the downturn, Asia (including ASEAN) remains the fastest growing region in the world (projected by the IMF to expand by 5.5 per cent in 2009), in stark contrast to disappointing growth rates in advanced economies (–2 per cent) and global economy (0.5 per cent). Indeed, Asia's economic dynamism will be pivotal in future global recovery and adjustment.

Asia will definitely be tested in 2009, particularly its contribution to global recovery. Global recovery can be facilitated if Asia is able to sustain its growth in 2009 the medium term. If Asia falters, it will be a disastrous outcome for the global economy considering Asia's growing contribution to world GDP.

Notes

[1] Date used in this report are as at end-September 2008 unless otherwise stated. Figures refer to the weighted average of real GDP growth rates for "ASEAN-5" namely Indonesia, Malaysia, Philippines, Singapore and Thailand, where preliminary data for GDP and their components were available at the time of writing this article. Unless otherwise indicated, reference to regional average in this article refers mainly to statistics for ASEAN-5.

[2] Include Brunei Darussalam, Cambodia, Lao PDR, Myanmar and Vietnam.

MANAGING ARMED CONFLICT IN SOUTHEAST ASIA
The Role of Mediation

MICHAEL VATIKIOTIS

The Southeast Asian region is more peaceful than it has been in the past six decades. Interstate conflict is a distant memory, and many — though not all — of the internal conflicts that erupted in the process of nation building after the colonial era have either subsided or have been resolved. ASEAN is proud of the fact that compared with neighbouring regions, relations among member states are relatively harmonious and security is for the most part assured.

There are glaring exceptions, however. In several parts of the region stubborn irredentist conflict sustains low intensity armed violence. In recent years, internal conflicts in the Southern Philippines, Southern Thailand and parts of Indonesia have flared up. In Southern Thailand, more than 3,500 lives have been lost since 2004. In 2008 a flare up of violence in the Southern Philippines resulted in the loss of 300 lives and the displacement of almost half a million people.

The fact that most of these conflicts pit Muslim against non-Muslim communities (in Indonesia's Maluku province, Mindanao in the Southern Philippines and Southern Thailand) has meant they attracted wider attention because of the dangers of wider international terrorist involvement.

Management of these conflicts has been partially successful. Over the years, governments have forged temporary ceasefire agreements, implemented some special local political arrangements, or placated communal feelings sufficiently enough to keep violence at a manageable level. But resolution in terms of reaching effective agreements to permanently end hostilities and address grievances through far reaching political and legal arrangements has been rare.

MICHAEL VATIKIOTIS is Asia Director at the Centre for Humanitarian Dialogue, Singapore.

One notable exception appears to be Aceh. The long running conflict between the Indonesian authorities and the Free Aceh Movement was settled after the signing of a Memorandum of Understanding in Helsinki in August 2005. The settlement, which allowed the former rebel groups to set up their own political parties, came after more than six years of efforts by private mediators from the Centre for Humanitarian Dialogue, and latterly the Conflict Management Initiative, to bring the two sides together.

The successful settlement of conflict in Aceh has raised the profile of mediation as a tool of conflict resolution in Southeast Asia and inevitably prompted questions of whether similar strategies of facilitation and mediation by a third party in an internal armed conflict can help effectively reduce violence and settle long standing grievances. This article argues that this is indeed the case, and offers a general set of suggestions aimed at encouraging parties conflicting in the region to embrace modern mediation strategies.

Traditionally, governments in Southeast Asia are strongly averse to infringements of sovereignty. A collection for the most part of modern states with memories of relatively recent colonial rule, Southeast Asian nations have stoutly resisted embracing collective formal security mechanisms that provide for intervention in internal disputes. ASEAN was established formally more than forty years ago as a cooperative economic grouping, whereas in reality the five original member states were economic competitors in need of more assured collective security.

Yet underlying these rigid positions on interference is an equally strong tradition of *informal* diplomacy that has generated some successful instances of mediation. In the 1980s and 1990s, for example, ASEAN member states cooperated to help resolve the Cambodian conflict. In many other instances, one country has helped another deal with violent conflict, as when Thailand and Malaysia cooperated in the late 1980s to settle a long running communist insurgency aimed at Malaysia, or when Indonesia helped broker a deal between the government in Manila and the Moro Nationalist Liberation Front in 1996.

Despite their success, all these instances of third party mediation have been presented as exceptions that prove the rule. Rather than embrace the need for an institutionalized process of mediation and conflict resolution within the region, ASEAN member states have preferred to stand solidly behind a firm insistence on non-interference. So much so that when Indonesia and Malaysia offered to help mediate in the resurgent conflict in Southern Thailand after 2004, Thailand said it preferred not to have the involvement of a third country settling an internal conflict. More than a decade after the MNLF agreement brokered by Indonesia, attempts to sustain a peace process through mediation with the

Moro Islamic Liberation Front, although facilitated by Malaysia, were also meeting resistance in Manila to a more overt internationalization of the conflict resolution process.

Part of the problem is the lack of consensus on any regional mechanism for dispute resolution. Indeed, while there has always been a popular expectation that ASEAN would evolve into a community of nations sharing a common set of principles and abiding by a code of conduct, it was only in late 2008 that a formal ASEAN Charter was adopted by all ten-member states. One whole chapter of the Charter involving five articles covers the settlement of disputes. Article 22 states that "ASEAN shall maintain and establish dispute settlement mechanism in all fields of ASEAN cooperation." Article 23 states that parties to a dispute "may request the Chairman of ASEAN or the Secretary General of ASEAN, acting in an ex-officio capacity, to provide good offices, conciliation or mediation".

The blueprint for an ASEAN Political Security Community, unveiled at the ASEAN Summit in Thailand at the beginning of March 2009, reinforces the spirit of the charter. It embraces an ambitious early warning mechanism to defuse conflict, fight terrorism, combat piracy and promote good governance.[1] The blueprint declares that: "More efforts are needed in strengthening the existing modes of pacific settlement of disputes to avoid or settle future disputes." However, as a blueprint it remains very much a set of aims to foster closer cooperation between security and political bodies. Nothing concrete has been put in place.

Although clearly stated in the Charter, the prospect of the ASEAN Chair or Secretary-General playing an overt mediation role in a regional dispute is far from assured. Far more likely for the time being is the kind of scenario that played out in October 2008 when Thai and Cambodian troops started firing at each other along a disputed area of the border between the two countries. ASEAN Secretary-General Surin Pitsuwan immediately swung into action with appeals for calm and a flurry of consultations with ministerial colleagues around the region. For one brief moment, it looked like war.

Tragedy was averted, but not necessarily as a result of high-level diplomacy or mediation. Within a matter of hours, local commanders saw sense and pulled back, agreeing on joint patrols. There were light casualties, only two Cambodian soldiers were killed and seven Thai troops injured in the clashes, which were over disputed land near the ancient Preah Vihar temple. Like so many potential flashpoints, so many times before, the instinctive avoidance of conflict, which is rooted deep in the region's cultural DNA, helped defuse a potential crisis, without the need for high level diplomacy or mediation.

Even so, the incident serves to remind us that there is no formal mechanism at a high level for resolving these disputes, and hence the frantic scattershot of phone calls and ad hoc initiatives that tend to ensue whenever crisis looms.

Strengthening Regional Capacity

A critical question therefore is what could be done to strengthen the regional capacity for conflict management, in particular the scope for effective mediation.

The first and most important priority is to build political support in ASEAN for a more proactive and coherent mediation role. On one level, there are those who argue that it is time for governments to recognize reality. "The days when domestic political controversies could not be discussed in regional settings are over", argues ASEAN Secretary-General Surin Pitsuwan.[2] It is here, Surin writes "in the cracks between sovereignties, the spaces between states", that hard choices are being made, and sovereignty is no longer a barrier to flexible and, let us say humanitarian intervention.

This can be seen in the many and varied responses to internal conflict in contemporary Southeast Asia that stem from private groups of citizens, academics and non-governmental organizations — the space between states, as Surin Pitsuwan describes them. It was Indonesian President Abdurrahman Wahid who first helped open up this space when he suggested to a small private foundation based in Geneva that it might help facilitate dialogue between the Aceh Freedom Movement and the Indonesian government in 1999. That opening led eventually to a peace deal six years later.[3] In Southern Thailand, where violence has taken the lives of more than 3,200 people since 2004, Thai academics and civil society activists have reached out to the shadowy insurgency in bid to engage in dialogue.

On a bureaucratic plane, however, nothing much is moving. Security officials for the most part regard the tools of mediation — dialogue and compromise and binding agreement — as signs of weakness and threats to sovereignty. Offers of third party help are mostly rejected. The ASEAN Charter is regarded as a vehicle for adapting rather than completely changing the twin ASEAN traditions of consultation and consensus and it is hard to imagine ASEAN-wide support for an overt intervention at the state level in an internal conflict so long as officials can throw up the consensus rule. Rather what will happen for the time being is the kind of ad hoc and episodic activism that for example characterized ASEAN's response to the September 2007 uprising led by the Buddhist clergy in Myanmar. Here, the international community was impressed by then ASEAN Chairman Singapore's strident criticism of the violent crackdown on Buddhist monks, but after this it became hard for ASEAN to agree on any concrete course of action.[4]

In the face of this inertia, ASEAN needs to strike a balance: weighing the preservation of sovereignty against the costs of violent conflict in a more interdependent and connected region.

Secondly, it is important to provide resources for ASEAN to develop as an institution in line with what the new Charter stipulates. Mediation is certainly provided for in the ASEAN Charter, but for the good offices of the ASEAN Chair and Secretary-General to be deployed effectively, ASEAN's resource and institutional capacity needs strengthening. Is it really adequate that a regional organization comprising almost 600 million people is served by a secretariat with a mere sixty officers?

Thirdly, ASEAN should take advantage of the global trend towards working alongside other institutions and international organizations in hybrid coalitions to achieve humanitarian and security goals. In this regard, ASEAN's groundbreaking role in paving the way for international aid to reach the victims to Cyclone Nargis in May 2008 was a tipping point for the association.

Cyclone Nargis struck the Irrawaddy delta region of coastal Myanmar on 2 May 2008. The very severe cyclone devastated the region, killing more than 140,000 people and displacing hundreds of thousands of others in an already impoverished region of the country. Amidst the anxiety in the international community about the Myanmar government's initial reluctance to allow in international aid and relief for the victims of Cyclone Nargis, ASEAN Secretary-General Surin Pitsuwan stepped in with an offer to send a less intrusive ASEAN Emergency Rapid Assessment Team. This was groundbreaking in the sense that it put officers from the ASEAN Secretariat on the ground in a crisis situation. This quickly led to the creation of an ASEAN-led coordinating mechanism named the Tripartite Core Group to facilitate international aid.[5] This creative mechanism enabled international organizations like the UN and the World Bank to operate under a less threatening ASEAN umbrella. Surin himself shuttled between Myanmar and the United States, working the government on the ground and UN agencies and the World Bank in New York and Washington. It was precisely the kind of mediating role envisaged by the Charter and did in the end result in aid being pledged and relief workers being allowed into the areas worst hit by the cyclone.

All the same, apart from much deserved praise for the individual political skills of ASEAN Secretary-General Surin Pitsuwan, a former Thai foreign minister, it is hard to see much more than a very minimal shift in ASEAN's bedrock principal of respect for sovereignty and non-interference. Humanitarian disasters like Cyclone Nargis, even if they do help establish institutional models and precedents for intervention, are a far cry from the kinds of political and security challenges presented by ongoing violence and displacement of people in Southern Mindanao.

Starting at the Community Level

Perhaps the least path of resistance to more effective conflict management in the region is to promote a creative approach to mediation, one that harnesses the region's considerable experience in peacemaking at the community level and within civil society to a more flexible and receptive attitude at the state level with informal, private diplomacy. There are some signs of this in the Philippines, where efforts to revive the stalled peace talks between Manila and the MILF have received a boost from the assistance of private organizations, informal diplomatic initiatives, and the efforts of eminent persons groups.

In Indonesia as well, conflict management at a community level has spawned a variety of initiatives and non-governmental organizations, which have helped ameliorate the potential for violence in areas like Maluku, Kalimantan and Central Sulawesi.

In Maluku a civil society effort helped lay the foundations of the government-led peace process that resulted in the signing of the Malino II Declaration between the Christian and Muslim communities after a conflict that erupted in 1999 killed more than 5,000 people and displaced half a million. Local NGOs along with members of the local communities were among the first to spearhead reconciliation efforts between the conflicting parties in Maluku when fighting and communal violence was still at its height in 2000–01. As violence has subsided and stability gradually returned to the region following the signing of the peace accord, these community level activities have helped keep the peace with the occasional support from the government.

The downside is that government mediated peace agreements in Maluku and central Sulawesi have not been fully implemented and many residents appear poorly informed of the contents of these agreements. Issues such as the return of internally displaced people and land disputes between different ethnic or religious groups plague these communities and remain significant sources of tension and conflict. In West and Central Kalimantan, conflict simmers over the competition for resources and continued mistrust between the Dayak and immigrant Madurese communities, but no peace agreement has been reached.

Government officials admit their response to these tensions has been hesitant and weak, but they are wary of solutions that could be criticized as tacit support for one side or the other. In a number of districts in West and Central Kalimantan, it is determined community action that has rejected being drawn into a cycle of violence and where traditional leaders still command influence over the local communities, the government recognizes their authority to assist in conflict resolution.

Conclusion

Low intensity internal conflict is a common security challenge in Southeast Asia, one that presents governments more often than not with the temptation to manage rather than resolve or settle the conflict. However, as standards of governance and levels of transparency have increased across the region, so have the pressures on governments to engage in genuine dialogue and seek peaceful settlements to long standing grievances. All too often these fledgling efforts at mediation struggle in the face of hesitant government support, interference from military quarters, and an overall lack of commitment and coherence. It would be helpful if peaceful strategies to resolve conflict in Southeast Asia received more high level political support and benefited from greater institutional back up from regional and international organizations.

Notes

Rohaiza Ahmad Asi, Project Assistant at the Centre for Humanitarian Dialogue in Singapore, contributed to this article.

[1]   See "ASEAN Security Community Plan of Action" at <http://www.aseansec.org/16826. htm>.

[2]   Surin Pitsuwan, "Foreword", in *Hard Choices: Security, Democracy, and Regionalism in Southeast Asia* (Singapore: Institute of Southeast Asian Studies, 2008), pp. xix–xi.

[3]   David Gorman, "Non-Governmental Actors in Peace Processes, the Case of Aceh", in *Third Parties in Conflict Prevention* (Sweden: CKM Forlag, Uppsala University, 2007).

[4]   In a statement issued in New York on 27 September 2007, Singapore Foreign Minister George Yeo said that ASEAN Foreign Ministers "were appalled to receive reports of automatic weapons being used and demanded that the Myanmar government immediately desist from the use of violence against demonstrators. They expressed their revulsion to Myanmar Foreign Minister Nyan Win over reports that the demonstrations in Myanmar are being suppressed by violent force and that there has been a number

of fatalities. They strongly urged Myanmar to exercise utmost restraint and seek a political solution. They called upon Myanmar to resume its efforts at national reconciliation with all parties concerned, and work towards a peaceful transition to democracy. The Ministers called for the release of all political detainees including Daw Aung San Suu Kyi." Source <http://www.aseansec.org/20974.htm>.

5   The Tripartite Core Group (TCG) was formed after the 19 May 2008 Special Association of Southeast Asian Nations (ASEAN) Foreign Ministerial Meeting in Singapore, and the 25 May 2008 ASEAN-United Nations International Pledging Conference held in Yangon, Union of Myanmar. The aim of the TCG is to act as an ASEAN-led mechanism to facilitate trust, confidence and cooperation between Myanmar and the international community in the urgent humanitarian relief and recovery work after Cyclone Nargis hit Myanmar (2 to 3 May 2008). Source <http://www.aseansec.org/21691.htm>.

MARITIME SECURITY IN SOUTHEAST ASIA
Two Cheers for Regional Cooperation

Ian Storey

It would be difficult to overstate the geostrategic and economic importance of Southeast Asia's maritime domains. The sea lanes of communication (SLOCs) that criss-cross and pass through Southeast Asia function as vital arteries of world trade. Southeast Asian SLOCs have been instrumental in the success of the ASEAN countries' export-led economic growth, while countless maritime communities dotted across the region continue to depend on the sea for their livelihoods. Further north, the economic powerhouses of Northeast Asia — Japan, the People's Republic of China (PRC) and South Korea — rely on Southeast Asian SLOCs for the safe passage of 80–90 per cent of their energy supplies from the Middle East and Africa, and as conduits for transporting their manufactured goods to other parts of Asia, Europe and beyond. For the world's Great Powers, especially the United States and Japan, but increasingly China and India, Southeast Asia's SLOCs and maritime chokepoints such as the Malacca, Sunda and Lombok-Makassar Straits have strategic value beyond measure, linking as they do Northeast Asia and the Western Pacific with the Indian Ocean.

Over the past several decades, globalization contributed to a phenomenal increase in the volume of seaborne trade: in 2007, 8.02 billion tonnes of goods were moved by sea, up from 6.27 billion in 2000 and 2.6 billion in 1970.[1] The dynamic economies of Asia accounted for much of this growth: in 2007 Asia took the lion's share, accounting for 40 per cent of loaded goods, followed by the Americas (23 per cent), Europe (18 per cent), Africa (10 per cent) and Oceania (9 per cent).[2] Of the world's 20 busiest ports in 2005, 15 were located in Asia;

Ian Storey is a Fellow at the Institute of Southeast Asian Studies (ISEAS), Singapore.

and of the 20 busiest container terminals 13 were in Asia, including seven in the PRC alone.[3] China's spectacular economic growth since the late 1970s has been a major, if not the primary, driver of maritime trade expansion, forcing the global shipping industry to struggle to keep pace with demand for vessels to carry raw materials into China and transport Chinese-manufactured goods to overseas markets.

The global shipping market, however, is notoriously prone to boom-and-bust cycles, and the international economic crisis that unfolded in 2008 seems set to bring an end to the current period of unprecedented maritime growth. As the recession bites hard in the United States and Europe, demand for Asia's manufactured goods has slowed, forcing countries like China to slash commodity imports. The global shipping industry, which had until recently complained of a shortage of vessels of all kinds, now faces excess capacity. The industry's bellwether, the Baltic Exchange Dry Index which tracks sea freight prices of major commodities, plunged 87 per cent between May and October 2008, hitting a five-year low.[4] Container traffic at Asian ports is slowing, putting expansion plans on hold, while the world's three biggest shipbuilders, South Korea, China and Japan, find themselves faced with shrinking order books. At the time of writing it is impossible to predict whether the global economic downturn will be deep and prolonged or deep but short-lived. Nevertheless, even if the downturn is protracted, Southeast Asia's SLOCs will continue to hold their economic and strategic value until the inevitable recovery leads to the next upsurge in global maritime commerce.

Maritime security in Southeast Asia has attracted a great deal of attention from scholars, analysts and journalists over the past decade, and especially since the Al Qaeda attacks in the United States on 11 September 2001 (9/11). Salient issues under examination include incidents of piracy and sea robbery, the threat of maritime terrorism, illegal trafficking in weapons, people and narcotics, territorial and maritime boundary disputes and the transit by sea of weapons of mass destruction (WMD). In meeting these challenges the need for regional and international cooperation is paramount. The purpose of this chapter is to review progress and identify remaining problems in two main areas: the fight against piracy and sea robbery in Southeast Asia, and attempts to mitigate or resolve maritime territorial and boundary disputes in the region. In both cases regional cooperation has bred success; but much more needs to be done to secure Southeast Asia's sea lanes and resolve contested maritime boundaries. As is often the case, sensitivities over sovereignty hinder the attainment of these goals.

Piracy, Sea Robbery and the Threat of Maritime Terrorism[5]

In 2004 the issue of how to enhance maritime security in Southeast Asia resulted in a squabble between regional countries and the United States. The genesis of the furore was the rising number of piracy and sea robbery incidents reported by the London-based International Maritime Bureau (IMB).[6] Since the late 1990s violent incidents at sea in Southeast Asia had been growing in number and intensity (see Table 1). The root causes of this phenomenon are contested, but likely include a combination of factors including weakened political authority, poor governance and socio-economic distress triggered by the Asian financial crisis of 1997–99, as well as readily available high-technology and advanced weaponry (such as high speed boats, satellite navigation and automatic weapons) used by pirates to mount attacks, and increased vessel traffic through Southeast Asia's SLOCs which created more "targets of opportunity".

The problem of maritime predations was particularly acute in Indonesia where the economic crisis and fall of President Soeharto in May 1998 deprived the Indonesian Navy (Tentara Nasional Indonesia — Angkatan Laut, TNI-AL) of the budgetary resources and capabilities necessary to patrol the country's vast archipelagic waters. In addition, the crisis also led to increased levels of corruption in the armed forces and law enforcement agencies, and forced some unemployed mariners and fishermen to turn to crime. The Free Aceh Movement (GAM), emboldened by East Timor's violent separation from Indonesia in 1999, also stepped up its campaign for independence and, according to the Indonesian authorities, employed piratical attacks as a means to raise funds. Between 2002 and 2006 approximately two-thirds of reported piracy and sea robbery attacks in Southeast Asia occurred in Indonesian waters, earning them the unenviable reputation of being the world's most pirate-infested waters.

Following 9/11, piracy and terrorism were conflated. Security analysts expressed concern that terrorists might join forces with pirate gangs to conduct atrocities in Southeast Asian waters, especially in the strategically important Straits of Malacca (SOM), through which 65,000 vessels per year transit, carrying an estimated one-third of world trade and one half of global energy supplies. The two most commonly cited scenarios included terrorists sinking one or more large vessels in an attempt to block the Strait and dislocate the world economy, and militants using a crude oil or natural gas tanker as a "floating bomb" in a major Asian port.

Southeast Asia is no stranger to acts of maritime terrorism. In the Philippines the radical Abu Sayyaf Group (ASG) has been active in the maritime domain since it was formed in the early 1990s, and in February 2004 the group committed

TABLE 1

Reported Piracy and Sea Robbery Attacks in Southeast Asia, 1994–2007

Location	1994	1995	1996	1997	1998	1999	2000	2001	2002	2003	2004	2005	2006	2007	2008
Indonesia	22	33	57	47	60	115	119	91	103	121	94	79	50	43	28
Malacca Strait	3	2	3	0	1	2	75	17	16	28	38	12	11	7	2
Malaysia	4	5	5	4	10	18	21	19	14	5	9	3	10	9	10
Singapore Strait	3	2	2	5	1	14	5	7	5	2	8	7	5	3	6
Philippines	5	24	39	16	15	6	9	8	10	12	4	0	6	6	7
Thailand	0	4	16	17	2	5	8	8	5	2	4	1	1	2	0
Myanmar	0	0	1	2	0	1	5	3	0	0	1	0	0	0	1
South China Sea	6	3	2	6	5	3	9	4	0	2	8	6	1	3	0
Cambodia	1	1	1	1	0	0	0	0	0	0	0	0	N/A	N/A	N/A
Vietnam	2	4	0	4	0	2	6	8	12	15	4	10	3	5	11
Total	46	78	126	102	94	166	257	165	165	187	170	118	87	78	65

Source: International Maritime Bureau, "Piracy and Armed Robbery Against Ships Annual Report", various issues 2001–08. Figures include actual and attempted attacks.

the world's worst act of maritime terrorism to date by sinking SuperFerry 14 in Manila Bay with the loss of 116 lives. In December 2001 Singapore's security services arrested 13 members of Al Qaeda-linked Jemaah Islamiyah (JI) whose plans included suicide attacks against visiting U.S. naval vessels using high-speed boats packed with explosives.[7]

The threat of a major maritime terrorism incident in Southeast Asia may well have been overstated, but it was a threat that could not be ruled out, and one that many countries, particularly the United States, took very seriously. In testimony before the U.S. Congress on 31 March 2004, Admiral Thomas Fargo, Commander of the U.S. military's largest combatant command, Pacific Command (PACOM) based in Honolulu, Hawaii, unveiled a new programme called the Regional Maritime Security Initiative (RMSI) which was designed to increase cooperation between the United States and Southeast Asian countries to address transnational security threats at sea including terrorism, piracy, proliferation of WMDs and illegal trafficking.[8] In his testimony, Fargo stated that in operational terms, PACOM was considering "putting Special Operations Forces on high-speed vessels" to conduct effective interdiction. But press reports in Indonesia erroneously claimed that PACOM intended to station Special Operations Forces in the Straits of Malacca to combat rising piracy attacks. The Malaysian and Indonesian governments bristled at the reports, condemned the proposal as a violation of their sovereignty and warned that the presence of U.S. forces in the Strait would only fuel Islamic radicalism in Southeast Asia.[9] Singapore, dependent for its prosperity on the unimpeded flow of maritime trade and perceiving itself as the target of groups such as JI and Al Qaeda, took the threat of maritime terrorism much more seriously than Kuala Lumpur or Jakarta, and offered tacit support for RMSI.[10] It was left to then U.S. Defense Secretary Donald Rumsfeld in June to soothe Indonesian and Malaysian ire by stating that it was never America's intention to permanently station military forces in the SOM. The damage to RMSI, however, could not be undone, and PACOM ceased using the acronym though, as described later, the programme's intent survived. Nonetheless by rejecting RMSI the ball was now firmly in the court of the SOM's three littoral states, Indonesia, Malaysia and Singapore.

Enhanced Security Cooperation Pays Off

Fearing U.S.-led military intervention in the Straits — as had happened in Iraq in 2003 — Indonesia responded by proposing trilateral coordinated naval patrols, an idea readily accepted by Malaysia and Singapore. On 20 July 2004 the first Malaysia-Singapore-Indonesia (MALSINDO) year-round naval patrols were launched. However, due to sensitivities over sovereignty, the trilateral naval patrols are coordinated, not joint: each country is responsible for patrolling its own sector of the Strait and each ship remains under national command with limited "hot pursuit" rights into the sovereign waters of the other participating states. In September 2005 an aerial surveillance component was added with the "Eyes in the Sky" (EIS) initiative. Under the EiS, each country allocates maritime patrol aircraft to conduct two air sorties per week along the Malacca and Singapore Straits: each flight carries a combined maritime patrol team made up of military personnel from each of the participating states. To improve the effectiveness of the naval and air patrols, the three countries signed terms of reference and standard operating procedures in April 2006, and renamed the initiative the Malacca Straits Patrols (MSP). The MSP comprises three elements: the Malacca Straits Surface Patrols (MSSP), the EiS and the Intelligence Exchange Group (IEG). The IEG went on to develop the Malacca Straits Patrols Information System (MSP-IS) to improve coordination and situational awareness at sea among the three countries. In September 2007 the MSP-IS was instrumental in the apprehension by the TNI-AL of a tanker in the Singapore Straits that had been hijacked by pirates.[11]

Of equal, if not greater, importance to the MSP were the actions undertaken by Indonesia to tighten security in the country's maritime domain. In response to international criticism, in 2005 the government ordered the armed forces to increase naval patrols in the country's territorial waters and step-up intelligence gathering operations in fishing communities along the coast of Sumatra and on the Riau Islands.[12]

The security initiatives put in place by the littoral states since 2004 have paid strong dividends. Figures published by the IMB demonstrate a significant downward trend in the number of reported incidents of piracy and sea robbery in Southeast Asia between 2004 and 2008. As shown in Table 1, the number of reported attacks fell from 187 in 2003 to 65 in 2008. Incidents of maritime depredations in the SOM declined from 38 in 2004 to just two in 2008 (though the number of attacks in the Singapore Strait doubled from three attacks in 2007 to six attacks in 2008). Particularly striking has been the improvement in Indonesian waters; attacks are down from a high of 121 in 2003 to 28 in 2008. No longer deserving of the epithet "most pirate infested waters in the world", in 2008 Indonesia dropped into third place behind the Gulf of Aden (92) and Nigeria (40). With Somalia ranked fourth (19) and Tanzania fifth (14), Africa is now the global piracy black spot.[13]

The overall downward trend is also reflected in statistics compiled by the Singapore-based Information Sharing Centre (ISC) which was set-up in 2006 under the auspices of the Regional Cooperation Agreement on Combating Piracy and Armed Robbery Against Ships in Asia (ReCAAP). ReCAAP is a 2001 Japanese initiative agreed to by 16 countries in 2004 (the ten ASEAN members, China, Japan, South Korea, India, Sri Lanka and Bangladesh). ReCAAP came into effect in September 2006, though Malaysia and Indonesia, citing sovereignty concerns, have declined to ratify the agreement. In its 2008 third quarter report, ReCAAP-ISC reported 42 incidents in Southeast Asian waters between January and September, down from 53 during the same period in 2006.[14]

The decrease in acts of maritime violence in Southeast Asia during the period 2004–08 may be attributed to a number of positive developments. First, although the littoral states have not made quantitative data available, the MSP seems to have acted as a strong deterrent to pirates and sea robbers — the maritime equivalent of a cop on the beat. In its 2008 third quarter report, the IMB highlighted the importance of the MSP when it praised the littoral states "for the continued and enhanced cooperation that has been in existence since 2004 which is directly attributable to keeping the overall number of incidents in this important strategic chokepoint down".[15] In March 2008 PACOM Commander Admiral Timothy Keating congratulated the three countries for "markedly improving maritime domain awareness and law enforcement capabilities in the strategically important Strait of Malacca".[16] Political leaders from the littoral states themselves have been full-throated in their praise for the MSP. In October 2008, for instance, Malaysian Deputy Prime Minister Najib Razak commended the "significant and unprecedented" security cooperation undertaken by the three countries in the SOM since 2004."[17]

In September 2008 the MSP was given a boost with the admission of Thailand.[18] Under revised arrangements, Thailand will participate in the MSSP beginning in October 2008 and the EiS in January 2009. Thailand's area of operations will be the northern approaches to the SOM in the Andaman Sea.

Second, increased and sustained patrols by the TNI-AL have led to a sharp decline in the number of attacks in Indonesian waters. In its annual report for 2008, the IMB applauded Indonesia for its "tireless efforts in curbing piracy and armed robbery in its waters.[19] The August 2005 Aceh Peace Agreement may also have contributed to a fall in the number of incidents off the northern tip of Sumatra as GAM disarmed and disbanded.

A third reason for the improvement in the security situation is assistance provided by external powers. As the RMSI controversy highlighted, Indonesia and Malaysia are strongly opposed to foreign military forces undertaking patrol duties in Southeast Asian waters. However, both countries welcome support from external powers in the form of capacity building (e.g. training, exercises and equipment transfer) and information sharing. Japan has played an active, though low-key, role in helping the littoral states with capacity building efforts since the 1960s, and continued to fulfill this role in 2007–08. In September 2007 the Japanese government reportedly pledged financial support of US$300 million to the Marine Security Coordinating Agency (Bakorkamla, in Indonesia the body that coordinates the activities of various law enforcement agencies) in Indonesia and in January 2008 donated US$4.34 million to the Malaysian coast guard, the Malaysian Maritime Enforcement Agency (MMEA), for the upgrade of surveillance radars.[20]

The United States has played a central role too. Although the 2004 controversy turned RMSI into a toxic acronym, the aim of assisting Southeast Asian countries improve maritime surveillance and interdiction capabilities was given significant financial backing by the Bush administration. These financial resources have been used in part to help Indonesia and Malaysia improve security in the SOM, but because the MSP and other initiatives have brought that problem under control, the U.S. redirected its efforts towards improving security in the so-called tri-border sea area. The tri-border sea area covers two main bodies of water: the Sulu Sea in the southwestern Philippines and off Sabah province in eastern Malaysia, and the Celebes Sea which is enclosed by Sabah, the Sulu archipelago and Mindanao in the southern Philippines and Indonesia's Sulawesi Island. Over the years, the tri-border area has gained a notorious reputation for illegal maritime activities such as piracy, smuggling and illegal trafficking, and, more seriously, as a transit route for members of terrorist groups such as ASG and JI to move between the southern Philippines, Sabah and Indonesia. Neglected for decades by the governments of Jakarta and Manila, the tri-border area has been characterized by some analysts as an "ungoverned space" and "theater of jihadi operations".[21]

Concerned about dangers posed by such ungoverned spaces, Section 1206 of the U.S. National Defense Authorization Act for Fiscal Year 2006 (FY06) authorized the Department of Defense (DoD) to assist foreign countries build and sustain capable military forces to conduct counterterrorism operations. Section 1206 funding is primarily designed to help countries improve maritime, riverine, border and port security efforts, particularly in Southeast and South Asia. Southeast Asian maritime states, particularly Indonesia, Malaysia and the Philippines, have been among the biggest recipients of Section 1206 funds, also known as the Global Train and Equip Program. In FY06 and FY07 the U.S. provided Indonesia with US$47.1 million in equipment to enhance maritime security, including five coastal surveillance radars situated along the Indonesian side of the SOM and seven in the Makassar Strait and Celebes Sea. During the same period, Malaysia received US$16.3 million, including US$2.2 million to enhance its EiS capabilities and US$13.6 million for nine coastal surveillance radars along the coast of Sabah. In FY06 and FY07 the Philippines received US$15.5 million to upgrade the maritime surveillance and interdiction capabilities of the Philippines armed forces.[22] The FY08 request includes US$9.5 million for coastal surveillance radars to be sited in the Sulu archipelago and US$3.5 million for additional radar facilities for Indonesia.[23] According to one agency, the Global Train and Equip Program is considered DoD's "single most important tool to shape the environment and counter terrorism outside Iraq and Afghanistan".[24] With the RMSI controversy in mind, equipment under Section 1206 authorization has been provided to Southeast Asian countries with minimal publicity. In addition to Global Train and Equip, the United States has also been providing capacity-building support to Southeast Asian navies through the annual Cooperation Afloat Readiness and Training (CARAT) and Southeast Cooperation Against Terrorism (SEACAT). The U.S. government has also funded the transfer of 30 patrol boats to the Indonesian Marine Police.[25]

Next Steps Forward

The security situation in maritime Southeast Asia has improved significantly since 2004, thanks mainly to the cooperative efforts of regional states and capacity-building support from external powers. However, there remains considerable scope for improvement. In the SOM, the littoral states need to maintain the current tempo of operations. As the number of attacks decline, and international pressure eases, a danger exists that the littoral states might let down their collective guard and the frequency of patrols will be reduced. As IMB Director Captain Pottengal Mukundan warned: "There is no room for complacency. It is vital that law enforcement resources remain deployed in [the Straits] if the attacks are not to resume."[26] And as Captain Noel Choong, head of the IMB's Piracy Reporting Centre, noted: "What we see is that the pirates aren't being detained, they're just lying low because of the aggressive patrols ... We maintain our piracy warning for the Malacca Straits despite the stability of the region".[27] The most important participant in the MSP, Indonesia, is particularly at risk of "patrol fatigue" both because it does not see piracy as a major threat (compared with illegal fishing and smuggling), and because the patrols consume a high proportion of limited resources, particularly ships, fuel and manpower. Due to rising energy prices and the global financial crisis, Indonesia's already modest defence budget for 2009 has been slashed by 15 per cent.[28] Only 30 per cent of the Indonesian navy's 120 vessels are operational at any one time, and the navy admits that it needs 376 ships to adequately patrol the country's vast maritime areas.[29] Continued vigilance is paramount, especially as both the Indonesian and Malaysian navies have warned that incidents of piracy may experience an upsurge due to deteriorating socio-economic conditions associated with the global economic downturn.[30]

Since 2005, Indonesian anchorages and territorial waters have become much safer. But overlapping jurisdictions among competing law enforcement agencies have created inefficiencies and rivalries. Bakorkamla, TNI-AL, Marine Police, Sea and Coast Guard, Customs Department and Fisheries Department share responsibility for maritime security in Indonesia: all are underfunded, under-equipped and undertrained, and interagency cooperation is very limited. Jakarta would do well to emulate its neighbour Malaysia, which resolved the problem of overlapping jurisdictions in 2005 by transferring responsibility for enforcing maritime law and order from 11 different agencies to the MMEA. Unfortunately, however, due to lack of financial resources, a unified Indonesian coast guard is unlikely to be established in the near future.[31]

The pan-Asian anti-piracy initiative ReCAAP Information Sharing Centre has done excellent work since it began formal operation in late 2006, including issuing insightful quarterly reports and conducting capacity-building seminars and exercises across the region. However, although the MMEA and Bakorkamla have agreed to cooperate with the ISC in Singapore, ReCAAP would be greatly strengthened if Malaysia and Indonesia were to formally ratify the agreement.

The tri-border sea area remains a haven for transnational criminals and militants, though according to some reports increased cooperation among the Philippines, Indonesia and Malaysia has slowed the number of JI operatives moving into the southern Philippines from Indonesia via Sabah.[32] Nevertheless, bilateral and trilateral security interaction remains patchy and episodic and an MSP-style initiative for the tri-border sea area would be a major step in the right direction. More fundamentally, in both the SOM and tri-border area, resident countries need to devote more resources to tackling the root causes of piracy and sea robbery, especially raising socio-economic conditions in maritime communities and improving good governance.

Maritime Territorial and Boundary Disputes

History, and especially the decolonization process after World War II, bequeathed Southeast Asia a myriad of contentious territorial disputes, both on land and in the maritime domain. The problem of unresolved maritime boundary claims was compounded as regional states enthusiastically adopted 200 nm exclusive economic zones (EEZs) as codified in the 1982 United Nations Law of the Sea Convention. Asian states have jealously sought to protect their sovereignty and sovereign rights, rendering some of the disputes seemingly intractable. Nevertheless, since the end of the Cold War qualified progress has been made in terms of mitigating interstate tensions through the application of confidence-building measures (CBMs) and, in some cases, even negotiated settlements. Such progress, however, has proved glacially slow. The following sections examine progress and remaining obstacles in two maritime territorial and boundary disputes that made headlines in 2008: the South China Sea and Pedra Branca/Pulau Batu Puteh (hereafter Pedra Branca) disputes.

The South China Sea Dispute: Two Steps Backwards

Among all of Southeast Asia's territorial problems none is more complex and contentious than the South China Sea dispute. For much of the 1990s the issue was a source of serious interstate tension between several ASEAN states and China. The focus of the dispute is contested sovereignty over two chains of islands, the Paracels and Spratlys. The Paracel Islands, which lie off the central coast of Vietnam and southeast of China's Hainan Island, are claimed by both the Chinese and Vietnamese governments. In 1974 China's People's Liberation Army (PLA) expelled South Vietnamese forces from the Paracels when Hanoi and Beijing were still nominal allies. Since 1975 Hanoi has consistently rejected China's claim to sovereignty over the islands. This dispute truly is intractable as Beijing considers the matter closed and refuses to even discuss the issue with Vietnam. The Spratlys archipelago, located in the southern part of the South China Sea, is composed of over 170 geographical features, less than 50 of which can technically be called islands. Sovereignty of the features is claimed by six parties: China, Taiwan, Vietnam, the Philippines, Malaysia and Brunei. The islands, rocks and atolls that make up the Spratlys have no intrinsic value in themselves: sovereignty is contested because of the potential for rich hydrocarbon deposits under the seabed, and because the Spratlys lie adjacent to the vital SLOCs that pass through the South China Sea. Since the 1950s each of the disputants except Brunei has occupied islands and stationed military forces on their possessions.

In the 1990s China's assertive behaviour in the South China Sea stirred anxiety in the ASEAN capitals. While China's paramount leader Deng Xiaoping had called on the disputants to put aside their sovereignty claims and engage in joint exploration and exploitation of maritime resources, actions taken by the Chinese government suggested it was intent on enforcing its irredentist claims. In 1992 China passed legislature which laid claim to almost the entire South China Sea; in 1995 it rattled the ASEAN states by occupying and building military structures on Mischief Reef, a small atoll within the Philippines' 200 nm EEZ; and throughout the 1990s China and Vietnam verbally sparred over ownership of off-shore oil fields close to the Vietnamese coast. China's "creeping assertiveness" was interpreted by some as a worrying portent of how a powerful China might behave in the future: as Philippine President Fidel Ramos warned in 1995, the Spratlys issue was "a litmus test of whether China as a Great Power intends to play by international rules, or make its own".[33]

In the second half of the 1990s the Chinese government recognized that its assertive behaviour in the South China Sea had been counterproductive in that it was fuelling fears of a "China threat". Accordingly Beijing began to show greater tactical flexibility by agreeing to discuss the dispute with ASEAN in multilateral settings. These discussions culminated in the Declaration on the Conduct of Parties in the South China Sea (DoC), signed by ASEAN and China in November 2002. Though non-binding and falling short of a formal code of conduct — which the signatories agreed to continue negotiations with — the DoC aimed to freeze the status quo by enjoining signatories not to occupy presently unoccupied features, and encouraging the disputants to adopt CBMs.

The most promising CBM was an agreement reached in September 2004 between the national oil companies of the Philippines and China to conduct "pre-exploration" studies in the Spratlys to identify oil and gas reserves. Vietnam was initially opposed to the agreement but after talks with the Philippines agreed to participate. In March 2005 the state-owned energy companies of the Philippines, China and Vietnam signed the Joint Marine Seismic Undertaking (JMSU), an agreement to jointly prospect for oil and gas deposits in the disputed waters of the South China Sea over a three year period beginning on 1 July 2005. The JMSU received a mixed reception. At the official level, it was widely praised: Philippine President Gloria Macapagal Arroyo called the JMSU an "historic diplomatic breakthrough for peace and security" while China's *People's Daily* lauded the agreement as the first step towards putting Deng's sovereignty-shelving formula into action.[34] Detractors of the agreement pointed to the JMSU's lack of transparency: the contents of the agreement were never made public, nor the exact locations of the survey sites.

In 2008 the JMSU became engulfed in a firestorm of controversy in the Philippines. An article in the January–February issue of the *Far Eastern Economic Review (FEER)* contended that in agreeing to the initial agreement in 2004, the Arroyo government had not only broken ranks with its ASEAN partners by cutting a bilateral deal with China without consulting them, but, more seriously, Manila had made "breathtaking concessions" to Beijing since approximately one-sixth of the area designated for the seismic survey lay within Philippine territorial waters, and outside the claims of both China and Vietnam.[35] The contents of the *FEER* article were quickly seized on by Arroyo's opponents, who accused the government of prejudicing the country's territorial claims in the South China Sea and violating Article 12 of the 1987 Constitution which stipulates that any consortium undertaking exploratory activities in Philippine waters must be 60 per cent owned by Filipinos. Critics assailed the government for selling out the national patrimony; some even called for the President's impeachment for treason. An even more explosive insinuation followed: that the Philippine leader had agreed to the JMSU as a quid pro quo for several large PRC-funded overseas development aid (ODA) projects, including a national broadband network and the upgrade of two railway lines, all of which had come under scrutiny by the Philippine Senate in response to allegations of overpricing and bribery (these projects were subsequently cancelled).[36]

The Philippine government offered a three-point defence: it argued the JMSU was a critical component of the country's search for energy independence; that it was a commercial agreement that did not prejudice the Philippines' territorial claims; and that it served as an important CBM that would transform the South China Sea from a region of conflict into a region of peace and cooperation. Critics of the JMSU remained unconvinced and called on the Supreme Court to declare the agreement unconstitutional. At the same time, the PRC came under fire for trying to exert undue pressure on Manila over a bill being discussed in the legislature to update the Philippines' archipelagic baseline claims in preparation for submission to the United Nations before May 2009. The bill, which reaffirmed Philippine claims to sovereignty over part of the Spratlys, had passed two readings but stalled on the third and final one. It was alleged that the Chinese Embassy in Manila had expressed opposition to the bill as a violation of the DoC and inimical to Sino-Philippine relations.[37] China's objections to the bill could be seen as hypocritical because Beijing had passed legislation in December 2007 creating a county-level city in Hainan Island called Sansha to administer China's claims in the South China Sea, including the Paracels and Spratlys.

This potent combination of scandal-tainted Chinese-funded ODA projects, questions surrounding the constitutionality of the JMSU and allegations of strong-arm tactics by Beijing over Philippine maritime legislation persuaded the Arroyo administration to distance itself from the tripartite seismic study to avoid further controversy. When the JMSU lapsed on 30 June 2008, the Philippine government announced that it would not be extended.[38] Interestingly there was no official comment from Beijing or Hanoi.

The South China Sea dispute also overshadowed Vietnam's relations with the PRC during 2007–08. As noted earlier, Hanoi had signed on to the JMSU in March 2005 after initially protesting the agreement. At the signing ceremony, Vietnam explained it had changed tack in the interests of regional stability.[39] It now seems clear, however, that Hanoi was prepared to join the JMSU only because the survey area covered by the agreement was not located in Vietnamese-claimed waters. The JMSU may have contributed to an easing of Sino-Vietnamese tensions in the South China Sea during 2005–06, but in 2007 developments led to a sharp deterioration in relations. Three sets of incidents riled Vietnam. The first concerned overlapping sovereignty claims in the Con Son Basin, 230 miles off Vietnam's southeast coast. In April the PRC accused Vietnam of infringing its sovereignty by allowing a consortium of energy companies led by British Petroleum (BP) to develop two gas fields in the basin.[40] As had become customary practice, Vietnam rejected China's protest and reaffirmed sovereignty over the area in question. However, in June, BP announced it was suspending work in the two fields, leading to speculation that Beijing had put pressure on the company by threatening to exclude it from future energy projects in the PRC.[41] Energy hungry Vietnam, which has prioritized the extraction of natural gas to help fuel the country's rapid economic development, was furious that China had apparently leaned on BP.

The second set of events concerned Chinese activities in the Paracels. In July, Chinese naval vessels fired on a Vietnamese fishing boat in the vicinity of the archipelago, killing one sailor. Vietnamese officials travelled to Beijing, and both sides agreed to maintain stability in the area.[42] In the second half of 2007, however, Hanoi felt compelled to reaffirm its sovereignty claims over the Paracels when Beijing announced the start of tourist cruises to the islands and conducted military exercises in the area, actions which Hanoi felt were not "conducive to a friendly bilateral relationship".[43]

The third set of incidents provoked the most serious crisis in Sino-Vietnamese relations since the two countries normalized relations in 1991. As noted earlier, in December 2007 China passed legislation creating Sansha city to administer the country's claims over the Paracels and Spratlys. The Sansha legislation proved to be the last straw for Vietnam: over two consecutive weekends in December it allowed hundreds of students to conduct anti-China protests near the Chinese Embassy in Hanoi and consular office in Ho Chi Minh City. The demonstrators expressed anger over China's claims in the South China Sea and accused China of invading Vietnamese territory and pursuing hegemonic ambitions.[44] The Vietnamese government claimed the protests had been spontaneous, though few believed this given the authoritarian nature of Vietnam. Clearly Hanoi had taken a leaf out of China's playbook and was using the demonstrations to register its indignation with Beijing. In response, the PRC declared it was "highly concerned" at the rallies and demanded the Vietnamese authorities adopt a "responsible attitude" and "avoid bilateral ties from being hurt".[45] Relations took another hit in January 2008 when China accused Vietnamese fishermen of attacking Chinese trawlers in the Gulf of Tonkin, a semi-enclosed body of water in the South China Sea which China and Vietnam had partially delimited in a 2000 treaty.

In keeping with their long-standing commitment to resolve outstanding disputes peacefully, and not to let territorial issues hinder the forward momentum of ties, Vietnam and China moved quickly to stabilize relations. The China-Vietnam Steering Committee met in Beijing on 23 January 2008 to douse the flames: co-chairs Chinese State Councilor Tang Jiaxuan and Vietnamese Deputy Prime Minister and Foreign Minister Pham Gia Khiem agreed to "properly handle the problems in bilateral relations" through "dialogue and consultation", and accelerate negotiations on the delineation of remaining areas of the Gulf of Tonkin and issues relating to the South China Sea.[46] During a visit to China by Vietnamese Communist Party (VCP) General Secretary Nong Duc Manh in June 2008, the two countries agreed to "uphold the use of peaceful negotiations to search for basic and long-term solutions acceptable to both sides, and at the same time to actively study and discuss the issue of joint development to find a suitable model and areas".[47] Agreement was also reached to undertake demarcation of waters outside the mouth of the Gulf of Tonkin.

Controversy returned, however, in July when a Hong Kong newspaper reported that executives of the world's largest energy company, ExxonMobil, had been approached by Chinese officials and warned not to proceed with a deal the company had signed in June to explore for energy resources off the Vietnamese coast. The report suggested other foreign energy companies had received similar warnings from China.[48] In a departure from the usual practice, China's foreign ministry confirmed the story by stating it had made clear its position to the "relevant side".[49] Vietnam brushed off China's warning: a foreign ministry spokesman noted that "We have confirmed that all Vietnamese cooperation with foreign partners in the field of petroleum is conducted in Vietnamese territorial waters and in the exclusive economic zone".[50] By October, official harmony had once more been restored, at least on the surface. During a visit to Beijing by Vietnamese Prime Minister Nguyen Tan Dung, the two countries agreed to "collaborate in maintaining peace and stability" in the South China Sea.[51]

There are several possible explanations to account for Sino-Vietnamese friction in the South China Sea during 2007–08. First, it may have been an attempt by Beijing to pressure Hanoi into accepting a joint exploration and production agreement covering energy fields located off the Vietnamese coast, similar in nature to the June 2008 pact between China and Japan to jointly develop the Chunxiao gas field in the disputed waters of the East China Sea. If so, Beijing's efforts were never likely to succeed, as the off-shore energy fields lie within, or at the edge of, Vietnam's declared 200 nm EEZ. Moreover, Vietnamese nationalism suggests that Hanoi will resolutely resist perceived attempts by China to bully it into accepting such an arrangement. As a tactic in pursuit of this goal Beijing seems to be ratcheting up the pressure on foreign oil companies not to enter into energy deals with Vietnam, with the implicit threat that corporations that do so will be excluded from future energy projects in the PRC. Thus far this tactic has proven unsuccessful, as both BP and ExxonMobil have indicated their intention to proceed with existing deals".

Second, China may be signalling to Vietnam its strong disapproval of deeper U.S.-Vietnam security ties. Since Vietnam and the United States normalized relations in 1995, Hanoi has been careful to calibrate its defence relations with the U.S. so as not to offend the PRC. However, in recent years the pace of development of U.S.-Vietnamese military-security ties has noticeably quickened. In June 2008 Vietnamese Prime Minister Nguyen made a high-profile trip to the United States where he met with President George W. Bush and became the first Vietnamese premier since 1975 to visit the Pentagon. In a joint statement released after the Bush-Nguyen meeting, both sides agreed to hold regular high-level talks on security and strategic issues. Moreover, President Bush also stated that the U.S. supported "Vietnam's *national sovereignty*, security and territorial integrity" (italics added).[52] Bush's unprecedented comment was open to interpretation, as it did not explicitly identify the South China Sea. However, it reinforced comments made by U.S. Defense Secretary Robert Gates earlier in the year in Singapore: "In my Asian travels, I hear my hosts worry about the security implications of rising demand for resources, and about *coercive diplomacy* and other pressures that can lead to disruptive complications... All of us in Asia must ensure that our actions are not seen as pressure tactics, *even when they coexist beside outward displays of cooperation*" (italics added).[53] The U.S. position is that it does not recognize the claims of any of the disputants in the South China Sea; taken together, however, the comments made by Bush and Gates suggest Washington is warning Beijing not to blackmail foreign and especially U.S. energy companies into non-participation in Vietnam's oil and gas sector.

A third possible reason is that Beijing has reverted to a more assertive policy in the South China Sea. This assertiveness may be driven by China's increasing thirst for off-shore energy deposits, the modernization of the Chinese navy which has given Beijing the military wherewithal to enforce its claims, and the growing importance of Southeast Asian SLOCs to China's strategic interests and Great Power ambitions. It remains to be seen whether the Chinese government will risk damaging greatly improved relations with ASEAN in pursuit of these goals.

Pedra Branca: A Breakthrough of Sorts

One avenue open to states with conflicting territorial and boundary claims is to submit their dispute to the International Court of Justice (ICJ) in The Hague for adjudication. It is unlikely that the Spratlys dispute will ever be heard before the ICJ as none of the claimants has a strong case and one of the disputants — Taiwan — is not recognized as a sovereign state by the PRC or any of the ASEAN disputants. Nevertheless, some Southeast Asian countries have pursued the adjudication option, including Malaysia and Singapore who submitted a bilateral maritime territorial dispute to the ICJ in 2003. The Court's May 2008 ruling, however, was not entirely clear cut.

The dispute centred on Pedra Branca, a small island lying at the eastern end of the Singapore Straits, 24 nm east of Singapore and 7.7 nm south of the Malaysian state of Johor. The sovereignty dispute emerged in 1979 when the Malaysian government published a map showing Pedra Branca situated in its territorial waters. In 1980 Singapore rejected the claim and asked Malaysia to amend the map. Two rounds of bilateral discussions in 1993 and 1994 not only failed to resolve the issue but also brought into contention ownership of two nearby features, Middle Rocks and South Ledge. In 2003 Singapore and Malaysia agreed to submit the dispute to the ICJ, and in November 2007 the case was heard.

The ICJ issued its judgement on 23 May 2008. The Court awarded Singapore sovereignty over Pedra Branca, and Malaysia ownership of Middle Rocks. The status of South Ledge was left undetermined: the Court ruled that it fell within overlapping territorial waters generated by Malaysia, Pedra Branca and Middle Rocks, and that sovereignty belonged to the state in whose territorial waters it was located.[54] In awarding Singapore Pedra Branca the Court concluded that while the Sultanate of Johor had possessed original title, after 1850 the Johor authorities and its successors had taken no action on the island; by reference to the conduct of Singapore and its predecessor (the United Kingdom) — including the operation of the Horsburgh lighthouse, investigation of marine accidents and the installation of naval equipment — and Malaysia's failure to respond to that conduct, by 1979 sovereignty had already passed to Singapore. In addition, the Court noted that a 1953 letter from the Acting Secretary of State for Johor to the British colonial authorities stated that Johor did not claim ownership of Pedra Branca, and that official maps produced by Malaysia in the 1950s and 1960s indicated appreciation of Singapore's sovereignty. Regarding Middle Rocks, the Court ruled that as original title belonged to the Sultan of Johor, and Singapore had not exercised conduct as a sovereign, ownership still lay with Malaysia.

It was not the outcome either side had hoped for, though both governments put a brave face on the ruling. Singapore's Deputy Prime Minister Professor S. Jayakumar called it a "good example to the region of how such disputes can be resolved in a peaceful and amicable manner", while Malaysia's Deputy Prime Minister Najib Razak praised the ICJ's "balanced decision".[55] Nonetheless, despite agreeing to abide by the decision, Malaysia indicated it would continue to search for evidence proving the Sultanate of Johor still possessed title to Pedra Branca, as the ICJ can review cases within a ten-year period.[56]

Within a few months of the ruling controversy erupted after a Singapore government minister stated in parliament that Pedra Branca could generate a 12 nm territorial sea and 200 nm EEZ.[57] Despite having referred to Pedra Branca as an island (Pulau Batu Puteh or White Rock Island) before the ruling, the Malaysian government averred that Pedra Branca did not meet internationally recognized criteria as an island. Malaysian Foreign Minister Rais Yatim claimed Singapore's action violated international law and warned the city-state that it risked "stirring a hornet's nest".[58] Despite the rhetoric, however, both sides have reiterated their commitment to abide by and fully implement the Court's decision.[59] Prior to the ruling the two sides established a joint technical committee to enforce the judgement. This committee is now tasked with the complex task of delimiting the territorial waters around Pedra Branca and Middle Rocks, and resolving ownership of South Ledge.

The ICJ ruling on Pedra Branca, Middle Rocks and South Ledge is reminiscent of its 2002 decision concerning a territorial dispute between Malaysia and Indonesia. On 17 December 2002 the Court ruled that sovereignty of Sipidan and Ligitan, two small islands off the east coast of Borneo in the Celebes Sea, belonged to Malaysia.[60] As with the Pedra Branca case the key factor which led the ICJ to award sovereignty to Malaysia was Kuala Lumpur's ability to demonstrate effective exercise of authority over the islands, including the operation of British-built lighthouses, which neither Indonesia nor its predecessor (the Netherlands) had protested. The ICJ did not, however, determine the maritime boundaries between Malaysia and Indonesia in the vicinity of the two islands (because as with the Pedra Branca case it was not asked to do so). As with Malaysia and Pedra Branca, Indonesia refused to accept that Sipidan and Ligitan could generate territorial seas and EEZs. Thus, in March 2005 Indonesia accused Malaysia of violating its sovereignty by awarding exploration licences to a foreign oil company in two deep-water oil concession blocks in the so-called Ambalat area. Unable to reach a diplomatic solution, both sides moved naval forces into the disputed area resulting in a tense stand off. Conflict was avoided when both sides agreed to resolve the issue peacefully and quietly withdrew their forces. A joint technical committee was established to discuss the issue, but it has yet to reach a settlement. In October 2008 the dispute flared up again when Indonesia accused the Malaysian armed forces of territorial violations in the Ambalat area.[61] As in 2005, Kuala Lumpur and Jakarta beefed up their military forces in the area.

In the case of the maritime boundary dispute over Pedra Branca the stakes are considerably lower because of the absence of nearby oil fields. However, the Ambalat dispute underscores two points. First, negotiations aimed at resolving overlapping maritime jurisdictions are invariably prolonged; and second, political and military posturing by one or both parties runs the risk of an accidental military clash. It is to be hoped that Malaysia and Singapore can resolve their overlapping maritime claims in a timely and amicable fashion.

Conclusion

It has become axiomatic that no one country has the resources to tackle security threats in the maritime domain: interstate cooperation is vital if threats to freedom of navigation and the free flow of global commerce are to be extinguished. In Southeast Asia over the past four years solid progress has been achieved through enhanced regional and international cooperation, especially in the strategically important Straits of Malacca where piracy and sea robbery attacks have fallen to their lowest levels since the early 1990s. The world's attention is now transfixed on the situation off the Horn of Africa where well-armed and highly-organized pirate gangs perpetrated 111 attacks against shipping in 2008, including 42 hijackings and the seizure of 815 hostages. In comparison, Southeast Asian waters seem positively placid and well-ordered. Yet higher levels of regional cooperation are required, especially in the notorious tri-border sea area. The same holds true for the South China Sea dispute, where recent developments have proved discouraging. The JMSU was fundamentally flawed and its expiration essentially puts the dispute back to square one. Negotiations between ASEAN and China to frame a formal code of conduct have led nowhere, snagged no doubts on the contentious issue of sovereignty. More ominously China's actions in the South China Sea over the past 18 months suggest a more assertive stance than at any time since the mid-1990s. Two cheers for regional cooperation.

Notes

The author would like to express his thanks to Clive Schofield and Bronson Percival for their insightful comments on an earlier draft of this paper.

[1]   United Nations Conference on Trade and Development (UNCTAD), *Review of Maritime Transport 2008* (New York and Geneva: United Nations, 2008), p. xiii.

[2]   Ibid., p. 8.

[3]   American Association of Port Authorities <www.aapa-ports.org> and UNCTAD, *Review of Maritime Transport 2006* (New York and Geneva: United Nations, 2006), p. 78.

[4]   "Global storm hits China's sea commerce", *Asia Times Online*, 21 October 2008.

[5]   For a more detailed account of these issues see Ian Storey, "Securing Southeast Asia's Sea Lanes: A Work in Progress", *Asia Policy*, no. 6 (July 2008): 95–127.

[6]   Under international law an act of piracy is defined as an illegal act of violence or detention involving two or more ships on the high seas, i.e. outside a coastal state's territorial waters. This definition is employed in the 1982 United Nations Convention on the Law of the Sea (UNCLOS) and was adopted by the International Maritime Organization (IMO), an agency within the United Nations (UN) specializing in maritime safety. According to this definition, acts of depredation which occur within a state's territorial waters are acts of "armed robbery against ships" (also known as sea robbery) and subject to the national jurisdiction of the state. See Article 101, *United Nations Convention on the Law of the Sea* (New York: United Nations Publication, 1997), p. 57.

[7]   For a complete account see *The Jemaah Islamiyah Arrests and the Threat of Terrorism* (Singapore: Ministry of Home Affairs, January 2003).

[8]   Testimony of Admiral Thomas B. Fargo, United States Navy, Commander, U.S. Pacific Command, Before the House Armed Services Committee, U.S. House of Representatives, Regarding U.S. Pacific Command Posture, 31 March 2004 <http://pacom.mil/speeches/sst2004/040331housearmedsvcscomm.shtml>.

[9]   "S'pore can't invite US to patrol straits: KL", *Straits Times*, 12 May 2004.

[10] Keynote address by Minister for Defence Rear Admiral (RADM) (NS) Teo Chee Hean, at the opening of the 2nd Western Pacific MCMEX and DIVEX, 26 April 2004 <http://www.mindef.gov.sg/display.asp?number=2073>.

[11] "Date sharing system boost for Malacca Strait security", *Straits Times*, 29 March 2008.

[12] Author interview with senior TNI-AL officers, Western Command Headquarters, Jakarta, 15 September 2006.

[13] IMB, "Piracy and Armed Robbery Against Ships: Annual Report 1 January–31 December 2008", January 2009, pp. 5–6.

[14] ReCAAP-ISC, "Quarterly Report: 1st January 2008–30th September 2008", available at <www.recaap.org>.

[15] IMB, "Piracy and Armed Robbery Against Ships: Report for the Period 1 January–30 September 2008", October 2008, p. 26.

[16] Statement of Admiral Timothy J. Keating, U.S. Navy Commander, U.S. Pacific Command, Before the House Armed Services Committee on U.S. Pacific Command Posture, 12 March 2008.

[17] Malaysia has spent more than RM300 million to ensure safety in the Straits of Melaka", Bernama, 21 October 2008.

[18] "Thailand joins 4-nation joint patrol of Straits of Malacca", Thai News Agency, 18 September 2008.

[19] IMB, "Piracy and Armed Robbery Against Ships: Annual Report 1 January–31 December 2008", January 2009, p. 26.

[20] "Japan to provide assistance to RI's maritime security agency", Antara News Agency, 19 September 2007 and "RM14 boost for Straits of Malacca security", *Star Online*, 25 January 2008.

[21] Angel Rabasa et al, *Ungoverned Territories: Understanding and Reducing Terrorism Risks* (Santa Monica, CA: RAND Corporation, 2007), p. 116.

[22] Nina M. Serafino, "Section 1206 of the National Defense Authorization Act for FY2006: A Fact Sheet on Department of Defense Authority to Train and Equip Foreign Military Forces", Congressional Research Service Report for Congress, 15 May 2008 <http://ftp.fas.org/sgp/crs/natsec/RS22855.pdf>.

[23] See <http://www.stimson.org/budgeting/Data/1206_Project_Data_Tables.pdf>.

[24] See Fiscal Year (FY) 2009 Budget Estimates Defense Security Cooperation Agency, February 2008 <http://www.defenselink.mil/comptroller/defbudget/fy2009/

budget_justification/pdfs/01_Operation_and_Maintenance/O_M_VOL_1_PARTS/
DSCA%20FY%2009%20PB%20OP-5.pdf>.

25 "US gives 15 boats to Indonesia, demands no return", *Jakarta Post*, 18 January 2008.

26 Cited in "No pirate attacks in Malacca Strait in first quarter", *Business Times* [Malaysia],
    21 April 2008.

27 "Southeast Asia winning Malacca Straits battle for now, says watchdog", Channelnewasia.
    com, 20 November 2008.

28 "MP: defense budget far from sufficient", Antara News Agency, 16 August 2008.

29 "Indonesia short of warships", *Jakarta Post*, 2 August 2007.

30 See "Indonesian Navy says credit crunch will lead to rise in piracy: report", Agence
    France-Presse, 26 November 2008 and "Navy puts focus on security in Straits of
    Malacca", *New Straits Times*, 7 January 2009.

31 "Coast guard argument continues", *Jakarta Post*, 22 October 2007.

32 John McBeth, "Choking off the Sulu connection", *Straits Times*, 18 October 2008.

33 "Spratlys will show if China plays by the rules: Ramos", *Straits Times*, 8 May
    1995.

34 "All-win rational choice", *People's Daily*, 18 March 2005.

35 Barry Wain, "Manila's Bungle in the South China Sea", *Far Eastern Economic Review*,
    January–February 2008.

36 "RP may lose Kalayaans by default", *Newsbreak,* 6 March 2008 <http://www.newsbreak.
    com.ph/index.php?option=com_content&task=view&id=4263&Itemid=88889051>.

37 "China objection stalls OK of bill on RP territory-solon", *Philippine Daily Inquirer,*
    12 March 2008.

38 "Joint exploration pact lapses", *Philippine Star*, 12 July 2008.

39 "Philippines, China, Vietnam to conduct joint marine seismic research in South China
    Sea", *People's Daily*, 15 March 2005.

40 "Vietnam's actions on Nansha Islands infringe on China's sovereignty: FM spokesman",
    People's Daily, 10 April 2007.

41 "Vietnam sees second weekend of anti-China protests", *Straits Times*, 17 December
    2007.

42 "Vietnamese, Chinese negotiators meet on territorial issue", *Straits Times,* 24 July
    2007.

43 "Nation reasserts sovereignty over Hoang Sa, Truong Sa", *Thanh Nien News*,
    25 November 2007.

44 "Vietnam sees second weekend of anti-China protests", *Straits Times,* 17 December
    2007.

45 "China pays close attention to so-called protest in Vietnam over South China Sea",
    Xinhua News Agency, 11 December 2007.

46 "China, Vietnam agree to properly handle the South China Sea dispute", Xinhua News
    Agency, 23 January 2008.

47 "China-Vietnam Joint Statement", Xinhua News Agency, 1 June 2008.

48 "Tussle for oil in the South China Sea", *Sunday Morning Post*, 20 July 2008.

49 "China opposes any act violating its sovereignty", Xinhua News Agency, 27 July 2008.

50 "Vietnam signals it wants ExxonMobil deal despite China warning", Agence France-Presse, 24 July 2008.

51 "Vietnam, China vow to deepen cooperation", Vietnam News Agency, 23 October 2008.

52 Joint Statement Between the United States of America and the Socialist Republic of Vietnam, 24 June 2008 <http://www.vietnamembassy-usa.org/news/story.php?d=20080627045153>.

53 International Institute for Strategic Studies (Singapore) speech as delivered by Secretary of Defense Robert M. Gates, Singapore, 31 May 2008 <http://www.defenselink.mil/speeches/speech.aspx?speechid=1253>.

54 For the full text of the judgement see <http://www.icj-cij.org/docket/files/130/14492.pdf>.

55 "World Court awards contested island of Pedra Branca to Singapore", *International Herald Tribune*, 23 May 2008 and "Pedra Branca belongs to Singapore", *Straits Times*, 24 May 2008.

56 "Malaysia not giving up hope on Batu Puteh yet", *Star Online*, 1 June 2008.

57 Transcript of Senior Minister-of-State Balaji Sadasivan's replies to Parliamentary Questions and a Supplementary Question, 21 July 2008 <http://app.mfa.gov.sg/2006/press/view_press.ap?post_id=4202>.

58 "KL's warning on Pedra Branca", *Straits Times*, 18 August 2008 and "Don't stir a hornet's nest, KL warns S'pore", *Straits Times*, 27 July 2008.

59 "Pedra Branca: New joint panel formed", *Straits Times*, 2 September 2008.

60 For a full account of the dispute see Clive Schofield and Ian Storey, "Energy Security and Southeast Asia: The Impact on Maritime Boundary and Territorial Disputes", *Harvard Asia Quarterly* IX, no. 4 (Fall 2005): 36–46.

61 "Malaysian territorial violations in Ambalat draw strong criticism", Antara News Agency, 24 October 2008.

Brunei Darussalam

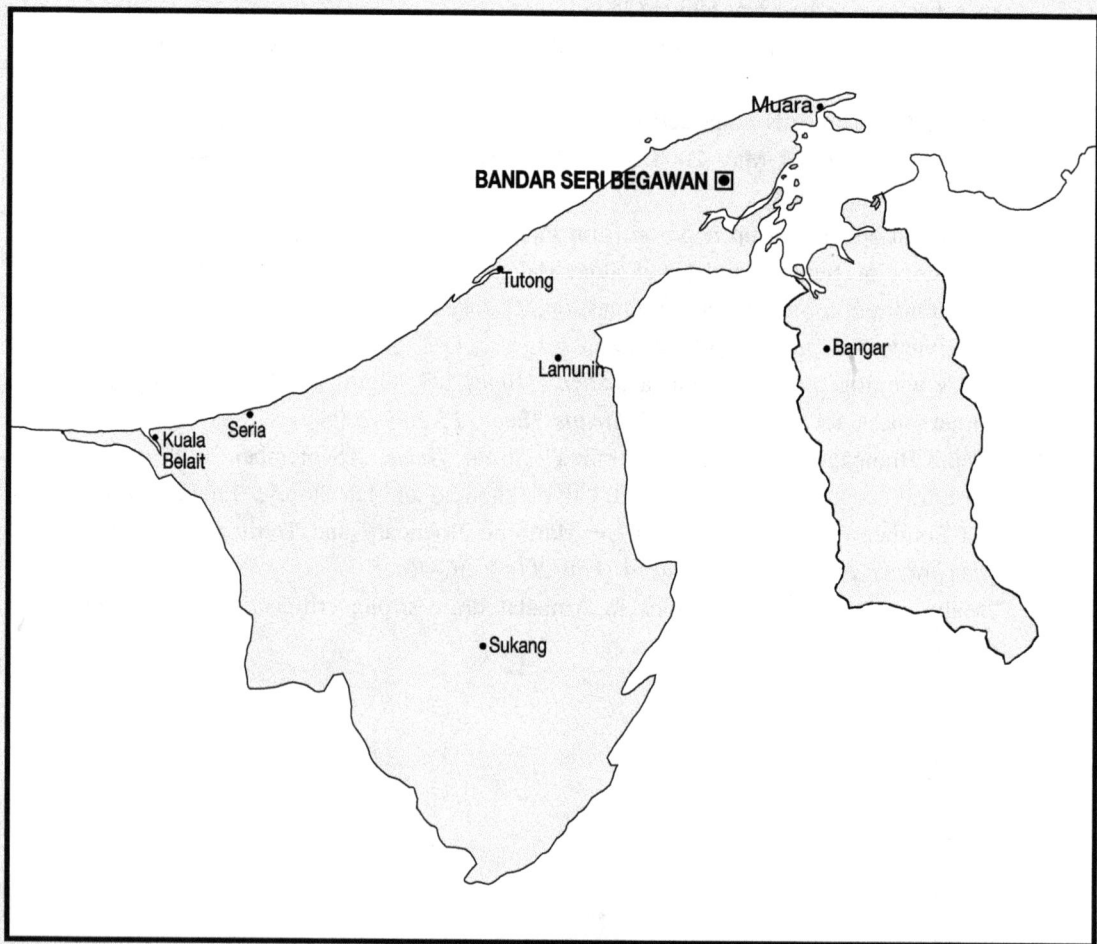

BRUNEI DARUSSALAM
Cautious on Political Reform, Comfortable in ASEAN, Pushing for Economic Diversification

Christopher Roberts and Lee Poh Onn

Domestic Politics

By the end of 2008, the political scene in Brunei was dominated by preparations for the commemoration of Brunei's Silver Jubilee celebrating twenty-five years of independence from colonial rule. On the eve of the National Day in early 2009, Sultan Haji Hassanal Bolkiah delivered a *titah* (a speech or decree) where he declared his intention to increase the growth of industries, to continue to reduce poverty, to increase rice production, and to ensure the continued development of an efficient and outstanding public service. The Sultan contended that both 'regeneration' and 'change' in Brunei will need to be engineered through the 'Brunei Vision' which itself will need to take 'into account not only the nation's status but also global trends'. Implicit in the Sultan's address to the nation was the recognition of the difficult global economic climate which had already affected Brunei.[1]

Since independence on 1 January 1984, Negara Brunei Darussalam has remained a monarchy where the Sultan's powers include the prerogative of mercy in the judiciary, the regulation of Islam and the ability to rule by decree. While the Sultan stated that the Malay Islamic Monarchy will 'ceaselessly remain a sovereign nation, independent and democratic', his pre-National Day *titah* was also notable for the fact that it did not discuss any of the political reforms he had

CHRISTOPHER ROBERTS is Lecturer in International Relations and Asian Studies, Faculty of Business and Government at the University of Canberra, Australia.

LEE POH ONN is Fellow at the Institute of Southeast Asian Studies (ISEAS), Singapore.

previously outlined for the nation. One of the most significant of these reforms concerned the Legislative Council (LegCo or *Majilisi Masyuarat Negeri*) that was reconstituted by royal decree in 2004 as a wholly appointed chamber following a twenty-year respite.[2] A new LegCo was reconvened on 24 September 2005 with an enlarged membership totalling thirty delegates including five indirectly elected members representing the Village Councils. During the meeting, the members voted to further increase the number of representatives to a total of forty-five with the new members being selected via popular vote. However, and through to the conclusion of 2008, there had been no announcement as to when such an election (the first since 1968) would take place.

Since the reopening of LegCo, the Assembly's role has been primarily limited to the deliberation of the national budget in March each year. Nevertheless, and in the context of the 2008 national budget, the Minister for Finance II was questioned about whether there was any financial provision for increased personnel in the fight against drug abuse and corruption. On the issue of narcotics, the Minister replied that in 2008 the size of the anti-narcotics bureau had been increased from 146 to 152 personnel, but added that over thirty new positions had been added during the course of the last few years. The Minister also outlined that the Br$7,100,530 budget for the Anti-Corruption Bureau included provision for 'officers, prevention, enforcement and other issues that may arise'.[3] A further issue that was deliberated during the March 2008 sitting was the longstanding problem of a national brain drain. The government announced that it would establish 'a special scheme for technical experts' and a review of salary for the civil servants — the largest category of employment in the sultanate.[4]

Importantly, the Sultan delivered a *titah* shortly before the sitting of LegCo to incite a discussion of some of his grander visions for the country. These included a 'zero poverty rate' by 2035, as alluded to during his *titah* in the lead-up to the 25th National Day celebrations.[5] In response to a number of questions asked during the deliberations, the Speaker of LegCo sought to refine the role of the Assembly, arguing that some of the issues being brought before it were too small and were therefore undermining the importance of the Assembly.[6] The 2008 session was also notable for taking place in the newly constructed legislative building which the Sultan officially opened on 4 March 2008.[7] Importantly, members of the public were invited to attend the deliberations of parliament during its five days of sitting and to inspect the new building.[8] Such an invitation is symbolic of the Sultan's publically declared intention to provide increased transparency and awareness concerning the government's decision-making processes.[9] Further, The Economist Intelligence Unit contends that LegCo has already set a trend where it is likely to become more assertive as a 'scrutinising body' in future years.[10]

A further area of reform, which had previously taken place in 2005, concerned a reshuffle of the Council of Ministers, or cabinet, which reportedly replaced conservative or divisive ministers with younger technocrats who are more experienced in such matters as commerce and industry. Further reshuffles have been made since, this time including the appointment of the former High Commissioner to Australia, Awang Mohd Sahrip bin Othman, as the new Deputy Permanent Secretary (Policy and Development) to the Ministry of Defence on 1 March 2008.[11] Nonetheless, and in addition to the position of Prime Minister, the Sultan holds the positions of Minister for Finance and Minister for Defence. Further, one of the Sultan's brothers, Prince Mohamed, serves as Minister for Foreign Affairs while the Sultan's son, Crown Prince Al-Muhtadee Billah, serves in the powerful but non-specific post of Senior Minister in the Prime Minister's Office.[12]

The limitations to the government's plans concerning greater political pluralism can also be seen in the context of the Societies Order of 2005 that requires all Associations with more than ten members to be registered and supervised by the government. In recent times, this requirement has provoked some discussion, if not debate, and in September 2008, for example, a government official conceded that activities like a visit to the cinema by more than ten friends would not require registration. While officials in Brunei contend the registration process is not as burdensome as some have claimed, the current cost of Br$200 still remains relatively prohibitive for some. While the government has indicated that it will seek to simplify the registration process so that it can be done via the internet, it is apparent that the government does not intend to amend the order to the point where genuinely autonomous civil society could evolve.[13]

The Societies Order was utilized by the government in late 2008 to disband at least fifty-five Associations for failing to comply with its provisions; a notable increase from the forty-one Associations that were deregistered the previous year. Under the Order, an Association can be deregistered for reasons such as failing to report the names of committee members or submitting the minutes of a meeting. The order also provides the government with an effective tool to regulate and/or disband opposition parties. In early 2007, the *Parti Kesedaran Rakyat* (PAKAR, People's Awareness Party) was disbanded while in February 2008 the *Parti Perpaduan Kebangsaan* (Brunei National Solidarity Party) was officially disbanded. No explanation was provided in the case of the latter.[14] The only legal opposition party that remains is the *Parti Pembangunan* (PP, National Development Party) which was legalised under the Order in August 2005. However, the party only has a few hundred members and Jane's Intelligence contends that the principal purpose of the party 'appears to be to serve as an example of political reform to foreign critics'.[15]

Further, given the country's low taxes, its social welfare policies and the high standard of living, there is no discernable pressure for change by the Bruneian people. However, in the long term, the Sultan has likely calculated that a degree of democracy will be necessary when Brunei's oil reserves run out — a possibility that is predicted to occur within the next twenty to thirty years. With such a scenario, and at a time when the government may no longer be able to provide the kind of economic and social welfare benefits of the past, democracy may provide a necessary 'safety valve' for debate on politicized issues. For example, should unemployment rise as a result of resource depletion then the issue of immigrant labour, such as from the Philippines, could become problematic. Democratization has also been viewed as a way to forestall the emergence of extreme Islamist groups in the country.[16] Nonetheless, for the time being the position of the Monarchy remains secure and a lack of urgency regarding domestic reform was evident when the Sultan attended Indonesia's forum on democracy in December 2008. At the forum, His Majesty discussed the idea of social contract — i.e. the provision of economic development and security to a nation's citizens — but completely avoided the issue of democracy.[17]

Brunei maintains a relatively positive human rights record.[18] For example, while capital punishment is permitted as a penalty for serious crimes, such as rape and murder, it has not been implemented during the entire period of independence. However, in some other areas the country is not entirely free from human rights issues. Thus, the 2008 Human Rights Report by the U.S. Department of State listed such issues as '... arbitrary detention; limits on freedom of speech, press, assembly, and association; discrimination against women; restricted labour; and exploitation of foreign workers' as being problematic in the country. Nonetheless, in recent years there have been a number of positive developments concerning some of these issues. In the context of women's rights and domestic violence, a special unit exists inside the police department that is staffed entirely by women for the purpose of investigating domestic abuse and child abuse. Criminal penalties apply — including caning — and 225 cases of domestic violence were reported during 2008. Further, the country's Islamic courts recognize assault as a ground for divorce.[19] Concerning the issue of 'arbitrary detention', the British installed 'Internal Security Act' (ISA) permits the government to detain suspects without the right to legal counsel for renewable two-year periods. However, during 2008 the government released a number of individuals held under the ISA. For example, on 14 July three individuals who had been accused of leaking government secrets and information and detained under the ISA were released.[20] On 1 September, Haji Sarbini bin Haji Junit was also released after being held under the ISA for allegedly being involved in a counterfeit ring. Following the release of Aji bin Ajak in early January 2009, the last suspect from the alleged counterfeit ring, it would appear that the Government of Brunei is no longer holding any prisoners under the ISA.[21]

In terms of religious freedom, the Constitution provides that while the official religion is Islam, other religions are permitted so long as they are 'practiced in peace and harmony'. There are however a number of restrictions. The Societies Order 2005 requires all non- Islamic religious groups to be 'registered' and to provide the names of their members. Proselytizing by any group other than the official Shafi'i sect is prohibited and the government has not permitted other religions to construct new shrines, temples or churches in recent decades. Further, the government has banned the minority faiths from importing religious materials such as bibles and non-Muslims have 'sometimes faced social or, less frequently, official pressure to conform to Islamic guidelines on behaviour'.[22] Nevertheless, there have been no reports of religious prisoners or detainees in the country and for the 2008 period the government showed a greater tolerance of alternative faiths. For example, in February the Sultan and other members of the royal family attended a number of Chinese New Year celebrations (sponsored by the Chinese community) and later, in 2008, several senior government officials attended the annual *Hari Gawai* ritual conducted by the Iban indigenous tribe where 'thanks' is given to the 'God of Paddy'. The fact that government officials attended the ritual was widely reported in the local media. Further, while multi-faith dialogue has been discouraged *within* the country by the continued application of a 1964 fatwa issued by the State Mufti, in recent years the government has sponsored interfaith dialogue and other ecumenical events through the Asia-Europe Meeting (ASEM). In December 2007, the Government also sponsored a multi-faith delegation to the inaugural Regional Youth Interfaith forum in Australia.[23]

Brunei continues to have problems with illegal immigrants including those that have overstayed their visa. By the turn of 2009, Brunei was forced to defend itself when it was reported in the international press that it had caned 396 immigration offenders during the past five years, with 68 canings having occurred in 2008.[24] According to government data, approximately 88,000 foreigners worked in the country during 2008 and the U.S. Department of State contends most foreign workers are excluded from labour protection laws. Nonetheless, the government has been making an effort to improve protective measures including 'briefings for workers, inspections of facilities, and a telephone hotline for worker complaints'. However, many of those subject to abuse are reportedly unable or unwilling to lodge a complaint. In 2007, only 26 domestic helpers and 108 corporate/garment workers lodged complaints. The government did not provide statistics for 2008. In these instances, the '2008 Human Rights Report' noted that the government was 'usually quick to investigate and impose fines and punishment'.[25] The Brunei government has been particularly active in combating the trafficking of persons having made the activity a specific offence in 2005. Consequently, the February 2009 'Global Report on Trafficking in Persons' UNODC (United Nations Office of Drugs and Crime) stated that no individuals were identified as victims of trafficking during 2008.[26] However, the UNODC at least partially relies on government data and the U.S. Department of State, by contrast, did reveal some 'limited' examples of trafficking. One incident provided a positive example of cooperation where local immigration officials assisted a foreign mission in the rescue of four trafficking victims who had been exploited in a neighbouring country and had entered Brunei to obtain work visa re-entry permits.[27]

Drug abuse, particularly among the nation's youth, has also been a problem in Brunei. In 2007 there were 732 drug related arrests representing around a one-third increase from the previous year.[28] Throughout 2008, the issue of illicit drug abuse featured prominently in the local press and was significant enough to draw the attention of the Sultan. In February 2008, His Majesty outlined how drug abuse was already a 'tragedy' in the nation and questioned how the next generation of leaders will arise if 'even from a young age they are already weak and undermined by drugs?'[29] The escalation of domestic crime rates, particularly in regard to theft, also caught the attention of Brunei's Imams who stated that by committing crimes such as fraud, theft, robbery, kidnapping and rape these people were 'challenging the very power of Allah the almighty in their criminal behaviour'.[30] The Government of Brunei has sought to address the problem through a number of initiatives including the implementation of a proactive 'community policing' approach and the purchase of new high-tech crime-scene equipment to enhance operational efficiency of law enforcement officers.[31] Nonetheless, and despite one report suggesting that both Malaysia and Brunei have been used as a transit point for illicit narcotics,[32] the country has not faced any significant problems with major transnational crime issues due to the high capacity of the state and its professionalized security sectors. The marginal nature of transnational crime in Brunei was reflected in the fact that Brunei receives very little attention from the UNODC and is not even included as a country for analysis in the annual U.S. Department of State's 'International Narcotics Control Strategy Report'.[33]

Military Procurements, Foreign Relations and ASEAN

Given Brunei's weakening economy during the course of the past year, it was not surprising that the Sultanate announced a 2.13 per cent decrease in the Fiscal Year 2008–09 defence budget amounting to a total expenditure of Br$509 million. Nonetheless, the reduced budget was rationalized by the Deputy Minister for Defence as being due to a more systematic management of defence programmes that was initiated by Brunei's 2004 Defence White Paper and the related update in June 2007. However, it is important to note that expenditure for the acquisition of 'major capabilities' is budgeted for separately.[34] Importantly, 2008 witnessed the continued diversification of actual and potential sources for military cooperation and defence acquisitions including meetings and negotiations with Indonesia, Singapore, China, the United States and the United Kingdom. For example, General Cao Gangchuan, the Vice-Chairman of the Central Military Commission, State Councillor and Minister for National Defence, China, made an official visit to Ministry for Defence at the Bolkiah Garrison in January 2008 where he discussed further bilateral cooperation.[35] Meanwhile, Brunei entered into agreements with Harris Corporation from the United States for the supply of battlefield radio systems. Brunei also entered into discussions with Indonesia concerning the possible purchase of additional CN-235 transport aircraft together with what was rumoured by Jane's Intelligence to be an interest in the Indonesian PT Pindad Company's Panser 6×6 armoured personnel carriers.[36] In May 2008, the Royal Brunei Technical Services, Brunei's military procurement and maintenance agency, also secured agreements with Singapore Technologies Engineering (ST Engineering) for the delivery of defence related services including the establishment of a 'communications maintenance centre', and a defence warehouse management system. During the previous twelve months, ST Engineering had also entered into a contract to supply 100 Ultimax machine guns and to expand capabilities in the joint maintenance, repair and overhaul of Brunei's military vehicles.[37]

Brunei's Ministry of Defence also hosted a workshop on defence acquisition cooperation with the United Kingdom and was active in its ongoing efforts to promote the Brunei International Defence Exhibition and Conference (BRIDEX) scheduled to take place on 11 August 2009. In this regard, Brunei marketed BRIDEX by hosting a reception at the Defence Services Asia exhibition in Kuala Lumpur in April 2008.[38] BRIDEX will be co-hosted by Jane's Intelligence and will bring together senior government ministers, defence force chiefs and leading defence industry experts for the purpose of exchanging ideas and information on the key defence issues facing the region and beyond.[39] Earlier, in January 2008,

Brunei's Ministry of Defence and the Royal Brunei Armed Forces announced the commissioning of the 'Defence Personnel Administration Information System' (DefPAIS) as a further step in the realization of the Ministry's goal of developing its information technology. However, the implementation of the system will be primarily limited to an increase in the efficiency of the administrative aspects of defence such as data concerning personnel and leave applications.[40] Despite the proactive nature of the Ministry of Defence's engagement with a diverse range of actors, Brunei's military has only a very limited capacity to undertake conventional warfare and there have been no major acquisitions of advanced weapons systems during the course of the past decade.

The Gurkha Reserve Unit (GRU), comprising two infantry battalions plus support elements, is controlled directly by the Sultan and is therefore outside the Army's chain of command. It is recruited from Gurkhas who have retired from the British Army, and the total number of personnel is believed to be around 2,100. They are used for guard and security services and are stationed in various locations around Brunei. Then there is the British military garrison, comprising a Gurkha infantry battalion, in Seria under British command. This is under a standing bilateral agreement between Brunei and the UK. The British Army also runs a jungle training school. The presence of British troops was negotiated with the British prior to independence and the terms and conditions of their presence are reportedly renegotiated periodically. The precise nature of the agreement has always been kept confidential. Given these unique circumstances, the Sultan's relations with Britain remain particularly important for both internal and external security. Thus, His Majesty the Sultan travelled to Britain to hold high level talks with Prime Minister Gordon Brown in June 2008 where they discussed bilateral relations including education, trade and defence.[41] Prince Charles and the Duchess of Cornwell reciprocated by visiting Brunei in late October.[42] Sound relations with Canada were also evident when thirty-six infantry troops from Canada's 3rd Battalion Royal 22nd Regiment's Reconnaissance Platoon conducted jungle war training exercises at the Seria jungle warfare training school in Brunei.[43]

2008 was also a very important year for Brunei's relations with the United States. In February, the U.S. entered into a land agreement with the Government of Brunei to construct a new embassy and the U.S. declared that it was looking forward to strengthening its people-to-people relationship with Bruneians beyond traditional commercial and diplomatic interests.[44] The U.S. also offered to help Brunei by sharing its expertise in disaster management and energy security — the Sultanate had been hit by flooding and landslides earlier that year — and promised to hold further dialogue in connection with these issues in the future.[45]

Importantly, the annual Cooperation Afloat Readiness and Training (CARAT) naval exercises took place in August 2008 and the U.S. pledged to increase the exchange of military information with Brunei.[46]

Meanwhile, Brunei has continued to maintain positive links with Australia in the security, economic and sociocultural spheres. In May 2008, the Royal Brunei Police Force and the Australian Federal Police Force signed a memorandum of understanding to enhance cooperation and collaboration. During the meeting, the Bruneian Commissioner of Police also thanked the Australian government for providing training in various fields of policing capabilities including the Police Management Development Programme, the Asian Law Enforcement Management Programme, and the International Management of Serious Crime Course.[47] On the military front, His Majesty the Sultan presented the Australian Chief of Air Force, Air Marshal Geoff Shepherd, with the award of the Royal Brunei Air Force Honorary Pilot Wing in recognition of his contribution in enhancing cooperation between the two air forces.[48] Australia was also reported in Brunei's press as representing a popular destination for tertiary education where more than 800 Bruneians are currently studying. In May 2008, the Australian High Commission hosted a Study in Australia Open Day with the theme of 'G'day Mate' to encourage more high school graduates to choose Australia as their study destination.[49]

In the context of extra-regional actors, both Brunei and China sought to enhance their bilateral ties with each other despite the continuation of conflicting claims in the South China Sea. Brunei received a visit from China's Foreign Minister in February where they reached a 'five point consensus' to boost the overall development of cooperation and relations between the two states. More specifically, China and Brunei agreed to maintain high-ranking visits and exchanges and to expand economic and trade cooperation particularly in the areas of agriculture, petroleum, engineering technology, port development and road and bridge constructions.[50] In July 2008 Brunei received a visit from Kuwaiti Prime Minister, Sheikh Nasser Al-Mohammad Al-Ahmad Al-Sabah, while in August Brunei established diplomatic relations with Kenya.[51] In November, Brunei also enhanced defence cooperation with Pakistan including joint military exercises and technology transfers.[52]

In the context of ASEAN, one of the most important partners for Brunei is Singapore. Singapore provides financial and diplomatic advice, is one of Brunei's most important sources of imports and the currencies of the two countries have been pegged at parity for forty-two years and they can be used in either country.[53] Their 'relationship reflects the pragmatism and shared concerns of ASEAN's two smallest and wealthiest member states amid a region dominated by countries with varying levels of economic, social and political dysfunction'.[54] While the defence relationship between the two countries has been kept low key, it is certainly significant with regular bilateral military exercise and exchange programmes and a continuous presence of the Singapore armed forces in Brunei for the purpose of jungle warfare training. The combined effect of these activities has been to enhance the Sultanate's umbrella of security.[55] During 2008, the closeness of the military relationship was highlighted by a five-day joint army exercise in March, a visit by one of Singapore's most advanced frigates to Brunei in June, a joint exercise between the two countries' cadet forces later in June, and the arrival of a thirty-member strong armed forces delegation from Singapore in August.[56] Brunei and Singapore also actively sought to build political, business and sociocultural ties throughout the year including a meeting to enhance educational ties and various student exchanges.[57] The nature of the relationship between the two countries is akin to a security community — albeit at the bilateral level.

Brunei has sought to maintain and/or enhance positive relations with other ASEAN members including Indonesia, the Philippines, Myanmar and Malaysia. During 2008, it conducted joint naval exercises with Indonesia and received a visit from the Indonesian Navy Chief of Staff to further enhance bilateral cooperation.[58] In April 2008, the Sultan of Brunei travelled to Indonesia to meet with President Susilo Bambang Yudhoyono where the two leaders focused on increasing cultural cooperation and His Majesty praised the continued strengthening of relations between the two countries during the course of the past two decades.[59] During the year, Indonesia opened its first bus route to Brunei and the two countries signed a memorandum to combat money laundering.[60] Brunei also made good progress in its relations with the Philippines and has played a significant role in sending peacekeepers to oversee a ceasefire agreement between the Philippine government and the Moro Islamic Liberation Front (MILF). It also expressed a willingness to lead the International Monitoring Team (IMT) following Malaysia's withdrawal between May and August 2008.[61] Brunei's relations with Malaysia have historically been tumultuous. As recently as April 2003, there was a brief naval standoff between Bruneian and Malaysian warships over the discovery of significant oil reserves in Limbang's offshore exclusive economic zone. However, relations have improved significantly since then. In August 2008 a major breakthrough occurred when the two countries were reported to have reached several agreements to resolve disputes concerning overlapping territorial claims along the sea and land boundaries.[62] The two countries have undertaken frequent activities in cooperation in all fields including joint defence meetings, anti-laundering and anti-drug agreements, joint efforts to combat communicable diseases, discount airfares between the two countries, joint training programmes, and meetings involving the two countries' leaders and the Malaysian King.[63] While there were few reports concerning relations with Myanmar, Brunei ranks as Myanmar's seventh largest trading partner and it was therefore not surprising that Myanmar's Prime Minister, Thein Sein, visited Brunei early in 2008.[64]

Given its small size in terms of its territory and population, the Sultanate places significant strategic importance on its membership in ASEAN. As Michael Leifer once stated, for countries such as Brunei, ASEAN provides a diplomatic voice that is greater than the sum of its parts.[65] While Brunei may not have fully supported some of the ideals that have been espoused in recent years, such as Indonesia's lead in pushing for greater democracy in the region, Brunei has largely managed to avoid having to publically choose between either the conservative or progressive positions that have become increasingly polarized within ASEAN's membership. Whether Brunei's silence on recent ASEAN debates — such as ASEAN's project for a security community, the related Charter and its human rights body — has been a deliberate strategy, or simply been neglected in regional analysis, remains open to conjecture. Nevertheless, Brunei's Minister for Foreign Affairs, Prince Mohamed Bolkiah, in delivering the Inaugural Southeast Asian Lecture in Singapore on 19 February, seemingly acknowledged some of the ideational problems and divides between the ASEAN members. In his address, he called on ASEAN to find common ground arguing that the achievement of such an outcome will necessitate thinking beyond the current list of issues, blueprints and road maps that have been agreed to and/or debated in recent years. He added that '[i]t won't be easy of course. We are 10 members with 10 different ways of life, different faiths and at least half a dozen systems of government. But I hope that ASEAN will find the way.'[66] In any event, during the course of the current decade Brunei appears to have consistently managed to win friends on all fronts through its regional and international diplomacy and it was with little surprise that Brunei — together with Singapore, Malaysia and Laos — were among the first to ratify the new ASEAN Charter.[67] Further, and throughout 2008, Brunei was highly proactive in attending the broad range of ASEAN meetings and initiatives including the ASEAN Tourism Forum, the ASEAN Foreign Ministers Retreat in Sentosa, the ARF Defence Officials Dialogue, ASEAN Labour Talks, the ASEAN+3 Meeting, ASEANPOL and the ASEAN Taskforce in response to Cyclone Nargis. Further, Brunei's friendly relations with international actors such as the United States have only served to complement ASEAN's international diplomacy. During the course of 2008, Brunei was also actively involved in other multilateral fora including the Asia-Pacific Economic Cooperation leaders summit (APEC), the Organisation of Islamic Conference (OIC), and the Brunei Darussalam-Indonesia-Malaysia-Philippines East ASEAN Growth Area (BIMP-EAGA).

The Economy

The year 2008 was not an easy one for Brunei Darussalam, given the cloud of the U.S. subprime mortgage crisis (which surfaced in late 2007) which subsequently developed into a global financial crisis in September 2008. Oil prices plummeted later in the year and Brunei's travel industry was reported to be hit as early as November 2008, with a decrease in the number of tourists arriving from Korea and China.[68]

Demographic and Economic Trends

Brunei has a well educated workforce, and one of the highest adult literacy rates in the region. Two-thirds of its population is Malay, followed by the ethnic Chinese and other races. The indigenous Murut, Dusun, and Iban make up about 6 per cent of the total population.

In 2008, the population of Brunei stood at about 393,000. The annual rate of population growth rate decreased from 3.5 per cent in 2006 to about 1.8 per cent in 2007.[69] Brunei's literacy rates are among the highest in ASEAN with an adult literacy rate of 96.5 per cent for males and 93.1 per cent for females. Brunei is ranked 30th on the global Human Development Index.[70]

The labour force participation rate decreased from 71.7 per cent in 2006 to 71.2 per cent in 2007. Unemployment stood at 3.4 per cent in 2007 and stayed more or less the same in 2008.[71]

The year 2008 was an important year for Brunei in that the Wawasan 2035 or "Vision 2035" was unveiled on 19 January. In this document, the government stated its goal of elevating Brunei to the ranks of the top ten countries in the world by 2035 in terms of per capita income, quality of life and a dynamic and sustainable economy.

However, achieving a higher rate of growth has remained a serious challenge. Real GDP in 2008 is estimated to be about –0.5 per cent. This is in contrast to 4.4 per cent growth in 2006 and 0.6 per cent in 2007.[72] The fall in growth has been attributed to a lower output of oil and lower oil prices in the later part of

2008 as a result of reduced global demand due to the economic downturn. As can be seen from Table 1, the real GDP growth between 2004 to 2008 was only 1.08 per cent on average. On a positive note, inflation was still below one per cent as indicated in the same table.[73] The Bruneian economy would have to achieve higher growth rates if Wawasan Brunei is to be realized.

The production of oil decreased from 219,258 barrels per day in 2006 to 193,832 barrels in 2007.[74] The fall was due to a strategic curtailing in order to protect some wells as well as some other existing and new wells not producing as much as anticipated. For 2008, production is expected to hover below or around the 200,000 barrels mark. Gas production for which data is available for 2005 to 2006 indicates an increase of 4.6 per cent.[75] The oil and gas sector comprised 66.6 per cent of GDP in 2007,[76] with this trend expected to continue in the next few years. Exports in 2007 were dominated by oil and gas which accounted for 96.2 per cent of Brunei's total exports.[77] This is expected to be more or less the same in 2008.

Many of Brunei's other trading partners have also reported slowdowns in their economies in 2008.[78] Brunei's major export markets in 2007,[79] for which figures are available, include Australia (12.1 per cent), Indonesia (24.2 per cent), Japan (33.5 per cent), the Republic of Korea (12.1 per cent), and the USA (5 per cent) all of which were heading towards decelerations in their economic growth rates. Notably, Indonesia and Japan account for nearly 60 per cent of Brunei's exports. In terms of gas, Japan is the largest importer (about 92 per cent of Brunei's total output).

Policy-makers in Brunei realize that the economy is currently too dependent on oil and gas. It as been reported that supplies of oil in the country are expected to run out in about twenty years' time. As such, future growth prospects must look beyond oil and gas into the other relatively undeveloped sectors in the Bruneian economy that could prove promising to the country for the medium- to long-term economic growth.

The policy of economic diversification is beginning to show some fruit. From the latest figures available, the non-oil and gas sector has helped to boost year-on-year GDP by growing about 9.5 per cent in 2007. Government services recorded the highest growth rate (15.7 per cent increase), followed by the private sector of about 5.9 per cent.[80]

The U.S. announced its decision on 22 October 2008 to join the Trans-Pacific Strategic Economic Partnership Agreement (TPSEA), known as the P4, which is a plurilateral free trade agreement previously involving four countries: Brunei Darussalam, Chile, New Zealand, and Singapore. TPSEA is expected to

Christopher Roberts and Lee Poh Onn

TABLE 1
Brunei Darussalam — Main Economic Indicators

	2003	2004	2005	2006	2007	2008
GDP at constant prices (Br\$ bn)[1]	11.36	11.42	11.46	11.97	12.04	11.98
Real GDP (growth, %)[1]	2.9	0.5	0.4	4.4	0.6	–0.5
GDP Per Capita at constant prices (Br\$)[1]	32,575	31,916	30,974	31,703	31,268	30,503
Crude Oil Production (1,000 barrels/day)[2]	207	206	201	220	194	n/a
Gas Production (trn Btu/day)[2]	1,049	1,016	993	n/a	n/a	n/a
Consumer Price Inflation (av; %)[2]	0.3	0.3	1.1	0.2	0.3	0.8
Population (millions)[1]	0.349	0.358	0.370	0.378	0.385	0.393
Exports fob (Br\$ m)[2]	7,704	8,563	10,397	12,119	11,556	n/a
Imports cif (Br\$ m)[2]	2,312	2,413	2,481	2,659	3,166	n/a

Sources: (1) International Monetary Fund (IMF), *World Economic Outlook Database: October 2008 Edition* <http://www.imf.org> (retrieved 21 October 2008); and International Monetary Fund (IMF), *World Economic Outlook* (October 2008). USA: IMF, 2008. Most figures in 2008 are estimates derived from the IMF, *World Economic Outlook Database: October 2008 Edition.*
(2) Brunei: Country Report (United Kingdom: The Economist Intelligence Unit, September 2008).

further widen Brunei's export potential especially with the participation of the United States from 2008.

The continuing development of Brunei's trade links, ecotourism industry, progress in the methanol plant project, and the continuing development of Sungai Liang Industrial Park (SPark) project, halal products, among others, were some of the positive developments in the Bruneian quest for diversification.

Heart of Borneo Project

The Heart of Borneo (HoB) Declaration which was signed on 12 February 2007 by the Governments of Brunei Darussalam, Indonesia, and Malaysia has gained further traction. This declaration involves the conservation and sustainable management of one of the most important areas of biological diversity, covering approximately 220,000 km² of equatorial rainforests. So far, the HoB initiative has done much to generate publicity about this large area.

In 2008, an allocation of US$128 million was made for an environmental strategy of the Wawasan 2035 plan to finance 19 environmental projects which include a Tropical Biodiversity Centre for the HoB Project. In July 2008, the Convention on Biological Diversity (CBD) welcomed Brunei as its 191st member.[81]

In October 2008, Brunei Shell Petroleum and the Hong Kong and Shanghai Bank donated about US$333,000 each to conserve forests in Brunei.[82] This would go towards the establishment of the HoB Brunei Center that will implement the HoB initiative.

The Standard Chartered Bank also donated US$500,000 to the HoB Project. The first two projects that will benefit from this donation are the rehabilitation of Borneo's peatland forest, and the biodiversity survey of the Sungai Ingei protection forest to aid an understanding of the resources available, the discovery of new species and new ways to preserve biodiversity.[83] Standard Chartered Bank is joined by the British High Commission in the project.

Such developments in 2008 bode well for conservation as well as the future realization of Brunei as an attractive ecotourism destination. The potential to increase tourism, especially in the ecotourism sector, certainly exists. The Brunei International Airport is designed to handle 1.5 million passengers per year, and the Royal Brunei Airlines serves 21 destinations in Asia, Middle East, Australia, and Europe.

Pulau Muara Besar Deepwater Container Port

The development of Pulau Muara Besar as a deepwater container port, export processing zone, and manufacturing hub is another plus factor for Brunei. In

October 2008, the Memorandum of Understanding was signed with port operator International Container Terminal Services Inc from the Philippines, and the Master Planner agreement with the Surbana consortium from Singapore.[84]

The Pulau Muara Besar master plan includes developing an export processing zone for halal food, and a manufacturing complex for major industries including the possible establishment of an aluminium smelter to complement the port's operations. Tenders for major infrastructural projects in the port will be called in 2010.

In the years to come, the development of this container port will provide a boost to business opportunities for investors and contractors, local as well as foreign, and this would represent a new sector of potential growth, as well as aid in Brunei's quest for diversification. In line with the development of the port and other infrastructural activities, the construction sector in 2007 grew by 10.7 per cent.[85] In the year under review, growth in this sector is expected to be at double digit rates.

Sungai Liang Industrial Park

A huge potential exists for extending the oil and gas value chain in Brunei. At the Sungai Liang Industrial Park (SPark) which commenced construction in 2007 and continuing into 2008, Brunei is planning a world class petrochemical hub.[86] The first investor in SPark is the Brunei Methanol Company, formed by a partnership between Brunei's National Oil Company, Petroleum Brunei, and two leading Japanese companies, the Mitsubishi Gas Chemical and Itochu Corporation. When completed at the end of 2009, the plant will produce 850,000 tonnes of methanol per year mostly for export. Commercial production is expected to begin in early 2010.

In 2008, the Brunei Economic Development Board was in discussions with global investors for a US$1 billion ammonia/urea plant as well as for various methanol spin-off industries, for example, in the manufacture of acetic acid. If the urea project takes off, employment prospects would be enhanced.

Halal Products

The Brunei Halal Brand was set up in August 2007. By August 2008, according to the Ministry of Industry and Primary Resources in Brunei, about 90 products from nine local companies have been granted permits to use the Brunei Premium

Halal Brand since the enactment of the Halal Label Certificate and Halal Label Order 2005.[87] In 2008, the government was also planning to set up a Halal Products Academy.[88] This was in line Brunei's aim to be globally recognized for its quality Islamic food products.

The Fisheries Industry

In September 2008, a Memorandum of Understanding on cooperation in fisheries was signed between the Department of Fisheries in Brunei and the Guangdong Provincial Oceanic and Fishery Administration, the People's Republic of China. Prior to this, the local fisheries sector was already growing from strength to strength. In January 2008, it was announced that the fisheries sector is expected to gain more than US$60 million annually from the production output of two allocated sites in the Tutong district to facilitate aquaculture activities and entice both local and foreign businesses to invest in the opportunities presented. Once both sites are completely occupied, Brunei should expect a huge boost to its fisheries revenue in the years to come.[89]

Conclusion

While the status quo was predominately maintained in the context of domestic politics and reform, 2008 represented a very successful year for Brunei diplomacy. One of the most significant developments concerned the resolution of some of the biggest territorial disputes that Brunei had held with neighbouring Malaysia. Brunei has also successfully managed to deepen and expand its web of allies without explicitly entering into formal alliances of the kind that could generate mistrust or resentment by those outside such a formal alliance framework. Brunei has also been more than willing to participate in training and exchange programmes with ASEAN and non-ASEAN countries alike. Brunei's involvement in these activities, both in 2008 and in preceding years, has undoubtedly helped the government to professionalize its security sectors, which has in turn led to a more stable environment that has largely avoided the worst aspects of a recent proliferation in transnational crime endured by some other ASEAN countries. Certain political and religious freedoms may be lacking but the social and economic benefits provided by the Sultanate provide some compensation. In the very least, the general wealth of the population has been sufficiently beneficial to deter any mass dissent at the grassroots level and this situation is likely to continue for the foreseeable future.

On the economic front, planning for economic diversification has to be tempered with caution and sound policy-making, as the Bruneian government would have to carefully deliberate on the kind of development that it wants the country to achieve when oil and gas run out. The government has been developing downstream industries based on the oil and gas sector, tapping on the benefits that can be raised from the economies of agglomeration. On the other hand, it has also been looking at non-oil and gas options and is now increasingly moving into developing its ecotourism sector. The private sector in Brunei has also been involved in this initiative as demonstrated by the participation of banks in funding conservation initiatives. The private sector would need to be further involved in developing the hotel and retail sector to attract eco-tourists. Careful planning and management plans must be on the table to protect nature sites from "overexposure" and unintended destruction. The big question is not just how to create opportunities for economic growth and development, but rather which sectors in the economy should be playing this pivotal role in the coming years.

Notes

Christopher Roberts wrote the sections on politics and military and foreign relations, while Lee Poh Onn authored the section on the economy.

1   "Brunei's Vision Needs to Identify Global Trends", *Borneo Bulletin*, 23 February 2009.

2   Pushpa Thambipillai, "Brunei Darussalam: Making a Concerted Effort", in *Southeast Asian Affairs 2008*, edited by Daljit Singh and Tin Maung Maung Than (Singapore: Institute of Southeast Asian Studies, 2008), p. 91.

3   James Kon, "Brunei: Concerns on Drug Abuse, Corruption", *Borneo Bulletin*, 7 March 2008.

4   Azlan Othman, "Initiatives to Curb Brain Drain from Brunei", *Borneo Bulletin*, 8 March 2008. The national brain drain has been compounded by the fact that only a few Chinese have been granted citizenship status resulting in significant patterns of emigration by the Chinese from the country.

5   Azlan Othman, "Legislative Council Members Respond to Sultan's Titah", *Borneo Bulletin*, 5 March 2008.

6   "Smaller Issues Should Be Solved Outside the Council", *Borneo Bulletin*, 12 March 2008.

7   "Sultan Opens New LegCo Building", *Borneo Bulletin*, 5 March 2008.

8   "Public Called to Attend LegCo Meet", *Borneo Bulletin*, 7 March 2008.

9   An intention that has been publicly declared and reported in the press. *Negara Brunei Darussalam* [Internet] (New Zealand Ministry of Foreign Affairs & Trade 2009 [cited

7 March 2009]); available from <http://www.mfat.gov.nz/Countries/Asia-South-and-Southeast/Brunei.php>.

10 "Brunei Country Report", *The Economist Intelligence Unit*, March 2009, p. 6.

11 "New Deputy Permanent Secretary of Defence", *Borneo Bulletin*, 1 March 2008.

12 "Brunei: Internal Affairs", *Jane's Sentinel Security Assessment*, 7 July 2008.

13 "Brunei Country Report".

14 Rosli Abidin Yahya, "PPKB Formally Deregistered", *Borneo Bulletin*, 1 March 2008.

15 "Brunei: Internal Affairs".

16 "Brunei Country Report".

17 "Sultan Addresses Bali Democracy Forum", *Borneo Bulletin*, 11 December 2008.

18 The relatively positive human rights situation in Brunei is reflected in the fact that the major organizations to frequently report on human rights and other related abuses – such as Amnesty International and Human Rights Watch — have not issued any reports on the country in recent years.

19 *2008 Human Rights Report: Brunei Darussalam* [Internet] (U.S. Department of State 2009 [cited 5 March 2009]); available from <www.state.gov/g/drl/rls/hrrpt/2008/eap/119034.htm>.

20 "His Majesty Pardons 3 Detainees", *Borneo Bulletin*, 15 July 2008.

21 "Internal Security Act Detainee Released", *Borneo Bulletin*, 11 January 2009.

22 *International Religious Freedom Report 2008*, U.S. Department of State 2009; available from <http://2001-2009.state.gov/g/drl/rls/irf/2008/108401>.

23 Ibid.

24 "Brunei Defends Whipping 400 Immigrants in 5 Years", *Associated Press Newswires*, 7 March 2009.

25 *2008 Human Rights Report: Brunei Darussalam* (cited).

26 "Global Report on Trafficking in Persons" (UNODC 2009), p. 168.

27 *2008 Human Rights Report: Brunei Darussalam* (cited).

28 Thambipillai, "Brunei Darussalam: Making a Concerted Effort", p. 95.

29 "Brunei: Combat Crime and Drug Abuse Urges Sultan", *Borneo Bulletin*, 23 February 2008.

30 "Imams Lament over Soaring Crime", *Borneo Bulletin*, 29 March 2008.

31 "Brunei to Use UK, German High-Tech Crime-Scene Equipment", *BBC*, 30 January 2009; "Preventing Crime through Community Policing", *Borneo Bulletin*, 22 May 2008.

32 "Malaysia, Brunei Used as Transit Points for Drugs", *Borneo Bulletin*, 27 August 2008.

33 See <www.state.gov>.

34 Jon Grevatt, "Brunei Announces Defence-Spending Cuts", *Jane's Defence Industry*, 11 March 2008.

35   "Ministry of Defence Receives General Cao Gangchuan", *Borneo Bulletin*, 15 January 2008.

36   Jon Grevatt, "Brunei, Indonesia Discuss Transfer of 'Weaponry'", *Jane's Defence Industry*, 28 April 2008; "Harris Corporation Awarded Contract by Brunei Ministry of Defence", *M2 EquityBites*, 20 February 2008; "Harris Gets $25 Million Contract to Provide Tactical Radios to Brunei Ministry of Defence", *Wireless News, M2 Communications*, 24 February 2008.

37   Jon Grevatt, "Brunei Clinches Defence Deals with St Engineering", *Jane's Defence Industry*, 7 May 2008.

38   "MINDEF Promotes 'Boutique' Defence and Security Exhibition in KL", *Borneo Bulletin*, 24 April 2008.

39   "Bridex 2009 Conference to Be Organised by Jane's Information Group and Brunei Ministry of Defence", *M2 Presswire*, 17 July 2008.

40   "Ministry of Defence and RBAF Launch DefPAIS", *Financial Times*, 25 January 2008.

41   "Sultan Holds Talks with British PM", *Borneo Bulletin*, 25 June 2008.

42   "Charles Smitten by Heart of Borneo", *Borneo Bulletin*, 2 November 2008.

43   "Canadian Troops Train Alongside Gurkhas in Brunei Jungle", *BBC*, 26 October 2008.

44   "US Looks to Improving 'People-to-People Relationship' with Brunei", *Borneo Bulletin*, 26 November 2008.

45   "US Keen to Help Brunei on Disaster Management", *Borneo Bulletin*, 8 February 2009.

46   "Brunei, US to Increase Exchange of Military Information", *BBC*, 8 December 2008.

47   Junaidi Yusrin, "RBPF Signs MoU with Australian Federal Police", *Borneo Bulletin*, 20 May 2008.

48   "Honorary Wing for Australia's Air Force Chief", *Borneo Bulletin*, 16 February 2008.

49   "Australia Increasingly Popular with Local Students", *Borneo Bulletin*, 17 May 2008.

50   "China, Brunei to Further Promote Bilateral Ties", *BBC*, 3 February 2008.

51   "Kuwait: PM Starts Tour of Asia", *Stratfor*, 23 July 2008.

52   "Pakistan, Brunei Cooperate in Defence, Joint Military Exercises, Technology Transfer", *Pakistan Press*, 22 November 2008.

53   "Singapore and Brunei: Close Friends in an Uncertain World", *Business Times*, 26 February 2009.

54   "Brunei: External Affairs", *Jane's Sentinel Security Assessment*, 7 July 2008.

55   Xueying Li, "MM Underscores Singapore's Special Ties with Brunei", *Straits Times*, 26 February 2009; "Singapore and Brunei Conclude Military Exercise", *Channel News Asia*, 13 January 2009.

56   Singapore and Brunei also conducted a further joint military exercise in January 2009. "Brunei Welcomes Singapore Armed Forces Delegation", *Borneo Bulletin*, 27 August 2008; "Brunei, Singapore Cadets Attend Joint Military Exercise in Temburong", *Financial Times*, 23 June 2008; "Singapore Frigate Visits Brunei", *BBC*, 3 June 2008; "Singapore, Brunei Conclude Bilateral Army Exercise", *Channel News Asia*, 9 March 2008.

[57] "Brunei Hosts Meeting to Enhance Education Ties with Singapore", *Borneo Bulletin*, 15 January 2008; "Singapore Students Visit Brunei's Cultural, Natural Heritage", *Borneo Bulletin*, 3 December 2008.

[58] "Indonesian Navy Chief Visiting Brunei, Then Malaysia", *BBC*, 13 January 2009.

[59] "Brunei Sultan Praises Closer Ties with Indonesia During Jakarta Visit", *BBC*, 24 April 2008; "President Yudhoyono Recieves Bruneian Sultan", *LKBN Antara*, 22 April 2008.

[60] "Brunei, Indonesia Sign Memorandum on Cooperation against Money Laundering", *BBC*, 21 December 2008; "Indonesia to Open First Bus Route to Brunei", *Thai News Service*, 8 July 2008.

[61] "Brunei Willing to Assume Malaysia's Role as Head of Imt", *Philippine Daily Inquirer*, 10 July 2008.

[62] "Malaysia, Brunei Agree on Border Solution", *New Straits Times*, 27 August 2008; "Malaysia, Brunei Reach Agreement on Overlapping Areas", *BBC*, 27 August 2008.

[63] For examples, see: "Brunei-Malaysia Defence Meeting at Bolkiah Garrison", *Borneo Bulletin*, 29 January 2009; "Brunei and Malaysia Underscore Cooperation in Drug Fight", *Borneo Bulletin*, 11 June 2008; "Malaysia, Brunei to Combat Non-Communicable Diseases", *BBC*, 21 November 2008.

[64] "Myanmar Prime Minister to Visit Indonesia, Brunei", *Thai News Service*, 15 January 2008.

[65] Michael Leifer, *ASEAN and the Security of Southeast Asia* (London: Routledge, 1989) p. 152.

[66] "Prince Calls on ASEAN to Find Common Ground", *Borneo Bulletin*, 20 February 2008.

[67] "Laos, Malaysia and Brunei Latest to Ratify ASEAN Charter", *Business Times*, 21 February 2008.

[68] "Brunei Travel Industry Hit by Raging Global Financial Crisis", *Brunei Times*, 27 February 2009 <http://www.bt.com.bn/en/home_news/2009/02/27/brunei_travel_industry_hit_by_raging_global_financial_crisis>.

[69] *Key Economic Indicators for Asia and the Pacific 2008* (Philippines: Asian Development Bank, August 2008).

[70] *Key Economic Indicators for Asia and the Pacific 2008*, op. cit.

[71] Ibid.

[72] Country Report, Brunei (United Kingdom: The Economist Intelligence Unit, September 2008), p. 5.

[73] For percentage changes in average consumer prices (Index 2000 = 100), see International Monetary Fund (IMF), *World Economic Outlook Database: October 2008 Edition* <http://www.imf.org> (retrieved 21 October 2008).

[74] *Brunei Economic Bulletin*, "Brunei Darussalam Economic Review Outlook and Recent Economic Developments", Department of Economic Planning and Development, Prime Minister's Office, Volume 5 — 2007 Special Edition, May 2008.

75   *Brunei Darussalam: Statistical Appendix* (Washington, D.C.: International Monetary Fund, May 2008).

76   Country Report, Brunei (United Kingdom: The Economist Intelligence Unit, December 2008), p. 4.

77   Ibid.

78   Ibid.

79   *Brunei Economic Bulletin*, op. cit.

80   *Brunei Economic Bulletin*, op. cit.

81   "$128m for green projects under Wawasan 2035", *Brunei Times*, 30 June 2008 <http://www.bt.com.bn/en/home_news/2008/06/30/128m_for_green_ projects_under_ wawasan_2035>.

82   "Shell, HSBC put $665,000 towards Borneo Rainforest Conservation Project", Mongabay.Com, 28 October 2008 <http://news.mongabay.com/2008/1026-borneo. html>.

83   "SCB Donates $700,000 to HoB Project", BruDirect.Com, 27 October 2008 <http://www.brudirect.com/DailyInfo/News/Archive/Oct08/271008/nite02.htm>.

84   "Big Leap towards Realization of PMB", BruDirect.Com, 29 October 2008 <http:// www.brudirect.com/DailyInfo/News/Archive/Oct08/291008/nite01.htm>.

85   See *Brunei Economic Bulletin*, op. cit.

86   The Brunei Forum, co-organized by the Brunei Economic Development Board and the Institute of Southeast Asian Studies, 19–20 February 2008.

87   "Brunei to set up company for Halal brand promotion", *Brunei Times*, 17 August 2008 <http://www.bt.com.bn/en/home_news/2008/08/17/ brunei_to_set_up_company_for_ halal_brand_promotion>.

88   "Halal Academy to Boost Ulama-Industry Ties", *Brunei Times*, 17 August 2008 <http://www.bt.com.bn/en/local_business/2008/08/17/halal_academy_ to_boost_ulama_ industry_ties>.

89   See "Brunei Fisheries Sector Gets Shot on the Arm", *Brunei Times*, 31 January 2008, cited at <http://www.fisheries.gov.bn/whatsnew/whatsnew 2008-01-31ae.htm>.

Cambodia

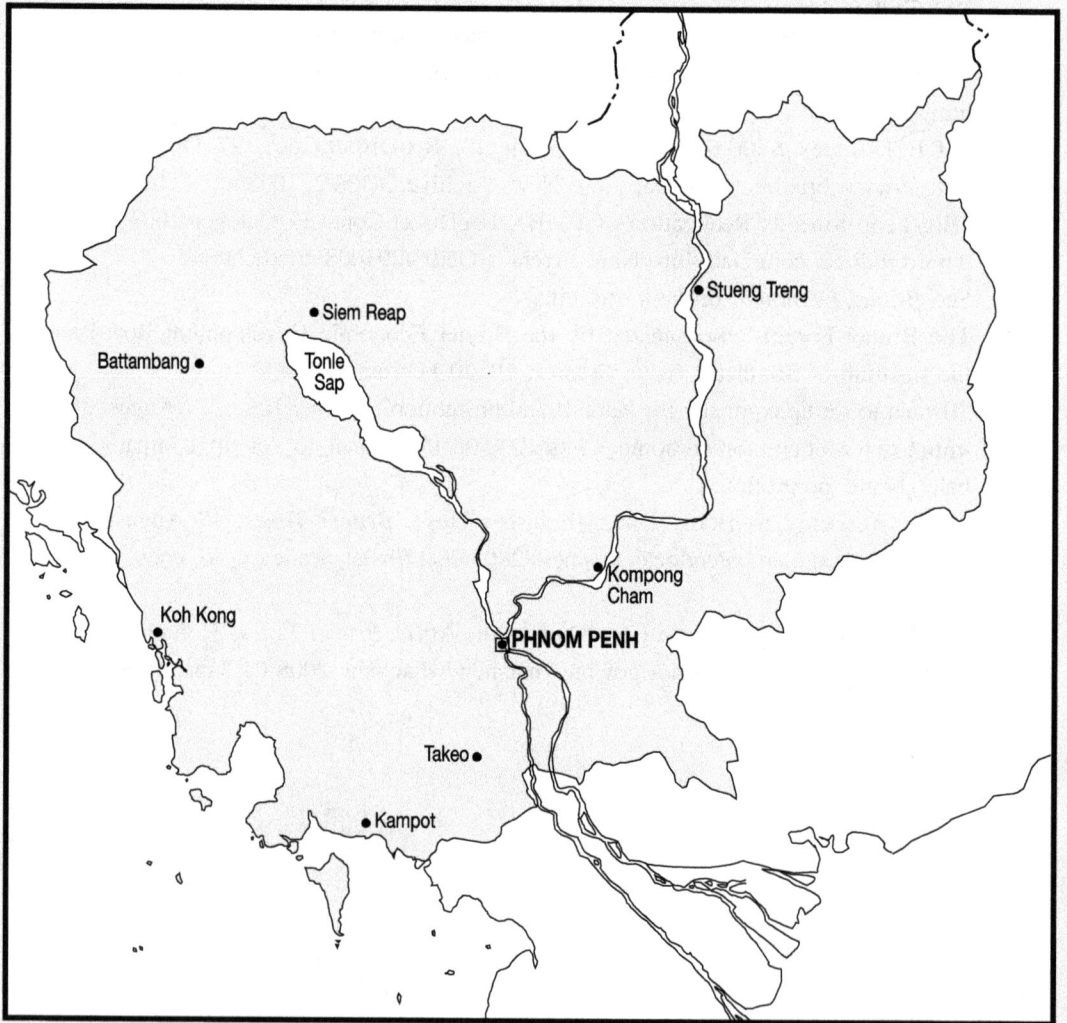

CAMBODIA
The Cambodian People's Party Consolidates Power

Carlyle A. Thayer

This chapter reviews major domestic and foreign policy developments in Cambodia in 2008. Three major issues are highlighted: the fourth national elections, the border dispute with Thailand, and the proceedings of the Khmer Rouge Tribunal. The chapter concludes with a brief overview of economic trends and a review of Cambodia's external relations.

National Elections

Cambodia held national elections on 27 July; they were the fourth general elections to be held since the end of the Cambodian conflict in 1991. In 2007, the National Electoral Committee (NEC) revised its national voter list and removed 586,160 names due to death, duplication and other reasons. The list of deregistered voters was displayed publicly for thirty-five days and citizens were given the right to contest their deletion. According to a U.S. Embassy assessment, "virtually all who took steps to protest the deletion of their names were re-instated".[1] Nonetheless, an audit by the National Democratic Institute (NDI) found that as many as 57,401 voters (or 0.7 per cent of the total) were deleted. This figure was challenged by the NEC and reduced to 49,340 voters (or 0.6 per cent of the total) who "may [have been]… improperly and unintentionally" disenfranchised.[2] The U.S Embassy noted that the deletion of as many as 57,000 legitimate voters "was a high price to pay for the successful removal of over 450,000 ghost voters".[3] The final official list totalled 8,125,529 registered voters.

CARLYLE A. THAYER is Professor of Politics, School of Humanities and Social Sciences, University College, The University of New South Wales at the Australian Defence Force Academy. Professor Thayer was a U.N.-accredited observer for the 1993 Cambodian elections.

In 2008 Cambodia had fifty-three officially registered political parties. Only twelve parties applied to contest the elections during the official registration period from 28 April to 12 May. Eleven political parties were approved (see Table 1).[4] The NEC also approved a total of 2,479 candidates (titular and alternate) and rejected the applications of 213. Only five political parties won seats: Cambodian People's Party (CPP), Sam Rainsy Party (SRP), Human Rights Party (HRP), FUNCINPEC (National United Front for Independent, Neutral, Peaceful and Co-operative Cambodia) and the Norodom Ranariddth Party (NRP).

The elections were monitored by a combination of international and domestic observers and political party representatives. According to NEC figures, there were 584 international observers from twenty-seven states and organizations.[5] The European Union-Election Observer Mission (EU-EOM) sent 221 observers, the largest foreign contingent. EU-EOM deployed both long-term observers to monitor the election campaign and short-term observers to monitor voting and counting on election day. The United States provided 116 observers, the second largest contingent. Japan, Australia, Russia and Vietnam among other countries provided observers but there were none from China.

The NEC accredited seventy-two domestic civil society organizations and registered 31,261 local observers. Two major election monitoring bodies, Committee for Free and Fair Elections (COMFREL) and Neutral and Impartial Committee for Free and Fair Elections in Cambodia (NICFEC) provided, respectively, 11,691 and 7,612 observers, the largest contingents. Both organizations provided long- and

TABLE 1
Results of the Cambodian National Election, 27 July 2008

Party	Valid Votes	Per cent	Seats
Cambodian People's Party	3,492,374	58.11	90
Sam Rainsy Party	1,316,714	21.91	26
Human Rights Party	397,816	6.62	3
Norodom Ranariddh Party	337,943	5.62	2
FUNCINPEC Party	303,764	5.05	2
League for Democracy Party	68,909	1.15	—
Khmer Democratic Party	32,386	0.54	—
Hang Dara Democratic Movement Party	25,065	0.42	—
Social Justice Party	14,112	0.23	—
Khmer Republican Party	11,693	0.19	—
Khmer Anti-Poverty Party	9,501	0.16	—
Total	6,010,277	100	123

Source: National Election Committee.

short-term monitors. The NEC also approved 78,981 political party representatives.[6] In sum, there were over 110,800 observers to monitor the elections.

According to Jerome Cheung, country director for the NDI, "[i]t is what happens before the election that does not make it fair, including CPP's total domination of broadcast media and intimidation of journalists and opposition".[7] In the five years since the last national election, and more particularly since the 2007 local elections when the CPP secured control of 98 per cent of the communes, the opposition functioned in an almost continuous environment of threats, harassment and intimidation according to Human Rights Watch.[8] Between February and May, CPP pressure on the SRP induced at least six of its deputies and a number of high-level officials to defect.

In April, prior to the start of the official campaign, Deputy Prime Minister Hor Namhong filed a criminal lawsuit for defamation against the leader of the main opposition party, Sam Rainsy. The following month the government shut down Angkor Ratha FM 105.25 radio in Kratie province for selling airtime to opposition parties.[9] In June, police arrested Dam Sith, editor of *Moneaksekar Khmer* newspaper, on charges of libelling Hor Namhong. Dam Sith was also a registered SRP candidate.[10] On 11 July, shortly after Dam Sith's release, an unknown assailant murdered Khim Sambo and his son in a drive by shooting.[11] Khim was a journalist working for *Moneaksekar Khmer* who wrote on election irregularities, illegal logging and land grabbing. These events led a coalition of forty Cambodian civil society groups to express their deep concern over the increase in political violence in the first half of the year when five members of political parties were assassinated and twenty-one cases of "political persecution" were reported.[12]

Both the CPP and the SRP "jumped the gun" and began their campaigns early in an attempt to enlist more supporters. Senior members of the CPP used opening ceremonies for schools, hospitals and other infrastructure as campaign platforms. Sam Rainsy undertook a "campaign style tour" of the provinces. The official campaign commenced on 26 June and ended on 25 July. The following day (26 July) was a "day of calm". Voting was held on 27 July at 15,255 polling stations in twenty-four electoral constituencies (provinces and municipalities) to elect 123 deputies to the National Assembly. Only eight political parties fielded candidates in all of the electoral districts.

The opposition parties stressed three main themes during the campaign: government corruption, land grabbing and economic mismanagement (poverty alleviation and failure to curb inflation). Other issues included: illegal migration, human rights abuses, misuse of state resources, failure to prosecute Khmer Rouge leaders, civil service salary reform, and national sovereignty. The CPP ran its campaign by touting economic prosperity, infrastructure development (schools, hospitals, pagodas, roads, irrigation canals), continued stability and the border dispute with Thailand. Under election regulations, all political parties received access to state television and radio and free airtime on Women's Media Centre's FM102. Two major dailies, *Moneaksekar Khmer* and *Samleng Yuvachun Khmer* openly supported the SRP and NRP, respectively, and published articles critical of the CPP.

Only two of the eleven political parties contesting the election had substantial appeal in the countryside. According to observers, electoral competition diminished in rural areas where the CPP took advantage of its incumbency to use state resources to bolster its campaign and to obstruct the opposition parties from conducting scheduled events. Only the SRP was able to mount a challenge to the CPP's hegemony. Throughout Cambodia, opposition supporters were personally intimidated and opposition posters were torn down or defaced. More significantly, the CPP conducted a major campaign of inducements, threats and reprisals against opposition party members, the SRP in particular, to defect. SRP sources complained that as many as twenty high-profile lawmakers and thousands of grassroots members switched sides as a result. The EU-EOM concluded, "[t]he pattern and frequency of opposition defections to the CPP support claims that the CPP offered large sums of money, expensive goods such as motorbikes, and government positions to attract opposition leaders and key activists".[13]

The NEC released the results of the elections in two phases. Preliminary results were released on 9 August and the final official results were issued on 2 September (see Table 1).[14] According to the final figures, the 2008 election witnessed a voter turnout of 75 per cent, the lowest for all four national elections held since 1993. The CPP won a landslide victory garnering 58 per cent of the popular vote. As a result of constitutional amendments adopted in 2006, the requirement of a two-thirds majority to form a government was amended to a majority or 62 seats. This proved superfluous as the CPP won 90 seats or 73 per cent of the total.

The Sam Rainsy Party consolidated its position as the major opposition party. It increased its number of seats from twenty-four in the previous National Assembly to twenty-six. The second most successful party was the newly formed Human Rights Party which won only three seats. The royalist FUNCINPEC party suffered a disastrous defeat with its representation dropping from twenty-six to just two seats. FUNCINPEC, by all accounts, imploded as a result of internal disunity following the expulsion of party leader Prince Norodom Ranariddth. Ranariddth founded his own party, the NRP, before fleeing to Malaysia to avoid imprisonment for a fraud conviction. The NRP won just two seats.

Cambodia's electoral regulatory system makes provision for the submission of complaints for breaches of election laws and rules at four levels: commune (Commune Election Committee or CEC), provincial (Provincial Election Committee or PEC), national (National Election Committee or NEC) and Constitutional Council. During the 2008 elections 184 complaints were submitted to CECs, 82 per cent filed by the SRP alone.[15] Ninety-one cases were resolved locally and the remaining ninety-two cases were referred to the PECs. The PECs also received eighteen direct complaints (for a total of 111). Only six complaints were accepted and all the others were rejected. Fifty-two cases were appealed to the NEC where they joined three cases that had been directly submitted. Sixteen cases were accepted and referred to the Ministry of Interior for disciplinary action. Most concerned allegations that commune officials fraudulently issued Form 1018. Form 1018 was designed to allow commune officials to certify that a citizen was qualified to vote in cases were identity documents had been lost.

On 27 July the four major opposition parties — SRP, HRP, FUNCINPEC and NRP — issued a joint statement rejecting the preliminary election results on the basis that voter lists had been manipulated at the expense of the opposition. Sam Rainsy variously claimed that 60,000 to 200,000 voters in Phnom Penh alone, and a total of one million persons nationwide, had been disenfranchised.[16] Election monitors from around the country confirmed that there were cases where voters were left off the list. But assessments by the EU-EOM and the United States Embassy failed to confirm opposition charges that voter deletions were specifically aimed at opposition supporters or materially affected the results of the election. The EU-EOM Final Report stated unequivocally "there is no clear evidence of systematic deletion of opposition supporters".[17] The U.S. Embassy concluded that only a small percentage of the voter population was affected that this was mainly a result of problems in issuing Voter Information Notices, reassignment of voters to different polling stations from one election to the next and the deletion in 2007 of legitimate voters.

The opposition's protests against electoral fraud were undercut on 12 August when the NRP broke ranks to declare that it "considers the election... was transparent, free, fair and in accordance with the democratic process in Cambodia".[18] On the same day FUNCINPEC issued a statement that noted despite "technical irregularities, FUNCINPEC party publicly supports and accepts the temporary [preliminary] results of the election".[19]

In August, the SRP and HRP separately filed complaints to the Constitutional Council and jointly appealed to the international community. They also announced they would file a complaint against the election results to the United Nations and European Union. Immediately after the Constitutional Council rejected the complaints by the SRP and HRP, they jointly wrote to the leaders of the eighteen countries which had been signatories to the 1991 Cambodia peace agreement charging "systematic and massive electoral fraud". In September, Sam Rainsy and Kem Sokha, head of the HRP, travelled to Paris and Brussels to press their case.

While virtually all of the major international and domestic election monitoring organizations found faults and irregularities in the conduct of the 2008 elections, none concluded that the elections were not free and fair. There was consensus that the official campaign period was better run administratively than the previous three national elections. COMFREL declared, for example, "the election was better. We saw irregularities but they were fewer than we saw before." The Final Report of the EU-EOM declared that "the 2008 National Assembly elections fell short of a number of key international standards for democratic elections".

In addition to the short comings discussed above, the EU-EOM highlighted four main areas of concern: (1) "lack of confidence in the neutrality and impartiality of the NEC and election administration among stakeholders"; (2) the distribution of money and goods to voters by most parties, most notably by the CPP; (3) the CPP's near total domination of the electronic and print media; and (4) the inadequacy of electoral complaints and appeals processes to address the main issues raised by political parties. The level of politically-motivated killings, threats and intimidation also diminished. Human Rights Watch declared "the legacy of violence continues to intimidate opposition supporters, but this campaign was run more peacefully than in the past".

While threats, intimidation and electoral fraud may explain why the opposition failed to do well in the general election, they are not sufficient to explain the CPP's landslide victory. The U.S. Embassy concluded that voting irregularities "were relatively low in number and they do not appear to have affected the outcome or to have distorted the will of the Cambodian people".[20] Phnom Penh based diplomats and other observers pointed to the opposition's disarray and lack of a coherent political programme as other factors. In short, FUNCINPEC's loss was the CPP's gain. More importantly, there is a body of evidence that the CPP government under the leadership of Hun Sen was genuinely popular, especially in rural areas.[21] A poll of public attitudes prior to the election indicated that 70 per cent thought Cambodia was heading in the right direction. In other words, the CPP reaped a political dividend for having delivered political stability and double-digit economic growth.[22]

The official swearing in ceremony for elected deputies was held at the Royal Palace on 24 September in the presence of King Norodom Sihamoni and Buddhist Patriarchs. In the lead up to this event both the SRP and NRP declared they would boycott the ceremony. However a last minute deal was brokered. Hun Sen agreed to amend the internal rules of the National Assembly to acknowledge the official role of the opposition and opposition leader, to provide budgetary support and full immunity for all deputies. SRP and HRP deputies attended but to demonstrate their dissent did not wear the traditional dress uniform.[23]

The fourth National Assembly met for the first time on 25 July with 94 deputies present. Both the SRP and HRP boycotted proceedings to protest the CPP's use of bloc voting. The National Assembly unanimously elected Heng Samrin as its president. Next the National Assembly re-elected Hun Sen to his fourth term as prime minister. Hun Sen's government was also approved; it consisted of twenty-six ministries and ministry-level bodies, nine deputy prime ministers and sixteen high-level ministers. All ministerial posts were filled by the same persons who served in the previous Cabinet. All were members of the CPP. The chairmanship of the National Assembly's nine committees also went to CPP deputies. Hun Sen also appointed over thirty-five SRP defectors and several members of nominal coalition partner FUNCINPEC to sub-ministerial posts at secretary to undersecretary of state level.[24]

Immediately after Hun Sen was elected prime minister, the king, acting on the advice of his prime minister, granted a royal amnesty to Prince Ranariddth who immediately returned to his residence in Siem Reap. A spokesperson for Ranarridth announced "the Prince does not plan to become actively involved in politics".[25] In January, the opposition SRP and HRP announced the formation of a Democratic Movement for Change to jointly contest the first indirect elections at commune level scheduled for May 2009.

Border Dispute

In 2008, in a bid to boost tourism, Cambodia applied to the United Nations Educational, Scientific and Cultural Organization (UNESCO) to have the Preah Vihear temple listed as a World Heritage Site. Preah Vihear temple had been awarded to Cambodia in a 1962 decision by the International Court of Justice (ICJ). At that time the ICJ declined to rule on the question of who had sovereignty over an area of 4.6 square kilometres surrounding the temple. Cambodia included this disputed area in its initial bid to UNESCO. In May, in return for Thai support, Cambodia removed this area from its application and resubmitted its bid.[26] Thailand's foreign minister then signed a joint statement supporting Cambodia's application.[27] On 7 June the World Heritage Committee approved Cambodia's request. A month later the 32nd session of the World Heritage Committee formally inscribed Preah Vihear temple on its World Heritage List. UNESCO's actions set off a political controversy in Thailand when the opposition People's Alliance for Democracy (PAD) criticized the government for mismanaging this case. Thai activists took the matter further on 15 July when they were arrested for illegally crossing the border in an attempt to plant the national flag at Preah Vihear.[28]

In short order a minor incident was turned into a major border dispute that steadily escalated during the year. Thailand and Cambodia share an 803-kilometre border that has never been demarcated. In 2000, the two countries signed a memorandum of understanding (MOU) that set up a Joint Commission on Demarcation for Land Border to resolve the boundary issue. Little was accomplished. Attempts in 2008 to resolve the border dispute foundered as a result of domestic politics in both countries. Hun Sen used the heritage listing of Preah Vihear to boost his domestic standing in the run up to the 27 July election. For much of 2008 Thai officials were hamstrung by domestic instability and a constitutional requirement that border negotiations be referred to parliament for endorsement. A series of violent incidents on the border eroded good faith on both sides.

On 15 July, Cambodia charged that Thai soldiers intruded into its territory and occupied a Buddhist pagoda located on disputed land.[29] Cambodia responded by sending troops to the border. Both sides then reinforced their border positions with additional forces, artillery and armoured personnel carriers. Soon 1,500 or more Thai and Cambodian troops faced off against each other.[30] Cambodia raised the matter at the UN and a meeting of the Association of Southeast Asian Nations (ASEAN) in Singapore. Both the UN Secretary General and the ASEAN Secretary General declined to become involved stating that the matter was best resolved bilaterally.[31]

The first in a series of bilateral talks on the border dispute took place on 21 July with the meeting between the Thai Supreme Commander and the Cambodian Minister for Defence. It ended inconclusively with vague pledges to refrain from using force. The Thai and Cambodian foreign ministers held two rounds of meetings, the first on 27 July in Siem Reap and the second on 18 August in Cha-am. The first meeting resulted in agreement to set up a bilateral committee to discuss troop redeployments. The second meeting agreed to initiate the first-phase of troop redeployments.[32] The two foreign ministers met again on 29 September on the sidelines of the annual meeting of the UN General Assembly.

The slow pace of negotiations was interrupted on 3 October when a firefight erupted between opposing forces at Veal Antri.[33] Two Thai and three Cambodian soldiers were wounded. Both sides provided conflicting accounts of what occurred. Matters turned worse on 6 October when two Thai paramilitary rangers lost their legs in a mine explosion.[34] Thailand was adamant that the area had been cleared previously and the mines that exploded were newly planted. An investigation by the Thai Mine Action Centre discovered new Russian-manufactured PMN2 anti-personnel land mines.[35] Thailand alleged that Cambodia violated the 1997 Ottawa Convention banning land mines to which it was a signatory.

On 13 October, Sompong Amornwiwat, Thai Deputy Prime Minister and Foreign Minister, flew to Phnom Penh to discuss the border situation with his counterpart, Hor Namhong. The Thai visitor paid a courtesy call on the king and met briefly with Prime Minister Hun Sen. When the two foreign ministers met they agreed to hold a meeting of the Regional Border Committee later that month. This positive development was overshadowed by an ultimatum delivered by Prime Minister Hun Sen after his meeting with Sompong. Hun Sen declared. "At any cost we will not allow Thai troops to invade this area. I would like to be clear about this. It is a life-and-death battle zone."[36] He set a deadline of noon, 14 October, for the withdrawal of all Thai forces.

On the afternoon of 15 October, after the deadline had passed, three armed skirmishes broke out along the border. In one intense exchange two Cambodian soldiers were killed and seven Thais wounded (one later died of his wounds).[37] Cambodia also captured ten Thai rangers. Ironically, Cambodian Foreign Minister Hor Namhong had telephoned his Thai counterpart in the morning to discuss border issues. Both ministers expressed regret and agreed that peaceful means should be used to settle the dispute. The Thai foreign minister also promised to seek approval from parliament for the reactivation of the Joint Commission on Demarcation for Land Border.[38] After the shooting incidents an emergency meeting of the joint Regional Border Committee was convened to work out measures to prevent further violence.[39] Correspondents at the border, however, reported that both sides were reinforcing their positions with additional troops, tanks and artillery.[40] Cambodia later announced it would double the size of its military budget to $500 million.[41]

There were no further violent incidents for the remainder of the year as both sides used diplomacy to keep tensions from boiling over. The eleventh annual meeting of the Regional Border Committee was held in Siem Reap on

24 October. Military leaders signed an agreement to reduce tensions.[42] The Thai and Cambodian prime ministers held a conciliatory meeting in Beijing at the same time on the sidelines of the 7th Asia-Europe Meeting (ASEM 7).[43] On 10 November, the Cambodia-Thai Joint Border Commission finally met in Siem Reap. Both parties agreed to accept the 2000 MOU as the framework for discussions and to lower troop levels in the disputed area.[44] The MOU divides border demarcation into seven sections and gives priority to non-disputed areas first. Instability in Bangkok prevented further progress on this issue.

New life was breathed into the negotiating process with the election of Abhisit Vejjajiva as prime minister of Thailand in late December. Thailand's new foreign minister, Kasit Piromya, visited Phnom Penh on 26 January 2009 to restart border discussions with his counterpart, Hor Namhong. The two ministers agreed in principle to drawn down troops in the disputed area and to hold further high-level talks. Meetings of the Joint Border Committee, Defence Ministers and Prime Minister were scheduled for February 2009.[45]

Khmer Rouge Tribunal

The Extraordinary Chambers in the Courts of Cambodia (ECCC or Khmer Rouge Tribunal) was set up in 2004 to try the most responsible leaders of the Khmer Rouge for war crimes and/or crimes against humanity during their rule.[46] By the end of 2007 five high-level leaders had been detained. During 2008 court proceeding were delayed due to allegations of corruption and nepotism, disruptive tactics by defence counsel,[47] and disagreement among the prosecutors. Budget projections presented to donors in January revealed that there were only enough funds to prosecute three individuals at the most.[48]

In August, investigating judges finally issued their first indictment against Kaing Gech Eav, alias Duch, the head of the S-21 interrogation centre. At year's end the ECCC rejected a request by the prosecutors to try Duch under the legal principle of Joint Criminal Enterprise that would have made him liable simply for having participated in the operation of S-21. Instead, the prosecutors ruled that Duch would have to be found guilty for each murder.[49] The ECCC then set 17 February 2009 as the trial date. In December, a major disagreement erupted between the two co-prosecutors over whether or not to pursue further indictments against additional members of the Khmer Rouge hierarchy. Roger Petit, the international prosecutor, argued for expansion, reportedly identifying six new compelling cases. Chea Leang, the Cambodian prosecutor, argued to the contrary that such action would violate the original mandate of the

ECCC, overstretch its duration and budget, and undermine national stability and reconciliation.[50]

Economy

In 2008 Cambodia's dream run of double-digit economic growth came to an end. After averaging 10–11 per cent for the three previous years, growth of the Gross Domestic Product (GDP) for 2008 was estimated at 6.5 per cent.[51] High growth had been fuelled by "three gems" — garments, agriculture and construction.[52] Garments alone accounted for nearly 80 per cent of export earnings. Demand dropped steadily throughout the year and analysts forecast that the situation would worsen in 2009 when U.S. restrictions on Chinese textiles were lifted. Tourism fell due to the border dispute and Thai domestic instability. The International Monetary Fund and the World Bank separately estimated that growth would decline to 4.8–4.9 per cent, respectively, in 2009.[53] Hun Sen stated his government would ensure economic growth around 7 per cent.[54]

Cambodia's economy was hit by strong inflationary pressures. In January, when inflation rose to 18.7 per cent, the government stopped issuing data on the Consumer Price Index for three months.[55] Inflation peaked at 25 per cent in May and reached an annual average of 20 per cent by the end of the third quarter.[56] On a more positive note, donors pledged a record US$951.5 million in development assistance for 2009, up from US$750 million in 2008.[57] Cambodia attracted US$750 million in foreign investment in 2008 and announced plans to open a stock exchange in 2009.[58] At year's end Russia cancelled 70 per cent of Cambodia's outstanding debt.

In December, the National Assembly approved a budget of US$1.88 billion for 2009. Emphasis was placed on health, education and agriculture. Due to pressure from donors the military budget was not doubled but military funding was raised to US$160–200 million to meet rising salary and pensions costs.[59]

Foreign Relations

In 2008 China continued to expand its considerable economic influence in Cambodia. In February, the Chinese Foreign Minister visited Phnom Penh and announced a major one billion dollar investment package in the energy sector. Funds would be used to construct several major dams to generate electricity for the countryside and electricity for an estimated three thousand Chinese companies already operating in Cambodia. The Chinese foreign minister donated a further US$55 million in development assistance and waived import duties on four hundred Cambodian goods.[60] Also in February, Cambodia established a special economic zone in Sihanoukville to produce goods for duty free export to China. In October, Prime Minister Hun Sen met with Premier Wen Jiabao on the sidelines of ASEM 7 in Beijing. In response to a request by Hun Sen, Wen pledged US$280 million in loans for infrastructure development.[61]

Cambodia's relations with the United States improved markedly after the lifting of legislative restrictions on direct funding to the central government that had been in place from 1997–2007. In September, Deputy Secretary of State John Negroponte paid a three-day visit to strengthen bilateral ties. Negroponte announced that the U.S. would provide US$24 million to aid economic development and would also provide US$1.8 million through the UN to support the work of the Khmer Rouge Tribunal.[62] Although the United States is Cambodia's largest trade partner, economic data indicates that garment sales are now in decline.[63] The U.S. also refuses to forgive Cambodia's debt of US$339 million dating back to the 1970s.[64]

Cambodia and Vietnam describe their bilateral relations with the slogan "good neighbourliness, traditional friendship, comprehensive and long-term cooperation". Cambodia's Defence Minister, Tea Banh, visited Vietnam in March for discussions with his counterpart. They agreed to continue joint maritime patrols and to initiate exchanges between military medical institutions.[65] In October, Vietnam hosted the tenth meeting of the Joint Commission for Economic, Cultural and Scientific-Technological Cooperation. The joint commission mapped out a wide variety of cooperative activities. This meeting also pledged to raise bilateral trade to US$2 billion by 2010 and to complete border demarcation by 2012.[66]

In November, Hun Sen paid an official visit to Vietnam as well as to attend two sub-regional summit meetings. Prime Minister Nguyen Tan Dung responded positively to Hun Sen's request for increased investment in Cambodia's rubber, oil and gas, electricity, post and telecommunications sectors.[67] Five agreements were signed at this time: visa exemption, goods transit, railway linkages, and information exchanges between their respective ministries and national radio stations.

Conclusion

The CPP's landslide victory in the 27 July national elections has brought about a realignment of the political forces that squared off in the early 1990s after peace was restored to Cambodia. The royalist cause is shattered with the stunning defeat of its main vehicle, FUNCINPEC, and its main representative, Prince Norodom Ranariddth. The secular Ram Rainsy Party is now the official opposition.

The dominance of the CPP and Prime Minister Hun Sen raise serious questions about the future of economic reform and liberal democracy in Cambodia. The CPP's commanding majority in the National Assembly, coupled with the CPP's grip over the judiciary, police and military and state apparatus at all levels, could undermine Cambodia's fragile system of check and balances. According to Kek Galabru, a leading human rights activist, "[t]he ruling party will have the right to amend laws and strip parliamentary immunity from critics. We are afraid our democratic state will shrink and shrink."[68]

Cambodia's new opening with the United States contains the prospect that there will be continued support for economic reform, transparency and better governance. But Cambodia's reliance on China for developmental assistance will mean that CPP officials will not have to fear external pressures to act on corruption.

The Cambodian government faces a challenging agenda that includes poverty alleviation, land disputes, youth employment, weeding out corruption, judicial reform (including the ECCC), and transforming a political culture based on violence and impunity. The CPP's consolidation of power could translate into a "business as usual" approach and a lack of urgency to address pressing issues. These trends could be reinforced by Cambodia's weakening economic climate. In sum, Sam Rainsy and his SRP have their work cut out for them in trying to keep the CPP government focused on needed reforms.

Notes

[1] "U.S. Embassy's Assessment of the Recent Cambodian National Elections", U.S. Embassy Press Release, Phnom Penh, 1 August 2008.

[2] The NDI conducted two voter registration audits: *Report on Voter Registration Audit (VRA) in Cambodia* (September 2007) and *The Results of the Voter Registration Audit II in Cambodia* (13 June 2008). These reports may be located on the NDI homepage at <http://www.ndi.org/>. See also: National Election Committee, "NEC's Response to NDI's Voter Registration Audit II", 7 July 2008.

[3] "U.S. Embassy's Assessment of the Recent Cambodian National Elections".

[4] National Election Committee, "Eleven Political Parties Officially Recognized by NEC", 22 May 2008. All NEC documents cited in this article may be found on its website <http://www.necelect.org.kh/English/Home.htm>.

[5] National Election Committee, "Number of National and International Observers Accredited by the NEC", 25 July 2008.

[6] National Election Committee, "Number of Representatives of Political Parties Observing in the National Assembly Election", 25 July 2008.

7   Quoted by Andrew Nette, "Cambodia's One-Sided Polls", Inter Press Service, 6 July 2008.

8   Human Rights Watch, "Cambodia: Threats, Intimidation Mar Campaign", 26 July 2008.

9   Both of these incidents are reported in European Union-Electoral Observation Mission, Preliminary Statement, 29 July 2008, p. 7. For the NEC's response to the EU-EOM's report in general see: National Election Committee, "The National Election Committee (NEC)'s Clarification to EU EOM Preliminary Statement on the 2008 National Election in Cambodia", undated.

10   Cambodian Association for the Protection of Journalists, "Post-election report on the media situation in Cambodia", Asian Press Alliance, 1 August 2008.

11   EU-EOM, Preliminary Statement, p. 7.

12   Nette, "Cambodia's One-Sided Polls".

13   EU-EOM, Preliminary Statement, p. 6.

14   National Election Committee, "Press Conference on Dissemination of the Temporary Election Results of 4th Mandate Election of Members of the National Assembly", 9 August 2008 and NEC, "The Total of Voices That Each Political Party Obtained throughout the Country for the 4th Mandate Election of Members of the National Assembly 27th July 2008", 3 September 2008. The final results were in fact issued a day early.

15   The home page of the Sam Rainsy Party has a section entitled Election 2008 which contains a table of complaints made to the NEC and the international community; see <http://www.samrainsyparty.org/>.

16   Lisa Murray, "Cambodia's ruling party claims victory", Financial Times.com, 27 July 2008; Angus Grigg, "Cambodian ruler increases seats", The Australian Financial Review, 28 July 2008; Ker Munthit, "Cambodia's ruling party claims large election lead", Associated Press, 28 July 2008; and "Post election shakeout", Phnom Penh Post, 31 July 2008.

17   EU-EOM, Final Report: National Assembly Elections, 27 July 2008, 13 October 2008, p. 2.

18   Agence France-Presse, 12 August 2008.

19   Agence France-Presse, 12 August 2008.

20   "U.S. Embassy's Assessment of the Recent Cambodian National Elections".

21   "After a dirty election, the prime minister tightens his grip", The Economist, 31 July 2008 and Fergal Quinn, "Landslide poll victory for Cambodia's ruling party", Irish Times, 29 July 2008.

22   Patrick Falby, "Cambodia's Hun Sen set to dominate polls", Agence France-Presse, 20 July 2008.

23   Meas Sokchea, "HRP hold steady on NA boycott", Phnom Penh Post, 25 September 2008.

24   Agence France-Presse, "Hun Sen elected as Cambodian PM for five more years", 25 September, 2008; Associated Press, "Cambodian Parliament Endorses New Cabinet",

25 September 2008; and "SRP defectors get top posts as Sam Rainsy complains to UN", *Phnom Penh Post*, 13 August 2008.

[25] Meak Sokchea, "King pardons exiled prince", *Phnom Penh Post*, 26 September 2008.

[26] Bunn Nagara, "Thailand defensive as Cambodia acts tough", *The Star*, 30 July 2008 and Bryan Havenhand, "Making New Ruins", *New Matilda*, 11 November 2008. In June, the Thai Constitutional Court ruled that the foreign minister had breached the constitution without first seeking parliamentary approval.

[27] "An autopsy of the Thai-Cambodian information war", *The Nation*, 28 October 2008.

[28] "Thai troops 'cross into Cambodia'", BBC News, 15 July 2008 and Sopheng Cheang, "Cambodia, Thailand deploy more troops", Associated Press, 17 July 2008.

[29] "Thai troops 'cross into Cambodia'".

[30] Agence France-Presse, "UN Security Council to discuss Thai-Cambodia dispute", *Borneo Bulletin*, 24 July 2008.

[31] Agence France-Presse, 24 July 2008; Puy Kea Puy Kea, Kyodo News Service, 27 July 2008; and "An autopsy of the Thai-Cambodian information war".

[32] Thailand Ministry of Foreign Affairs Briefing, "ASEAN member countries briefed on latest developments regarding Thai-Cambodian border issue", Thai News Service, 15 October 2008.

[33] Thanida Tanssubhapo and Wanana Nanuam, "Border shoot out prompts protest to Cambodia govt", *Bangkok Post*, 5 October 2008.

[34] "Two killed, several hurt in Preah Vihear clashes", *Phnom Penh Post*, 16 October 2008.

[35] "ASEAN member countries briefed on latest developments regarding Thai-Cambodian border issue".

[36] Quoted by Seth Mydans, "2 Killed on Thai-Cambodian Border", *New York Times*, 16 October 2008.

[37] Mydans, "2 Killed on Thai-Cambodian Border"; Simon Montlake, "Gunfire erupts along Thai-Cambodian border", *Christian Science Monitor*, 16 October 2008; and "Two killed, several hurt in Preah Vihear clashes", *Phnom Penh Post*, 16 October 2008.

[38] "ASEAN member countries briefed on latest developments regarding Thai-Cambodian border issue" and "Fighting stops, one Cambodian killed, 5 Thais injured", Thai News Service, 16 October 2008.

[39] Richard S. Ehrlich, "Temple tiff teeters towards war", *AsiaTimesOnline*, 7 October 2008.

[40] Associated Press, "Thai, Cambodian militaries agree to joint patrols", *International Herald Tribune*, 16 October 2008 and "More troops at Thai-Cambodian border", *Bangkok Post*, 16 October 2008.

[41] Ek Madra, "Cambodia doubles military budget after Thai clash", Reuters, 9 October 2008.

[42]   Ian Ransom, "Thailand, Cambodia to step up efforts to fix border", Reuters, 24 October 2008 and Xinhua News Agency, 24 October 2008.

[43]   Ransom, "Thailand, Cambodia to step up efforts to fix border" and Marianne Barriaux, "Thailand, Cambodia agree to prevent further border clashes", Agence France-Presse, 24 October 2008.

[44]   Thai News Service, 10 November 2008 and Saritdet Marukatat, Thanida Tansubhapol, and Associated Press, "Border temple talks start today", *Bangkok Post*, 10 November 2008.

[45]   Associated Press, 27 January 2009. The two Prime Ministers were scheduled to meet on the sidelines of the ASEAN Summit to be held in Thailand from 27 February to 1 March 2009.

[46]   For background see Milton Osborne, "The Khmer Rouge Tribunal: An Ambiguous Good News Story", *Perspectives* (Sydney: Lowy Institute for International Affairs, August 2007).

[47]   See Claire Duffett, "Khmer Rouge Genocide Tribunal Stumbles as French Defense Lawyer Demands New Translation", in International News, Law.com, 10 December 2008.

[48]   Sara Colm, "Killing Field Trials", Human Rights Watch, 2 March 2008.

[49]   Duffett, "Khmer Rouge Genocide Tribunal Stumbles as French Defense Lawyer Demands New Translation".

[50]   Duffett, "Khmer Rouge Genocide Tribunal Stumbles as French Defense Lawyer Demands New Translation"; Cat Barton, "Court casts wide net, but at what cost?", *Phnom Penh Post*, 24 December 2008; Brendan Brady, "KRT prosecutors at impasse", *Phnom Penh Post*, 31 December 2008 and Brendan Brady, "No more KR suspects: Cambodian prosecutor", *Phnom Penh Post*, 6 January 2009.

[51]   Agence France-Presse, 7 November 2008 and 10 December 2008.

[52]   Kounila Keo, "Work safety worsens as Cambodian construction booms", Agence France-Presse, 9 October 2008.

[53]   Agence France-Presse, 7 November 2008 and 10 December 2008.

[54]   Agence France-Presse, 9 November 2008.

[55]   Agence France-Presse, 6 June 2008, 25 June 2008 and 7 November 2008.

[56]   AFX Asia, 7 November 2008.

[57]   Agence France-Presse, 5 December 2008.

[58]   AFX Asia, 7 November 2008 and Agence France-Presse, 21 November 2008.

[59]   Associated Press, 9 December 2009 and Xinhua News Agency, 9 December 2008.

[60]   "China presence in Cambodia grows", *AsiaTimesOnline*, 30 May 2008 based on original reporting in Khmer by Radio Free Asia.

[61]   Xinhua News Agency, 24 October 2008.

[62]   "Remarks by Deputy Secretary Negroponte in Cambodia", U.S. Department of State, 16 September 2008.

[63]   Geoffrey Cain, "Hun Sen's diplomatic juggling act", *AsiaTimesOnline*, 18 July 2008.

[64] Scot Marciel, Deputy Assistant Secretary for East Asian and Pacific Affairs, "The United States and Cambodia: Bilateral Relations and Bilateral Debt", Testimony before the Subcommittee on Asia, the Pacific, and the Global Environment, House Foreign Affairs Committee, 14 February 2008.

[65] "State President reiterates good ties with Cambodia", *Nhan Dan*, 25 March 2008 and "Cambodia thanks Vietnam for military assistance", *Thanh Nien*, 26 March 2008.

[66] Agence Kampuchea Presse, 8 October 2008.

[67] Vietnam News Agency, 3 November 2008 and Commentary, "Vietnam, Cambodia promote comprehensive cooperation", Voice of Vietnam Radio, 4 November 2008.

[68] Quoted in Patrick Falby, "Fears for Cambodian democracy after Hun Sen's win at polls: observers", Agence France-Presse, 28 July 2008.

Indonesia

INDONESIA IN 2008
Democratic Consolidation in Soeharto's Shadow

Marcus Mietzner

Indonesia's political and socio-economic developments in 2008 were marked by two contradictory trends. On the one hand, the process of democratic consolidation continued, with Indonesia further strengthening its political institutions, making progress in its anti-corruption drive and generally maintaining healthy economic growth. Indeed, with very low levels of political and communal violence, Indonesia in 2008 appeared like a bulwark of stability in the Southeast Asian region, as Thailand was crippled by incessant mass demonstrations and the Philippines saw the Mindanao insurgency escalating once again. However, Indonesia's democratic consolidation was also challenged by a very divergent phenomenon: that is, the increasing proliferation of some form of nostalgia for the effectiveness of Soeharto's New Order, which had ruled the country with an iron fist between 1966 and 1998. Significantly, the year 2008 not only witnessed Soeharto's death after a long struggle with illness and the post-authoritarian judiciary, but also the tenth anniversary of the democratic regime change. Using both occasions to reflect on Soeharto's achievements, many Indonesians concluded that his regime had been superior to the existing polity in several important aspects, particularly health services, prices of basic goods and security. This sentiment was also reflected in the names that emerged as contenders for the 2009 presidential elections: several of Soeharto's former generals threw their hat into the ring, trying to profit from the growing sympathy for New Order policies.

This chapter aims to take account of both developments: the remarkable stabilization of Indonesian democracy *and* the latent support in society for Soeharto's authoritative and tough leadership. Accordingly, it will discuss events,

MARCUS MIETZNER is Lecturer in Indonesian Studies, Faculty of Asian Studies, Australian National University.

trends and patterns that dominated Indonesia in 2008 by looking at five different areas: first, the progress that Indonesia has made in advancing key democratic institutions and procedures, including elections and the fight against corruption. Second, the public reaction to Soeharto's death in January 2008, which highlighted the attitudes of Indonesians toward the New Order and the current polity. Third, the field of candidates for the parliamentary and presidential elections in 2009, and the way many of them have attempted to tap into the prevalent Soeharto nostalgia. Fourth, the state of the economy, with healthy growth in the first half of 2008 overshadowed by the emerging global financial crisis and the uncertainty associated with it. And fifth, the area of foreign policy, in which Indonesia continued its long-lasting struggle to become a relevant player on the world stage. In the conclusion, I will argue that despite the threat of an economic crisis and continuous criticisms of the incumbent multi-party system, Indonesia's democracy in 2008 was more stable than at any other point in its history.

Democratic Consolidation

The effectiveness and competitiveness of Indonesia's electoral democracy continued to increase in 2008, with minor revisions to existing laws and regulations leading to a further opening of the political system. Most importantly, non-party candidates were allowed from mid-2008 onwards to participate in the direct elections for governors, district heads and mayors. Previously, only nominees supported by political parties had the right to compete, but a decision by the Constitutional Court in July 2007 forced the government to annul this stipulation.[1] While non-party figures had to clear high administrative hurdles to register their candidacy, the new rules resulted in a more diverse field of nominees. In October 2008, Arya Zulkarnaen became the first independent candidate to win a direct local election in Indonesia outside of Aceh (which had allowed for non-party candidates since 2006, based on its special autonomy law). Winning the elections in the district of Batubara in North Sumatra, Zulkarnaen beat the second-placed GOLKAR candidate by a large margin. Independent candidates also did well in district elections in East Nusa Tenggara, Jambi, West Kalimantan and West Nusa Tenggara. Another important change to the laws on local elections saw the authority to rule on electoral disputes transferred from the Supreme Court to the Constitutional Court. In the past, the Supreme Court had often issued rather erratic verdicts, which were then ignored by both the government and the contestants. By contrast, the Constitutional Court enjoys much greater respect. Thus when the Court issued its first ruling on an electoral conflict in November 2008, all parties involved accepted the outcome. As a result of these and several other legal changes, the 153 elections held in 2008 registered much less violent protest than previous rounds of local ballots.

In preparation for the 2009 national elections, Indonesia took additional reform steps. Mostly, these innovations addressed widespread societal concerns about the lack of "representativeness" in the electoral system used in 1999 and 2004. For example, in 2004 only 2 out of 550 members of parliament had been directly elected; the rest had entered the legislature because of their ranking on a list determined by their parties. Hence, in early 2008 parliament at first agreed that seats won by parties in the upcoming elections would be allocated to those nominees who personally received more than 30 per cent of an electoral quota (i.e., the number of votes required to win a seat), regardless of his or her ranking on the party list. But in December 2008 the Constitutional Court went even one step further, declaring party lists in conflict with people's sovereignty and therefore unconstitutional. Consequently, parties that win a seat will now have to hand this mandate to the nominee with the highest number of votes, without paying attention to the initially agreed threshold and ranking.[2] This new system has already forced nominees to campaign much harder at the grassroots than they were used to. In late 2008, around half a year before the legislative elections scheduled for April 2009, many seasoned politicians who had previously won their seats through backroom negotiations in Jakarta were now seen spending significantly more time in their districts than ever before.[3] Banners that in the past only featured party symbols now placed the photographs of the nominees in the foreground. While one of the side effects of this more personality-based campaigning was a higher level of intra-party competition, the goal of a closer relationship between voters and nominees apparently has been achieved.

In addition, Indonesia introduced measures to consolidate the party system and encourage more stable coalitions between its actors. Since 1999, one of the most frequent complaints by academic observers and the public alike had focused on the large number of political parties. No less than 17 parties were represented in the 2004 parliament, many of them tiny splinter parties with an unclear mission and purpose. Accordingly, the political elite decided in 2008 that beginning with the 2009 elections, a parliamentary threshold of 2.5 per cent will apply. Parties that do not reach this threshold at the national level will no longer have representatives in parliament, forcing them in the longer term to rethink their strategy and possibly merge with larger parties. Such mergers would make the party system more effective and parliamentary proceedings less dependent on the narrow group interests of small parties. In the same vein, all key parties agreed to raise the threshold for presidential nominations. In 2004, parties (or coalitions between them) needed to have achieved only 3 per cent in the parliamentary polls in order to nominate a candidate for the subsequent presidential ballot. In 2009, by contrast, 20 per cent of the seats or 25 per cent of the votes will be necessary to make such a nomination.[4] This new regulation will encourage parties to build larger coalitions to name a presidential candidate, giving the eventual president-elect a better chance of establishing a solid and coherent government.[5]

While the reform of the electoral system is a precondition for Indonesia's further democratic consolidation, no institution can work properly if it is undermined by corruption. Corruption remained Indonesia's biggest political problem in 2008, and it is likely to stay that way in the foreseeable future. Many politicians continued to misuse their legislative and executive positions to siphon off state funds, shift contracts to their financial donors or draft laws ordered by their lobbyists. But although Indonesia still ranks as one of the most corrupt places in the world, it has made significant progress in its attempt to address the problem. In Transparency International's 2008 Corruption Perception Index, Indonesia climbed 17 ranks from its position in the same survey conducted in the previous year.[6] This improvement reflected the successful performance of the Corruption Eradication Commission (KPK, Komisi Pemberantasan Korupsi), which in 2008 intensified its campaign against corrupt legislators, prosecutors and government officials. In March 2008, the KPK arrested a senior prosecutor from the Attorney-General's office, who had accepted money from a close associate of fugitive tycoon Syamsul Nursalim in exchange for closing the latter's case. In September, the law enforcement official was sentenced to 20 years in prison, one of the stiffest sentences ever issued in an Indonesian corruption case. In the same vein, the KPK detained a member of parliament from the Islamic United Development Party (PPP, Partai Persatuan Pembangunan). The legislator had not only demanded money from a local government official to facilitate the conversion of a natural reserve area into commercial land, but was also involved in a host of other cases. In January 2009, he was sentenced to eight years in prison.

The impact of the KPK's campaign on the daily lives of state officials and politicians cannot be overestimated. In addition to prison sentences and hefty fines, culprits now face considerable social shame and marginalization. The KPK has chosen to conduct its operations in a very public manner, inviting the media to film the arrests and releasing tapped phone conversations with intimate details to the press. In one such conversation, the PPP legislator mentioned above described the physical attributes of the prostitute he wanted supplied as a reward for using his political influence. Shortly after the tapes were played in court, the suspect's celebrity wife filed for divorce, and PPP fired its member from the party and the legislature. Obviously, there is now widespread anxiety among elite politicians that they may be the next in line, forcing them to be much more careful in conducting their financial operations. In a recent interview with the author, a senior party functionary and member of parliament nervously checked his three mobile phones each minute for updates, explaining that one of his colleagues who was currently being investigated by the KPK had threatened to "sing", i.e. to openly implicate all other politicians associated with the case. This fear of the KPK was compounded by the fact that its investigations have now begun to reach the highest political echelons. In November 2008, even President Susilo Bambang Yudhoyono's brother-in-law Aulia Pohan was arrested for his alleged involvement in the cover-up of a massive banking scandal, sending a clear message that virtually nobody is off-limits for the KPK.

Indonesia's progressing democratic consolidation in 2008 was also assisted by the remarkable absence of large-scale political and communal violence. To begin with, the Aceh peace accord celebrated its third anniversary in August 2008, amid largely favourable political and security conditions in the formerly troubled province. The situation in Papua was also stable, although the levels of dissatisfaction of native Papuans with Jakarta's rule remained high and are unlikely to decline in the short to medium term. Similarly, not a single terrorist attack took place in 2008, with further arrests of Jemaah Islamiyah figures undermining the strength of jihadist underground cells. There was, however, an increase in intolerance and physical violence towards religious minorities. According to a report published by the Wahid Institute in December 2008, the number of cases involving religious discrimination and intimidation rose from 197 in 2007 to 232 in 2008.[7] Most of these cases related to forced church closures in majority Muslim areas, but there was also a significant number of attacks by Islamic groups on followers of the Ahmadiyah sect, which mainstream organizations view as heretic. The worst of these attacks occurred on 1 June in Jakarta, when members of the radical Islam Defenders Front (FPI, Front Pembela Islam) attacked a pro-Ahmadiyah demonstration, injuring 70 people. The instigators of the attacks were later tried and sentenced to short prison terms, but many observers have accused the government of not doing enough to protect religious freedom in Indonesia. However, while these developments are certainly a source of concern, they have not seriously disturbed the general stabilization of Indonesia's democratic polity in 2008.

Soeharto Nostalgia

Despite the generally satisfactory performance of Indonesia's democracy, the year 2008 was also characterized by renewed interest in and sympathy for former President Soeharto and his authoritarian rule. Two main events highlighted this trend: the death of the long-time autocrat and the 10th anniversary of his downfall. When Soeharto died after a long illness in January 2008, many Indonesians genuinely mourned their former leader. His funeral attracted more attention than that of any other Indonesian figure since Sukarno's death in 1970, with hundreds of thousands of people lining the streets along which his coffin passed. Many had tears in their eyes, and when interviewed on television, they called on the nation to forgive Soeharto for his mistakes and honour his achievements. In talk-shows broadcast during the week following Soeharto's passing, commentators tried to outbid themselves in their praise for the ex-despot, describing him as "peace-loving" and "despising violence".[8] Soeharto, who had presided over one of the bloodiest political massacres of the twentieth century, now appeared as a benevolent, grandfatherly patron who had brought Indonesia stability and prosperity. The excesses of his regime — from the murder of dissidents and the invasion of East Timor to extrajudicial killings of street criminals and the rampant corruption of his family — were all blamed on manipulative advisers and greedy relatives. While some of this proliferation of revisionist historiography was certainly the result of the universal observance of *de mortuis nil nisi bonum* ("Of the dead say nothing but good"), the emotional Soeharto obituaries produced by the Indonesian media and ordinary citizens also revealed deeply rooted admiration for the New Order and its political principles.[9]

Soeharto's death ended a decade of long and painful discussions within Indonesian society on how to relate to the former president in political and legal terms. While student groups and liberal civil society organizations vocally demanded that he be tried for corruption, successive post-New Order presidents had felt reluctant to bring Soeharto to court. The Wahid government, for instance, had laid corruption charges against Soeharto in May 2000, but only several months later declared that he was too ill to stand trial. Soeharto's lawyers and state-appointed doctors asserted repeatedly that his brain functions were severely reduced after several minor strokes, and that he therefore could not defend himself in court. However, doubts about the seriousness of his illness were widespread. This was largely due to the fact that Soeharto was often seen at family functions walking unaided and chatting alertly to his guests. Needless to say, such events were invariably followed by media commentaries that proposed to re-examine Soeharto's health.[10] But whether coincidental or not, Soeharto would be admitted to hospital with "acute" medical problems whenever fresh demands for his prosecution were made. In late April 2006, for example, then Attorney-General Abdurrahman Saleh announced that the government had established a team of doctors to look into Soeharto's health once again. Only two weeks later, Soeharto entered hospital with "intestinal bleeding".[11] Concluding that the medical obstacles were insurmountable, the government eventually decided to initiate civil charges against Soeharto's foundations instead. The civil trial ended only in March 2008 — after Soeharto's death — with a verdict that acquitted Soeharto personally but ordered his foundations to return a small part of the money.

To be sure, it was not only fear of Soeharto's residual influence or the endless legal conflicts inherent in his case that discouraged the political elite from seriously pursuing his imprisonment. More importantly, there was also a growing awareness in elite circles that while the students and some media outlets were strongly advocating for Soeharto's legal prosecution, only very few ordinary Indonesians actually wanted to see him behind bars. In fact, the nostalgic support for Soeharto that erupted on the occasion of his death had built up gradually during Indonesia's difficult and decade-long struggle to develop a functioning democratic system. In May 2008 — the tenth anniversary of Soeharto's resignation — a public opinion survey undertaken to review the performance of the post-authoritarian polity recorded that 58 per cent of Indonesians preferred their living conditions under the New Order to those under the current regime.[12] Evidently, many Indonesians feel that some public services were better under Soeharto, prices were lower and jobs more secure. While such results do not yet indicate an active societal push for a return to autocratic rule, they do point to the existence of a significant pool of voters who are susceptible to pro-New Order rhetoric.

The competition for this large segment of the Indonesian electorate intensified throughout 2008. Parties as diverse as GOLKAR and the Prosperous Justice Party (PKS, Partai Keadilan Sejahtera) openly reached out to politically conservative voters, trying to translate the ongoing Soeharto nostalgia into electoral support. A senior GOLKAR functionary stated that in the 2009 elections, "we intend to appeal to those Indonesians who believe that the New Order had its good sides as well; especially those who are convinced that their economic situation was better."[13] PKS, for its part, triggered a major controversy both inside and outside the party by calling on the government to pardon Soeharto and — after his death — broadcasting a television advertisement that classified him as a "national hero". As an Islamic party whose older members still remember the intimidation they suffered under the New Order, PKS created considerable confusion with its pro-Soeharto turn. But its move had less to do with a new-found sympathy for Soeharto than with a strategic reading of the polls. In making its decision, PKS referred to a 2008 survey conducted by the independent research institute LP3ES, which found that 34 per cent of Indonesians viewed Soeharto as the most effective president; in the same poll, founding president Sukarno received 24 per cent support, and the incumbent Susilo Bambang Yudhoyono only 12 per cent.[14] Through its posthumous "reconciliation" with Soeharto, PKS thus hoped to soften its image as a puritan Islamic party, and open its door to new constituencies.[15] Apparently, PKS's new strategy reflected broader electoral trends: by mid-2008, the field of presidential contenders for the 2009 elections began to be dominated by a remarkably high number of former Soeharto generals and aides.

Presidential Candidates

In the run-up to the 2009 presidential elections, a wide variety of prospective and less prospective candidates emerged. Most of these challengers felt encouraged to throw their hat into the ring in the middle of 2008, when Yudhoyono experienced a crisis of public confidence that saw him temporarily falling behind in the polls.[16] Yudhoyono's popularity ratings had been dropping for a number of reasons. Most importantly, the dramatic increase in global oil prices forced the government in May 2008 to cut fuel subsidies, driving up the living costs for ordinary Indonesians. In addition, voters were generally dissatisfied with Yudhoyono's perceived lack of leadership, and many complained about deteriorating public services. It was in this period that many political figures sensed that they might have a chance to unseat the president in the 2009 elections. But before these would-be nominees could set their electoral machines in motion, Yudhoyono made a surprisingly fast comeback in opinion surveys. After the government put a cash assistance programme in place that compensated poor Indonesians for the escalating inflation, Yudhoyono's numbers began to rise again. In addition, Yudhoyono was assisted by the sharp decline of international oil prices from August 2008 onwards, which allowed him to reduce the cost of fuel several times in December. By the end of the year, most polls showed him again as the front-runner for 2009, and some initially hopeful candidates withdrew their candidacies. However, five or six fairly credible contenders remained in the race.

In opinion polls conducted throughout 2008, former president Megawati Sukarnoputri appeared as the most serious challenger to Yudhoyono. In June and July 2008, she even momentarily overtook him in the polls, triggering both panic in Yudhoyono's camp and immediate policy responses by the government. Megawati owed her relative strength in the surveys largely to the fact that her Indonesian Democratic Party of Struggle (PDIP, Partai Demokrasi Perjuangan) was the only major established party not represented in Yudhoyono's cabinet. For that reason, voters dissatisfied with the performance of the incumbent government initially felt little alternative but to shift their support to her. However, as new parties and candidates emerged, her popularity began to decline. In addition, Megawati failed to demonstrate that she had changed significantly since her landslide defeat in 2004. At that time, Megawati had been widely seen as arrogant, aloof, elitist and complacent. Four years later, she still did not seem to have understood that this negative personal image was partly to blame for her 2004 rout. Despite the best efforts of her advisers who wanted Megawati to go into the 2009 elections with a "more friendly and more open" attitude,[17] the former president continued her belligerent approach to the press, often barking at journalists when she deemed a question inappropriate. At internal party events, she blamed her own cadres for the loss of her presidency in 2004, showing no awareness that she might have been responsible as well. While Megawati continued to command a sizeable core of loyalist voters, by the end of 2008 it appeared as if another presidential term would be a long shot for Sukarno's favourite daughter.

One of the most controversial presidential candidates to emerge in 2008 was Prabowo Subianto, Soeharto's former son-in-law and a feared military leader under his rule. Prabowo had been "honourably" dismissed from the military in 1998 after units under his command admitted to the kidnapping of several regime dissidents. Subsequently, Prabowo divorced Soeharto's daughter and concentrated on the development of his businesses, which included lucrative oil enterprises in Kazakhstan. He unsuccessfully sought the presidential nomination of GOLKAR in 2004, losing in that party's convention to his archrival Wiranto. It was this defeat that led him to conclude that he needed to build up his own grassroots network. Accordingly, he took over the chairmanship of an influential peasant association in December 2004, giving him access to one of the largest segments of the Indonesian electorate.[18] Furthermore, he initiated the founding of a political party, which would serve as his political vehicle to run for president in 2009. Gerindra (Partai Gerakan Indonesia Raya, Great Indonesia Movement Party), which pledged to restore Indonesia's past "greatness" by reducing its dependence on foreign capital, quickly became one of the most popular new parties in the political landscape. Using his considerable wealth to finance an aggressive media campaign,[19] Prabowo began to figure prominently in opinion surveys by the end of 2008. However, he was still significantly behind Yudhoyono and Megawati, suggesting that the fight for the presidency might turn out to be an uphill battle for the ambitious ex-general.

Prabowo was not the only New Order military leader who tried to tap into the nostalgic sympathies of some voters for Soeharto's tough but efficient regime. Wiranto, Soeharto's last commander-in-chief and his former adjutant, also based his campaign on the disappointment of many Indonesians with the performance of successive post-Soeharto governments. In 2004, Wiranto had been GOLKAR's official candidate for the presidency, but he had finished only third in the first round of the elections and thus did not even make it into the run-off. Blaming his defeat on the lack of support by GOLKAR's electoral network for his campaign, Wiranto decided — much earlier than Prabowo — to develop his own political party as the foundation for another run. Therefore, he established Hanura (Partai Hati Nurani Rakyat, People's Conscience Party), which attracted many of Wiranto's former military colleagues and politicians who had left other parties for a variety of reasons. But despite its well-funded organization and successful penetration of both urban and rural areas, Hanura did not play a significant role in the opinion polls published in 2008. While stronger than other new parties, it did not reach the levels of support enjoyed by GOLKAR, PDIP or Yudhoyono's Democratic Party (PD, Partai Demokrat). In the same vein, Wiranto's personal popularity ratings remained in single-digit territory,[20] making victory a very unlikely scenario for Soeharto's former military chief.

Another former Soeharto loyalist running for the presidency was Sutiyoso, the ex-commander of the Jakarta military area and recently retired governor of the capital. In July 1996, Sutiyoso had ordered his troops to violently suppress the emerging pro-Megawati movement, and Soeharto had installed him in the Jakarta governorship in the following year. As head of the Jakarta government until 2007, Sutiyoso tried to convey the image of a decisive leader willing to enforce his ideas against partisan opposition by narrow-minded politicians. But major floods that hit Jakarta in 2002 and 2007 exposed Sutiyoso's poor preparations for such a predictable disaster, and his reputation declined as a result.[21] In addition, a new system of special bus lanes — offered by Sutiyoso as his solution to the notoriously bad traffic congestion in Jakarta — not only suffered from the usual ills of corruption, inefficiency and inadequate maintenance, but in effect exacerbated the traffic problems in the city. Undeterred by such setbacks, Sutiyoso launched his bid for the presidency immediately after leaving office. Believing that Yudhoyono's image as a procrastinator would provide his hard-headed campaign with a strategic opening, he began to tour the country and offer himself as the long-awaited alternative.[22] But unlike Prabowo and Wiranto, Sutiyoso decided not to build up his own political party. Instead, he lobbied already existing parties to nominate him, but with little success. As his poll numbers remained low, there were few indications in late 2008 that Sutiyoso's campaign could gain the momentum that he had initially hoped for.

Among the civilian presidential hopefuls declaring their candidacy in 2008 was the Sultan of Yogyakarta, Hamengkubuwono. As the traditional ruler and governor of Yogyakarta, Hamengkubuwono drew his electoral capital largely from widespread Javanese beliefs in the mystical powers of the sultanate. In addition, Hamengkubuwono had been a critical figure in the 1998 protests against Soeharto, allowing the students in his city to stage the largest anti-government demonstration outside of Jakarta. But Hamengkubuwono lacked the charisma and intellectual sharpness of his father, who had been a national leader in the revolution, a minister in several cabinets and eventually Soeharto's vice-president. Without a clear campaign message, Hamengkubuwono found it difficult to reach out to electoral constituencies other than Central Javanese royalists. However, the loyal support by his core electorate guaranteed Hamankubuwono a place in the upper ranks in the opinion polls, and made him interesting for several political parties. Most importantly, Hamengkubuwono became the main option for GOLKAR elements that rejected the plan of their chairman Jusuf Kalla to seek another term as vice-president at Yudhoyono's side.[23] Arguing that GOLKAR was too large and important to be content with the deputy post, these dissidents pushed openly for Hamengkubuwono — who had previously been the head of the party's provincial chapter in Yogyakarta — to become GOLKAR's presidential nominee.[24] But at the end of 2008, Kalla's opponents did not appear to have gained the upper hand in this dispute, making Hamengkubuwono's candidacy for the party increasingly unlikely.

In the last quarter of 2008, the presidential campaign became more and more influenced by the rapidly escalating global financial crisis. For many candidates, the economic downturn was not only an important policy issue that they suddenly had to address with their political programmes; more crucially, the financial interests of some nominees were so severely affected by the crisis that they no longer had the money to sustain their campaigns. Sutrisno Bachir, for example, the chairman of PAN (Partai Amanat Nasional, Nantional Mandate Party), had spent millions of dollars before the crisis on an aggressive advertising campaign in the media. But after the collapse of the stock markets, he was forced to suspend this effort and quietly leave the presidential race.[25] In the same vein, political observer Rizal Mallarangeng, who was sponsored by the affluent entrepreneur and cabinet minister Abdurizal Bakrie, withdrew his candidacy in November 2008 after the value of some Bakrie companies dropped a stunning 90 per cent on the Jakarta stock exchange. But while all nominees witnessed their monetary resources declining, for the politically and financially more established candidates the crisis also offered strategic opportunities. For Yudhoyono's opponents, the prospect of an economic meltdown provided welcome campaign material against the incumbent president. In fact, many nominees began to exclusively focus on the crisis, hoping that the collective fear of an uncertain economic future would seriously damage Yudhoyono. The president, however, also saw positive elements in the historic decline of the world economy: the sharp drop in international oil prices allowed Yudhoyono to lower domestic fuel costs in late 2008, just in time for the beginning of the campaign. Whatever impact the crisis may have had on the political fortunes of the individual nominees, it quickly became clear that the outcome of the 2009 elections would to a large extent be determined by the state of the economy at the time of the ballot.

The Economy: From Success to Crisis

The global financial crisis — which erupted in the United States in September 2008 but spread swiftly to other parts of the world — tainted what would otherwise have been an extraordinarily successful year for the Indonesian economy. Continuing several years of strong growth, Indonesia's GDP expanded by a very healthy 6.4 per cent in the second quarter of 2008.[26] Investment grew 12.8 per cent in comparison to the previous year, with the transport and communication sectors even recording growth rates of 39.9 per cent and 36.7 per cent, respectively. Exports were also stronger than in 2007, increasing by 15.5 per cent in the first quarter and 16.1 per cent in the second.[27] Most importantly, there were clear indications that middle-income earners profited from the overall expansion of the economy, with motorcycle sales growing by 44 per cent.[28] In the same vein, domestic car sales increased by around half to almost 300,000, making Indonesia the largest car market in the Association of Southeast Asian Nations (ASEAN) in June and July 2008. Before the crisis began, average income per capita was projected to reach around US$2,400 by the end of the year, up from US$1,946 in 2007. This strong performance of the economy apparently also helped to reduce poverty, with the number of poor Indonesians declining from 37.17 million in March 2007 to 34.96 million (or 15.4 per cent of the population) by March 2008. As Yudhoyono proudly pointed out, this was the lowest level of poverty since 1998.[29] Similarly, official unemployment decreased from 10.55 million people in 2007 to 9.43 million in 2008.[30] With figures like these, Indonesia was on a good way to finally complete its recovery from the 1997/98 crisis, which had crippled the country for more than a decade.

But the crisis put an abrupt end to this success story. While Indonesia appeared less exposed to the financial turmoil than its neighbouring countries Malaysia, Thailand and Singapore, it nevertheless suffered tremendously. Companies trading at the Jakarta Stock Exchange lost more than half of their value between June and October 2008, with some sectors recording particularly dramatic losses. The index for mining shares dropped 75.15 per cent, the agriculture sector declined 73.7 per cent, and the trade, services and investment listings shed 65.66 per cent of their prices registered earlier in the year.[31] Embarrassingly for Indonesia, trading in Jakarta's stock market had to be suspended for several days in October, after massive losses incurred by some of Abdurizal Bakrie's companies had threatened to send the whole stock exchange into an unstoppable downwards spiral. In the wake of the declining financial markets, the Rupiah temporarily reached 10-year lows, and the government was forced to spend billions of dollars of its foreign reserve to stabilize the currency. The government subsequently revised its growth forecast for 2009 from 6 to between 4.5 and 5 per cent, with the World Bank and other international financial institutions announcing similar figures. Some private analysts even put the estimates for 2009 growth as low as 2.5 per cent.[32] Consequently, the government prepared itself for a significant increase in unemployment numbers in 2009, with jobs in the export industry especially threatened and many Indonesian workers overseas likely to be sent home. While the exact extent of the crisis remained unknown in late 2008, it was obvious that the earlier streak of strong economic growth would at least be interrupted, and that the fight against poverty and unemployment would suffer severe setbacks as a result.

Amid the constant stream of bad news, however, the government was also able to partly profit from the economic crisis. As indicated earlier, Yudhoyono was now in a position to reduce domestic fuel charges as a consequence of the collapsing international oil prices. Not surprisingly, Yudhoyono tried to make the most of this welcome development. In May, when his government felt forced to increase fuel prices, the president had left it to his aides to announce the politically hurtful measure. By contrast, in December he called for a special press conference to announce that he personally had "decided" to lower the cost of gasoline. With the 2009 elections only months away, the political implications of this move were evident. Yudhoyono's critics, however, were quick to point out that reducing fuel prices alone was an inadequate response to the overall decline of the economy.

Indeed, the fallout from the global financial downturn is likely to aggravate the already deeply seated disenchantment of many citizens with the liberal economic policies favoured by most post-Soeharto governments. Even before the crisis began and economic growth was still solid, an opinion poll showed that 79 per cent of respondents were unhappy with Yudhoyono's management of the economy.[33] Such figures were very similar to those received by other presidents after 1998, highlighting societal discontent with general living conditions as the most significant weakness of the post-authoritarian polity. One of the major sources of this frustration has been the high level of inflation, which remained above 10 per cent throughout 2008. In fact, consumer prices rose 17.9 per cent in August and core inflation (which excludes food and fuel prices) stood at 10.2 per cent.[34] The high cost of living, which is a particular burden for the lower classes, has contributed to a general feeling in Indonesian society that it is largely the elite that benefits from economic development. In a poll of young voters taken in August, 76 per cent of respondents stated that the government's economic strategy "does not side with the people".[35] While the available economic data suggests that ordinary Indonesians actually *have* profited considerably from the strong growth in recent years, this negative sentiment is nevertheless widespread and has fuelled, among others, the nostalgia for Soeharto described above. More effective, socially balanced and participatory economic governance thus remains the most important challenge for Indonesia's post-New Order leaders if they want to complement the remarkable political progress since 1998 with similar achievements in the economic field.

International Relations

Towards the end of 2008, the global financial crisis also began to dominate Indonesia's international relations. In November 2008, Yudhoyono attended the crisis summit of the G-20 states hosted by outgoing U.S. President Bush in Washington, and he was also a participant in the APEC summit in Lima shortly afterwards. In its discussions with other nations, Indonesia's primary interest was to lobby against traditional concepts of financial crisis resolution that it believed had failed disastrously in the past. Most significantly, Yudhoyono rejected the involvement of the International Monetary Fund (IMF) in negotiations over emergency loans to affected countries, including Indonesia itself.[36] Blaming the

IMF for Indonesia's economic turmoil in 1997 and 1998, Yudhoyono instead supported proposals to set up an East Asian emergency fund, from which nations in the region could draw if they needed assistance. At the same time, however, Indonesia also applied for bilateral assistance in case its economy deteriorated further in 2009. In December 2008, Jakarta announced that it had secured 5 billion dollars in standby loans from Australia, Japan, the Asian Development Bank and the World Bank, allowing it to ignore offers of fresh IMF funds. [37]

But while Indonesia had succeeded in using its international relationships to obtain financial help for its troubled economy, its contribution to larger debates on the reform of the world economy was peripheral. Despite Yudhoyono's exceptional English language skills and his good grasp of international affairs, his role in the crisis summits remained largely unnoted. This stood in sharp contrast to Yudhoyono's self-proclaimed goal of raising Indonesia's status on the world stage — an agenda in which he has invested significant amounts of time and energy. Since taking office in 2004, Yudhoyono has received much praise from international leaders for his moderate stance on issues ranging from climate change to Islam and democracy, but concrete foreign policy successes for Indonesia have been rare. In fact, many of Yudhoyono's initiatives have been widely criticized as ineffective, focused more on political symbolism than hands-on problem-solving. In 2007, Yudhoyono had famously convened an international conference to seek a solution to the conflict in Iraq, but none of the invited parties involved in the civil war showed up when the event was held in Jakarta. In 2008, such insufficiently prepared foreign policy initiatives continued. In September, Indonesia — represented by Vice-president Kalla — hosted informal peace talks between the Muslim "rebels" in Thailand's South and the Bangkok government. But not only did the Thai cabinet deny any knowledge of the negotiations, the alleged "rebels" turned out to be figures with no or only loose connections to the insurgents.[38] The ensuing public relations debacle led to tensions between Jakarta and Bangkok as well as within Yudhoyono's government, and the initiative soon faltered.

Indonesia's two-year term as a non-permanent member of the UN Security Council also ended in late 2008 without significantly boosting Jakarta's international stature. To some extent, this was because Yudhoyono needed to take the possible domestic impact of decisions made in New York into account when directing Indonesia's representative at the UN to vote on sensitive international matters. As a result, Indonesia's ability to manoeuvre effectively and flexibly in such a high-profile diplomatic arena was severely constrained. The Iran nuclear issue was a telling example in this regard. After Jakarta's support of Resolution 1747 on sanctions against Iran in March 2007 had earned the president a protest note from parliament, Yudhoyono instructed that subsequent Indonesian decisions on the matter should not appear as if they simply paraphrased the American and European positions. Therefore, when the Security Council passed another resolution in September 2008 that reiterated the existing sanctions, Indonesia claimed it had successfully lobbied the Council to refrain from additional threats against Iran, including military action.[39] Whether Indonesia indeed played a decisive role in this debate is questionable, however. China and Russia would have never agreed to the inclusion of military action as a possible sanction anyway, making Indonesia's objections supplementary at best. Jakarta's statement, it seemed, was more designed to appease its political audience at home than to influence its counterparts in the Council. Thus while the Council membership put Indonesia temporarily on the map of international diplomacy, it is unclear whether its impact was great enough for it to remain there in the longer term.

Indonesia's mixed foreign policy record in 2008 was also evident in the role it played in ASEAN. Crucially for Yudhoyono, Indonesia's weight in international relations has traditionally been measured by its influence in the organization it co-founded in 1967. Under Soeharto, Indonesia was ASEAN's leading force, often determining the course of the group and representing it in international contexts. But the domestic political chaos associated with Indonesia's regime transition after 1998 distracted many post-New Order governments from engaging extensively in ASEAN affairs, and Jakarta lost its leadership status as a result. Yudhoyono had pledged to reverse this trend, and he consequently devoted much attention to ASEAN and its many forums and sub-groupings. The results of this increased effort have been uneven, though. During much of his term, Yudhoyono had tried to use Indonesia's power to push for a fundamentally revised ASEAN Charter — one that would make the group more flexible in its decision-making and give it more authority to sanction troublesome members like Myanmar. In November 2007, however, ASEAN adopted a new Charter that included very few of Indonesia's initial proposals. Indeed, Indonesia's parliament was so unhappy with the document that it withheld ratification until October 2008.[40] When Yudhoyono formally launched the Charter in Jakarta two months later without any other ASEAN head of state or government present, it was difficult to escape the conclusion that Indonesia's influence in ASEAN — and in international affairs as a whole — was still a far cry from what Yudhoyono and the majority of Indonesians would want it to be.

Indonesia in 2008: Consolidation and Continued Challenges

Despite the emerging economic crisis, widespread nostalgia for Soeharto and unfulfilled foreign policy aspirations, the most remarkable feature of Indonesia in 2008 was its exceptional stability. Post-New Order Indonesia's tenth anniversary was marked by the absence of large-scale political, separatist or communal violence, the orderly conduct of elections at the local level and generally strong support for democratic institutions. This achievement not only contradicted many predictions made by political observers a decade ago, but also contrasted sharply with the current crises of other democratic or semi-democratic states in the Southeast Asian region. Unlike Thailand and the Philippines, which saw their democracies undermined by political divisions and armed conflict, Indonesia's democratic system consolidated further in 2008. To be sure, many problems and challenges remain. The fact that the field of candidates for the 2009 elections is dominated by figures associated with the New Order points to difficulties in the political regeneration process, and is also evidence of a lack of comprehensive public debates about Indonesia's recent past. In the same vein, the genuine respect shown for Soeharto when he died in January 2008 demonstrated the deep-seated affinity of many Indonesians with notions of harsh but decisive leadership. Should the economy continue to deteriorate and even fall into recession, such dispositions might negatively affect the long-term resilience of Indonesian democracy. So far, however, the post-Soeharto state has not only performed significantly better than anybody could have expected. It has also outperformed its only democratic predecessor (the short-lived parliamentary system of the 1950s), making the current polity the most stable and durable non-authoritarian regime in Indonesian history.

Notes

The author would like to thank Harold Crouch and Rodd McGibbon for their comments on an earlier draft of this paper.

[1] "'Welcome' Calon Independen", *Lampung Post*, 24 July 2007.

[2] "MK Hapus Nomor Urut", *Suara Merdeka*, 23 December 2008.

[3] Interviews with parliamentary candidates Gandjar Pranowo, Jakarta, 9 December 2008; Fachri Hamzah, Jakarta, 5 December 2008; and Jeffrey Geovanie, Jakarta, 12 November 2008.

[4] "UU Pilpres Disahkan", *Harian Jogja*, 30 October 2008.

[5] Interview with Hardisoesilo, member of parliament for GOLKAR, Jakarta, 10 December 2008.

6   "Peringkat Indeks Persepsi Korupsi Indonesia Membaik", *Koran Tempo*, 24 September 2008. In the 2008 index, Indonesia ranked 126th among 180 countries.

7   "Cases of Religious Violence Up: Report", *Jakarta Post*, 11 December 2008.

8   Indonesian TV coverage of Soeharto's death, personal observations by the author, 28 January to 5 February 2008.

9   See, for example, "Jasa HM Soeharto dalam Membangun Citra Islam", *Antara News*, 29 January 2008.

10   "Tutut: Keluarga akan Taat Peraturan", *Suara Merdeka*, 24 April 2006.

11   "Soeharto Kembali Menjalani Operasi", *Gatra*, 19 May 2006.

12   Lingkaran Survei Indonesia, "Reformasi Setelah 10 Tahun" [Reform After 10 Years], Jakarta, May 2008, p. 6.

13   Interview with Rully Chairul Azwar, deputy secretary-general of GOLKAR, Jakarta, 10 December 2008.

14   "Iklan Pahlawan Partai Dakwah", *Tempo*, 17 November 2008.

15   Interview with Anis Matta, secretary-general of PKS, Jakarta, 14 November 2008.

16   "Hasil Survei, Peluang Megawati Menguat", *Berita Sore*, 8 August 2008.

17   Confidential interview with a senior PDIP politician, Jakarta, 12 November 2008.

18   "Letjen. Purn Prabowo Jadi Ketua Umum HKTI", *Pikiran Rakyat*, 6 December 2004.

19   "Partai Berlomba Iklan, Dongkrak Popularitas", *Lampung Post*, 1 December 2008. According to data collected by AC Nielsen, by the end of November 2008 Prabowo had already spent 43 billion Rupiah (around 4 million US$) on media advertising.

20   "Tak Pusingkan Hasil Survei: Wiranto Soal Capres", *Duta Masyarakat*, 22 November 2008.

21   "Jakarta Darurat", *Kompas*, 5 February 2008.

22   "Sutiyoso Akan Kampanye di Yogya dan Bali", *Detik.com*, 26 November 2008.

23   Interview with Sukardi Rinakit, head of Hamengkubuwono's campaign team, Jakarta, 13 November 2008.

24   "Survei Capres Partai Golkar, JK Dikalahkan Sultan", *Sinar Indonesia Baru*, 17 October 2008.

25   "Soetrisno Bachir: Berhemat, Saya Siap Jual Alphard", *Kompas*, 28 November 2008.

26   "RI Economy Expands 6.4 per cent in Q2", *Jakarta Post*, 14 August 2008.

27   I am indebted to Ross McLeod from the Australian National University for providing this data. See also Ross McLeod, "Survey of Recent Developments", *Bulletin of Indonesian Economic Studies* 44, no. 2 (2008): 183–208.

28   Cyrillus Harinowo, "Economic Growth: The Rise of the Indonesian Middle Class", *Jakarta Post*, 16 September 2008. The following data on per capita income is also taken from this article.

29   "President's Speech Likened to Campaign", *Jakarta Post*, 16 August 2008.

30   "Number of Poor Falls by 2.21m, Says Statistics Body", *Jakarta Post*, 2 July 2008.

31   "The Stock Market's Spectacular Crash", *Jakarta Post*, 22 December 2008.

32   "Fiscal Stimulus Key for Economy", *Jakarta Post*, 22 December 2008.

33   "Hasil Survei, Peluang Megawati Menguat", *Harian Berita Sore*, 8 August 2008.

34   "Indonesia's Inflation Accelerates More Than Expected On Food", *Jakarta Post*, 27 August 2008.

35   "Pembangunan Kurang Akomodasi Kepentingan Rakyat", *Antara News*, 7 August 2008.

36   "Presiden: Indonesia Tidak Akan Minta Bantuan IMF", *Harian Berita Sore*, 17 November 2008.

37   "Indonesia Secures $5b Loan to Shield Economy", *Jakarta Post*, 6 December 2008.

38   "Govt 'Not Party' to Peace Talks", *Bangkok Post*, 22 September 2008.

39   "RI Backs Revised UN Resolution Against Iran's Nuclear Program", *Jakarta Post*, 29 September 2008.

40   "Beholden to ASEAN?", *Jakarta Post*, 25 July 2008.

LEGACIES OF HISTORY, PRESENT CHALLENGES, AND THE FUTURE

Jusuf Wanandi

Introduction

Of the many myths and legends in Indonesia, the notion of the "Great Majapahit" has been the most attractive to many Indonesians. Mohamad Yamin, regarded as Sukarno's ideologist, was the main proponent of this legend. He believed that the Majapahit Hindu Kingdom in the fourteenth to sixteenth century was a vast and strong Kingdom, covering the entire archipelago and extended its influence as far as Madagascar in the West and Taiwan in the North.

In reality, however, Indonesia came into being only in the twentieth century, when nationalism began to grow in certain parts of the archipelago, and more specifically since the Youth Oath or Pledge in 1928 that recognized "one country, one nation and one language, namely Bahasa Indonesia", as the national movement was taking shape. In 1945 this modern state was established by the Nationalist Movement. Thus, the Indonesian state and nation were only established some 63 years ago. It is quite a young nation.

The Legacies of Sukarno and Soeharto

The first era of this young nation was led by President Sukarno. This period began after World War II and the four years of the revolution. The economy was in shambles and political development highly unstable. Following the Dutch model, we had many political parties, and in 1947 developed a liberal parliamentary democracy which deviated from the presidential system under the 1945 Constitution. Unstable coalitions came and went during this phase with the government on average lasting only 11 months.

JUSUF WANANDI is Vice Chair, Board of Trustees, Centre for Strategic and International Studies (CSIS) Foundation, Jakarta, Indonesia.

The general election in 1955, the first of its kind, and an honest one, produced four main parties, but there was no stability. Bung Karno (or Brother Karno, as Sukarno was affectionately called) tried hard to have the PKI (Indonesian Communist Party) included in the government but he did not succeed. Some of the regions, especially Sumatra and Sulawesi, rebelled and martial law was proclaimed in early 1958. On top of that the Constituent Assembly failed to formulate a new constitution because of its inability to decide on the ideology of the Republic: Pancasila or Islam. To overcome the stalemate, Bung Karno in 1959, with support of the Army, declared a return to the 1945 Constitution, which provided for a stronger role for the President.

Because of his idea of permanent revolution, Sukarno prepared to take back Papua (Irian Jaya) by force which was accomplished in 1962 through negotiations between Indonesia and the Netherlands and mediation of the UN. He nationalized the Dutch companies in 1958, resulting in a worsening of the economy that had never recovered from the earlier setbacks. After that, in 1963, he started a confrontation against Malaysia (and Singapore, as part of Malaysia), which he considered to be a creation of a neo-colonial plot by the British. In the meantime the Indonesian Communist Party underwent a transformation because it lined up with the CCP (Chinese Communist Party) in 1962. When Sukarno fell seriously ill in early August 1965, the PKI thought they should do something to prevent the Army from taking over the country in the event of Sukarno's death. They instigated a coup that failed. Soeharto, with the support of the middle class, especially students and intellectuals, disbanded the PKI because Bung Karno continued to resist holding the PKI to account for the attempted coup. This was preceded by much political tension and physical clashes between the pro and anti-communist camps since the early 1960s. In the end Bung Karno was demoted by the MPRS (People's Consultative Assembly) and Soeharto became President in 1968.

Sukarno was the founding father of the Republic. He did an extremely important job in keeping the country together and giving self-confidence to the Indonesian people. However, in the end his political and ideological adventures made the country bankrupt. His extreme idea to maintain a permanent revolution and a NASAKOM (Nationalism, Religion, Communism) government consisting of all the major parties, including the PKI, was rejected by the people. Furthermore, his foreign policy of leaning towards China was a diversion from the non-aligned stance that had been scrupulously followed by the Indonesian elite since 1948.

Soeharto was the hero of the non-communist political elite and of the student activists because he was the only general that was brave enough to stand up to Bung Karno. He was also the one who dared to ban the PKI after

Bung Karno conferred power on him on 11 March 1966. He was definitely the leader who transformed the Indonesian economy and developed it into an East Asian economic miracle. However, he stayed too long as president and made the Indonesian economy a personal and a family affair. His governance was full of KKN (acronym for corruption, collusion, and nepotism).

His second mistake was that he did not want to prepare a new generation of leaders for the future. He appeared to have been greatly influenced by his idea of the Javanese kingship, wherein the King ruled until death unless he was dethroned by one of his relatives. That is why he always removed any aspirant for national leadership immediately after the person showed such an interest. As a result he was never serious about political development, because he was the only "anointed one" from above and everybody else was dependent on his "wahyu" (inspiration) and had to follow him.

After 32 years in power he had to step down because the financial crisis undermined all his belated efforts to undertake economic and political reforms. Until the end he was still trying to save his children's economic interests, and he thought he could still organize the political reforms needed, until he found that his most trusted assistants like Habibie (his Vice-President), Harmoko (Speaker of the House and Chair of his GOLKAR Party), and Ginandjar (Head of Planning and protégé of Soedharmono, his former loyal aide and Vice-President) double crossed him and asked him to step down.

Both presidents, Sukarno and Soeharto, were strong leaders who would not step down until they were made to so. And both had an autocratic streak in their psychology and their governance. They also could not adjust to changes that were happening in the country. Soeharto did well in managing the economy in the first 20 years. After that he became corrupt or allowed corruption around him to take place, to his own detriment. Sukarno, on the other, simply did not pay any attention to the economy.

On political development and political liberalization, there were no major improvements under both of them. And both also instituted a highly centralized style of governance that put the regions outside Java always on the receiving end, creating a lot of resentment from 1958 when local rebellions started against the dominance of Java.

Indonesia developed economically under Soeharto, resulting in the emergence of a middle class of 30 to 40 million people. They could not accept an autocratic rule so easily anymore and demanded more political space and freedom. They got their chance when Soeharto stepped down and Habibie replaced him in May 1998, which happened only because of the financial crisis of 1997/98.

The Four Presidents Since 1998

With the above background on Indonesia under its first two presidents, there can be a better understanding of the transition periods involving the subsequent four presidents and why they faced enormous difficulties in changing the system of governance, structuring the relationship between the centre and the regions, and fully rehabilitating the economy.

Habibie was only an extension of Soeharto, having served under him for over 25 years and was a party to Soeharto's KKN. He has never accounted for the state funding and financing of the 15 strategic corporations he was managing during Soeharto's rule, including the aerospace conglomerate IPTN, Krakatau Steel, arms producer Pindad, nautical engineering firm Pal and Batam Development Agency. Tens of billions of U.S. dollars were involved. And then there was the case of procurement of the naval ships from Germany which happened under very cloudy circumstances. When Tempo magazine tried to publish the case, its printing licence was revoked by Soeharto. The country was still in the depths of the economic crisis when Habibie took over as President and he was assisted mainly by members of Soeharto's old guard. Therefore, there was nothing he could do other than follow the agreements with the IMF.

Habibie tried to demonstrate his democratic credentials by getting many laws passed through the DPR Parliament that was still dominated by the old Soeharto network of GOLKAR's majority rule. However, it is not quite true that he did a great deal to establish democracy in Indonesia. How could a person who had for over 25 years served an authoritarian ruler like Soeharto change overnight into a democrat as he claimed?

In a proposed new law governing the media, he attempted to curb the freedom of the media by requiring all journalists to be licensed to be able to practice just as lawyers and accountants are licensed. This was rejected by civil society and parliament. His proposal to limit the activities of civil society by introducing a new security law to replace the old anti-subversive laws of Soeharto was also strongly opposed by all political parties in parliament except the military faction.

Habibie was responding to the pressures from the people, including the pressure to hold a general election in 1999, and to push the new law on decentralization through parliament. His biggest political blunder was the way in which East Timor was given independence, which was one of the main reasons why his accountability speech to the MPR (the People's Consultative Assembly) was rejected which in turn prevented him from being chosen as a candidate for the presidency at the MPR session. He was also not able to control the armed forces that went on the rampage in East Timor after the plebiscite. Withdrawing his candidacy for the presidency was the only way out for him, and he was lucky to leave almost unscathed.

Gus Dur, a great Muslim leader from the Nahdlatul Ulama, became Indonesia's president by default after the 1999 elections. This happened because Megawati, whose party won the biggest number of seats in the parliamentary (DPR) elections (33 per cent), did not make any effort to gain the presidency. Instead, she expected to be offered the position by the MPR on a golden platter. This was not how the system worked. Her passivity provided the opportunity to the Muslim parties to outmanoeuvre her and to put Gus Dur in the presidency. To defuse the expected strong reaction from Megawati's supporters (especially in Jakarta, Central Java and Bali), who felt that she was cheated and betrayed by Gus Dur, she was immediately approached by Gus Dur to become his vice president. This solved the one-day crisis.

Gus Dur was already in poor health when he became Indonesia's fourth president. Instead of having a qualified and solid team to assist him, he squandered his opportunity by having a rainbow coalition in his cabinet. Above all he did not give them the chance to make any decision because he himself would decide on as many issues as possible. Because he was so erratic and capricious nothing much improved under his presidency. He went abroad too often, and continued to behave like an activist from an NGO in conducting foreign policy. He achieved little because his foreign policy initiatives were not prepared in collaboration with the Foreign Ministry. There was never any follow up on his "official" escapades.

In the end parliament could no more stomach it and asked that the MPR be convened to assess Gus Dur's competence, especially after he allegedly misused Bulog's (Logistics Bureau) funds. The result of this was his removal from the presidency by the decision of the MPR. He was replaced by Megawati, his Vice-President. His efforts over several months to oppose the impeachment process were to no avail because too many people and the political parties withdrew their support for him.

The new President, Megawati, had been a leader of PDI-P (Partai Demokrasi Indonesia Perjuangan, Indonesian Democratic Party-Struggle) since 1982. She rose to the top largely because she was the daughter of Bung Karno. She had little interest in governance or politics, but she believed that she had the task to complete Bung Karno's mission. She could have prepared herself for the job during the Soeharto years when she was a member of parliament representing PDI. Unfortunately, she failed to use that opportunity.

Megawati's cabinet was a mixed bag, and amongst her entourage there were individuals that were known to be not clean. Her minister for labour, a hero to her during the PDI leadership struggle in the Soeharto years, was himself a labour leader. His attention was solely on the interests of labour and not on the health of the economy as a whole. Although Megawati was able to stabilize the macro-economy, her government failed to attract new investments, in large part because the new labour laws became a major disincentive for investors.

Her main weakness was her unwillingness to listen to advice and to reach out to the people. She did not want to talk to the media. She was also very hands off in her style of governance. Although her party had 33 per cent of the seats in DPR, and as such was the biggest faction, she was not able to create coalitions that fully supported her.

When the September 11 terrorist attack took place in the U.S., she could have worked with Indonesia's moderate Muslims to strongly condemn the extremist groups in Indonesia but she did not. That kind of passivity was again demonstrated at the time of the Bali bombing in October 2002. On Aceh, she was very reluctant to find a compromise and a political solution to the conflict because her only reference paradigm was of NKRI (the unitary state of the Republic of Indonesia) as advocated by Bung Karno, her father and her role model. That was also the case on the issue of Papua. She created by Presidential Decree the province of West Papua, which was in violation of the Law on the Special Status of Papua. Ironically, the Constitutional Court did not reverse the decision on the argument that the province was already created.

In conclusion, Megawati was in essence only a transition figure, and as such should not be evaluated as a full president. Her record was mixed. While she was a pluralist and a nationalist, she was very much a hands-off president. In some instances it was good to have left matters to the respective ministers.

When she was running for president for a full term, she was advised to select better people for her cabinet if elected and to announce this during the presidential campaign. She was also advised to reach out to the people to mobilize their support. Alas, none of these happened. That was why she could not win against SBY in the first direct presidential election of 2004. Her party, PDI-P, also lost seats in the parliamentary election from 33 per cent in 1999 down to 19 per cent in 2004. The first direct presidential election showed that popularity was the main reason for people's support and for their votes. SBY made good use of his position as Megawati's Coordinating Minister to become known to the people. He also became the popular spokesman of the government, because Megawati was not inclined to talk to the people directly or through the media.

SBY talked well and in a measured way, and has the looks of a leader. But in fact, he lacks decisiveness, even after four years of being president. He is too cautious, would like to please everybody (and therefore ends up displeasing many), would like to see all aspects of a problem and get everybody's ideas first before he is willing to decide, which can be a lengthy process. One example is the decision to increase fuel prices and to cut fuel subsidies. The cabinet made the decision on 5 May 2004, but it was announced only on 26 May because the president was still hesitant. There were 11 cabinet meetings in between the decision and the announcement to deliberate again and again on the issue.

In a dire situation, as Indonesia's economy is obviously in, one cannot let the momentum slip away. In early 2005, at the first Infrastructure Summit, SBY promised to issue or amend 14 laws and regulations in order to improve the investment environment. As late as in 2007 only the Investment Law was concluded, and the Taxation Law was passed only in mid-2008. In his military career, his indecisiveness was perhaps a major reason why he never became a regional commander except for a short stint at Sriwijaya Command (South Sumatra Command) in Palembang.

What has he achieved thus far? Much has happened in the arena of political development because of new circumstances and new developments that have generated pressures for change rather than primarily because of his leadership. Democracy has developed and deepened as a result of the active involvement of the people in NGOs, the media, mass organizations like NU and Muhammadiyah, scholars, and think-tanks, as well as some elements in the political parties and the parliament to establish democratic principles and practices. Others in the cabinet and in the bureaucracy have also made their contribution. Foremost is the Minister of Finance, Sri Mulyani, who has undertaken major reforms of the bureaucracy in the Department of Finance. The business sector, such as APPINDO (Employers' Federation of Indonesia) (headed by Sofyan Wanandi), has also participated in the efforts to promote and implement reforms.

What is true is that SBY has not hampered the initiatives taken by others, in the society at large as well as in the government, such as Jusuf Kalla's efforts to negotiate a peaceful solution to the Aceh rebellion. He also supported the efforts of the Anti-Corruption Commission on corruption cases at the Central Bank and at the Attorney General's office. Unfortunately, when it comes to ideological or religious issues, he has not come out strongly to act against the unlawful actions of radical groups like the FPI (Front Pembela Islam or Islamic Defenders Front) in the Ahmadiyah case. His belated effort to implement the rule of law and public order on that case has been weak.

He has also not taken action against more than 50 regencies (out of over 450) that have introduced the syariah law, which is in violation of the constitution. According to the law of decentralization, the Central Government can annul the local regulation within 30 days of its issuance if it is considered against the Constitution or against another national law. In fact, the regions proclaiming syariah have not been able to implement it because the rules for its implementation have not been formulated. However, this has been damaging to SBY, because it showed the inability of the Central government to implement the Constitution and national laws in the political arena. Except for Aceh where syariah is stipulated in the special law for that province, the adoption of syariah in other regions should be firmly opposed by the Central Government. Hopefully, the Constitutional Court that is now looking into the case will make the right decision.

The other area that has been neglected because of the indecisiveness of SBY is the economy. He has not been able to move it enough to overcome poverty, unemployment and underemployment resulting in an increase in the number of people living below the poverty line. He has achieved macro-economic stability, which was already achieved under Megawati's presidency, and he has achieved 6 per cent growth since 2006, but this is not enough to provide jobs for over 2 million new workers that enter the labour force annually. That is why unemployment is still over 12 per cent and underemployed around 20 per cent. He has not been firm enough in removing obvious obstacles, and is very sensitive to anti-globalization and anti-foreign protests, especially from parliament and the labour unions.

As has been said above, the legal reforms were not achieved as promised. Judiciary reforms have been too slow, the labour market has become very rigid and the bureaucracy is stalling. On corruption some efforts have been made and some real cases at the highest level have been prosecuted by the Anti-Corruption Commission, such as the cases against two former Governors of the Central Bank and the Attorney General's Office, as well as members of DPR, but this has not yet happened across the board and in a more consistent way. SBY has been defending his minister and financier Aburizal Bakrie to the hilt, especially in relation to very dubious cases which are against the interest of the people, such as the Bumi Resources fiasco on the Jakarta Stock Exchange, on top of the Lapindo mudflow case. Thus, SBY's governance has not been as consistent and above board as some people have thought. This will complicate the country's efforts to deal with the international financial tsunami.

What Has To Change?

Following the above examination of all the presidents of Indonesia from independence until today, the question is why Indonesia had to go through all that it went through. If one considers the many endowments Indonesia has, namely ample supply of good human resources, abundance of commodities and minerals and other resources such as forestry and fisheries, why could it not prosper and have good governance? In 1998 Kishore Mahbubani asked me what road Indonesia will take and how long will the economic crisis last. Will we take the Korean way of resoluteness or the Thai way of muddling through, or will it be the Russian way after the Cold War, which has been messy and complicated and protracted? I answered then that most probably Indonesia will follow its own model of overcoming the crisis. And that is exactly what has happened! Why? And what do these developments mean for the future development of Indonesia?

The follow up question is what have we learned from the political developments so far, and how will this influence our future development?

We had a chaotic democratic development during the revolution, due to the armed struggle against the Dutch, and internal uprisings challenging the existence of the Republic during the period 1945–50. We experienced a leftist uprising in 1948 that was organized by the Indonesian Communist Party (PKI) and from 1947 rebellion by religious groups wanting to establish a Muslim state in several regions such as West Java, South Sulawesi and Aceh. But the nation and its leaders were also inexperienced and lacked the skills of governance that were necessary to build a state and a nation under conditions of great stress.

The economy had deteriorated rapidly during World War II and the revolution. It became worse after 1958 due to the total negligence of Bung Karno. During the 1950–58 period the country was under a liberal democratic system, and because of continued bickering among political parties, each government lasted for an average of only 11 months.

When the Constituent Assembly could not agree on the principles of the state, Pancasila or Islam, Bung Karno (under pressure from the Army), declared that the Provisional Constitution of 1950, with a parliamentary system, was replaced by the 1945 Constitution with a presidential system that would have a stronger executive. However, in practice it led to the concentration of power with Bung Karno, especially after he disbanded the DPR and the Constituent Assembly.

The main lesson from this period was that without a stronger middle class, better educated people and a minimum of economic development, democracy could not be properly implemented.

The "guided democracy" with Bung Karno as the centre was not a real democracy because it lacked the three basic criteria that define a democracy. They are: (a) the supremacy of law, namely that the rule of law should be the basis of the state and society and no one is above the law; (b) equality before the law, namely that everybody, whether a street cleaner or a president, is equal before the law; and (c) there is the possibility of changing the government democratically, namely through general elections.

The situation under guided democracy deteriorated rapidly because Bung Karno became increasingly dependent on the PKI since only the PKI supported his leftist ideas and policies consistently. Bung Karno became increasingly worried about the army which was seen as a major hindrance to the implementation of his leftist policies.

The 1965 abortive coup of the PKI was the result of this confrontation. Although Bung Karno did not support it, he did not want to condemn it. Therefore, the majority of the elite, with the support of most of the people, removed Bung Karno from the presidency in 1967. The Indonesian people could not accept Communism as their ideology and political system, although the PKI was then the third largest Communist Party in the world (after the Communist parties of the USSR and China). The PKI crumbled within a short time, even with the continued support of Bung Karno.

Another lesson was that anarchy, as caused by the divided leadership between Bung Karno and Soeharto, can easily happen and cause great devastation. This happened when the people (with some help and encouragement from the local military in several places) took the law into their own hands and killed members and alleged members of the Communist Party. It took place mainly because these people were worried about possible retaliation by the PKI if in the end they won the political struggle. It should be noted that when the PKI was at the height of its power they were very oppressive and often took matters into their own hands such as seizing land by force from Muslim leaders and sometimes killing them as well. Furthermore, the Army was unable to uphold law and order as their discipline broke down because they were internally divided. And human rights were not much of a concern then, since they had not become part of Indonesia's political culture.

The events of 1965 were traumatic and should never happen again. They constituted one of those catharses in Indonesian political development and were a watershed. People are still reluctant to talk about the killings that occurred because they are still too raw emotionally. It will take perhaps another generation before the matter can be re-opened completely.

When Soeharto took over the leadership of the country, he was considered a hero. The Army that supported him was also politically more astute. They formulated their dual role, which was accepted by the people then, because they were seen as the saviour of the nation against the real threat of a Communist take over. Above all, they became the last arbiter in political life.

The overall tendency in the region then was to follow the so-called "Korean model" or "East Asian model" of development, in which priority was given to economic development. Only when the middle class has grown large can democracy and political development become viable. Soeharto stayed too long in power and the longer he was in power the more reluctant he became to prepare a new generation of leaders to take over. That is why we have great difficulties today in finding capable leaders.

The so-called "45 generation" (founders of the Army during the revolution) who came from all walks of life had the experiences and knowledge about politics and the society. They were able to organize "politics" for Soeharto. The succeeding generation of military academy trained officers were not up to that job and simply became Soeharto's praetorian guards.

When he lost trust in the leadership of General Benny Moerdani, his Commander-in-Chief during the period 1983–88 and a long time associate as well as his intelligence chief, he started to look for alternative support from Muslim groups. He supported the creation of the Association of Muslim Intellectuals (ICMI), with Habibie put as its head. He believed that Habibie was his main protégé and confidant, but found out later that he could not trust the man and never wanted to see him again after Habibie took over the presidency, not even on his death-bed.

After so many years in power, the military began to abuse its power. We have learned one thing about them: they are effective as a group because they are well-trained, but basically they are a machine that the national leader should use only for the defence of the country. Their power should be limited and they must come under democratic and civilian control. They have now retreated from politics, from all state organs including the legislative councils. However, the structure of the military still has to undergo more reforms because it still has a certain political role. They have not fully accepted civilian control and continue to maintain their sense of impunity from wrong-doing. Their businesses have largely become empty shells and are not worth much because of corruption and incompetence in managing them. And most of all they do not want to be accountable to the civilian judiciary for their violation of laws and abuses of human rights.

The military cannot keep its political role much longer, because there is almost no patriotism left among many officers. They are no longer concerned about the nation and the people but only about their own plight and pocket. This is so because for over a decade they acted as mere security guards for Soeharto, completely dependent on him for everything. Moreover, they have lost their legitimacy in the eyes of the Indonesian people. In that sense, they have no chance to take over in a military *coup d'etat*. The more the Indonesian democracy is consolidated, the more difficult, indeed impossible it will be for them to return to politics.

The transition period after Soeharto stepped down was marked by instability and civil strife in several regions (Aceh, Papua, Central Sulawesi, West and West Kalimantan, and Riau). The deep economic crisis of 1997–98 caused serious unemployment and poverty. Soeharto had opened up the economy, particularly after Indonesia hosted the APEC Summit in 1994, but he had continued to protect the businesses of his children and cronies. Therefore, there was no coherent policy to face globalization, and the people were not being prepared to deal with the effects and consequences of globalization.

Indonesia's structure of government under Soeharto was too centralized for such a diverse nation and a large archipelago. Several regions had rebelled against this "Javanese imperialism", but ended up being clobbered. With the end of the Soeharto era, this structure could no longer be sustained. The policy of decentralization adopted in 1999 was the right answer to put an end to the pressures from the regions. As an integral part of democratization, decentralization is the way to keep Indonesia united and intact. The process of decentralization has been rather messy, but it has brought about some positive results. Provinces and *kabupaten* (regencies) have greater authority in deciding what is good for them and thus they have greater ownership in the development programmes.

Indonesian politics is now to a large extent dependent on what the moderate Muslims are going to do in political life and development. They are represented in two large mass organizations for social and educational purposes, namely Nahdlatul Ulama (40 million supporters), which is a rural based organization, and Muhammadiyah (30 million supporters), which is an urban based one. Muslims in the country are well-versed in Islamic laws and rites. If asked whether some parts of the syariah should be implemented, most would tend to say yes, because they are and want to be good Muslims. However, polls about their political affiliation and aspirations suggest that most of them have chosen the national Pancasila ideology and political parties that are based on pluralism and democracy.

That is why in the last two democratic elections (1999 and 2004) the more conservative Muslim parties (those that advocate the implementation of syariah) received no more than 23 per cent of the seats in parliament. If parties influenced by Islamic ideas (such as PAN — National Mandate Party — which is aligned to Muhammadiyah and PKB — National Awakening Party — aligned to NU) are included, the combined votes they received translated into about 38 per cent of total seats in parliament, which is less than the general election of 1955 (43 per cent). But, it should be noted as well that certain laws initiated by the Muslim parties such as the anti-pornography law (passed by the DPR in November 2008), tend also to be supported by many other parties, including GOLKAR.

This means that policy proposals related to values and religion, unless they call for stark syariah laws, could be supported by many of the Muslim parties as well as Muslim members of certain nationalist parties such as GOLKAR — which in turn means that on these issues the "secular" groups have always to be watchful. The political leadership and the government have to be clear about their role: that they should not only be above the political parties, but they are responsible for maintaining public order and implementation of public laws. The recent pressures on the Ahmadiyah sect and the declaration of the syariah in 50 districts suggest that much remains to be desired on this front.

There will always be some extremists among the 200 million Muslims, but they have been small in number although very vocal and extremely active, including in instigating rebellions (1947–65) or trying to achieve their objectives through terrorist acts as the Jamaah Islamiyah has done. The latter appears to have become a part of the global terrorist movement under Al-Qaeda. The government, especially the police, with the support of the international community, have done their part to overcome and prevent those acts without compromising the law and human rights.

The Future

The above review of the state of political development leads me to make the following concluding remarks about the future.

First, democracy has taken root in Indonesia following a messy transition period, and is maturing for the future. What has made this possible is the struggle of the elite to keep democracy intact. Efforts by some politicians and ex-army leaders to limit democracy for the sake of stability have been effectively opposed by NGO leaders and the media as well as influential political leaders. One example of this is the move by Habibie in 1999 to introduce a new law to replace the anti-subversive laws created under Bung Karno and Soeharto which he had to abandon in the face of opposition. Similarly, the moves by General Wiranto and several other military officers to create vigilante groups of extreme Muslim groups in 1999 to confront the students' demonstrations against the Habibie presidency were widely condemned.

Second, unity has been preserved, despite some real dangers in the first five years after Soeharto stepped down that Indonesia could split up into four to five states. A major success was the resolution of the Aceh conflict through a peaceful political solution on the initiative of Vice President Jusuf Kalla with help from former President Marti Arthisaari of Finland and from the EU. The agreement to allow local political parties to be established in Aceh and the acceptance of an ex-GAM leader as the first elected governor mean that peace is going to stay. Another special effort to keep Indonesia's unity is reflected in the law on the Special Autonomy for Papua and the establishment of the Papuan Council, consisting of regional government and civil society representatives, which will decide first on every major policy concerning Papua.

Third, minorities, such as the Indonesian Chinese, feel that they are more accepted as equals and will contribute more.

Fourth, the military has become almost non-political, but it has yet to reform its institutions and show its willingness to be accountable for its abuses.

Fifth, Muslim organizations and Muslim political parties in general are now willing to accept Pancasila as the state ideology and understand that they cannot impose syariah laws. However, the moderates among them should always be on the alert, because some groups/political parties still attempt to wholly or partially implement the syariah in the future.

Sixth, in the end economic development is critical for political stability and the consolidation of democracy. There are always dangers, especially if the global economic crisis inflicts great damage to the economy. Efforts to work together with East Asians in the ASEAN Plus Three or the East Asia Summit (EAS) have to be intensified as a *conditio sine qua non* for economic recovery, in addition to efforts in the global context (G-20 and the WTO).

Seventh, one lacuna has to be recognized. A generation of political leaders has been lost due to Soeharto's unwillingness to prepare for a young generation to take over from him. That is why no young leaders have emerged to contest the 2009 presidential election. Since the threshold to propose a presidential candidate has been raised (a minimum of 20 per cent of the seats in parliament or 25 per cent of the total votes in the parliamentary elections), there could most probably be only three candidates, namely SBY, most probably supported by his own Partai Demokrat plus PKS (Partai Keadilan Sejahtera or Prosperous Justice Party) (in case it has less than 20 per cent of the DPR seats, with Hidayat Nur Wahid as SBY's VP candidate), Megawati from PDI-P, and Jusuf Kalla as GOLKAR's candidate. In the last Leaders Meeting of GOLKAR in October 2008 a decision was made that if the party emerged as the leading party in the parliamentary election the Board would propose its own presidential candidate. It is not inconceivable that GOLKAR could become the number one party again.

This suggests that a presidential candidate from the new generation could only emerge in 2014. There can be many potential candidates by then that will come from the ranks of local leaders (successful governors or *bupati*/district heads), young politicians in parliament, NGO leaders, business leaders, and from within the bureaucracy. But all of them need time to be known at the national level, and the next few years will be critical for that purpose.

In conclusion, it can be ascertained that democracy and unity will stay as part of Indonesia's future. Challenges still exist, especially from the right-wing extremists (fundamental Muslims or from the military), who could create anarchy if the economy collapses in order to take over the government. But this is only a remote possibility, because the Indonesian elite and the people, including moderate Muslims, will oppose such action. A political collusion between Muslim extremists and the Army leadership is now more remote than in 1998. History has shown that despite some lacunas the Indonesian elite and the Indonesian people have rejected authoritarianism as a political system and will continue to support the unitary state. With a growing middle class and with a better group of leaders in the future that determination is likely to be maintained.

Laos

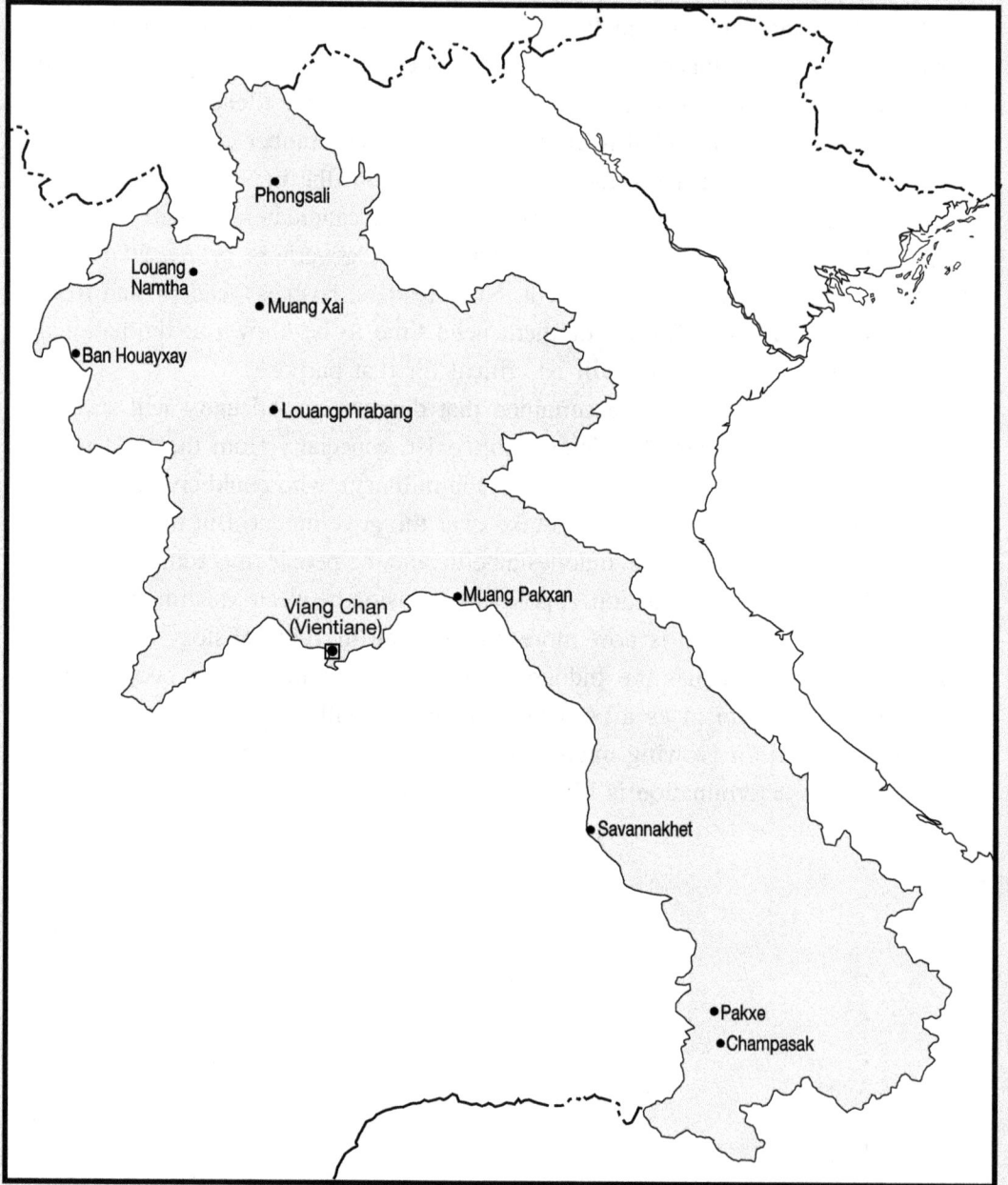

Phongsali

Louang
Namtha

Muang Xai

Ban Houayxay

Louangphrabang

Viang Chan
(Vientiane)

Muang Pakxan

Savannakhet

Pakxe

Champasak

Southeast Asian Affairs 2009

LAOS
The Chinese Connection

Martin Stuart-Fox

The title of my first contribution to Southeast Asian Affairs in 1980 was "Laos: The Vietnamese Connection". A great deal has happened in the Lao People's Democratic Republic (LPDR) over the past three decades, both internally, and in its relations with its neighbours. The Lao People's Revolutionary Party (LPRP) is still in power, but it is a party riven by ambition and greed. The country is wealthier than it was thirty years ago; but the urban-rural divide is more marked than ever. Wealth is concentrated in the cities, most of it in the hands of Party members and their families. The resources of the country, which the French had glimpsed a century before, most of which are located in rural areas, are now being rapidly exploited, but not for the benefit of the rural majority. Neighbouring states have hungrily eyed these resources, and seized their opportunities to obtain a share — none more so than China. So just as what was interesting about Laos in 1980 was the Vietnamese connection, so in 2009 what is interesting is the developing Chinese connection, and what this means for Lao politics and policies.

To focus on the Chinese connection is not to suggest that the Vietnamese connection no longer matters. It certainly does. Rather it is to focus on economic and political changes that are now taking place. What I want to do in this article is to examine the changes that were becoming apparent in 2008 in three areas: in politics; in economic development; and in international relations. But I shall deal with these in the reverse order, for Lao politics are all but opaque in the absence of any media reporting or discussion, and it is only by examining the shifting influence of neighbouring states, and popular responses to the impact of development policies, that some light can be cast on Lao politics.

Martin Stuart-Fox is Professor Emeritus, University of Queensland, Brisbane, Australia.

International Pressures

(a) The Rise of China

In early 2008, for the first time the growing Chinese presence became a matter of popular concern and debate in the LPDR. The trigger was an announcement in September 2007 that a consortium of three Chinese companies would build a new 20,000-seat stadium in Viang Chan (Vientiane) in time for Laos to host the Southeast Asian games in December 2009. In return, the consortium, coordinated by the Suzhou Industrial Park Overseas Investment Company, would be given a 50-year concession to develop 1,640 hectares of swampy land known as the That Luang marshes, not far from the hallowed That Luang stupa.[1]

The agreement had been secretly negotiated through the China Development Bank, which had agreed to provide credit of US$100 million to build the stadium, on the surety of the land concession. A Lao company, whose political associations are unclear, was given a five per cent stake in the project, which would include not just up-market housing, but also an industrial zone, a shopping complex and hotels. Buildings would be sold or leased for the duration of the concession, which according to the agreement could be extended for a further 25 years. Thereafter ownership would revert to the Lao government.

On the face of it, the "New City Development Project" looked like a good deal: Laos would obtain a stadium free, plus a modern housing estate in the heart of Viang Chan. But then concern grew and the rumour mills began to grind. People were unsure how much land would be resumed and what compensation would be paid. Promised compensation is often not paid in Laos, but rather ends up in the pockets of officials. Rural victims have no recourse, but reportedly some of the land covered by the That Luang development belonged to Party members, who began to ask questions.

Of greater popular concern, however, was Chinese ownership of the project, and what the consortium intended to do with it.[2] The Lao are well aware that the Chinese business presence is expanding in Laos, and they know how Chinese businesses operate. Already there is a large shopping complex in Viang Chan, known simply as the Chinese Market, where mainly Chinese shopkeepers sell consumer products imported from China through business networks that effectively exclude Lao from competing. Moreover Chinese businesses usually employ only Chinese workers. The Chinese company contracted to build the stadium has brought in as many as 3,000 Chinese construction workers rather than employ Lao labourers.

It was not entirely surprising therefore that a rumour was soon circulating that the "new city" was being built exclusively to house 50,000 Chinese residents.

So persistent was the rumour that the Party felt it necessary to hold a rare press conference specifically to deny it. Deputy prime minister (and former foreign minister) Somsavat Lengsavat, who reportedly facilitated the deal, revealed to reporters many of the details given above, and assured them that anyone with the necessary means would be able to buy a house in the new estate, for there would be "no discrimination among buyers and no special concessions for Chinese citizens".[3]

More details were released about the development itself, which an artist's impression depicts as modern and multi-purpose, overlooking open water. But rumours about the project persisted — particularly that it would become a luxury "Chinatown" for wealthy Chinese who would come to control the Lao economy. By August, Voice of America was quoting unnamed "Lao authorities" as saying that many landowners were refusing to relocate because of inadequate compensation, and that as a result the government was looking for land elsewhere.[4] Another rumour was that the That Luang development would be cut to one third of the original plan.

What feeds such rumours is the lack of transparency that characterises most government and Party business in Laos, where decisions backed by powerful political figures can overrule any existing regulations. But the furore over the That Luang marshes development project reflects growing unease over the Chinese presence in Laos. That presence is evident for all to see, as is the influence of Chinese business, which is willing to pay for useful political connections.

A small Chinese presence in Laos goes back centuries, but the Chinese population grew steadily during the French and Royal Lao periods (1893 to 1975) to reach more than 40,000.[5] Most of this Sino-Lao community left after the LPRP seized power in 1975 and relations between Laos and China deteriorated in 1979. But with the restoration of normal relations in 1987 and transition to a market economy, a few began to return. By 1997, the Chinese population in Laos was estimated to be around 10,000,[6] divided between Sino-Lao families who had returned to reclaim property and restart businesses in the Mekong towns of central and southern Laos, and an influx into northern Laos of new entrepreneurs and small traders from Yunnan, who can enter Laos with no more than Chinese identity papers and a border pass.

Today the Lao government puts the number of Chinese living in Laos at 30,000. This is widely believed to be a gross underestimate, but even the government's figures still represents a tripling of the Chinese population over the last decade. In the northern Lao provinces down to Udomxai, the Chinese presence is very evident. Many shop signs are in Chinese, and in some towns most commerce is now in Chinese hands. Over the last five years, Chinese from Kunming and further away still, many of them young single men, have begun trading in Luang Phrabang and Viang Chan. Some have moved even further south.

These newcomers have little in common with the older Sino-Lao community. Many hardly speak Lao and most have little sensitivity towards Lao culture. They are more brashly nationalistic and tend to stick together.[7] But the Chinese are nothing if not adaptable. Already intermarriage is occurring (partly due to the gender imbalance in China), and once young men acquire Lao wives they are more likely to stay in Laos, learn Lao, and adapt to Lao ways.

Another recent trend has been a rapid increase in large-scale Chinese investment in Laos, principally in mining and agriculture, but also in energy production, telecommunications, and construction materials. Chinese companies are involved in mineral exploration, and are exploiting deposits of limestone (for cement) and potash. A consortium in which the Aluminium Corporation of China holds a 51 per cent stake and another Chinese company holds 19.5 per cent has been awarded the right to mine half of a vast bauxite deposit in southern Laos,[8] while a second Chinese-led consortium has applied to develop the other half. The investment needed, including power stations, will run into billions of dollars.

China's rapidly growing demand for agricultural and forestry products, particularly rubber and food, has driven investment in plantations in northern Laos. Rubber was first planted in northern Laos (400 ha in Luang Namtha province) in 1994. By 2006 the area under cultivation had increased to 7,341 ha, with planned expansion that will take the total to 119,000 ha by 2010. This is almost double the planned cultivation area for central and southern Laos over the same period.[9]

Much of this massive expansion is in the form of plantations run by Chinese companies. Some, however, is being driven by smallholders who are planting rubber on their own land, usually with inputs provided by Chinese buyers. Rubber trees take seven years to come into production, but thereafter the return for the farmer per hectare (US$880) is almost as much as for opium (US$903). Agarwood and teak are also being grown on plantations for the China market.

Food crops include corn, cassava, bananas, sesame, and soy beans. These too are either produced on land leased to Chinese companies, or grown by smallholders who sell to Chinese buyers on contract (usually for a period of fifteen years). If land concessions are less than 100 ha, deals can be concluded with provincial authorities. For larger plantations central government approval is required. Abuses occur when land to which peasant farmers claim traditional rights is expropriated on the grounds that they do not have legal title.[10]

The areas of land involved are substantial. Over a ten-year period from 1996 to 2006, the area contracted to grow corn for China in Udomxai province alone increased from 3,000 ha to 13,000 ha, producing around 100,000 tonnes. Meanwhile in Luang Namtha province, closer to China, 40,000 ha were devoted to growing sugarcane and 60,000 to cassava. Production of each crop was expected to reach 1 million tonnes in 2008.[11]

Chinese construction companies have also been active in Laos. Most of the construction work has been on Chinese aid projects, but a Chinese construction company was contracted to build the Malaysian-owned Don Chan Palace Hotel, the tallest building in Viang Chan, in time for Laos to host the ASEAN Summit of 2004. Chinese construction companies have also been successful in bidding for road construction projects funded by the Asian Development Bank. A Chinese airline has bought a stake in Air Lao.

The figures for Chinese direct investment in Laos tell the story. From 2001 to August 2007, according to the Lao Committee for Planning and Investment, US$1.1 billion of Chinese investments was approved, second only to Thailand's US$1.3 billion.[12] But for the fiscal year 2006–07, Chinese investment accounted for over 40 per cent of the total US$1.1 billion approved; and 45 out of the 117 projects were Chinese.[13]

In view of the increase in Chinese investment project designed to produce goods that China needs, from food to minerals, it is not surprising that trade is growing. China has unilaterally reduced tariffs on a wide range of imports from Laos, and the target is for two-way trade to reach US$1 billion. That goal is some way off, however. In 2006, China imported US$45.1 million from Laos and exported US$185.6 million; so trade runs strongly in China's favour. What is surprising is that these figures are still but a fraction of the trade in both directions between Laos and Thailand (see below).[14]

Chinese aid has focused on improving communications between China and Laos. Chinese engineers have been building roads in northern Laos since the early 1960s. Until they were withdrawn in 1979, the work was done by military construction units. With the resumption of normal relations, a selective Chinese aid programme also resumed. For example, a ground satellite reception centre was built in 1990–91, and the capacity of the Vang Viang cement factory was expanded in 1992–94. (A second factory has subsequently been built.)

The expansion of China's aid programme to Laos dates from 1999, when China provided a substantial loan to enable Laos to weather the Asian economic crisis. The Lao were grateful for the assistance, and relations warmed between the two countries. China undertook two showy projects in Viang Chan: construction of the Lao National Cultural Hall, and reconstruction of the Avenue Lan Xang, and the gardens around the Patouxai monument at the head of the avenue, leaving Japan (by far the largest aid donor to Laos) to deal with the other major thoroughfares with their more demanding associated sewage and drainage problems.

Over the last several years Chinese financial assistance has mainly been in the form of cash grants and no-interest loans for projects agreed upon with the Lao government, plus credits for commercial ventures by Chinese companies in Laos. Roads and bridges continue to be a priority. In 2008, National Route 3 from the China-Laos border at Boten to the Mekong River port of Huayxai opposite Chiang Saen in Thailand was completed.[15] China will build a connecting bridge to be jointly financed with Thailand and completed by 2011, after which it will be possible to drive from Singapore to Beijing. Other road construction is underway or planned, notably in Udomxai province. Commercial credits have gone towards building hydropower stations on three rivers in northern Laos, to the Hongsa lignite-fired power station in Xainyaburi province, and to power transmission lines and telecommunications. China has also built part of the GMS Information Super highway in Laos, which went into operation on 31 March 2008.[16] Total Chinese development aid granted to Laos to mid-2007 has been estimated at US$280 million, but China has reportedly also cancelled loans to the value of US$1.7 billion.[17]

Since 1991, China has provided scholarships (currently 55 per annum) for Lao students to study in China; Chinese advisers are assigned to work with Lao counterparts on specific programmes; and Chinese youth volunteers spend six-month terms teaching IT and languages (Chinese and English), coaching in various sports, or performing medical service. Groups of Lao government and Party officials attend management and training courses in China, including military training for young officers.

Laos and China exchange official government, Party and military delegations on a regular basis. In November 2000, President Jiang Zemin became the first Chinese head of state to visit Laos, following an official visit to China by Lao president Khamtay Siphandone. Premier Wen Jibao attended the 2004 ASEAN Summit in Viang Chan, and arrived again for the 2008 Greater Mekong Subregion (GMS) Summit, an indication of the importance China attaches to the regional grouping. While in Laos, the Chinese premier signed seven agreements covering aid, trade, investment, infrastructure, communications and power generation, including provision of a US$100 million export credit facility for the purchase, among other items, of a Z9 military helicopter.[18] The Chinese have said they are happy with the state of military relations, which "have developed very well";[19] and China is believed to provide military equipment to the cash-strapped Lao army, though no details have ever been published.

China and Laos have no outstanding problems to resolve. The border has been demarcated. They do, however, share concern over such transnational problems as smuggling (especially of drugs, but also of people) across their porous common border, and the spread of infectious diseases (from HIV/Aids to bird flu). There is reportedly some Chinese concern about the operation of the Boten casino, just across the Chinese border in the Lao province of Luang Namtha. The turn-off to the casino is actually north of the Lao immigration and customs post, which means that Chinese visitors do not have to pass through any Lao checkpoint. The casino operates solely for a Chinese clientele, catering for gambling, prostitution and money laundering. For this cosy arrangement, the Hong Kong Chinese operators pay Lao provincial authorities.

There has been much debate over the evolving Chinese relationship with the states of mainland Southeast Asia, and speculation over Chinese intentions towards the region.[20] As the smallest and most under-populated state, Laos is the most vulnerable in the face of China's growing might. There is little doubt that both the Chinese presence and Chinese influence will increase. But Laos has little to fear as long as Chinese interests are kept in mind in Viang Chan. And there is every indication that they are. When Wen Jiabao visited Laos in March 2008, the Chinese media quoted Lao prime minister Bouasone Bouphavanh as assuring him that Laos highly valued its ties with China and would make "concerted efforts ... to step up the friendly and cooperative relations".[21]

What the Chinese want for their grant aid and loans are three things: backing for Chinese policy on everything from Taiwan to Tibet; access for Chinese companies to exploit Lao resources; and lines of communication through Laos to Thailand. The Lao provide all three. What the Lao regime seeks in addition to aid and investment is political support in the face of Western pressure for reforms, both economic and political, that the Lao are reluctant to accept. It receives this support in the guise of China's policy of non-interference in the internal affairs of sovereign states. Not only will China exert no such pressure itself, but as in the case of Burma/Myanmar, China looms as a potential alternative source for any aid or investment the West can provide, thus vitiating Western influence.

As China's own influence is undoubtedly on the rise, the obvious question is: what implications does this have, both for the Laos' relations with other neighbouring states, particularly Vietnam and Thailand, and for Lao politics? Let us take Vietnam first.

(b) Party-to-Party: The Continuing Influence of Vietnam

Just as there has been debate over China's intentions towards Laos, and mainland Southeast Asia more broadly, so there has been discussion over whether China and Vietnam are actively competing for influence in Laos.[22] And if so, whether this has resulted in, or reflects, divisions within the Central Committee of the LPRP.

For several years there has been speculation over whether there exist defined pro-Vietnamese and pro-Chinese factions in the LPRP. Some observers have suggested that the basis for such a division is generational: the old revolutionaries have close ties to Vietnam, while younger Party members have no such historical baggage and look rather to China. Others point to geographical factors: northerners, led by former foreign minister Somsavat Lengsavad (who is ethnic Chinese and speaks fluent Mandarin) favour China,[23] southerners less so. But neither argument is very convincing.

The only time when there may have been pro-Vietnamese and pro-Chinese factions was in 1979, when some in the Party were purged following the Vietnamese invasion of Cambodia to overthrow the Khmer Rouge, and during the subsequent Sino-Vietnamese conflict when Laos fell into line with Vietnam. But those purged were not so much pro-Chinese as anti-alignment: though they may have had some sympathy for China, they argued that Laos should remain neutral in the conflict between China and Vietnam. Their expulsion from the LPRP was engineered by the Vietnamese.

Historically the Lao have been adept at balancing one external power off against another, and it is part of their international relations culture to do so. This is true whether they are of the revolutionary or the younger generation. As for Somsavat, he is Sino-Lao, but formed by his immersion in the Lao revolutionary movement. He has benefited from Chinese contacts, but there is no evidence that he ever took the risk of being labelled pro-Chinese. Besides, he had little influence in a party dominated by military men with close ties to Vietnam.

Lao policy is to be as even-handed as possible between China and Vietnam. When the new leadership team of Lieutenant General Choummaly Sayasone as Party and state president and Bouasone Bouphavanh as prime minister were appointed in 2006, both men first visited Hanoi, then immediately went on to

Beijing. This would suggest that Vietnam still retains an edge over China in the closeness of its relations with Laos.

But if there are no pro-Vietnamese versus pro-Chinese factions, are the two countries nevertheless competing for influence in Laos? Some indication may be provided by figures for aid, trade and investment. Like China, Vietnam releases few figures or details of its aid to Laos, though over the years this has been substantial. Occasionally announcements are made of emergency aid or aid for specific projects. Thus in 2008, Vietnam gave US$100,000 of aid for flood victims in Laos, and said it would assist Laos in preparing to host the 2009 Southeast Asia games by building a training centre and sending instructors (with no dollar value attached). Assistance is also provided from one organization to another, such as medical supplies donated by a hospital in Vietnam to a hospital in Laos, or by one province to another with which a "sister" relationship exists.

Vietnam avoids giving large sums for prestige projects of the kind China favours; nor can it provide anything like the assistance China gave Laos during the Asian economic crisis (though Vietnam did do what it could). Vietnam has funded major road and bridge construction, and built airstrips. Overall, however, Vietnamese aid is more comprehensive than Chinese aid, and many more Vietnamese experts are sent to work with their Lao counterparts in fields as diverse as the media, education and agriculture. Vietnamese experts also advise in such sensitive areas as Party organization, security, and in the military.

As for trade, Vietnam is ahead of China as a destination for Lao exports (at US$107.2 million as against US$45.1 million for China for 2006, the last year for which figures are available), but provides half the value of imports that China does (with US$90.8 compared with US$185.6 for China in 2006).[24] Two-way trade, though more evenly balanced, thus lags behind China, and the gap is likely to have widened in the last two years. As with China, however, the goal is to increase two-way trade between Laos and Vietnam to US$1 billion per annum by 2010, and to double that again by 2015.[25] This is overly ambitious, but by then Vietnam will be purchasing substantial amounts of Lao electricity, and a number of Vietnamese investment projects will be in production. Vietnam has facilitated trade by building roads and making the port of Danang available for Lao exports. A railway to connect Savannakhet with the Vietnamese rail network is also planned.

Vietnamese investment in Laos comes in third after Thailand and China, but is not far behind and on the rise. Total investment in 117 projects underway or planned was put at US$1.28 billion, with US$600 million committed in 2007 alone and another US$240 million in the first seven months of 2008.[26] A large proportion of this sudden increase is in hydropower. Dams under construction or planned on the Xekaman River in Attapeu province will be producing 4 billion kWt of electricity for sale to Vietnam by 2013.[27] A more controversial hydropower dam is planned on the Mekong River in northern Laos.[28] Other projects include mining and mineral exploration, rubber and agricultural plantations, wood processing, garment factories, and other light manufacturing. Vietnamese commercial banks also operate in Laos. Just as most Chinese investment is located in northern Laos (but for bauxite), so most Vietnamese investment is concentrated in the south and east.

Vietnam certainly does not rely on historical ties between aging revolutionaries as the sole basis for its continuing influence in Laos. Up-and-coming Lao Party members regularly attend ideological training courses at the Ho Chi Minh National Politics Institute in Hanoi,[29] which enables Vietnam to build contacts with successive generations of Lao Party leaders. Far more Vietnamese than Chinese possess good Lao language skills, and many Lao speak Vietnamese (including ten out of the eleven Lao Politburo members, the exception ironically being prime minister Bouasone who was educated in Moscow). This allows the Vietnamese embassy (the largest in Viang Chan) to maintain contacts across the LPRP. As a result, the Vietnamese have a better understanding of Lao politics than any other foreign embassy.

Even though the 25-year Treaty of Friendship and Cooperation that comprises the core of the "special relationship" between Vietnam and Laos expired in 2002, Vietnam does all in its power to keep the memory alive. A joint history of the relationship is being written, and Vietnam has funded a US$1.6 million Laos-Vietnam History Museum near Savannakhet. The military debt has been acknowledged in the form of memorials, and small, but well publicized, ceremonies take place as the remains of Vietnamese soldiers killed in Laos are repatriated. The phrase "special relationship" may no longer be used in official communiqués, but it has simply been replaced by reference to the two countries' "traditional friendship, special solidarity and comprehensive cooperation".[30]

Like China, Vietnam has no outstanding issues with Laos. The border is delineated, including the crucial tri-border marker between Vietnam, Cambodia and Laos (placed in August 2008). Development of the tri-border area is a priority for all three countries. Smuggling from Laos to Vietnam remains a problem, including notably timber and illegally caught wildlife. Despite a ban on the export of whole logs dating from 1999, timber smuggling continues on a large scale, abetted by the military of both countries, to feed the voracious Vietnamese furniture trade.[31]

So in view of the evidence, are Vietnam and China competing for influence in Laos? On the face of it, it would appear so. The recent upsurge in Vietnamese investment in Laos suggests that Hanoi is determined to match China in obtaining a share in Lao resources. And both countries foresee a similar increase in trade. Their aid programmes are very different, however, and so may be their unstated political goals.

For China, political influence appears to be directed mostly towards obtaining economic opportunities,[32] though a strong Chinese presence in Laos also offers some strategic benefit to Beijing. For Vietnam, the strategic importance of Laos for the defence of its long and vulnerable wester border has always been of primary concern. The price Hanoi was prepared to pay to maintain control of eastern Laos was demonstrated during the Second Indochina War. For Vietnam, a politically friendly regime in Laos is essential. Thus for Vietnam the first priority is to preserve the closest possible political relationship, which for Hanoi has always taken precedence over the economic relationship. And the political relationship rests squarely on party-to-party relations between the Vietnamese Communist Party and the Lao People's Revolutionary Party. This is why Hanoi's political goal in Laos is to promote a strong and cohesive LPRP.

Of course China also supports Laos politically, and will continue to do so for as long as its economic interests are served; but China could obtain concessions from, and dominate, any Lao regime of any political persuasion simply by virtue of size. Because China does not need to have particularly close party-to-party relations, Beijing sees no need to overtly challenge Hanoi's political influence. The continuing cohesion and effectiveness of the LPRP is thus a Vietnamese responsibility, and Vietnam takes it very seriously.

Vietnam takes a close interest not only in Lao politics, but also in how the Lao government is performing. Marxist-Leninist instruction of Lao Party members in Vietnam emphasises their moral responsibility to improve the lot of the "masses". Vietnamese advisory teams visit important ministries (including finance and defence) to suggest improvements in administrative efficiency. Reforms are designed to make the Party more responsive to popular demands, in particular to limit corruption, which is the principal criticism many Lao voice in private. There is no suggestion of regime change, which the Lao always suspect lies behind Western advice: just the opposite for the Vietnamese.

Apart from corruption, another concern the Vietnamese reportedly have is over the cohesion of the LPRP, not in relation to ideological differences, but rather with regard to the ambitions and activities of powerful individuals and their patronage networks. Where these are in conflict, rivalries and jealousies may cause divisions that have the potential of weakening Party cohesion, and so need to be managed. Already the wealth accumulated by certain families is a cause of envy on the part of others. For these reasons, according to some sources, the Vietnamese have lent cautious support to moderate reforms that prime minister Bouasone has indicated he would like to introduce.[33]

(c) ASEAN and the West

Lao membership of ASEAN has significantly altered the perception the country has of its place in the region and the world. Lao leaders repeatedly stress their commitment to regional integration, through which landlocked Laos will become landlinked, as the mantra goes. Certainly Laos is strategically situated, for it shares common borders with the other four mainland states.[34] But of these two loom much larger than the others. Vietnam is one, of course: the other is Thailand.

Relations between Laos and Thailand have been bumpy at times, as several outstanding issues create difficulties for both sides. These include border demarcation, refugees and security, trafficking, and smuggling. The border problem has been dragging on for years. While the land frontier (with Xainyaburi province in the north and Champasak province in the south) is determined but for a small stretch over which the two countries fought a brief border war from December 1987 to January 1988, there has been no agreement even on the principles of demarcation of the longer river frontier.

Over the past decade, security concerns have mainly focused on the Hmong minority. A small remnant group of Hmong in the mountains to the south of the Plain of Jars have refused Lao government offers of amnesty and continued their armed insurgency, though few insurgents now remain. Others have escaped to Thailand as refugees. The Thai want to send them back to Laos, but Lao authorities have been reluctant to accept them. The Hmong themselves do not want to return; nor are they keen to take up offers of resettlement in the U.S. or elsewhere.[35]

The Lao have also accused the Thai of harbouring Lao dissidents responsible for making armed incursions into Laos, attacking a border post, and probably exploding a number of small bombs between 2000 and 2004. On the other hand, several such dissidents have been mysteriously assassinated in Thailand, in which, if rumour is to be believed, the Lao secret service has been implicated. These murky events have done nothing to improve Lao-Thai relations.

Trafficking and smuggling are other perennial problems that bedevil Lao-Thai relations. Young Lao women are trafficked for prostitution and young Lao men for employment in conditions of virtual slavery. Drugs are also trafficked through Laos, from Burma and China into Thailand. Smuggling is two-way, of timber and livestock into Thailand and of manufactured and consumer goods into Laos. If one route is closed off, others open along the long and porous border.

Concerted efforts have been made on both sides to deal with these problems. Thai and Lao representatives meet regularly, from the local to the national level. There is close cooperation on health matters in particular (HIV/aids, bird flu). Moreover there is political goodwill on both sides — with good reason, for despite the rise of China and the political influence of Vietnam, in trade terms Thailand is more important than both combined. Over half of all Lao exports go to Thailand, while Thailand accounts for almost 70 per cent of Lao imports.[36]

Amounting US$1.3588 billion to 2007, Thai investment in Laos still remains greater than that of China, although it slowed in 2007, and in 2008 will again be less than for China, due to the political turmoil in Thailand and the world financial crisis. Large projects include power generation (mainly in the form of hydro-electricity), mining and agriculture. And there are also many smaller Thai investment projects (more than for any other country) in areas such as tourism, transport and manufacturing.

Thailand exercises influence by other means, however. Many Lao have extended family members in northeast Thailand. Most Lao can understand, and many can read Thai, and as relatively little is published in Lao, Thai publications provide much of the information educated Lao have about the world. Lao students study in Thailand, and a large, but unknown, number work there, legally or illegally. For many Lao, therefore, Thailand provides their model for development.

Of the other ASEAN countries, only Malaysia (with US$138.6 million) and Singapore (with US$100.6 million) have significant investments in Laos (in tourism and timber, industry and services).[37] Trade is on the increase, and will be boosted by full Lao accession to the ASEAN Free Trade Area (AFTA), but it will continue to be overwhelmingly with Thailand and Vietnam. Only Malaysia (for exports) and Singapore (for imports) currently figure in Lao trade statistics.

Japan (with US$420.3 million) and Korea (with US$296.9 million) also have significant investments in Laos,[38] Japan mainly for a hydropower project and plantations for woodchips in southern Laos and Korea in a wide variety of smaller enterprises, including garment manufacturing and plantations of cassava and jastropha (for biodiesel production). Ten Korean companies have teamed up with Lao partners to build an entire satellite city close to Luang Phrabang. The 3,000 ha development will include hotels, a shopping mall and a golf course in addition to residential housing, all at an estimated cost of US$2 billion.[39] An Indian multinational is investing US$350 million in eucalypt plantations and a paper pulp mill.

Japan has consistently been the most generous donor of bilateral aid to Laos, contributing more than the next four donors combined (France, Germany, Sweden and Australia), and more than the multilateral aid provided by either the World Bank or the Asian Development Bank. Major projects have included hospitals, bridges and roads, notably in Viang Chan, and the Viang Chan water supply.

Western aid donors have been less generous, though Laos still manages to attract one of the highest per capita aid provisions in Asia. After more than two decades of assistance, especially to the forestry sector, Sweden has announced it will terminate its aid to Laos as current projects are completed, but France as the former colonial power and Australia are committed to continuing their aid programmes. Germany is a late comer, and the United States has only had a very small programme focusing mainly on opium reduction along with some clearance of unexploded ordnance left over from the Second Indochina War.

The point of this brief overview is to note that no ASEAN or Western state is in a position to exert the sort of influence over the Lao government that Vietnam or China do. The Lao-Thai relationship has been too fraught for too long, and carries too much historical baggage for Bangkok to have a decisive influence in Viang Chan. Japan has a much more consistent relationship as the Lao PDR's principal aid donor, but has invested relatively little and would be reluctant to urge reform, for fear that the Lao regime might interpret it as covertly working towards regime change.

This leaves the multilateral donors. Both the World Bank and the Asian Development Bank provide substantial loans to Laos for infrastructure development and poverty reduction. Both are thus in a position to include provisions in contracts to improve governance and financial transparency. As both banks are avowedly non-political, however, there is a limit to how much pressure for reform they can exert.[40]

Domestic Pressures

Even in an authoritarian single-party state like Laos, the political leadership is not immune to domestic political pressure — as the Party's response to concern over the That Luang marshes development project demonstrated. Such pressures tend to be less acute when the economy is growing at a healthy rate, and the benefits are flowing, if not evenly, then to some extent throughout the population. Over the eight years since Laos shrugged off the effects of the Asian economic crisis of the late 1990s, economic growth has been sufficient to provide opportunities and satisfy some expectations. But as corruption has increased, social pressures have been building, and as the global financial crisis impacts on Laos, those pressures are likely to increase and even have political implications.

(a) Economic Development

For the first two years of the current five-year National Socio-Economic Development Plan (2006–10), key development indicators have been positive.[41] The plan covers five strategic areas: economic growth driven by the private sector; greater competition and increased trade through regional integration; human and social development; poverty reduction; and good governance. These in turn require appropriate socio-economic policies to encourage the development of human and natural resources, through the introduction of appropriate institutional, legal and regulatory frameworks.[42]

Of the five strategic areas, most success has been registered in the first two. Investment in the private sector, most of it foreign, has provided employment and driven economic growth. More than half of all foreign investment has gone into power generation, almost all of it hydropower. This has yet to bear fruit, however: electricity exports in 2007 were no more than they were in 2003.[43] The first big increase will come when the giant Nam Theun II project comes on stream. The dam began filling in June 2008, and power production is due to commence at the end of 2009. Almost all the electricity will be exported. Other smaller projects are due for completion from 2009 onwards. So from 2010 the government can expect a substantial boost in taxes and royalties from hydropower.

Minerals (copper and gold) have accounted for almost half of all Lao exports since 2006 when the Australian-owned Sepone mine came into full production.[44] Profit taxes and royalties on mining paid to the Lao government amount to just about 20 per cent of budget revenue, almost all of which comes from the Sepone mine.[45] Gold production is on the decline at Sepone, while copper production has risen, but gold exports will rise again in 2009 when another Australian-owned gold and copper mine near Phu Bia, northeast of Viang Chan, comes into production.

The value of timber exports in 2007 amounted to less than a third the value of minerals, but continued to provide more tax revenue to the government than hydropower, even though illegal logging continues unabated.[46] Agricultural products are of increasing value and importance as new plantations come into production. Coffee and corn are already significant exports, and will be joined by cassava, soy beans and rubber. Tourism is another growth industry, which will be taxed through introduction of a value added tax (VAT).[47] This is expected to contribute a substantial sum to government revenues.

The government is also expecting economic dividends from improved transportation links, both within Laos and with neighbouring states. An extensive all-weather road network is being constructed, and new international airports are planned for Viang Chan and Luang Phrabang. The first railway in Laos, connecting the Thai rail network at Nongkhai across the Friendship Bridge to a terminus on the outskirts of Viang Chan, was given a trial run in July 2008 and was due to open for regular traffic in March 2009. Another rail link has been surveyed from Thakhek on the Mekong River across the Annamite Cordillera to the port of Danang in Vietnam. And the Chinese are considering building a section of line from southern China, as part of a proposed 2,500 km line via Viang Chan to follow the Mekong River to Cambodia.[48]

The global financial crisis will certainly impact on Laos in 2009.[49] OZ Minerals, owner of the Sepone mine, has flagged production cuts as prices and demand for copper falls, and expansion plans for the Sepone mine are likely to be put on hold. Gold production may increase in 2009, but not electricity exports. Unless the VAT is introduced and customs dues and income taxes are collected more efficiently than at present, government revenues will decline and the budget deficit increase. In the longer term, however, the outlook is for more revenue from resource development, so pressures to raise revenue from other sources will be more easily resisted — along with relevant reform measures.[50]

(b) Social Pressures

Human and social development is closely linked to poverty reduction, both strategic priorities for the current five-year National Socio-Economic Development Plan. The goals for both were set out in the government's *National Growth and Poverty Eradication Strategy* of 2003, which calls for increased expenditure in education, health and welfare. Progress since has been patchy. In its 2007–08 Human Development Index, the United Nations Development Program (UNDP) ranked the Lao PDR at number 130.[51]

The percentage of GDP devoted to education in Laos (currently 2.8 per cent) has always been low.[52] In many remote rural areas, mostly inhabited by ethnic minorities, schools do not exist; or if they do, teachers are not paid and must earn their own living by other means. As a result, the UNDP estimates that 21.5 per cent of young Lao between the ages of 15 and 24 remain illiterate. Overall, the literacy rate hovers just below 70 per cent.[53]

Teachers are poorly qualified and lack textbooks. School enrolments stood at 84 per cent for the primary level, dropping to 37 per cent at the secondary level for the 2005 school year. Though both figures were improvements on the early 1990s, percentages for girls were lower and their drop-out rates higher.[54] Only about 8 per cent of students go on to the tertiary level, where standards are also low. As a result Laos has a serious skill shortage, especially in such key areas as IT and accountancy, despite the establishment over the last five years of a number of private institutions. The children of powerful Party leaders are often educated abroad.

There has been growing concern in Laos over the poor standard of education, and the need for educational reform has been recognized by the new education minister, Somkot Mangnormek. Additional resources are to be committed to teacher training, development of new curricula, and the extension of the school system by one year. The government has established an educational investment fund of US$60 million for these projects, 70 per cent funded by foreign aid.[55] It has also opened the way for foreign investment in tertiary education.

Health is another area of popular concern. Despite assistance from France, China and Cuba, health care in major urban hospitals is poor by international standards. In the rural areas it is often non-existent. Where rural clinics do exist they are usually understaffed and lack supplies of even the most basic medicines. According to the World Health Organization, Laos devoted 3.6 per cent of GDP to health in 2005 (the last year for which statistics are available), amounting to US$78 per capita.[56] While this compares favourably with many developing countries, it is anything but evenly distributed and depends on the level of foreign aid. A report by the UN World Food Program said half of all rural Lao children were chronically malnourished, with the level for some ethnic minorities even higher.[57]

Two other sources of popular discontent are the increasing divide between urban and rural living standards and the government's policy of resettlement of ethnic minorities. While small-scale commercial agriculture (rubber, coffee, corn) has contributed to rural incomes in some areas, elsewhere rising population has forced rural families either to migrate to the cities, or to send their sons and daughters in search of work, many of them in Thailand. In some villages in Laos only old people and young children remain.

The policy of resettling ethnic minorities practising shifting slash-and-burn agriculture in permanent villages at lower altitudes is justified by the government as necessary to protect the environment. In the case of the Hmong, two additional reasons are to limit opium production (which in Laos has been quite effectively done), and as a means of security control. Overall the programme has not been a success, however. Resettlement has often been on marginal land and promised government assistance has not been forthcoming. Some people who were relocated have returned to the hills; others have become impoverished and dissatisfied.[58]

(c) The Corrosion of Corruption

The most common criticism of the Party and government (between which, for most Lao, no distinction is made) is over the increasing level of corruption. Corruption now permeates every aspect of Lao society, or at least every interaction with officials, whether government bureaucrats, police, and even teachers and health workers. Much of it is petty corruption on the part of low-paid civil servants to make some additional income. So, for example, police impose on-the-spot fines for minor infringements, health workers charge a small fee for service or for medicines that should be free, and teachers do the same for school books.[59] Or officials may be paid to be elsewhere when some illegal activity takes place.

Corruption becomes more serious as the stakes become higher and more senior officials are involved. So, for example, judges accept bribes to decide court cases, especially in disputes over property and land ownership, or to hand down lenient sentences; officials from the ministry of finance accept bribes to reduce taxes imposed, including income tax; customs officials do the same for duties on imports; officials from other government departments take payments for signing documents, issuing permits, and awarding contracts for goods or services.

Just as insidious is corruption that diverts government property or national resources into private hands. This includes funds for maintenance of government property, such as offices, schools and health centres, all of which are poorly maintained. Or materials may be sold commercially, or diverted for private use (as when cement for an irrigation scheme is used to construct a private house). Smuggling of timber, particularly by the military, falls into this category.

Corruption is also rife in the banking sector. Despite bank restructuring, money continues to be loaned to state owned enterprises (SOEs) with a history of defaults, much of which finds its way into private pockets (especially from the military-controlled SOEs). Loans are also made to individuals and to businesses, frequently in defiance of existing regulations, often on the sole basis of their political connections. Non-performing loans have rendered government commercial banks technically insolvent twice over, and only refinancing with the assistance of multilateral lenders has kept them afloat.[60]

Foreign investment has also been riddled with corruption, both in the approval process (which under pressure has been progressively simplified to reduce abuses) and subsequently in the form of continued payments to officials. This may take the form of employment of politically well connected officials as consultants, or advisers, or board members. Foreign investors may also pay off officials to avoid certain requirements, such as an environmental impact assessment, or to facilitate acquisition of land or mining concessions.

Land has become a particularly contentious issue as local and provincial officials have accepted payment for signing over land to which communities have traditional use rights, but no legal title. Angry protests have resulted, and the matter was raised in the National Assembly. As a result the granting of land concessions was officially suspended. Since then the central and provincial authorities have been in dispute over rates to charge.[61] Protests have also been mounted by people forced to relocate from dam sites due to be flooded.[62]

There is no doubt that popular anger over corruption (including the advantages gained and immunity granted to family members of powerful politicians) is on the rise. The moment the draconian government control of the press is lifted slightly the issue surfaces, and the problem of corruption has been raised in the National Assembly. An anti-corruption law was passed in 2005,[63] but as yet only minor officials have been prosecuted — unlike in China and Vietnam. All that has happened to senior Party members in Laos is that they have been given another job, for to target one person would be to implicate too many others.

I have argued that the increase in corruption in Laos is linked to a resurgence of Lao political culture, which seeks to concentrate power and wealth through patronage networks centred on senior members of the ruling Party.[64] To oil these networks resources are needed, which are transferred from the state to favoured individuals. Increasingly, however, the fruits of corruption are unevenly distributed, and as a result jealously is beginning to divide Party members. The prime minister is aware of this and wants to prevent it going any further. So do the Vietnamese.

Both know that the problem of corruption will have to be tacked if the Party is to retain political credibility and a degree of popular support.

Politics and the Party

(a) Pressures for Reform

From the above it is clear that pressures for reform are building, and that these are both international and domestic. International pressures fall into three categories: from the need to meet requirements for Lao membership of international organizations; from Western agencies and countries concerned over the mounting levels of corruption; and, almost wholly non-transparent, from advice offered by Vietnam or China. Domestic pressures are coming from the urban educated class critical of corruption and nepotism (for example, in the area of employment); from popular discontent over rising living costs and poor government services; and from rural Lao and ethnic minorities alike who have been cheated and dispossessed by Party officials or are unhappy over rural poverty.

Apart from the reporting requirements and interaction that are part and parcel of membership of ASEAN, Laos must meet its obligations imposed by the ASEAN Free Trade Area (AFTA). Membership of the World Trade Organisation (WTO), which Laos hopes to join by the end of 2009, requires reform of the legal framework for foreign trade. A Lao working party that visited Geneva in July 2008 reported progress on such areas as customs procedures, trade facilitation, and protection of intellectual property.

Western pressure, as we have seen, has focused mainly on better governance and greater transparency in fiscal matters.[65] These include public expenditure, financial management, economic restructuring (for example, of SOEs), and the regulatory environment for small to medium private enterprises — all designed to limit corruption. By contrast, advice from Vietnam (and to a lesser extent, China) has the purpose of strengthening the LPRP through judicious partial relaxation of draconian Party control (for example, of the media), strengthening the State Inspection Authority,[66] and the strengthening of internal Party control procedures. But while Western pressure for reform is designed to promote civil society and so prepare the way for greater democracy, advice from Laos' communist neighbours aims to maintain the LPRP in power.

Domestic pressures for reform have been outlined above, but there is one additional source of pressure, and that is from within the Party. Because the LPRP is hierarchically structured does not mean that no debate takes place or that no criticisms are voiced. All but two National Assembly deputies are Party members, but criticisms of government have been increasing. In its debate on the 2008 budget, the NA called on the government to increase its tax revenue so that services could be improved, knowing full well that this would entail a reduction in negotiated "exemptions".

Internal Party criticism is the kind that can be least ignored. It is on the rise because it has been Party policy to recruit the educated and ambitious, including those educated in Western tertiary institutions; and it is precisely the technocratic, middle level of government that participates in foreign-funded programmes related to reform.[67] So they are well aware of systematic shortcomings.

One widely recognized problem within the Party is the fraught relationship between the central government and provincial administrations, even though almost all provincial governors are members of the Party Central Committee. Earlier attempts at decentralization in the 1990s only fuelled corruption at the provincial level. Teachers and health workers went unpaid as local Party officials helped themselves to funds they had been given the responsibility to disburse. Banks were plundered, and a decreasing proportion of taxes and customs dues found their way to the ministry of finance. Re-centralization is now underway in three large central provinces in relation to financial disbursements, customs and tax collection, with more to follow.[68]

(b) Political Culture and Politics

Where the Party is the state, as in Laos, the state of the Party is a matter of considerable concern. Today the LPRP is in danger of becoming little more than the political arena within which jealous personal and regional interests compete for power and wealth. Competition between such interests is deeply embedded in Lao history in the traditional structure of centre-periphery relationships,[69] and was one of the factors that weakened the Royal Lao regime prior to the communist seizure of power.

In 1975, the LPRP was a disciplined and committed revolutionary organization, led by its founding secretary-general, Kaysone Phomvihan. During its first decade in government, the Party succeeded in monopolizing political power, but at the cost of all but destroying the economy. By the mid-1980s, as the Soviet Union began to cut economic aid, a change in policy had become inevitable. Kaysone realised this, and argued for the introduction of some elements of a free market economy. He was opposed by a coalition within the Party comprising socialist ideologues led by Nouhak Phoumsavan (who died in September 2008, aged 98) and the military led by General Khamtay Siphandone. This "two-line struggle" lasted for much of 1986, and delayed the Fourth Party Congress for over six months. It was a struggle Kaysone might well have lost, were it not for Vietnamese support.

Ironically, however, as most of the former entrepreneurial class had fled the country, the army was in the best position to exploit the new economic opportunities. For a decade it had had to generate its own funding, in large part through business ventures, often in cahoots with former Vietnamese military allies. From 1984 onwards, the Lao army set up large corporations to exploit the country's natural resources, particularly timber. No questions were asked, and the army was not subjected to oversight by any government instrumentality. Senior military officers were thus able to pursue their activities unhindered.

When Kaysone died in 1992, he was succeeded as president of the LPRP by General Khamtay. Kaysone lived frugally, as befitted a committed revolutionary. But the army generals who dominated the Politburo under Khamtay had come to enjoy the wealth that power brought them. Over the decade that followed, a culture of corruption took hold as the example set by Politburo members permeated the whole Party. Western countries and lending agencies, which stepped in to provide foreign aid after the Soviets left, became alarmed at the growing corruption (and "leakage' from their aid programmes), and began to urge reform (better governance, greater transparency).

When Khamtay eventually stepped down in 2006, he was succeeded as LPRP president by his close colleague, Lieutenant General Choummaly Sayasone. But a younger man from a quite different background, Bouasone Bouphavanh, was appointed prime minister. Bouasone has spent his working life as a Party technocrat, and understands very well both the strengths and weaknesses of the Party. In his inaugural speech to the National Assembly he promised a reform agenda (without specifying details).

The problem for Bouasone, however, is that he owes his position to Khamtay. Like Khamtay, Bouasone is a southerner, but he did not have a strong patronage network of his own. Since any reform agenda threatens powerful interests within the Party, Bouasone has had to move carefully to build his own support base. This has taken time. He has had to win over others of his generation of Party leaders, including the minister for security, Thongban Sengaphone, whose police can provide some counterbalance to the military. Bouasone has also sought to build a base among middle-level technocrats, and outside the Party among the wider urban elite (many of whom work for foreign companies and aid projects where they have regular contact with foreigners, speak English, and are well informed). For example, in November 2007, Bouasone spoke to the Lao Business Forum, promising to simplify investment procedures, and followed this up by raising the

Committee for Planning and Investment to ministerial level. He decreed an end to land concessions (even though some have still been granted) and has backed re-centralization.

Two actions that Bouasone has taken indicate his intention of doing something about corruption. One was the Law on State Inspection that he presented to the National Assembly in September 2007. This law, which replaced an earlier decree, empowers the State Inspection Authority to examine transactions at all levels of government. Where positions are being used for personal gain, officials will first be warned, then either dismissed or prosecuted.

The second development was the government reshuffle of July 2008, which removed the finance minister, Chansy Phosikham, and replaced him with his deputy Somdy Duongdy. At the same time four new ministers were appointed to the office of the prime minister, effectively increasing Bouasone's direct influence on government. These moves were widely interpreted as aimed at curbing corruption, as they followed a clear statement by Bouasone that it was "time to crack down on corruption, the luxury [of officials] and wrongdoers who violate the laws". "No one can help us", Bouasone told Assembly members. "We must do it ourselves."[70]

That Bouasone has not gone further, faster, is an indication of how powerful his opponents are. In fact in view of continued dominance of the Politburo by military men under whose watch the culture of corruption developed, it is unlikely that Bouasone would get anywhere at all were it not for the additional support he receives from Vietnam and China. This brings us full circle. The Vietnamese have apparently concluded that the competition, both personal and regional, that is inherent in Lao political culture, which feeds and feeds on corruption, both threatens the cohesion of, and undermines popular support for, the LPRP. To preserve the Party both discipline and organization must be strengthened. So the Vietnamese are backing Bouasone to introduce the necessary reforms — just as before they backed Kaysone to introduce a market economy.

There is now the Chinese connection to take into account, however, and the Chinese are more ambivalent. But as long as Bouasone signs off on Chinese investment projects in Laos, Beijing will back him too. Only with the support of Vietnam and China can Bouasone curtail corruption. It remains to be seen how successful he and his supporters will be, but two things are certain: first, this is how politics are played in Laos — with the participation of powerful friends; and second, the outcome will bring little joy to those who hope for a transition to democracy in the Lao PDR.

Notes

1   The stupa is the symbol of Lao culture and identity, in the same way Angkor Wat is for Cambodia. When the LPDR introduced a market economy, the That Luang replaced the red star at the apex of the Lao national crest. A three-day national holiday marks the That Luang festival in November, the most important in the Lao Buddhist year.

2   Brian McCartan, "New-age Chinatown has Laotians on edge", *Asia Times Online*, 26 July 2008.

3   Editorial statement, "Govt [sic] explains That Luang Marsh Development", *Vientiane Times*, 12 February 2008.

4   Dara Baccam, "Laos: Chinese firms will not develop That Luang marshland", *Voice of America News*, 12 August 2008.

5   Prior to the French period, Lao contacts with China were via Yunnan, in the form of tribute (via Kunming) and trade (conducted by Yunnanese Muslims or Hui). Very few Chinese lived in northern Laos. The Chinese who arrived during the French period came via Saigon or Bangkok to southern and central Laos. Most were Chaozhou, Hakka, Hainanese and Cantonese, roughly in this order. See "Chinese in Laos" in Martin Stuart-Fox, *Historical Dictionary of Laos*, 3rd ed. (Lanham, MD: Scarecrow Press, 2008), pp. 54–55.

6   Florence Rossetti, "The Chinese in Laos: Rebirth of the Laotian Chinese community as peace returns to Indochina", *Chinese Perspectives* no. 13 (1997): 26.

7   See Bertil Lintner, "China Ascendent — Part 1: Checkbook diplomacy raises China's standing with Laos and Cambodia", *YaleGlobal*, 25 April 2008 at <http://yaleglobal. yale.edu/display.article?id=10702> (accessed 30 April 2008).

8   The other partners are Italian-Thai 19.5 per cent (Bangkok-based and owned by a Sino-Thai family) and Saha Bolisat Lao 10 per cent (a Lao company controlled by the family of former Lao state and Party president Khamtay Siphandone).

9   Sounthone Ketphanh, Khamphone Mounlamai, and Phoui Siksidao, "Rubber Planting Status in Lao PDR", paper presented to a workshop on Rubber Development in Laos held at the National Agriculture and Forestry Research Institute of Laos, Viang Chan, 9–11 May 2006 at <http://nafri.org.la/05_news/workshops/rubber/papers/Sess1_p2_rubber%20status.pdf> (accessed 12 November 2008).

10   Brian McCartan, "China Farms Abroad", *Asia Sentinel*, 1 August 2008 at <www.asiasentinel.com/index.php?option=com_content&task=view&id=1361&Itemid=32> (accessed 11 November 2008).

11   David Fullbrook, "Beijing pulls Laos into its orbit", *Asia Times Online*, 25 October 2006.

12   The figure for 2002–07, according to the IMF, was US$1.188 billion. *IMF Country Report* no. 08/340, Lao People's Democratic Republic, Statistical Appendix.

13   "Chinese investors invade Laos", *The Nation* (Bangkok), 8 October 2007.

14   Thailand accounts for 51.3 per cent of Lao exports and 70.6 per cent of imports, as against figures for China of 8.9 and 8.6 per cent. *EIU ViewsWire*, New York, 5 June 2008 and 23 September 2008.

15   The cost of US$97 million was shared between China, Thailand and the Asian Development Bank (US$30 million each), with the Lao government making up the remainder. "New overland route links Singapore to Beijing", *The Nation* (Bangkok), 1 April 2008.

16   Laos has announced suspension of further foreign investment in telecommunications because the sector is "saturated". *KPL Lao New Agency,* 28 October 2008. Mining concessions are also on hold until 2010.

17   "Chinese investors invade Laos", *The Nation* (Bangkok), 8 October 2007; *Radio Free Asia*, 12 May 2007.

18   Qin Jize, "China, Laos to enhance ties", *China Daily*, 31 March 2008.

19   "Sino-Laotian bilateral ties", *People's Daily Online*, as updated 16 November 2006 <http://english.peopledaily.com.cn/200611/16/eng20061116_322139.html> (accessed 13 November 2008).

20   Bertil Lintner calls the movement of Chinese into mainland Southeast Asian states "a creeping invasion", which Beijing is doing nothing to prevent (in "China's Third Wave, Part 1: A new breed of migrants fans out", *Asia Times Online*, 17 April 2007). Grant Evans prefers the term "drift' (in his paper "The Southward Drift of the Chinese" presented at the 17th Biennial Conference of the Asian Studies Association of Australia, Melbourne, 1–3 July 2008). With respect to Laos, Evans rejects C.P. Fitzgerald's alternative models of sinicization: the Vietnam model of wholesale adoption of Chinese culture; and the Yunnan model of Chinese settlement followed by political administration. Instead he favours a third model in which limited Chinese migration will bring some sinicization of Lao culture, but not political control. I have argued that the pattern of power relations between China and Southeast Asia that is emerging, while it is by no means a modern replay of the tributary relationship that existed until the nineteenth century, does preserve cultural and historical elements of it that both sides implicitly recognize. See Martin Stuart-Fox, *A Short History of China and Southeast Asia: Tribute, Trade and Influence* Crows Nest (Australia: Allen & Unwin, 2003). Milton Osborne argues similarly that China seeks recognition from Southeast Asian countries as the paramount power: Chinese interests will come first, but China also wants Southeast Asia to be a prosperous partner. Milton Osborne, *The Paramount Power: China and the Countries of Southeast Asia* (Sydney: The Lowey Institute for International Policy, 2006).

21   "Special Report: Premier Wen visits Laos, attends GMS Summit", *Xinhua*, 30 March 2008.

22   See, for example, Ian Storey, "China and Vietnam's tug of war in Laos", *China Brief from the Jamestown Foundation*, vol. 5, issue 13 (7 June 2005).

23   Bertil Lintner, "Laos: Signs of Unrest", in *Southeast Asian Affairs 2001*, edited by Daljit Singh and Anthony Smith (Singapore: Institute of Southeast Asian Studies, 2001), pp. 177–86.

24   *EIU ViewsWire*, New York, 5 June 2008. IMF Country Report no. 08/340 (Laos), October 2008.

25   "Laos sets to boost trade with Vietnam", *Vietnam News Agency*, 27 October 2008.

26   "Vietnam pours 1.28 billion USD in investment in Laos", *Vietnam News Agency*, 12 August 2008. According to the IMF, however, the total for 2002–07 was US$539.2 million. *IMF Country Report* no. 08/340, Lao People's Democratic Republic, Statistical Appendix. See also Andrew Symon, "Regional race for Laos" riches", *Asia Times Online*, 30 August 2007.

27   "Vietnam, Laos ink supplements to major hydro-power project", *Vietnam News Agency*, 16 June 2008.

28   To be constructed over 2010–16 at a cost of US$2 billion. *Voice of America News*, 30 October 2008.

29   According to the *Vietnam News Agency* (27 August 2008), since 2005, 947 Lao officials have graduated from the Institute.

30   Used twice in the joint statement issued on the occasion of Lao president Choummaly to Vietnam in 2006 at <http://www.vnanet.vn/pPrint.aspx?itemid=151083> (assessed 16 August 2006).

31   Supalak Ganjanakhundee, "Illegal logging hits Lao forests", *The Nation* (Bangkok), 1 April 2008.

32   Tina Qian argues in "Communist capital flows downstream: China's aid to Laos" (China Development Brief at <http://www.chinadevelopmentbrief.com/node/454/> accessed 11 November 2008) that China wants an economic quid pro quo for its aid, rather than greater political influence. Others argue that China is waiting for the revolutionary generation to pass on (Brian McCartan, "China and Vietnam square off in Laos", *Asia Times Online*, 30 August 2008), and that this is a deliberate long-term strategy (Storey, "China and Vietnam's tug of war over Laos"; Pavin Chachavalpongpun, "With a little help from Laos' friends" at <http://www.nationmultimedia.com/2006/12/04/opinion/opinion_30020631.php> (accessed 6 December 2006).

33   See, for example, his speech to the National Assembly in June 2007. "PM announces improvements to Govt [sic]", *Vientiane Times*, 25 June 2007.

34   Burma/Myanmar, Thailand, Cambodia and Vietnam; Malaysia being commonly grouped with the maritime states of Indonesia, the Philippines, Brunei and Singapore.

35   Of close to 8,000 Hmong refugees in Thailand, almost a thousand returned to Laos in May and June 2008 and have been resettled. Others refuse to go. The Lao have complicated things by preventing independent monitors from verifying that returnees have been properly treated.

36   Lao exports to Thailand have declined from 50 per cent in 2005–06 to 30 per cent in 2007–08, while imports remained at 68 per cent. Department of International

Cooperation, Ministry of Planning and Investment, Lao PDR, *Background Document: Achievements, Challenges and Future Directions within the Implementation of the National Strategies and Policies* (Roundtable Implementation Meeting, Vientiane, 24 November 2008), p 8. Major import items include petroleum products, vehicles and machinery; while exports include minerals, timber, and electricity. Two-way trade stood at almost US$1.5 billion in 2006, a figure both sides intend to double by 2010. *Mekong News*, 28 December 2006 at <http://209.85.173.132/u/sumernet? q=cache:FRYSamSaVAEJ:www.sumernet.org/news/mekongnews_detail.asp%3Fid% 3D28+investment+laos&hl=en&ct=clnk&cd=2&ie=UTF-8> (accessed 24 November 2008).

[37]   *IMF Country Report* no. 08/340, Lao People's Democratic Republic, Statistical Appendix.

[38]   *IMF Country Report* no. 08/340, Lao People's Democratic Republic, Statistical Appendix.

[39]   *Voice of America News*, 30 October 2008.

[40]   For an assessment of progress in such matters as public expenditure, financial sector reform and the reform of state-owned enterprises, all of which the World Bank has been pressing for. See The World Bank Office, Vientiane, *Lao PDR Economic Monitor*, November 2008.

[41]   World Bank, *Lao PDR Economic Monitor*, November 2008.

[42]   Department of International Cooperation, *Background Document*, p. 2.

[43]   *IMF Country Report* no. 08/340, Lao People's Democratic Republic, Statistical Appendix.

[44]   As of writing, China's Minmetals was negotiating to buy OZ Minerals, the Australian company that owns the Sepone mine, though the Lao government will persumably continue to hold a 10 per cent stake in the mine. Along with the proposed Chinese bauxite mine, ownership of the Sepone mine would give China an even stronger presence in southern Laos.

[45]   *IMF Country Report* no. 08/340, Lao People's Democratic Republic, Statistical Appendix. Of some 140 approved foreign-owned mining ventures in Laos, only a handful contribute something to government revenue. Most are small, but whatever they pay does not show up in the government's budget papers.

[46]   "Illegal logging hits Laos forests", *The Nation* (Bangkok), 1 April 2008. Most illegal timber is smuggled into Vietnam to feed the country's US$3 billion furniture export industry.

[47]   Introduction of a VAT was signed into law in January 2007, but its implementation has been delayed for technical reasons until 2009.

[48]   "Laos seeks investors for the national railway network project", People's Daily Online, 21 November 2008 at <http://english.people.com.cn/90001/90777/90851/6538363.html> (accessed 30 November 2008).

[49]   World Bank, *Lao PDR Economic Monitor*, November 2008. Ben Bingham, Statement by IMF Resident Representative, Roundtable Implementation Meeting, Vientiane, 24 November 2008.

50   Most pressure has come from the World Bank, which predicts revenue collection will rise to 14.9 per cent of GDP for the financial year 2007–08, but decline in 2008–09. World Bank, *Lao PDR Economic Monitor*, November 2008. Projections are for mining to contribute just under 15 per cent of revenue and hydropower more than double that. LPDR, *National Growth and Poverty Eradication Strategy*, October 2003, Table 4.1, p. 282.

51   Most recent figures for this report are from 2005.

52   Among ASEAN states, only Cambodia and Indonesia rank lower.

53   UNDP, *Human Development Report 2007/2008*, statistics for the Lao PDR at <http://hdrstats.undp.org/countries/data_sheets/cty_ds_LAO.html> (accessed 26 November 2008).

54   UNDP, *Human Development Report 2007/2008*, statistics for the Lao PDR.

55   *EIU ViewsWire*, New York, 5 June 2008.

56   WHO statistics at <http://www.who.int/countries/lao/en/> (accessed 29 November 2008).

57   "Half of Laos' rural children chronically malnourished, says WFP", *The Nation* (Bangkok), 8 November 2007.

58   See Olivier Evrard and Yves Goudineau, "Planned Resettlement, Unexpected Migrations and Cultural Trauma in Laos", *Development and Change* 35, no. 5 (December 2004): 937–62; Keith Barney, "The trouble with tenure security in Laos", *Watershed* 12, no. 2 (2007): 57–64.

59   The government has promised low-paid civil servants to increase salaries, but this is unlikely to ameliorate matters.

60   Reading between the lines of the World Bank, *Lao PDR Economic Monitor*, November 2008, indicates how reluctant the Lao government has been to restructure SOEs or to undertake financial sector reform. See also Nick Freeman, "Laos: Funding the Future", *The Banker*, October 2006.

61   The government wants to increase rates, which will squeeze payments made to provincial authorities, who are resisting any rise.

62   Susanne Wong, "Laos: Villagers Mount Unprecedented Protest Against Dam in Laos", World Rainforest Movement Bulletin no. 70, May 2003, at <http://www.wrm.org.uy/bulletin/70/Laos.html> (accessed 29 November 2008).

63   At <http://www.mfa.gov.sg/vientiane/Laws/Anti%20Corruption%20Law%20&%20Decree%20FINAL%2014-03-06.pdf> (accessed 30 November 2008).

64   Martin Stuart-Fox, "The Political Culture of Corruption in the Lao PDR", *Asian Studies Review* 30, 1 (2006): 59–75. See also Martin Stuart-Fox, "The Persistence of Political Culture in Laos and Cambodia", *Südostasien aktuell* 3 (2008): 34–57.

65   Laos comes in at number 151 out of 180 countries in Transparency International's Corruption Perception Index. See <http://www.transparency.org/news_room/in_focus/2008/cpi2008/cpi_2008_table> (accessed 30 November 2008).

66   "Laos to improve transparency", *The Nation* (Bangkok), 16 September 2007.

67   The list of these is impressive (World Bank, *Lao PDR Economic Monitor*, November 2008, pp. 30–39), and indicates how successful Party leaders have been in resisting reform. One way they have done this is to prolong discussion; another is to pass laws or issue decrees that are not implemented; while a third is to establish an institution which does no actual work (such as an independent audit authority that is not, and never can be, independent of government and the Party).

68   World Bank, *Lao PDR Economic Monitor*, November 2008, p. 15. The dispute over rates to charge for land concessions shows, however, how powerful province governors remain.

69   Or *meuang* dynamics. See Martin Stuart-Fox, "The Politics and Reform in the Lao People's Democratic Republic", Working Paper no. 126, Asia Research Institute, Murdoch University, at <http://wwwarc.murdoch.edu.au/wp/wp126.pdf>.

70   China Economic Net, "Laos cabinet reshuffled" at <http://en.ce.cn/World/Asia-Pacific/200707/04/t20070704_12058131.shtml> (accessed 1 December 2008). A second reshuffle was required in November 2008 following the unexpected death of Bosaykham Vongdara, the minister for energy and minerals. His place was taken by Soulivong Daravong, while the mayor of Viang Chan, Sinlavong Khoutphaythoun, a supporter of Bouasone, took over Soulivong's portfolio of planning and investment. The fast-rising Hmong governor of Xainyaburi province, Sombath Yialiheu, was appointed the new mayor of Viang Chan.

Malaysia

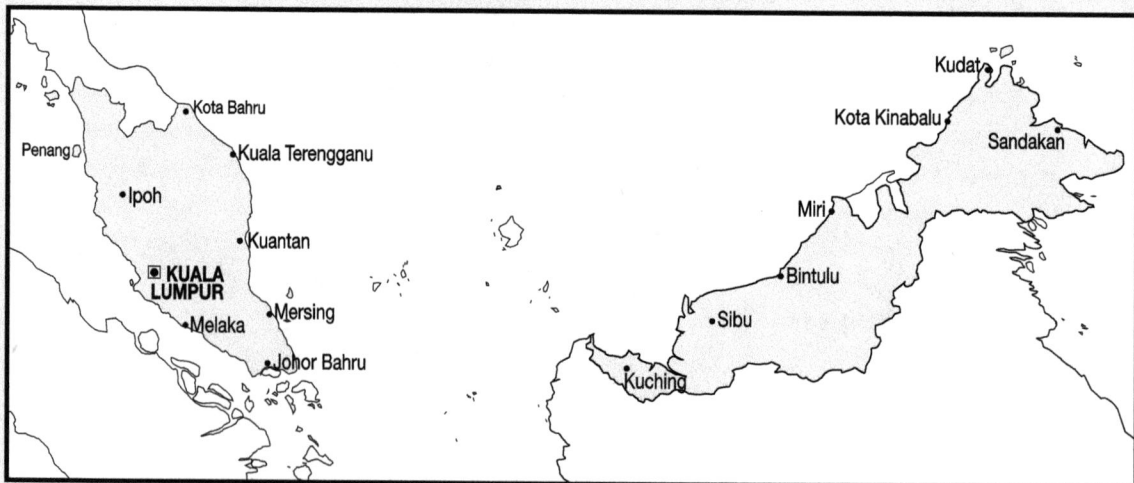

MALAYSIA
Political Transformation and
Intrigue in an Election Year

Johan Saravanamuttu

The year 2008 will be remembered as a watershed for the Malaysian political system and for the forward trajectory of Malaysian democracy. This election year saw a refurbished coalition of oppositional political forces, the People's Pact (Pakatan Rakyat), deprive the ruling National Front (Barisan Nasional) coalition of its two-thirds majority of seats in Parliament. Even more significantly, four state governments fell, making it a total of five governments in Opposition hands. I suggest here that this development has created a de facto two-party system for a maturing Malaysian democracy. Economically, Malaysians will be facing a severe downturn though not a technical recession. The year also saw the denouement of a leadership crisis within the United Malays National Organisation (UMNO) leading ultimately to the anticipated departure from the political stage in March 2009 of the fifth Malaysian Prime Minister Abdullah Ahmad Badawi. The political terrain remains fraught with pitfalls for premier-in-waiting Najib Abdul Razak and for Opposition Leader, Anwar Ibrahim, who awaits his sodomy trial.

The Malaysian Prime Minister Abdullah Badawi already had more than his fair share of a baggage of problems to deal with even before his tenure headed into 2008. Let me briefly recollect. After 25 November 2007, five HINDRAF lawyers remained in detention under the draconian ISA, while one was at large. The V.K. Lingam video expose in September 2007 and the Royal Commission inquiry into it in January 2008 remained much in the public consciousness,[1] so too the Altantuya murder trial which had dragged on from 2007. Inter-faith

JOHAN SARAVANAMUTTU is a Visiting Senior Research Fellow at the Institute of Southeast Asian Studies (ISEAS), Singapore.

fractures which had surfaced since 2005 remained largely unresolved and so too internal squabbles within the ruling coalition parties. Most sensationally, the MCA Minister for Health had to resign because of the circulation of a sex video by his detractors. Finally, the economy was not in great shape with petrol prices and inflation spiking and Mahathir still sniping from the sidelines. Yet speculation was rife by early 2008 that an early election would be called presumably to salvage the premier's beleaguered situation, more than one year in advance of the mandatory five years. In a CNN interview Abdullah did admit that a fresh mandate was necessary for him to address a host of new issues and to make good his unfulfilled anti-corruption agenda.

In the event, parliament and state assemblies, with the exception of Sarawak, were dissolved on 13 February 2008. The Election Commission called for nominations on 24 February for the 12th General Election of Malaysia to be held on 8 March 2008. An unusually long 13 days were given for campaigning and some 222 parliamentary seats were in contention along with 505 state seats. Malaysians were in for an exciting 2008, whatever the prospective outcome of the election. Hardly anyone got it right. Two days before election day, Malaysian analysts (including this one) speaking at a seminar at the Institute of Southeast Asian Studies (ISEAS) in Singapore were not prepared to concede that the Barisan Nasional (BN) would lose its two-thirds majority in parliament, let alone four more state governments.[2]

The Election Outcome

It could well be that the 8 March General Election (GE) has surpassed some of the outcomes of the 1969 watershed general election which led to the outbreak of riots in Kuala Lumpur on 13 May.[3] In 2008, the outburst of election rallies throughout the campaign period by Opposition parties was also reminiscent of May 1969, but perhaps eclipsing 1969 by the sheer numbers that attended such rallies throughout the country. One large rally in Penang, saw some 50,000 in attendance, clearly unprecedented.[4] Despite the ruling coalition of Barisan Nasional (BN) losing its two-thirds majority of seats held, no untoward events occurred after 8 March speaking well for the fact that Malaysian society had arrived at a political threshold where violence as an instrument of change was now no longer tolerated. Equally significant, I would argue, is that Malaysia edged closer to a formal parliamentary two-party system but as an outcome of 8 March already has a de facto two-party system at the state-level of governance. Let us now turn briefly to the election results (for a summary of the results, see Table 1).

TABLE 1
Results of Parliamentary Election, 2008

Party	Votes	%	Seats	%
Barisan Nasional	4,090,670	50.14	140	63.1
UMNO	2,381,725	29.19	79	35.6
MCA	849,108	10.41	15	6.8
MIC	179,422	2.20	3	1.4
Gerakan	184,548	2.26	2	0.9
Others	495,867	6.08	41	18.5
Pakatan Rakyat	3,786,399	46.41	82	36.9
DAP	1,107,960	13.58	28	12.6
PAS	1,140,676	13.98	23	10.4
PKR	1,509,080	18.50	31	14.0
Others	28,683	0.35	0	0
Independents	63,960	0.78	0	0
Spoilt Votes	175,011	2.14	—	—
Unreturned votes	41,564	0.51	—	—
Total	8,159,043	100	222	100

Source: Computed from Election Commission data.

Some of the salient outcomes of 8 March could be said to be the following:

- The BN barely got half (50.1 per cent) of the 7.9 million ballots cast nation-wide and lost the popular vote on the Peninsula, garnering only 49 per cent of the ballots.
- The BN lost its two-thirds majority in parliament, winning 140 federal seats and 307 state seats, the Opposition taking 82 and 198 respectively.
- The BN lost the state governments of Selangor, Penang, Perak and Kedah, while Kelantan remained in Opposition hands. (In its worst performances of the past, BN had failed to capture only two state governments, Kelantan and Terengganu in 1959 and 1999).
- BN casualties included the Women, Family and Community Development Minister, Sharizat Abdul Jalil; Information Minister Zainuddin Maidin; presidents of the Malaysian Indian Congress, S. Samy Velu; People's Progressive Party (PPP), M. Kayveas; and Gerakan, Koh Tsu Koon.
- Parti Islam Se-Malaysia (PAS)'s women's wing chief Lo' Lo' Mohd Ghazali became the second woman from the party to win a parliamentary seat (the first was Khadijah Sidek in 1959).

One of the more significant aspects of the 2008 GE in contrast to previous elections, was the comprehensive vote swing of all major ethnic communities away from the BN parties. Political scientist Ong Kian Ming has estimated that some 30–35 per cent of non-Malay voters swung to the Opposition parties, compared with the popular vote in the previous election of 2004. Although the overall corresponding swing for Malays was only about 5 per cent, Ong has argued the following:

> It is important to highlight that these vote swings are not uniformly distributed. For example, the Malay vote swing in the West Coast states, especially in Penang, Selangor and Kuala Lumpur was higher than the estimated 5 per cent and was closer to 10 per cent or even higher in certain constituencies like Balik Pulau, Gombak and Lembah Pantai. It would not have been possible for the opposition, PKR in these cases, to win without a sizeable swing in the Malay vote (Ong 2008).

Nationwide, in mixed seats where the electorate formed 40–60 per cent of Malay voters, the BN won 28 seats and the Opposition 26 seats, showing that the alternative People's Pact (Pakatan Rakyat, PR), had become a veritable contender to the BN and in some sense was emulating BN's model of electoral success.[5] It could well be argued that cross-ethnic voting accounted for a significant number of victories of the People's Pact and, had the pattern of cross-ethnic voting which occurred in Kelang Valley been replicated in states like Pahang, Malacca, Negeri Sembilan and Johor, the BN government would have been toppled on 8 March.[6]

A De Facto Two-Party System

The fact that Malaysia may have become a de facto two-party system at the state-level can be attributed to the stunning victories of the People's Pact coalition of forces led by Anwar Ibrahim as shown in Figure 1. In fact, some analysts have pointed out that the sixth state to fall was the federal territory of Kuala Lumpur, where all but one parliamentary seat out of 12 seats went to the People's Pact.[7]

Anwar further demonstrated about six months later that the 8 March outcome was no fluke by sweeping the Permatang Pauh by-election with a majority of well over 15,000 votes on 26 August and was subsequently officially anointed as Leader of the Opposition in Parliament.

First, it must be stressed that the major change in the political landscape is still the nascent, two-party (or two-coalition) system at the state level, where PR governments run five governments, namely, Selangor, Penang, Perak, Kedah

Figure 1
Malaysian Election 2008:
Distribution of Seats Won in Each State Legislature

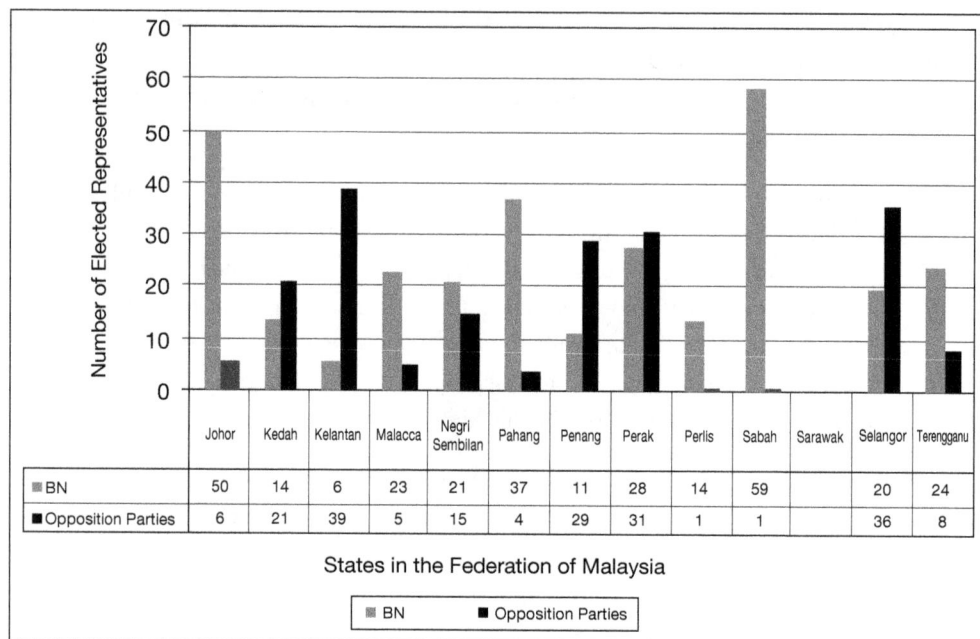

	Johor	Kedah	Kelantan	Malacca	Negri Sembilan	Pahang	Penang	Perak	Perlis	Sabah	Sarawak	Selangor	Terengganu
■ BN	50	14	6	23	21	37	11	28	14	59		20	24
■ Opposition Parties	6	21	39	5	15	4	29	31	1	1		36	8

States in the Federation of Malaysia

■ BN ■ Opposition Parties

Source: Computed form Election Commission data.

and Kelantan. In these states, the BN now finds itself in the unfamiliar role of opposition, except in Kelantan where this has been the case for about two decades. One could well argue that Malaysian democracy has perhaps arrived at a new threshold and that citizens can now have the opportunity to judge four alternative state governments and choose to re-elect or reject them the next time around. As such, the formalization of the People's Front as an alternative coalition to the National Front appears to be *fait accompli*. Unlike its predecessor, the Alternative Front (Barisan Alternatif) of 1998–99, the People's Pact governmental presence seems guaranteed for some time to come by virtue of power at the state level. The next move would be to have a common logo, like the BN.

Second, the obverse may be true for the BN coalition. This long-standing coalition is clearly in a state of transformation if not turmoil. Already one component party, the Sabah Progressive Party (SAPP) has abandoned the pact (on 17 September 2008) while the Gerakan and even the Malaysian Chinese Association (MCA) have sounded out their deep disaffection with UMNO politics. These two Chinese-based component parties are themselves in a state of political reinvention, spurning an earlier suggestion of merger. After the 8 March result, one senior woman leader and her supporters left the MCA and joined Anwar's party.[8] The suggestion by the new Gerakan President Koh Tsu Koon to have direct membership in the BN and to turn it eventually into a multiracial party hints at the current poor formula of racial power sharing within the National Front today. The leader of Sabah's native-based United Pasokmomogun Kadazandusun Murut Organization (UPKO), Bernard Dompok, has also expressed grave concern about the failure of the National Front government to deal with three urgent matters, namely, the unequal exchange of economic benefits to Sabah and its concomitant status as Malaysia's poorest state, the issue of religious freedom and the unresolved problem of the influx of more than one million illegal immigrants into Sabah.[9]

However, not all is rosy for the PR. Taking the example of Penang, the DAP-led People's Pact government may have weathered a number of UMNO-generated political storms and self-inflicted *faux pas* but the going has been tough, admitted as much by Chief Minister Lim Guan Eng.[10] Similarly, the PKR-led Selangor government has also had its fair share of challenges but it seems to be holding firm. The PAS-led governments of Perak and Kedah also have their own sets of political hiccups.

At the federal level, the formation of a strong parliamentary opposition with 82 seats seems to be having a noticeable impact on the BN, even without a no-confidence vote against the government.[11] The Malaysian budget for 2009 has been made somewhat irrelevant by the global financial crisis in October 2008, with the new Finance Minister introducing new measures such as the injection of a RM7 billion ringgit stimulus package for the economy.[12] As the country approached the end of 2008, all eyes were focused on UMNO's attempt to re-establish itself with its new leader, Najib Razak, who now held the crucial finance ministry. It remains to be seen how a Najib's cabinet would look after a likely reshuffle following UMNO party gathering in March 2009. To leave behind a legacy, Abdullah has in the month of December 2008 introduced three reform bills affecting the Judiciary, the Anti-Corruption Agency and the Police, which will be discussed further below.

Anwar's New Sodomy Trial[13]

Not long after successes of the People's Pact in 8 March came another accusation of the perpetration of sodomy by Anwar Ibrahim. Dubbed "Sodomy II", this sensational development surfaced in late June when a 23-year-old political aide of Anwar, one Mohd Saiful Bukhari Azlan, lodged a police report claiming that he had been sodomised by Anwar. Anwar's wife Wan Azizah immediately countered the allegation by revealing photographs that Mohd Saiful had been seen to be associated with political aides of Deputy Prime Minister Najib Razak. The suggestion was that the young man may have been a 'plant' who had offered to work for the PKR during the general election. It was also later revealed by Najib himself that Saiful had come to his residence to inform him of the alleged act and to seek advice before he lodged the police report. Almost immediately after the accusation, there was a dramatic incident of Anwar seeking asylum or refuge in the Turkish Embassy on 30 June alleging that his life was under threat.[14] In the event, charges were then proffered against Anwar for sodomy. A series of dramatic developments then occurred as follows:

- On 2 July, the police confirmed the charge of sodomy based on a Kuala Lumpur Hospital medical report by the alleged victim, Mohd Saiful Bukhari Azlan.

- On 9 July, Anwar asked an Islamic court to investigate his former aide. Under *syariah* law, accusations of a sexual crime, such as sodomy, needed four witnesses to support the claim.

- On 16 July, Anwar was arrested by a contingent of 10 police cars with 20 balaclava-clad officers, under Section 377A of the Penal Code, outside his home, one hour before he was due to make a statement at the police HQ.

- Anwar was released without charges filed on police bail after overnight detention, and after recording a statement.

- On 29 July, Anwar Ibrahim demanded that the police drop the sodomy investigation against him, producing a medical report he said showed no assault had taken place.

- In a statutory declaration on 1 August, Mohamed Osman Abdul Hamid of Pusrawi Hospital reiterated his findings that after examining Mohd Saiful, he found no evidence of sodomy. The doctor made his first public appearance after missing for more than a month since his medical report was leaked to the media.

- On 15 August, Mohd Saiful swore on the Qur'an at the Federal Territory Mosque that he was sodomized by Anwar Ibrahim. Imam Ramlang Porigi subsequently said that Mohd Saiful's Quranic oath or "sumpah muhabalah" was technically wrong. "I was only there as a witness, to listen in", he elaborated, noting that Saiful made two errors while reciting the oath: the first when he mispronounced the word for God and had Ramlang correct him;

and the second when he confused the date of the alleged sodomy incident and corrected himself.

- Anwar Ibrahim, on 7 August, pleaded not guilty to sodomy or "unnatural sex" (defined as "carnal intercourse against the order of nature") and was released by Sessions Court Judge Komathy Suppiah on a personal bail bond of RM20,000 (US$6,090).
- On 7 November 2008, the judge in the Sessions Court struck down the request by Malaysia's Attorney-General Abdul Gani Patail to transfer the case to the High Court. The reason given was that the certificate signed by the AG was invalid.

Despite Anwar's minor court victory, his political trajectory remains stymied as long as the sodomy trial is ongoing. It is difficult to see how he would function effectively even as the leader of the parliamentary Opposition when the trial gets into full-swing presumably in 2009. The worse-case scenario would be that he was found guilty and would have to serve another jail term, in which case he would be disqualified to be a parliamentarian.

An Aborted Numbers Game

The year 2008 was noted for the turbulent politics of a possible or impending takeover of the government by the People's Pact through the parliamentary move of attracting crossovers of government MPs to the Opposition bench. With the PR holding 81 seats,[15] it needed exactly 31 crossovers to give it a majority of one in a parliament of 222 MPs. This stratagem was the brainchild of Anwar Ibrahim, the newly crowned Opposition leader. With his resounding victory in his former constituency, vacated by wife and PKR leader Wan Azizah, Anwar's moment to topple the government seemed palpable as he cleverly kept alive a strategy of baiting crossovers of BN parties and politicians, especially from Sarawak and Sabah. However, the deadline of 16 September 2008 passed with a Parliament out of session and Anwar not making good his claim of toppling the BN. The Malaysian government has always designated 31 August as national day somewhat ignoring the sentiments of the two East Malaysian states which only joined Malaysia (indeed made it possible) on 16 September 1963.

Anwar's stratagem of choosing 16 September for a takeover seemed clever enough. He also called for 16 September to be a public holiday in the five PR-governed states, with the standing offer of a 20 per cent state royalty on oil and gas. Many have suggested that sequestering some 50 MPs in Taiwan from 7–19 September on a supposedly study trip was specifically aimed at blocking

Anwar's 16 September plan and discrediting him when it did not materialize. It seemed to many that the Abdullah government was genuinely worried that Anwar had the numbers and the Taiwan tour was a desperate attempt to foil Anwar's plan. Anwar on his part dispatched some five of his political lieutenants to Taiwan to pursue the BN MPs. Tian Chua, the PKR MP for Batu, who led the group was quoted as saying that: "We have the numbers already. We are just going there to have coffee and spend time with them and also learn about agriculture from Taiwan so that we do not get left behind when Pakatan Rakyat takes over."[16]

Anwar's sodomy trial could certainly be seen as another stratagem by his opponents not just as an attempt to block his takeover plans, but in the worst-case scenario take out the Opposition Leader with a 20-year prison sentence. The Session Court's decision to not transfer the case to the High Court is perhaps a minor victory for Anwar although the fact remains that as long as the trial is still on, this would mean that Anwar's overall political situation remains in limbo. 16 September arrived without the much anticipated crossovers which Anwar claimed he had. One hypothesis was that Anwar may have got enough crossovers (or pledges) to form the government but PAS was uncomfortable with an imbalance in favour of non-Muslims. There was also the prevalent suggestion that Anwar was either playing a psychological game or merely bluffing with the hope that his stratagem would bring about a bandwagon effect of a swing in his favour.[17] In the event, by October 2008, as the crossovers were not forthcoming, Anwar was forced to put his takeover plan on the backburner and probably even abandon it altogether.

Political Turbulence of a New Politics

The year 2008 will also definitely be remembered for the political turbulence it generated in Malaysian race relations, although one hastens to add, without any hint of a racial riot. Indeed, the idiom of a "new politics" in which a political society resists the worst attempts by extremist elements to tilt the political balance in the direction of violence has been greatly and assiduously practised. The racist outburst by one Ahmad Ismail of UMNO in September could have easily stirred a hornet's nest and led to undesired incidents but it did not. Indeed good sense seemed to have prevailed although the general public appeared to be somewhat dissatisfied with the Prime Minister's less then stern sanction against the offending individual. After his provocative act of smashing and ripping apart the framed portrait of the former Chief Minster of Penang, the UMNO Bukit Bendera chief was suspended by UMNO for three years.[18] Even so, the UMNO recalcitrant still refused to apologise for a serious alleged remark in which he alluded to all non-Malays as being "temporary visitors" to the country.

Politics took an ugly turn with the ISA arrests of Sin Chew reporter Tan Hoon Cheng and Seputeh MP Theresa Kok, and then the ISA detention of blogger Raja Petra Kamarudin, all occurring in the month of September. The Sin Chew journalist detained was the same person who had reported on the Ahmad Ismail statement, allegedly made during the Permatang Pauh election campaign. Although she was held for only a day, many thought it incredulous that the reason given for her detention was to protect her from harm, as stated by the Home Minister Syed Hamid Jaafar Albar.

However, Theresa Kok's detention was a much more convoluted affair. The DAP parliamentarian, winner of the largest parliamentary majority on 8 March,[19] was arrested under the ISA on 13 September and detained for seven days in an undisclosed location. Just before her arrest, the Malay daily *Utusan Malaysia* in an article had claimed that Teresa Kok "advised" a mosque in Puchong not to use loudspeakers while making the *azan,* the Islamic call to prayer, which she denied doing. It turned out later that a faulty loudspeaker system was the reason why the mosque did not broadcast the *azan* although it was true there was a petition to the mosque by a neighbourhood group requesting a mosque to lower the volume during ceramahs or sermons but not during *azan.* The administrator of the mosque as well as the petitioners also confirmed that Kok was not involved in the petition. PAS MP for Kota Raja, Siti Mariah Mahmood, lodged a police report against a blog website called Pembela Melayu and Selangor Opposition Leader Mohd Khir Toyo for defaming Kok by alleging that Kok had supported a petition by the Chinese in Kinrara against the *azan* in their area. After her release, Kok filed a RM30 million legal suit against the *Utusan Malaysia.* On 27 September, two Molotov cocktails were thrown into the Kok family home in Taman Rainbow, Jalan Ipoh, together with a warning letter containing threatening words but Teresa's parents and her siblings were not in the house and nobody was hurt.

What was rather unexpected was the release of Raja Petra on 7 November by the Shah Alam High Court after he had spent just over a month in Kamunting. The High Court ruled that the detention of Raja Petra under the ISA was illegal and ordered his immediate release. Judge Syed Ahmad Helmy Syed Ahmad said that Raja Petra's detention was unconstitutional and that the home minister had erred procedurally under Section 8 of the ISA to issue the detention order against Raja Petra.[20] Raja Petra, 58, had named the Home Minister as the defendant in the habeas corpus application which sought among others for his immediate release and an order that his detention under the ISA was unlawful.

The minister had given three reasons for Raja Petra's detention, namely, that he owns and operates the *Malaysia Today* website and published articles and readers' comments intentionally and recklessly which were critical of and insulting to Muslims, affecting the purity of their religion and the personality of Prophet Muhammad; published articles deemed defamatory or false concerning Malaysia's leaders, with the intention of undermining public confidence and inciting hatred against the government; and that these articles are alleged to be a threat to national security. The articles in question were "Malays, the Enemy of Islam", "Let's send the Altantuya murderers to hell", "I promise to be a good, non-hypocritical Muslim" and "Not all Arabs are descendents of the Prophet".[21]

It seems evident from the ISA detentions of Tan, Kok and Raja Petra that the UMNO-led government remained insensitive or impenetrable to the idiom of new politics ushered in by the 8 March General Election. The use of the draconian ISA against political opponents, for that matter, politicised trials such as the sodomy charge against Anwar Ibrahim, increases the government's credibility gap and tends to reinforce a public's declining confidence in government institutions such as the police or the judiciary. The Home Minister's own reasoning that the ISA detention of the Sin Chew journalist was to "protect" her was the butt of considerable public ridicule. Civil society groups have reacted to the draconian moves of the Home Minister by organizing such events as candlelight vigils, peaceful protests and signature campaigns. Spokespersons of the Gerakan have also called for the reform of the ISA.[22] Undoubtedly, political parties within the government coalition, such as Gerakan, MIC and MCA, are uncomfortable with the use of the ISA on these recent occasions.

A Minister's Resignation

As a matter of fact, the Abdullah government's use of the ISA in September directly led to the resignation of de facto Law Minister Zaid Ibrahim proving that the new idiom of politics had made inroads into UMNO itself. In a thoughtful open letter to the Prime Minister, on 30 September, Zaid wrote that events of the last three weeks compelled him to review his position within the government and that the way in which the ISA had been used led him to the conclusion that "the government had time and time again failed the people of this country in repeatedly reneging on that solemn promise made by Tunku Abdul Rahman", which he cited as follows:

> My cabinet colleagues and I gave a solemn promise to Parliament and the nation that the immense powers given to the government under the

ISA would never be used to stifle legitimate opposition and silent lawful dissent.[23]

In his letter, Zaid listed the many times Malaysian governments (including that of the Tunku) reneged on this promise, mentioning in particular its recent use by Abdullah on the HINDRAF 5 and on Tan, Kok and Raja Petra. He opined:

> Malaysians today want to see a government that is committed to the court process to determine guilt or innocence even for alleged acts of incitement of racial or religious sentiment. They are less willing to believe, as they once did, that a single individual, namely the minister of home affairs, knows best about matters of national security.[24]

Zaid goes on to write about his failure to bring about the sort of judicial reform he was trying to advocate in the Abdullah government. High on his list of priorities was the reinstatement of "judicial review" as a concept and practice which was virtually removed by the 1988 constitutional amendment during the Mahathir era after Operation Lalang. He writes that he sought to introduce the means by which steps could be taken to assist the judiciary to regain its reputation for independence and competence but "unfortunately, this was viewed as undesirable by some since an independent judiciary would mean that the executive would be less 'influential'."[25] Not long after writing this letter, Zaid Ibrahim was sacked from UMNO.[26]

Before his resignation, Zaid did try to salvage or repair the reputation of former Lord President Tun Salleh Abas and five other former supreme court judges of the Mahathir period. But even this attempt at resuscitation of the judiciary turned awry. In a dinner in April attended by the Bar Council and politicians, on the urging of Zaid, the Prime Minister made ex-gratia payments to these judges for the injustice meted out to them by the Mahathir government. Abdullah said that their pain and loss could not really be compensated by monetary payments although the Prime Minister would not apologise for the events of 1988. Apart from Salleh Abas, a second judge, Azmi Kamaruddin, and families of the other four judges were at hand. At the same event, the Prime Minister announced that he would set up a Judicial Appointments Commission. However, later developments soured Zaid's efforts when the amount of the ex-gratia payments was announced even though Zaid had promised not to do so in deference to the ex-judges and their families.[27]

Any form of judicial repair was further damaged by the controversial appointment of a new Chief Justice in Tan Sri Zaki Tun Azmi on 21 October who succeeded Datuk Abdul Hamid Mohamad. Zaki's appointment has been criticized by the DAP citing his swift promotion and the fact that he had been a legal adviser to the UMNO. Opposition Member of Parliament Karpal Singh said he was in possession of an audio recording of what Zaki allegedly said to the media: "It took me six months to be nice, to bribe each and every individual to get back into their good books before our files were being attended to." Zaki later issued a clarification, published in *New Straits Times* on 9 November, saying that the reporter misinterpreted what he said. He said "I have never in my life bribed or received any bribe."[28] Karpal has persisted in calling for Zaki to step down from his Chief Justice post and has upbraided the Bar Council for not objecting to Zaki's appointment.[29]

UMNO Transition

Ever since the Barisan Nasional's disastrous showing on 8 March, the likes of Mahathir and Tengku Razaleigh had been calling for Abdullah Badawi to step down as President of UMNO. The Kelantan politician-prince immediately offered himself as candidate for the UMNO presidency in the UMNO polls originally due for December. Abdullah managed to resist these calls until his own minister Muhyiddin Yassin also threw down the gauntlet in early May, stating that he was willing to contest one of the two top positions in the December UMNO polls.[30] The Minister for International Trade and Industry subsequently decided only to contest the Number Two spot. This left Najib Razak with only Tengku Razaleigh to take on but the latter's bid fizzled out in November when Najib's massive accumulation of nominations shut out any challenger. Meanwhile, UMNO provided a face-saving device for Abdullah when it postponed the polls till March 2009. Abdullah has indicated that he will not contest the presidency in March.[31] The UMNO contestants to key posts, with the requisite number of nominations, at the point of writing are as follows:

President:	Najib Tun Razak
Deputy President:	Muhyiddin Yassin, Ali Rustam, Muhammad Muhd Taib
Vice Presidents (3):	Hishammuddin Hussein, Ahmad Zahid Hamidi, Khaled Nordin, Shafie Apdal, Syed Hamid Albar, Mohd Isa Samad, Jamaluddin Jarjis, Rais Yatim, Rahim Tambi Cik
UMNO Youth Chief:	Mukhriz Mahathir, Khairy Jammaluddin, Mohd Khir Toyo
Wanita Chief:	Rafidah Aziz, Shahrizat Abdul Jalil

Abdullah Badawi has turned out to be the biggest casualty of the 8 March political tsunami and will step down in March 2009 in favour of the incoming UMNO president Najib Razak. Another casualty in the future may be the political fortunes of Abdullah's son-in-law, Khairy Jamaluddin, who at the time of writing trails far behind Mukhriz in nominantions.[32] With such major changes to the Malay political landscape, one could expect some political ramifications for Malaysian politics in 2009 such as a cabinet reshuffle with Najib loyalists. However, whatever happens at the March 2009 party gathering, UMNO's position of primacy within the ruling coalition is unlikely to change. The new leadership is likely to see the continued influence (if not interference) of former Prime Minister Mahathir Mohamad. Moreover, if his son, Mukhriz, assumes the leadership of the UMNO Youth Movement, he would act as a natural conduit for his father's continued presence and influence in UMNO. Najib, as UMNO's new leader with his likely deputy Muhyiddin Yassin are bound to be more accommodating to Mahathir and his ideas as compared to Abdullah Badawi before.

Coping with the Economic Downturn

Unlike the political realm, the economy has seen less turbulence. This notwithstanding, the Malaysian budget announced in September 2007 was clearly already in need of adjustment by the middle of 2008. The first change came with the anticipated petrol and diesel price hikes in June, post-general election. Pump prices for petrol went up by 40 per cent to RM2.70 while diesel shot up by 63 per cent to RM2.58 leading to several street demonstrations, organized by the Opposition and other groups. The unpopular hikes were nonetheless sweetened by cash rebates and a road tax reduction for smaller cars. By the end of 2008, owing to the severe plummeting of oil prices, petrol and diesel prices returned to almost 2007 levels. Declining oil prices would however have a negative impact for the profits of Petronas, the national oil corporation, which is known to take up the financial slack in periods of economic crisis.

Towards the end of 2008, the most serious problem for the government was the slowdown in the economy as a result of the global economic crisis. While Malaysia is not expected to go into recession in 2009, with its anticipated marked down growth of 3.5 per cent, the Malaysian bourse and the economy in general have already taken some hard knocks. The new Finance Minister Najib Razak, first announced in November, an injection of RM5 billion into the stock market through the government's Valuecap corporation.[33] The funds were to be sourced from the Employees Provident Fund (EPF), a move which invariably sparked a hue and cry by Opposition figures. The second measure came with the tabling of the 2009 budget, also in November by Najib, in which he announced a stimulus package of RM7 billion for the economy. Targeted programmes included low- and medium-cost housing, maintenance works, building schools, skills re-training, public transport, investment funding and broadband upgrading.[34]

As the year drew to a close, critics have suggested that Abdullah's regional economic corridors, proposed in the Ninth Malaysia Plan, may have become darkened alleys with little hope that economic activity will take off anytime in the near future.[35] This said, there were upbeat reports that the southern economic corridor, known as the Iskandar Development Area (IDR), and more recently just as Iskandar Malaysia, has seen some spectacular promises of investments and projects.[36] Some multiples of billions in overall investments are anticipated soon and Newcastle University has announced plans to set up the Newcastle University of Medicine (NUMed) in IDR by 2011.[37]

Foreign Policy

Since he took over Prime Minister, Abdullah Badawi was never quite able to fend off his predecessor's periodic outbursts against his policies. Mahathir's criticism of Abdullah was particularly evident with respect to foreign policy issues, especially in Abdullah's softer and more open polices towards such countries as the U.S., Australia and Singapore. Mahathir was especially acerbic about Abdullah's softening of relations with Singapore and matters hit the ceiling when the Abdullah government in 2005 scuttled the Scenic or Crooked Bridge project of Mahathir. When the IDR was launched in 2007, Mahathir had pounced on this development, at one point stating that it was a bridgehead for Singaporean and Israeli penetration. To the Abdullah government's credit, a first joint Ministerial Committee (JMC) meeting on the IDR was held with Singaporean counterparts in July 2007 although nothing much seems to have developed in 2008. However, as noted earlier, Iskandar Malaysia may now become the most important of the economic corridors and the gateway not just for Singaporean investment but also for inflows of Arab and other sources of finance. It is unlikely that the UMNO-led government will pay too much attention to the Northern Economic Corridor, lodged within Opposition territory.

For the most part of 2008 domestic issues seem to trump foreign policy questions except for the Pulau Batu Puteh/Pedra Branca decision of the International Court of Justice (ICJ) on 23 May, which had more than a minor ripple effect domestically. The ICJ ruled that Pedra Branca belonged to Singapore but that the outcrop known as Middle Rocks was Malaysia's. It left South Ledge, another outcrop, to be determined by negotiations between the two countries. Newly anointed Foreign Minister Rais Yatim (since March 2008), called the ICJ decision a "win-win" outcome although privately Wisma Putra circles as well as UMNO politicos were clearly smarting over the ICJ decision. There was also probably unnecessary worry that other islands like Pulau Pisang, near Johor, will also suffer the fate of Pulau Batu Puteh. By August, Rais Yatim assured Malaysians that the government was doing its best to establish its territorial waters as well as its Economic Exclusive Zone (EEZ) in negotiations with Singapore and that a joint committee of the two countries had already met twice.[38]

The Closing of the Abdullah Era

It is fitting that one ends with a section on the denouement of the Abdullah Badawi tenure. Abdullah's final curtain closes with the tabling of three bills to recoup a severely dented reputation and to presumably bestow some kind of belated legacy to his tenure as the fifth prime minister of Malaysia. The bills, presented in quick session during the December sitting of Parliament, were: the Malaysian Commission on Anti-Corruption (MCAC) Bill, Judicial Appointments Commission (JAC) Bill and the Special Complaints Commission (SCC) Bill. Had such bills been tabled during his earlier term, he may have been spared the criticism of doing too little too late. The SCC is now lambasted by critics as the watered-down version of the Independent Police Complaints and Misconduct Commission (IPCMC) submitted three years ago after a veritable study by a Royal Commission. Abdullah's failure to implement this was one of his egregious failures which cost the BN many votes on 8 March. The JAC is Abdullah's supposed answer to judicial reform which we have discussed at some length above but the legislation has now been critiqued for its various flaws, in particular the stipulation that judicial appointments still have to be ultimately screened by the Prime Minister.[39] Finally, the MCAC has been criticized for the requirement that corruption charges have to be made via the Attorney General's office and that the new commission, replacing the ACA, still has no power of prosecution.

It may be Abdullah's unfortunate fate that history may judge him harshly as the leader who showed more promise than he had the capacity to fulfill. Even on the question of foreign policy, Abdullah who began self-assuredly by debunking some Mahathirist stances and policies, unfortunately ended with even scandals[40] and with the personally damaging loss of a piece of territory, Pulau

Batu Puteh/Pedra Branca, to Singapore.[41] Worse, Abdullah's administration is now held responsible for the massive landslide on 6 December which saw five people killed and thousands evacuated at Bukit Antarabangsa, an up-market residential spot near Kuala Lumpur.[42]

Furthermore, two major unresolved issues will continue to exercise Malaysian political actors whether in government, opposition or civil society. First would be detention under the Internal Security Act (ISA) of five Hindu Rights Action Force (HINDRAF) leaders. Civil society groups and the opposition will continue to press for their release and the debunking of the ISA, while the credibility and legitimacy of the Malaysian Indian Congress (MIC) and its leader, Samy Vellu will remain in limbo until the HINDRAF issue is resolved. Malaysia has the dubious distinction of two persons "missing in action" abroad, *personae non grata* Waytha Moorthy of HINDRAF and P. Balasubramaniam, the private detective who made a statutory declaration about Najib Razak and his association with the murdered Mongolian model, Altantuya Shaariibuu.

The second serious issue in the immediate post-Abdullah period could be the progression of the Altantuya murder trial and the Anwar sodomy trial. Despite the unexpected acquittal on 31 October of political analyst Razak Baginda for abetment, a long trial may ensue for the two other accused whose defence has been called. This could still have grave implications for the new Prime Minister Najib Razak as the two who will be in the dock were special police officers assigned to Najib as Deputy Prime Minister. Similarly, the course and outcome of Anwar's sodomy trial will not only affect his own political fortunes but also his leadership of the People's Pact. Abdullah has left Malaysia with an uncertain political future. Both the leaders of the government and the opposition will have unpredictable political trajectories in 2009 and beyond. Who will navigate through the political minefields and emerge as the victor? As Malaysians edge gingerly into 2009, a still fluid and uncertain political scenario awaits them. What is certain is that the political terrain has palpably shifted after 8 March and politics of the old mould would have become ineffectual.

Notes

[1] The video clip showed lawyer V.K. Lingam allegedly speaking to former Chief Justice Fairuz Abdul Halim about his appointment as Chief Justice of the Federal Court. A commission of inquiry found the video to be authentic but till date, no action has been taken on the matter.

[2] Most pundits could not see the Opposition winning more than 40 seats. At a pre-election seminar in ISEAS, two days before polling day, main speaker Dato' Dr

Michael Yeoh of the Malaysian think-tank ASLI and other speakers were confident that the BN would retain its two-thirds majority.

3   Cf. Ooi, Saravanamuttu and Lee, *March 8: Eclipsing May 13* (Singapore: Institute of Southeast Asian Studies, 2008).

4   See Ooi's "the Opposition's Year of Living Demonstratively", in Ibid, pp. 17–20.

5   See Maznah Mohamad, "Malaysia: Democracy and the End of Ethnic Politics? *Australian Journal of International Affairs*, vol. 62, no. 4 (December 2008): 446.

6   This is the thesis proffered by Lee (Ooi et al. 2008, pp. 113–14).

7   See Lee's analysis of the Kuala Lumpur voting (Ooi et al. 2008, pp. 92–103).

8   On 17 July 2008, MCA former women's wing deputy chief and former cabinet minister, Tan Yee Kew, quit her party and in August joined the PKR with 1,700 supporters <http://anilnetto.com/malaysian-elections/tan-yee-kew-and-1700-mca-members-cross-over-to-pkr/>.

9   Dompok raised these issues in a 21-page keynote policy address in his party's 12th triennial meeting in October 2008 ("Dompok: Tide against BN in Sabah", *Malaysiakini*, 12 October 2008).

10 See Lim's statement in Malaysiakini.com, 21 December 2008 <http://www.malaysiakini.com/news/95227> (accessed 29 December 2008).

11 The threat of crossovers remains possible although Opposition leader Anwar Ibrahim appears to have dropped the idea, as will suggested in the section below.

12 Najib made this announcement on 4 November. The government had earlier also announced that there would be an injection of RM5 billion into Malaysian Bourse, the money being sourced from the Employees Provident Fund (EPF). *Malaysian Insider*, 4 November 2008. <http://www.themalaysianinsider.com/index.php/malaysia/11792-najib-epf-loan-to-valuecap-is-guaranteed-by-government> (accessed 29 December 2008).

13 I have sourced most of this set events from Wikipedia and corroborated them with other news reports, especially in Malaysiankini.com.

14 The Turkish Embassy denied that they were granting Anwar asylum.

15 Although there are 82 seats on the Opposition bench, one is held by an independent, Ibrahim Ali, MP for Pasir Mas, Kelantan.

16 Tian Chua said this when he was met by reporters at the KL International Airport before boarding, with five others, a 2.20 p.m. China Airlines flight to Taiwan on 12 September. See *The Star*, 3 September 2008.

17 I have made such an argument elsewhere. See "Are Malaysian Parliamentarians caught in a Prisoner's Dilemma?", *Opinion Asia*, 11 September 2008.

18 Compare this to Zaid Ibrahim's sacking. See below.

19 Kok's retained the Seputeh constituency with a majority of 36,492 votes.

20 See *Malaysiakini*, 7 November 2008 <http://www.malaysiakini.com/news/92620> (accessed 29 December 2008).

21 See Ibid.

22 Newly elected Gerakan president Koh Tsu Koon in October called for the government to expedite reforms to avoid a repeat of 8 March. Among others, he called for a judicial commission and reforms to the Internal Security Act (ISA), Printing Presses and Publications Act (PPPA) and the University and University Colleges Act (UUCA). See *Malaysiakini*, 11 October 2008 <http://www.malaysiakini.com/news/91078> (accessed 29 December 2008).

23 Zaid's open letter was carried in full by *Malaysiakini* <http://www.malaysiakini.com/news/90602> (accessed 30 December 2008).

24 Ibid.

25 Ibid.

26 On 2 December, the UMNO Supreme Council rescinded Zaid's membership in UMNO. Zaid has complained that he was not given a chance to defend himself and that UMNO practised a double standard <http://www.malaysiakini.com/news/94294> (accessed 30 December 2008).

27 Minister Mohd Nazri Aziz revealed that RM10.5 million was paid out and also insisted that the judges were not sacked and were paid government pensions. Salleh Abas received the largest amount of RM5 million <http://www.malaysiakini.com/news/92589> (accessed 30 December 2008).

28 As reported in *The Sun* <http://www.thesundaily.com/article.cfm?id=27751> (accessed 30 December 2008).

29 See report in *The Sun*, Ibid.

30 See *The Star* <http://thestar.com.my/news/story.asp?file=/2008/5/11/nation/21218890&sec=nation> (accessed 30 December 2008).

31 Najib Tun Razak had practically won the presidency with 134 nominations out of a possible 191 and would make him prime-minister-in-waiting. He will assume the UMNO presidency at the general assembly scheduled for 24–28 March 2009.

32 Mukhriz has obtained 63 nominations while Khairy has secured 36.

33 Valuecap Snd Bhd was set up in 2003 primarily to invest in the stock market. See *The Malaysian Insider*, 11 November 2008 <http://www.themalaysianinsider.com/index.php/malaysia/12190-valuecap-shareholders-to-refinance-rm51b-loan> (accessed 12 January 2009).

34 *Malaysiakini*, 4 November 2008 <http://www.malaysiakini.com/news/92461> (accessed 12 January 2009).

35 See Denis Hew, "The Malaysian Economy: Developments and Challenges", *Southeast Asian Affairs 2008* (Singapore: Institute of Southeast Asian Studies, 2008), pp. 217–20, for a discussion of the economic corridors including the IDR.

36 Johor Menteri Besar Abdul Ghani Othman announced in July that he was visiting Dubai with representatives of some 100 companies; a figure of RM38 billion in investments was mentioned. The Iskandar official webpage, citing the MB, states that in the first two years RM40.25 billion in investments was secured <http://www.irda.com.my/media-news.aspx?mid=7&smid=28&cid=0&itmid=285&title=Iskanda

r%20Malaysia%20In%20Great%20Shape,%20says%20MB> (accessed 12 January 2009).

37   *Bernama*, 14 November 2008 <http://www.bernama.com.my/bernama/v3/news_lite. php?id=371779> (accessed 12 January 2009).

38   *The Star*, 8 August 2008.

39   See the studied analysis of its various provisions, including those problems related to the central idea of a nine-member commission, by constitutional expert Shad Saleem Faruqi in his column, *Reflecting on the law*, "Many unanswered questions", *The Star*, 31 December 2008. Faruqi says that "the law is adroitly silent" on whether the PM is bound by the JAC's nominations.

40   The oil-for-food issue involving relatives and the transporting of centrifuges by a company headed by his son are two examples.

41   However, one should note that the agreement to have the Pulau Batu Puteh/Pedra Branca dispute adjudicated by the ICJ was already decided during the Mahathir period.

42   Derived from various news reports.

Myanmar

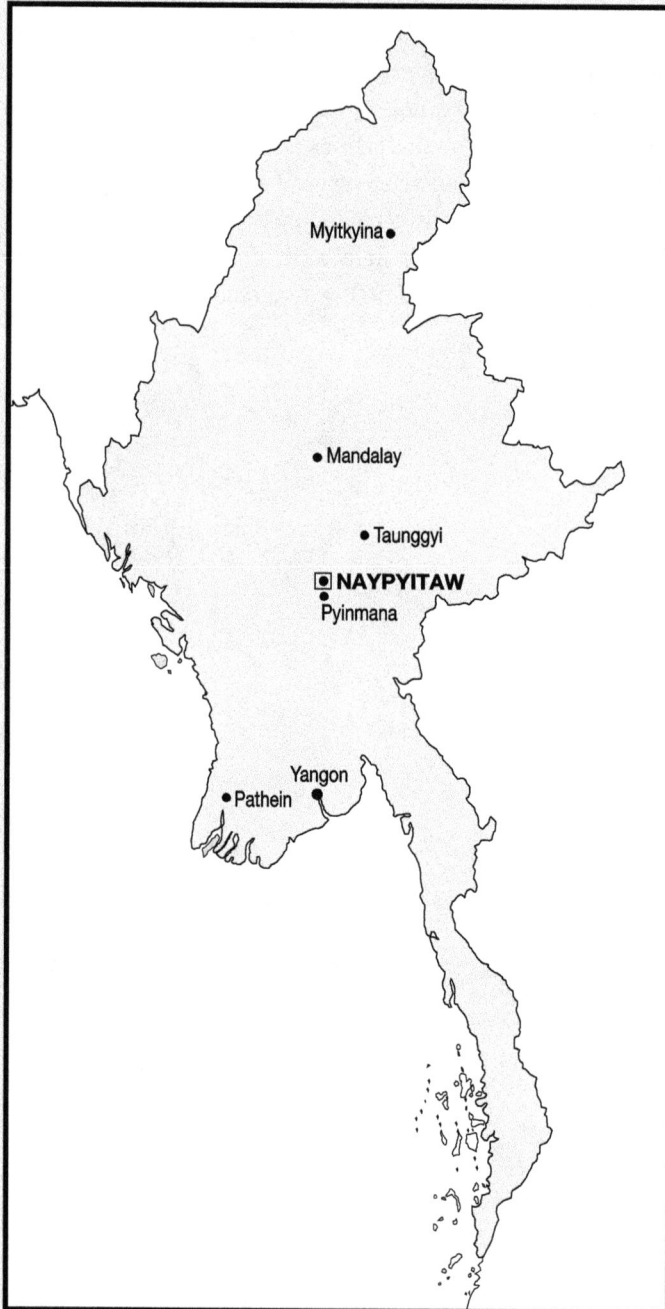

MYANMAR in 2008
Weathering the Storm

TIN MAUNG MAUNG THAN

The most significant events for Myanmar in the year 2008 were the devastating tropical Cyclone Nargis that wreaked havoc in the former capital Yangon and the Ayeyarwady Delta and the constitutional referendum that was conducted soon after the disaster. Both elicited strong emotional responses from the military government's detractors at home and abroad. In fact, the tragedy brought about by Nargis provoked a storm of protest and angry calls for humanitarian intervention from opposition groups, human rights advocates, and (mainly) Western politicians over the military government's seemingly lethargic response in the storm's aftermath and its attempts to control the flow of international aid as well as access to affected areas. At the same time, the timing of the referendum that was organized in two stages during the same month in which Nargis struck as well as the overwhelming (over 92 per cent) proportion of affirmative votes led to accusations of callousness and allegations of vote rigging on the government's part.

On the other hand, the extent of the devastation that required a sustained and massive relief and rehabilitation effort led to the active involvement of the United Nations (UN) — through the personal diplomacy of Secretary-General Ban Ki-moon — and ASEAN (Association of Southeast Asian Nations) in a tripartite arrangement with the Myanmar government to coordinate and oversee damage assessments as well as international assistance in personnel, money and material. Consequently, an opportunity was created for local civil society organizations (CSO), general public, and INGOs (international non-governmental organizations) to take part in a monumental effort aimed at helping the victims of Nargis. To some observers, this augurs well for the development of civil society in Myanmar.

TIN MAUNG MAUNG THAN is a Senior Fellow at the Institute of Southeast Asian Studies (ISEAS), Singapore.

Meanwhile, skeptics and critics continued to harp on the lack of progress in political dialogue between the government and the political opposition and the continued detention of opposition icon Daw Aung San Suu Kyi. Moreover, allegations of forced labour, ill-treatment of political prisoners, internal displacement, and religious persecution persisted while the United Nations Secretary-General's special advisor Professor Ibrahim Gambari failed to garner concessions from the government on issues relating to the release of Aung San Suu Kyi and 'political prisoners', political dialogue between the protagonists and an all 'inclusive' political process.

On the economic front, foreign trade continued to expand. With exports buoyed by natural gas sales to Thailand, Myanmar registered a huge trade surplus in spite of the fall in commodity prices in the last quarter of 2008. As a result, the foreign exchange reserves reached an all time high. Despite Western economic sanctions a substantial amount of foreign direct investment (FDI) proposed by investors from mainly regional states was approved. On the other hand, the growth of the domestic economy appeared to have slowed down though the full impact of the global economic crisis that exploded in the last quarter of the year had yet to manifest in Myanmar whose exposure to the global economy was perhaps the least among the ten ASEAN economies.

Nargis: More than a Storm?

The tropical cyclone, named Nargis, which formed in the Bay of Bengal took almost a week to reach Myanmar's shores. During the night of 2 May and the next morning, it battered the Ayeyarwady Delta with winds of up to 200 kilometres per hour and a 3.6 metre high storm surge that swept everything in its path across hundreds of kilometres inshore over flat plains inhabited mainly by families engaged in agriculture, fishing, and salt production. Though there were regular warnings issued by the state meteorological agency about the impending storm through radio, television and newspapers the significance of such warnings apparently went unheeded by the majority of the potential victims either because they had no means of receiving real time warnings or they remained unperturbed as they had never encountered such fury in their living memory and had weathered many lesser storms and tides. Given the extreme rarity of such an event the government also had little experience in taking preventive measures to minimize losses. Myanmar, unlike Bangladesh that usually bore the brunt of tropical storms, lacked a dedicated warning and shelter system. As a result, there were unprecedented and huge human and material losses estimated as:[1]

- 2.4 million people affected with 800,000 internally displaced
- 84,537 dead, 53,836 missing (presumed dead) and 19,359 injured
- 450,000 housing units totally destroyed; 350,000 damaged
- 50–60 per cent of public schools damaged or destroyed
- 75 per cent of health facilities damaged
- Damage amounting to around US$1.75 billion and losses (reduction in economic activity) estimated at US$2.26 to US2.38 billion (taken together the total came to about 21 per cent of Myanmar's gross domestic product for the previous fiscal year).
- Over 1.3 million acres of farmland flooded with saltwater.

But it turned out to be more than a straightforward case of coping with natural disaster given the long history of contention between the regime and its detractors, especially those in the West. Opposition groups, humanitarian and human rights lobbies, international non-governmental organizations, Western politicians and governments all seized the opportunity to kick up a storm of criticisms, protests and condemnations over the speed, scope and manner of the government's response to Nargis.[2] Many were reacting emotionally to vivid images of storm victims and physical damage obtained by foreign news media as well as those posted over the Internet by individual 'netizens' and bloggers. The government was accused of delaying the deployment of its vast military machine for relief and rescue operations and condemned for not allowing unrestricted influx of foreign relief workers, journalists and military personnel as well as direct relief operations by a United States naval flotilla and a French naval vessel.[3] The critics alleged that thousands who could have been rescued in a full scale and concerted international effort had perished and presumed that thousands more were dying as the rescue effort proceeded without an open invitation to outside help that would bring in quickly the much-needed expertise, appropriate equipment and adequate logistic support. As such, complaints arose against the denial of unfettered access to affected areas and restrictions on distribution of relief supplies. The French foreign minister even attempted to invoke the UN's "responsibility to protect" to justify humanitarian intervention without Myanmar's consent but it failed to get any support from the international community.[4] Further contentious issues included concerns over profiteering from exchange rate differences in currency conversion,[5] alleged eviction of cyclone victims from places of temporary refuge and arrests of some political activists engaged in relief work. The junta was also criticized for not postponing the constitutional referendum scheduled for 10 May.

On the other hand, regional states and neighbouring countries were more supportive of the regime's effort, promptly sending rescue teams and material assistance without any fuss or strings attached.[6] They did not question the SPDC's rules and regulations set up by the government in the Nargis response and strictly observed the "non-interference" principle in the internal affairs of Myanmar. Local offices of the United Nations Development Programme (UNDP) and other specialized agencies of the UN such as UNICEF, FAO, and WHO as well as many INGOs like Save the Children and Medicin Sans Frontieres which were already working in Myanmar also responded quickly in cooperation with their counterpart government organizations.

On its part, the SPDC activated the National Disaster Preparedness Central Committee (NDPCC, established in 2005) under Prime Minister General Thein Sein and subsequently formed ten functional Emergency Disaster Response Sub-Committees to oversee operational tasks in various sectors relating to the overall disaster response. The government immediately sanctioned an emergency Kyats 50 billion (about US$45.5 million at market exchange rate) in emergency funds and tasked selected ministers and military commanders to spearhead the relief effort mobilizing two light infantry divisions with support from naval and air force units as well as GONGOs (government organized non-governmental organizations) such as the USDA (Union Solidarity and Development Association), Myanmar Red Cross and Myanmar Medical Association. The Government agencies were also directed to provide construction materials and other necessary commodities at special prices. Tariffs on imports of construction materials were waived and private companies were allowed to import diesel fuel (hitherto a state monopoly) to ease the fuel shortage. Donations from the general public were also solicited and the overwhelming response of the people resulted in a registered total of some Kyats 13 billon in cash and kind in the first seven weeks notwithstanding an unknown amount (believed to be as large) of individual direct assistance that bypassed official channels and went unrecorded. The government also tasked prominent local business enterprises in the relief and rehabilitation work and the entire business community offered donations as well as their services in kind totalling some US$58 million in value within two months.[7] The government had also warned the well-wishers about the dangers of indiscriminate aid that could lead to the development of a 'crutch mentality' among the traumatized victims. Meanwhile, on 18 May, the SPDC Chairman Senior General Than Shwe toured the affected areas for the first time and met some of the survivors. On 19 May, the SPDC announced a three-day mourning period for the victims of Nargis, beginning 20 May.

Even though Myanmar had rebuffed attempts by the United States (U.S.) and France to conduct direct relief operations and did not allow their naval vessels to enter its territorial waters, airlifting of supplies by both military and civilian aircraft to Yangon Mingladon Airport were permitted as international aid began to arrive on 7 May. In fact, the U.S. military flew 185 airlift sorties with military aircraft from 12 May to 22 June.[8]

On the international front, the UN Secretary-General (UNSG) and the ASEAN Secretary-General (Sec-Gen) Surin Pitsuwan went to great lengths to extend their offers for help, urging the regime to swiftly facilitate the inflow of relief personnel and material aid as the SPDC and its (mainly) Western critics were in contention over the rules, regulations and modalities of international assistance, especially the restrictions on granting visas to foreign aid workers. The ASEAN Committee on Disaster Management dispatched the ASEAN Emergency Rapid Assessment Team (ERAT) to Myanmar a week after the disaster (9–18 May) to assist the UN team and Myanmar officials in the field. ASEAN convened a ministerial meeting on 19 May and persuaded the regime to accept the formation of the "ASEAN Humanitarian Task Force for the Victims of Cyclone Nargis" (AHTF) led by the ASEAN Sec-Gen who then went to Myanmar to meet Myanmar's Prime Minister on 21 May. The UN, on 9 May, launched a "flash appeal" amounting to US$200 million for immediate relief and the UNSG paid a visit to Myanmar on 22 May and called upon Senior General Than Shwe on the next day where he obtained the consent to allow the entry of "all" aid workers into the country. An international (aid) pledging conference followed on 25 May attended by 51 countries, 24 UN agencies, INGOs and international multilateral lending agencies. The Tripartite Core Group (TCG) chaired by Myanmar and comprising altogether nine representatives from the Myanmar government, the United Nations and the ASEAN Secretariat was also set up following the pledging conference. Subsequently, the Advisory Group to the AHTF was also set up with representatives from China, India and Bangladesh, the UN, the Red Cross and the Red Crescent, the World Bank, the Asian Development Bank and INGOs.[9]

The economic damage and losses, though considerable, were not so crippling as to force a crisis situation that could lead to serious unrest. Despite the popular notion of being Myanmar's rice bowl the Ayeyarwady Division, in 2007, produced only 22 per cent of total paddy production from 3.7 million acres of monsoon acreage and 0.58 million acres of summer harvest.[10] The amount of lost paddy was estimated to be equivalent to less than 10 per cent of the annual harvest and the government had held on to its buffer stock while putting a moratorium on private rice exports and controlling the domestic flow of rice. This averted a steep rise in rice prices in the following months. Losses of draft cattle and buffalo could be around 10 per cent of the national stock and could not be easily replenished. Tens of thousands of farm, fishery and salt workers were lost while many small business enterprises were wiped out. The task to rebuild businesses and replace lost workers would be formidable but it could be an opportunity for returning migrant workers from neighbouring countries who lost their livelihood to the impact of global recession. However, the government had been promoting agriculture mechanization as a viable alternative in the face of manpower and draft animal shortfalls despite the overall scarcity of fuel.

It was estimated that Nargis would result in a reduction in the national GDP by about 2.7–2.9 per cent and the cost for a three-year recovery programme to rebuild the shattered regional economy was estimated at around US$1 billion which, though large, is not prohibitive, given that the government has cash reserves estimated to be over US$3 billion and the annual trade surplus reached US$2 billion in the last fiscal year.[11]

Meanwhile the revised UN emergency "flash appeal" for relief and early recovery which stood at US$477 million in December garnered only 64 per cent funding up to 11 December. This could create problems for the vulnerable population amounting to hundreds of thousand who are still dependent on international support.[12]

The Constitutional Referendum

While the Constitution Drafting Commission (set up on 18 October 2007) with 54 members and chaired by the Chief Justice was still formulating the draft constitution based on the detailed principles endorsed by the National Convention (1993–2007) the SPDC made a surprise announcement on 9 February 2008 that a constitutional referendum would be conducted in May with "multi-party democracy general elections" scheduled for 2010. The completion of the draft constitution was eventually announced on 19 February. This was followed, on 26 February, by the promulgation of "The Referendum Law for the Approval of the Draft Constitution" and the formation of a 45-member "Commission for Holding Referendum for the Approval of the Draft Constitution" — chaired yet again by the Chief Justice. On 9 April, it was announced that the referendum would be held on 10 May in conformity with "international standards". Only then, the Myanmar version of the draft constitution went on sale in Yangon. It was apparent from all these successive pronouncements within a short period of two months (leaving little time for the opposition to mount an effective campaign) and the fact that the word "Approval" figured prominently in the titles of referendum law and referendum commission that the junta was determined to ensure that the new state constitution would be adopted, leapfrogging over the political dialogue process aimed at reconciliation between Daw Aung San Suu Kyi (the leader of the opposition National League for Democracy or NLD, the party that won more than 80 per cent of the seats in the 1990 elections; hereafter DASSK) and the government which was initiated in 2007 by Professor Gambari, the special advisor to the UNSG. Calls by Professor Gambari and some Western governments to allow international observers also went unheeded.

Contentious Features in the New State Constitution

The draft constitution drew harsh criticism and calls for rejection by the National League for Democracy (NLD) and other opposition groups, student activists, human rights and democracy advocacy groups and Western governments who accused the SPDC of perpetuating military control under the guise of a civilianized political regime and skewed electoral rules.[13]

The most contentious provisions that appeared unacceptable to those advocating liberal democratic norms are as follows:

- The military's complete autonomy to manage its own affairs (Chapter 1, Basic Principles, article 20);
- Designation of the armed forces Commander-in-Chief (C-in-C) as supreme commander of all armed forces (Chapter 1, Basic Principles, article 20);
- Reserved seats for the military in the form of C-in-C's nominees amounting to 25 per cent of the seats in both houses of the national parliaments (Chapter 4, The Legislature, articles 109 and 141);
- Reserved seats for the military in the form of C-in-C's nominees amounting to one-third of the other elected representatives in the parliaments of the (14) States and Regions comprising the Union (Chapter 4, The Legislature, article 161);
- Reserved positions for the nominees of the C-in-C as ministers and deputy ministers for defence, home affairs and border areas (Chapter 4, The Executive, articles 232 and 234);
- Exemption for military personnel to remain in military service while serving as ministers and deputy ministers whereas civilians have to resign from their positions as parliamentarians or civil servants or suspend their party affiliations (Chapter 4, The Executive, articles 232 and 234);

- The President, after coordinating with the National Defence and Security Council, may declare a national emergency and then hand over executive, legislative and judicial powers to the C-in-C in situations "if there is sufficient reason for a state of emergency to arise that may disintegrate the Union or that may cause the loss of sovereignty, due to acts or attempts to take over the sovereignty of the Union by insurgency, violence and wrongful forcible means" (Chapter 11, Provisions on State of Emergency, articles 417 and 418);
- Requirement for the powerful executive President to be "well acquainted with the affairs of the Union such as political, administrative, economic and military", have twenty years continuous domicile, and be born of full citizen parents. Moreover, the candidate, one of the parents, the spouse, any of the children or his/her spouse must not be a subject or citizen of a foreign country or have sworn allegiance to a foreign country, or enjoy the same privileges and benefits bestowed by the foreign country to its subjects and citizens (Chapter 3, Head of State, article 59);[14]
- The President has the authority to appoint and dismiss ministers and deputy ministers of the national government as well as chief ministers of the (seven) states and (seven) divisions who are going to be heads of provincial governments (Chapter 5, Executive, articles 232, 234, 235 and 264);
- Amendment of any of the major provisions in the constitution can only be made if it secures more than 75 per cent of the votes in the national parliament (a combined upper and lower house) together with more than 50 per cent votes of all eligible voters in a national referendum (Chapter 12, Amendment of the Constitution, article 436);
- An "immunity" clause that protects the junta and all government personnel from being persecuted for any act carried out "in the execution of their respective duties" (Chapter 14, Transitory Provisions, article 445).

The Contest for Votes

The announcement of the time line for the referendum and the elections elicited a deluge of critical comments, protests and condemnations from opposition activists, dissident monk groups, academics, pro-democracy lobbies, non-governmental organizations and political personalities from the West. Virtually all the pro-democracy groups and political parties (with the exception of the National Unity Party which was reincarnation of the disgraced and defunct Burma Socialist Programme Party) found fault in the proposed constitution and tried to campaign for a 'No' vote and the NLD openly endorsed the 'No' campaign on 2 April.

Overseas Myanmar language radio stations, mainly the BBC, VOA, RFA, and DVB as well as the Western media supported the 'No' campaign by broadcasting commentaries, news and interviews that argued against the adoption of the new constitution. Despite the harsh jail sentences (of up to three years) prescribed in the referendum law to deter any opposition moves, the 'No' campaign was waged by shadowy urban activists with sporadic poster and graffiti campaigns, clandestine circulars, symbolic T-shirt displays, some organizing trips into the rural heartland in a game of hide-and-seek with the authorities.[15] However, the silence of DASSK (under house arrest since May 2003), the extremely cautious and self restraining actions (or inaction according to many observers) of the ageing executives at the NLD headquarters and the continued incarceration of the "88 generation" student leaders and prominent democracy and human rights activists since August 2007 seemed to have deprived the vote 'No' movement of an inspiring and effective leadership and it remained patchy and ineffective inside Myanmar until Cyclone Nargis effectively extinguished it.

The government countered by arresting scores of demonstrators and activists, launching a media blitz, mobilizing its 26 million strong USDA and the "Swan Arr Shin" (a quasi-vigilante) members, and marshalling government-sponsored social and professional organizations comprising, *inter alia*, groups such as women, artistes, writers, war veterans and entrepreneurs as well as employing its military and administrative machinery from ministers downwards to ward and village leaders to garner support for a 'Yes' vote. The 2008 referendum law, the 1996 law protecting the constitutional convention and other security laws effectively neutralized any attempt to mobilize the people to reject the new constitution.

Finally, the unprecedented catastrophe brought about by Cyclone Nargis overshadowed the referendum debate as the SPDC refused to postpone it despite calls by many quarters in the light of the unmitigated disaster that warranted full attention and deployment of all available resources and massive international aid.

An Easy Victory

The junta went ahead with the referendum on 10 May except for the 47 townships (40 in Yangon Division and 7 in Ayeyawady Division) severely affected by the cyclone for which the date was postponed to 24 May. On 15 May the referendum commission announced that in the 278 township where the polls were staged there was an extremely high 99.06 per cent turnout with 92.4 per cent of the voters casting their votes in favour of adopting the draft constitution. Only 6.1 per cent voted against the constitution. With only 4.6 million left for the second phase from among the total of 27.4 million eligible voters (age 18 and above) there was no doubt about the success of the government campaign to implement the fourth step of the seven-step road map first unveiled in August 2003 by the then Prime Minister General Khin Nyunt as the only path towards a "discipline flourishing" democracy. Another announcement on 26 May confirmed what was expected: a turnout 93.44 per cent resulted in 92.9 per cent affirmative votes and only 6 per cent negative votes. The outcome was even better than that in the areas unaffected by the cyclone. The consolidated result showed that the overall turnout was 98.12 per cent and the 'Yes' votes comprised 92.48 per cent with only 6.1 per cent voting 'No' among the votes cast. Interestingly, it was also revealed that some 4.6 million votes or 17.3 per cent of the total votes cast were from advanced voting and this category achieved 98.4 per cent affirmative votes.[16] The results are hard to swallow for the regime's critics as they had assumed that much of the polity should have been angry and disillusioned with the government on account of its suppression of the September 2007 demonstrations and the perceived shortcomings in the government's response to Cyclone Nargis disaster.[17] There were allegations of incomplete poll lists and discrepancies in the registries and use of pre-marked voting tickets as well as block votes and proxy votes for USDA members, civil servants, military and security personnel, workers and uniformed groups.[18]

Domestic Politics

The opposition groups at home and abroad, having lost the bid to reject the regime-sponsored constitution in the polls, nevertheless refused to recognize the new constitution. And they continued pushing for negotiations among political stakeholders over the political rules of the game with or without the good offices of the UNSG whose special advisor Professor Gambari has been playing a bridging role between the junta and the opposition (Daw Aung San Suu Kyi in particular). The opposition is dead set against the implementation of the junta's road map towards what it has interpreted as institutionalized military control behind democratic trappings.

The NLD's refrain on the release of its leaders and all political prisoners and initiation of a political dialogue yielded no result in 2008 as had been the case in the past. Not surprisingly the house arrests of DASSK and the NLD vice-chair U Tin U were extended during the year resulting in the usual ritualistic round of deploring and condemning from the regime's adversaries and critics. Changing tack, the NLD released a "special statement" on 22 September in which it reiterated its rejection of the referendum result and called for the convening of a parliament with representatives elected in the May 1990 elections (a recurring demand since 1990) so as to enable it to establish a constitutional review committee (comprising elected representatives, constitutional experts and representatives of the military, ethnic groups and ceasefire groups) that would complete its review process within six months. The only tangible result was a summons from the police chief who reprimanded the NLD chairman and central executive committee members for "inciting the public" and told them they were liable to prosecution.[19] Nevertheless, the NLD had stuck to its position on a constitutional review and refused to contemplate the issue of contesting the 2010 election. Despite the release of several elected parliamentary candidates and some senior party cadres in the mass release of 9002 prisoners (on 23 September) the NLD remained emasculated and lethargic with the conservative executives at the headquarters trying their best to placate the restive grassroots while cautiously avoiding actions that could jeopardize its precarious existence under the watchful eyes of the authorities. Even U Win Tin a top NLD leader who was released from incarceration on 23 September admitted that the future of the NLD appeared dim and indistinct.[20]

On the other hand, the National Unity Party (NUP, refashioned from the Burma Socialist Programme Party that was dissolved at the height of the upheaval in 1988 that ended the Socialist era) accepted the new constitution and the referendum result. The NUP indicated its willingness to play by the SPDC rules and participate in the 2010 elections.

Other stakeholders among the major ceasefire groups like the KIO (Kachin Independence Organization) and NMSP (New Mon State Party) informally expressed their disappointment over the junta's disapproval of their proposals for more institutionalized autonomy but remained ambivalent about taking part in the 2010 elections.[21] Meanwhile, the powerful Wa ethnic ceasefire group (former troops of the defunct Burma Communist Party) also seemed disappointed on its base area not being accorded the status of a state or region in the Union but did not reveal its future course of action in relation to the SPDC road map.[22]

With most of the leading activists from various opposition groups under detention or on the run, opposition attempts to agitate the public had little impact during the year.[23] There were a number of short-lived demonstrations on a small scale as well as dissemination of posters and pamphlets and drawing of graffiti but no major protest occurred on the opposition's commemorative dates including the twentieth anniversary of the so-called 'four-eights' event.[24] The government also demonstrated its resolve to crush any opposition by sentencing prominent figures in the activist movement to long prison terms, while several lawyers defending opposition detainees were jailed for contempt of court or contravening the law.[25]

International Mediation Efforts

Though his predecessor Professor Paulo Sergio Pinheiro did not manage to return to Myanmar towards the end of his tenure, the new UN special rapporteur on human rights Mr Tomas Ojea Quintana who took over the job in April visited Myanmar in August. He seemed to have taken a more realistic position on Myanmar's situation on human rights and democracy and was reported to have said, right from the beginning of his stint, that the "restoration of democracy cannot happen overnight; it will take generations". He apparently placed more emphasis on establishing a rule of law, ensuring independence of the judiciary and "progressive release of all prisoners of conscience" as well as legal training and reforms to enhance human rights. There were no substantive developments in his mandated area in this early phase of establishing confidence with the authorities concerned.[26]

Similarly, Professor Gambari made no progress in his efforts to help reconcile the government with DASSK and encourage the emergence of an all-inclusive political process despite visiting Myanmar in March and August.[27] In fact, during his second visit he tried in vain to meet DASSK who cancelled their meeting in an apparent reflection of her dissatisfaction with his inability to achieve substantive progress. Later he admitted that the outcome of his visit fell below expectations.[28]

The UNSG who confined his mission solely to the issue of international assistance during his visit to Myanmar in the wake of Cyclone Nargis later indicated his wish to return and discuss issues relating to the political transition in Myanmar with the highest authorities in Naypyitaw (the new administrative capital located in Central Myanmar). However, given Gambari's lack of progress and the junta's strong resolve to dismiss any outside attempt to influence its decisions on Myanmar's internal affairs, he believed he could not go "without reasonable expectations of a meaningful outcome" and reiterated that the onus is on the "government to deliver substantive results, including freeing political prisoners and holding a dialogue with Aung San Suu Kyi".[29] Nevertheless, he continued consulting with the so-called "group of friends of Myanmar" comprising the five permanent members of the United Nations Security Council (UNSC), Australia, the European Union (EU), India, Indonesia, Japan, Norway, Singapore, South Korea, Thailand and Vietnam as well as leaders of regional countries which are 'friendly' with Myanmar.[30]

Government and Security Issues

As the SPDC prepared for the 2010 elections and the promised transition to constitutional rule by an elected government, there were minor cabinet changes and some shuffling of the command hierarchy just below the top echelon comprising the Chair, Vice-Chair, Chief of Joint Staff, Prime Minister and Secretary. In June the Navy Chief Vice-Admiral Soe Thein was posted to the ministry of Industry-2 while the incumbent Minister Major General Saw Lwin was shifted to the Ministry of Immigration and Population which was previously one of two ministries under the charge of another minister. The reported military shuffle was more significant in that four senior Lieutenant Generals who were in charge of the Bureaux of Special Operations (BSO, a powerful operational command position) and another who was the Chief of Military Training (all SPDC members), were replaced by younger regional commanders. This led to several promotions to fill the vacancies in regional commands and a reassignment of the commanders of two out of the 13 regional commands. Detractors would like to believe that these reshuffles indicate factionalism and jostling for power but it is more likely that the top leadership was consolidating the command hierarchy in preparation for leadership renewal in the post-2010 transition.[31]

There were a number of bomb explosions in Yangon and even in the environs of Naypyitaw, with the government putting the blame on Kayin insurgents and expatriate dissident organizations comprising former students and self-exiled political activists.[32] On 11 January 2008 a small bomb exploded in the toilet of the railways quarters at Naypyitaw-Pyinmana railway station killing one person. On the 13th of the same month, an explosion next to the public toilet near the ticket office of the Yangon main railway station wounded another. Yangon's central business district was the target of the next round of blasts on the night of 20 April when one explosion took place in the drain of the 36th street at 8 o'clock while another occurred one-and-a-half hours later underneath a saloon car parked in the 32nd street which is just behind the Traders Hotel. However, no one was hurt and no panic was reported. A bomb reportedly exploded at the entrance of the ward level USDA office in Shwepyitha township of Yangon on 1 July without injuring anybody. Another explosion of a time bomb, in the morning of 25 September, near the rubbish dump situated behind the bus stop at the Maha Bandoola Garden (where the Independence monument is located) injured seven persons and security forces had to defuse yet another time bomb attached to a cassette recorder found on a bench of the bus stop just ten feet away from the site of the first explosion. It was reported that there were no casualties from a small explosion in Yankin township of Yangon. However, the explosion on 19 October in a house in Shwepyitha township killed the occupant and later investigations revealed the victim to be a bomb-maker. In fact the authorities found physical evidence at the crime scenes suggesting that the explosions on 19 October and 25 September were related. All in all, apart from a security surge following the incidents, these small explosions in the major cities and elsewhere[33] failed to disrupt the daily life or erode the security situation in urban Myanmar.

The Shan State Army South (SSA-South) and the Karen National Liberation Army (KNLA — armed wing of the KNU or Karen National Union), the last remaining major ethnic armed groups holding out against the government, still refused to give up their armed struggle though the KNU espoused a willingness to consider a political solution to the six decades long conflict. There were some skirmishes with government troops as they continued to employ hit-and-run tactics against security forces and vulnerable targets. The SSA-South under Colonel Yord Serk or Ywet Sitt managed to hold onto their enclaves in the Thai-Myanmar border operating out of five bases.[34] On the other hand, the depleted ranks of the KNLA suffered significant psychological and organizational setbacks when KNU General-Secretary Padoh Mahn Sha Lah Phan was assassinated by two unknown gunmen in Mae Sot (Thailand) on 14 February and KNU Chairman Padoh Saw Ba Thin Sein died of natural causes on 22 May. This resulted in the appointment of the daughter and father team of Naw Zipporah Sein (general-secretary of the KWO or Karen Women's Organization) as Mahn Sha's replacement and the octogenarian General Tamla Baw (KNLA commander and vice-chair) as the new chairman.[35] The KNU seemed more emasculated than ever in its long history of armed struggle.

Narcotics in one of the non-traditional security issues confronting Myanmar and the government has been battling the production and distribution of opium and ATS (amphetamine type substances) all along. The government's opium eradication campaign seemingly supported by ceasefire groups residing in and around the notorious golden triangle had, according to the UNODC (United Nations Office on Drugs and Crime), resulted in substantial reductions in poppy acreage in the decade since 1997 (by around 86 per cent) and a steady downward trend from 2002 (the first year of the Myanmar government/UNODC joint survey) until 2007 when the acreage went up by 29 per cent. In 2008, this upswing continued, albeit slightly (by only 2.9 per cent), probably driven by high prices and lack of viable alternative livelihood for the impoverished farmers in the Kayah and Shan hills. Estimated to involve around 168,000 households and the total potential value of the yield reaching US$123 million, planting poppies remained a major industry in remote areas where the government's opium eradication drive was compromised by terrain, ecology and ceasefire arrangements with the Wa and Kachin ethnic groups.[36]

ATS is more difficult to eradicate than opium because of the synthetic nature of production and the ease of distribution, usually in the form of pills, despite the government's best efforts to block the inflow of precursor chemicals into the country and seize production facilities which are mobile and elusive. One high profile case of ATS abuse emerged during the year when it was revealed that Maung Weik, who was known as a very wealthy construction tycoon, was charged on 10 June together with six other accomplices for use of ectasy and ketamine tablets and distributing 'party drugs' at company functions and birthday parties. Apparently the substance abuse had been going on for about five years with supplies from a Malaysian dealer.[37]

International Affairs

Myanmar's relations with India and China were further enhanced in 2008. Driven by the imperatives of border security, cross-border trading and ever-rising energy demand the two giant neighbours of Myanmar extended economic and technical assistance to Myanmar while increasing their investments in infrastructure development and oil and gas sector, with Myanmar seemingly benefiting from their (at times competitive) attempts to enhance their positions in economic and political relations with the military regime.

Thailand's tumultuous internal political dynamics and the attendant uncertainty did not seem to affect its relations with Myanmar. The latter managed to work with the government of the day in Bangkok and Thailand, with its heavy dependence on Myanmar's natural gas and border trading, also kept the relationship on an even keel throughout the year. The much maligned Myanmar-DPRK (Democratic People's Republic of Korea) relations steadily improved and an agreement to exempt visa requirements for diplomatic and government officials was reached some one year after the resumption of diplomatic relations in 2007. While relations with Cambodia, Laos and Vietnam remained cordial, especially since the CLMV (Cambodia, Laos, Myanmar, and Vietnam) comprised an informal sub-grouping within ASEAN, and all three neighbours seemed to be most sympathetic to Myanmar's stand in its contentions with the West. Relations with Bangladesh, Myanmar's neighbour to the west, appeared to be greatly improved with the three-day visit of SPDC Vice-Chair and Deputy Commander-in-Chief of Tatmadaw (Myanmar Armed Forces) Vice-Senior General Maung Aye to Dhaka from 7 October but turned sour in the following month over a territorial dispute triggered by offshore oil exploration (see next section for details). However, the tensions that flared up were diffused within two weeks through negotiations though the issue was yet to be resolved.

Myanmar's personal diplomacy premised upon the exchange of goodwill and working visits between top leaders and high-level officials was, as usual, quite active during 2008, especially with China and India.[38]

There were a number of exchange visits of high officials between Myanmar and India beginning with Myanmar Foreign Minister's visit to New Delhi on 1 January. Vice-Senior General Maung Aye went to India on the invitation of the Indian Vice-President. This trip from 2 to 6 April resulted in several agreements on avoiding double taxation, preventing tax avoidance, a framework for infrastructure development along the Kaladan River and related protocols, as well as a memorandum of understanding (MoU) on sharing intelligence information between the two countries. India sent its permanent secretary of foreign affairs to Yangon who stayed from 7 to 10 February and again from 22 to 23 November. The Director General of Military Operations came calling with a delegation on 15 March. Other senior Indian military visitors included the Commandant of the National Defence College (6 September) and General Officer Commanding, Eastern Command (21 October).

Myanmar's Prime Minister General Thein Sein led a delegation to attend the opening of the Beijing Olympics on 7 August and also toured Yunnan Province on the way back. The prime minister again led a large delegation to China from 20 to 23 October to attend the Nanning Trade Fair and the China-ASEAN Economic and Investment Meeting. Member of SPDC and Chief of Joint Staff General Thura Shwe Mann led a military delegation to China in November and met the PLA (People's Liberation Army) Chief of General Staff on 29 November in Beijing. The Chinese visitors included the Vice-Chairperson of the Standing Committee of the National People's Congress who arrived on a goodwill mission on 10 January. Other prominent Chinese guests to Myanmar included the PLA Deputy Chief of General Staff whose delegation arrived for a two-day visit on 27 October, the CCP (Chinese Communist Party) delegation led by a member of the political bureau of party Central Committee and party chief of Tianjin municipality which came on a three-day visit from 18 to 20 November, and the foreign minister who arrived on 5 December.

Other high level visits included Thailand Prime Minister Samak who led a goodwill delegation on 14 March, Prime Minister of Kuwait whose delegation was in Myanmar from 6 to 8 August, Vietnamese Minister of Defence who arrived on 11 August, and an Iranian delegation led by its foreign minister.

Myanmar's diplomatic efforts to engage "friendly" countries not only involved high-level visits for bilateral discussions but also attendance at meetings involving various UN specialized agencies, multilateral institutions and sub-regional and regional organizations. The prime minister attended several multilateral meetings that included the fourth summit of CLMV countries and the third ACMES (Ayeyawady-Chao Phraya-Mekong Economic Cooperation Strategy) Summit held in Hanoi in the first week of November and the second BIMSTEC (Bay of Bengal Initiative for Multi-Sectoral Technical and Economic Cooperation) Meeting in New Delhi from 12 to 14 November. U Nyan Win, Myanmar's foreign minister, also attended the ASEAN-MERCUSO (*Mercado Común del Sur* or Southern Common Market), meeting in Brasilia on 23-24 November apart from a series of regular ASEAN ministerial meetings.

Myanmar also applied for observer status to SAARC (South Asian Association for Regional Cooperation) and was formally accepted at the 15th SAARC Summit held in Colombo from 2 to 3 August.[39] The SPDC ratified the ASEAN Charter on 21 July.

Contentious Issues

Korea's Daewoo International which won the tender to explore oil and natural gas at the Arakan offshore plot designated AD-7 began exploration work in September. However Bangladesh, claiming ownership of the site in the Bay of Bengal, demanded immediate cessation of all activities and sent three warships on 1 November (and one more on the 4th) in response to the two Myanmar naval vessels that had been dispatched to escort the Korean exploration rig. Tensions mounted as the Myanmar government rejected Bangladesh's claim as wrong and unlawful. As both sides brought in reinforcements to the border, the foreign secretary of Bangladesh led a delegation to Naypyitaw for discussions. By the second week of November, Myanmar had withdrawn its naval ships and both sides eventually stood down by the month's end though the territorial dispute remained unresolved.[40] Border trade was also disrupted during the stand-off but resumed quickly to attain normality in December.

Despite a substantial reduction in opium production in the last decade and the government's continuous efforts to control the production and distribution of ATS, Myanmar was still put on the "Majors List" of "countries identified as major drug transit or major illicit producing countries" by the United States. President Bush, in a memorandum of 16 September, also designated Myanmar (together with Bolivia and Venezuela) as "countries that have failed demonstrably during the previous 12 months to adhere to their obligations under international counter-narcotics agreements and take the measures" stipulated in the Foreign Relations Authorization Act (Fiscal Year 2003).[41] This had been happening every year and the Myanmar side had always felt that it was politically motivated and resented it.[42]

The sanctions debate continued unabated over the failure of punitive measures to bring about regime change. Nevertheless the U.S. led Western governments and the EU (European Union) maintained their economic sanctions and visa bans on junta-related persons. They even introduced so-called 'smart sanctions' targeting individual entrepreneurs suspected to be linked to the regime and exports of particular goods like gems and timber from Myanmar. For example, the U.S. Treasury Department, on 5 February imposed banking sanctions against U Tay Za (the most prominent tycoon in Myanmar) and several business partners and their companies as well as family members of the military regime.[43] On 1 May President Bush authorized adding some government-owned enterprises to the existing list covered by U.S. financial sanctions.[44] Similarly, the U.S. Senate on 22 July passed the JADE (Junta's Anti-Democratic Efforts) Act already approved by the House on 15 July. This Act prohibited U.S. companies from importing Myanmar gemstones through third parties while legislating financial sanctions against companies directly or indirectly linked to the government. President Bush endorsed the Act as well as the extension of Burma Freedom and Democracy Act of 2003 that banned all direct imports to USA.[45] The U.S. Treasury Department's Office of Foreign Assets Control, on 13 November froze the assets of 17 enterprises and 26 persons in Myanmar who were accused of drug-trafficking.[46] Meanwhile, in September, Switzerland reportedly came on board the existing EU sanctions on Myanmar and Australia announced on 22 October its decision to add 45 new names to the list of some 418 Myanmar individuals named for punishment with financial restrictions.[47]

On the other hand, in the U.N., an attempt by an opposition group to unseat the Myanmar government's representative did not even receive any consideration. The ill-advised effort by the expatriate Members of Parliament Union (Burma) to challenge the credentials of Myanmar government at the 63rd session of the UN

General Assembly by submitting a request to recognize its own representative (an exiled representative who was elected in the May 1990 elections from Mandalay) was rejected as it did not conform to the formal legal requirement of the rules of procedure in which only the government of the day could issue credentials for a country representative.[48]

Issues of human rights and democracy continued to be EU's main concern with Myanmar and its relations with the SPDC remained contentious. These were reflected in the statement of the European Council's Presidency on 20 June in which the EU regretted that "the way the [constitutional] referendum was conducted did not contribute to an inclusive and transparent process of national reconciliation" and reiterated its call for "the release of all political prisoners".[49] Similarly, Council conclusions at its meeting on 10 November 2008 deplored "the lack of progress ... towards a genuine democracy" and pointed out that the forthcoming elections, scheduled for 2010, would "have no credibility unless ... authorities unconditionally release all political prisoners", DASSK in particular "and initiate a political process with [UN] support on the basis of an inclusive, long-term dialogue in which the opposition and ethnic groups can participate fully". Meanwhile, the Council reaffirmed its "firm and unconditional support for" the effort by the UNSG to use his good offices to end "the current deadlock" in Myanmar. On the other hand, it was also stated that the EU "is prepared to revise, amend or reinforce the measures it has already adopted to keep pace with developments in the situation" and "remains ready to react positively to real progress towards democracy".[50]

The meeting of the UNSC, on 2 May 2008, considered the "Situation in Myanmar" and its Presidential statement on behalf of the Council underlined "the need for the Government of Myanmar to establish the conditions and create an atmosphere conducive to an inclusive and credible process [of political transition] including the full participation of all political actors and respect for fundamental political freedoms".[51]

On 11 November, at the 39th meeting of the Third Committee, France introduced a draft resolution on "Situation of human rights in Myanmar". On 21 November, at the 44th meeting, the Myanmar delegation, supported by China and Russia, moved a motion for adjournment of the debate on the draft resolution but was rejected by a vote of 90 to 54, with 34 abstentions. Subsequently, at the next meeting on the same day, the revised draft resolution (A/C.3/63/L.33) was adopted by a vote of 89 to 29 with 63 abstentions. This resolution forwarded to the 63rd Session of the UNGA called upon, *inter alia*, the Myanmar government to "cooperate on humanitarian access in all other [besides areas affected by

Cyclone Nargis] areas of the country" to deliver "assistance to persons in need" and "to cooperate with the international community in order to achieve concrete progress in areas such as human rights and political processes leading to a genuine democratic transition through concrete measures". While welcoming the "steps taken" by Myanmar "in implementing" the agreement between ILO and Myanmar "designed to provide a mechanism to enable victims of forced labour to seek redress" it called upon the government "to engage more actively to eliminate the use of forced labour". Moreover, the resolution emphasized that "without significant progress towards meeting [the] calls of the international community, the situation of human rights in Myanmar will continue to deteriorate" and it also strongly condemned what it deemed to be "ongoing systematic violations of civil, political, economic, social, cultural rights of the people".[52]

Myanmar categorically dismissed all allegations of human rights violations as well as criticisms over its conduct of the constitutional referendum and the implementation of its seven-step road map for political transition. Foreign Minister U Nyan Win, speaking during the general debate of the 63rd session at the UNGA, blamed "unwarranted" punitive sanctions imposed on Myanmar for inhibiting political and social progress. Pointing them out as being "unfair", "immoral" and "counter-productive", he asserted that the "sooner the unjust sanctions are revoked and barriers [to markets, technology and investment] removed, the sooner will the country be in a position to become the rice bowl of the region and a reliable source of energy", in an apparent allusion to the severe food and energy situation confronting the world..[53]

The Economic Situation[54]

The Asian Development Bank (ADB) in its annual Asian Development Outlook for 2008 cautioned that double digit GDP (gross domestic product) growth claimed by the government in recent years was doubtful and "[c]hanges in production inputs such as energy, fertilizer, and capital goods" were more "consistent with modest economic growth".[55] The forecast by the International Monetary Fund (IMF) for economic growth in 2008 was 4 per cent and the Economist Intelligence Unit (EIU) forecast only 0.9 per cent growth for 2008.[56] It was estimated that the Cyclone Nargis could depress the GDP for fiscal year 2008 (April 2008 to March 2009) by 2.7 to 3.1 per cent.[57]

However, the rising trend in external trade continued throughout the year with exports from January to November increasing by some 5.1 per cent year-on-year. The corresponding increase in imports was even higher at 25 per cent, probably driven by international assistance in response to Nargis. The trade surplus for the same eleven-month period was estimated to be around US$2.2 billion. Thailand remained the top destination for Myanmar's exports with its huge demand for Myanmar offshore natural gas, followed by Hong Kong, India and China, with Singapore at fifth place. In the same period, most of Myanmar's imports came from China followed by Singapore and Thailand.

Myanmar's foreign direct investment (FDI), calculated on approved basis, increased by US$975 million (for 5 projects) during the year, reaching a cumulative (since 1989) value up to November of over US$15 billion for over 420 projects.[58] The additional pledges came in the form of 3 projects in oil and gas exploration from Russia and Vietnam and 2 projects in mining (China and Singapore).

In recent years Myanmar had suffered from annual budge deficits with revenues not keeping up with rising expenditures. In 2008 the revenue situation improved significantly with custom duties increasing by over 130 per cent (to Kyats 82 billion)[59] year-on-year in the eleven-month period ending November while the amount of total taxes increased by 37 per cent (to Kyats 908 billion) over the same period.

Consumer price inflation remained a cause for concern as the general consumer price index (C.P.I.) in November registered a 23.5 per cent year-on-year increase though gold prices remained virtually unchanged on average when compared to 2007. Free market prices for diesel and gasoline that had been subjected to rationing rose in the aftermath of Nargis but the government promptly reacted by allowing selected private business organizations to import diesel fuel that eased the demand pressure and stabilized prices. The increased supply and reduced demand caused by an economic slowdown in the last quarter caused the free market price of fuel to dip below the official price towards the year's end.

The tourism industry that suffered a sharp drop in arrivals in the aftermath of the suppression of the monks' protest in September 2007 did not recover in 2008 either. The total number of visitors fell by 15.6 per cent for the eleven-month period as compared to the same period in 2007 with the number of airborne tourists falling by over 39 per cent.

The agriculture sector, still the backbone of Myanmar's economy after two decades of selective market reforms, proved quite resilient in the wake of the devastating storm. Earlier fears of rice shortage that led to a temporary ban on rice exports were not realized. In fact, the domestic rice price was stable even after Cyclone Nargis and fell towards the year's end as surplus stocks were released. According to a special report prepared by the UN Food and Agriculture Organization and World Food Programme the monsoon paddy production in the cyclone-affected areas was around 65 per cent of the output achieved in the 2007 planting season, while the corresponding figure for the combined Yangon and Ayeyarwady divisions as a whole was 91 per cent.[60]

Conclusion

The junta seemed to be staying its course in pursuing its seven-step road map to its logical conclusion. It weathered the political storm that arose in the wake of Cyclone Nargis by mobilizing its administrative and security apparatus and capitalizing on ASEAN's willingness to play a mediating role that would soften the international criticism and bring in some valuable international aid without losing control of the internal situation.[61] It appeared to have regained its usual self-confidence within a few weeks of the disaster though its detractors may interpret it differently as indication of a huge human security deficit.

On the other hand, the referendum has not ended the debate on the constitution and the government's road map for establishing a "discipline flourishing multi-party democracy". The 'imperfect storm' of 2008 physically destroyed much-needed human and material assets of Myanmar but failed to loosen the junta's grip over Burma's polity or reorient political change in a direction favoured by the opposition. However it seemed to have opened some space for the nascent civil society that came to the fore during the post-Nargis relief and rehabilitation effort. The disaster also "prompted a period of unprecedented cooperation between the government and international humanitarian agencies to deliver emergency aid". However, the recommendations by the influential International Crisis Group (ICG) to follow up on this small opening to engage positively with the military regime was largely ignored by the West in the ensuing months of 2008.[62]

Myanmar's relations with the international community remained largely unchanged and its strained relationship with the West continued, as has been the case for the last twenty years. Pragmatism prevailed among the regional states and Myanmar's neighbours in their dealings with the junta. China and India continued to favour expanding trade and investment and prefer order and stability over ideals of human rights and democracy as espoused by the (mainly) Western advocates and opposition groups.

The economy appeared to have slowed down due to structural constraints and policy inertia as politics took centre stage, with Cyclone Nargis further retarding growth though the worst fears were not realized. Myanmar, which has been least exposed among ASEAN countries to globalization and largely insulated from international finance and business, appeared to have been little affected by the global economic downturn that severely hit the developed countries in the last quarter of 2008. Nevertheless there were some indications towards the end of the year that falling demand and depressed energy and commodity prices were starting to bite into Myanmar's export sector and the knock-on effects of the global downturn on Myanmar's labour force at home and abroad were becoming increasingly evident.[63]

Notes

[1]   "Post-Nargis Joint Assessment" (hereafter referred to as PoNJA), a report prepared by the Tripartite Core Group comprising Representatives of the Government of the Union of Myanmar, the Association of Southeast Asian Nations and the United Nations (July 2006), pp. 1, 7, 9, 13, 20.

[2]   For illustrative examples of the litany of opposition's accusations see *Irrawaddy* (June 2008); and *Burma Bulletin* 17 (May 2008), 18 (June 2008), and 19 (July 2008) published by the Thailand-based opposition advocacy group ALTSEAN.

[3]   The U.S. Pacific Command (USPACOM) flotilla of four naval vessels led by the amphibious assault ship USS *Essex* (LHD-2) and comprising the amphibious transport dock USS *Juneau* LPD-10), dock landing ship USS *Harpers Ferry* (LSD-49), and guided missile destroyer USS *Mustin* (DDG-89) were on station off the Myanmar coast in international waters from 13 May to 5 June poised to deliver relief aid by helicopters and naval craft with the help of the 31st Marine Expeditionary Unit (comprising over 2,000 marines at full strength) on board. After making "at least 15 attempts to convince" the Myanmar authorities which failed, the USPACOM commander, who even went to Yangon to meet Myanmar's naval chief, finally decided to withdraw the Essex Group on 5 June. See Press Release 008/08PACOM, 3 June 2008 and <http://en.wikipedia.org/wiki/USS_Essex_(LHD-2)> (accessed 6 February 2009). The French sent their amphibious assault, command and power projection ship FS *Mistral* with 1,000 tonnes of relief supplies which arrived on 17 May off the Myanmar coast but was also denied permission to engage in relief operations. On 28 May, it offloaded its supplies at Phuket (Thailand) to be distributed by the UN's World Food Programme (see, e.g., Saline Prab "French supplies for Burma unload in Phuket", *Nation* [28 May 2008] in BurmaNet News, 28 May 2008).

[4]   For a critic of the French position see the comment by Gareth Evans, President of the influential International Crisis Group (ICG), in *The Guardian*, 12 May 2008, entitled "Facing Up to Our Responsibilities".

[5]   The government's ruling that the incoming donor funds must be exchanged into local currency (kyat) via the Foreign Exchange Certificate (FEC, stipulated as equivalent to the U.S. dollar in value) resulted in a controversy over huge potential losses as

the FEC was trading substantially below the greenback in the open market during the months following the disaster. The UN estimated the total losses due to exchange rate discrepancies up to August as less than US$1.6 million amounting to only one per cent of total contributions. See *Irrawaddy* (September 2008), p. 8.

6   Thai Prime Minister Samak made a day trip to Myanmar on 14 May to personally hand over satellite telephones and Thai contributions to the disaster relief fund. Medical and technical assistance teams from India, China, Thailand, Laos, Bangladesh, Singapore, Philippines and even France were accommodated in May and in June teams from Indonesia and Korea were accepted (see *Living Color* [Myanmar language magazine], July 2008, p. 22N).

7   See, PoNJA, op. cit., pp. 38–41.

8   See "USAID Fact Sheet #1 Fiscal Year (FY) 2009", 17 November 2008, p. 2.

9   See PoNJA, pp. 46–47.

10 See production data in *Chronicles of Development: Comparison between Period Preceding 1988 and After (Up to 31–12–2007)* (Yangon: Ministry of Information, 2008), pp. 341, 365.

11 Estimates are based on data in PoNJA, p. 34; and Central Statistical Organization website at <www.cso.org> (accessed 2 February 2008); and *International Financial Statistics*, January 2009.

12 See "Myanmar Cyclone Nargis OCHA Situation Report", no. 54 (12 December 2008), p. 1.

13 For a summary of reactions to the new constitution see, e.g., Robert H. Taylor, *The State in Myanmar* (London: Hurst, 2009), pp. 503–04.

14 This article effectively excludes the candidature of DASSK for president due to her marriage to an Englishman and her son's foreign nationality. However the constitutional provisions do not rule out her eligibility for becoming a member of parliament (article 120) or even a minister (article 232).

15 See *Burma Bulletin* 16 (April 2008) and 17 (May 2008), passim., for illustrative examples of opposition actions.

16 Compared to the 1990 elections in which the proportion of eligible voters comprised about 51 per cent of the population the proportion for this referendum at less than 48 per cent was a bit low. If the population distribution had not changed substantially (there is no reason for it to be changed), some 1.5 million seem to be missing. This number is very close to the combined number of those who were internally displaced and those who were working illegally in neighbouring countries.

17 Newspaper op-eds commenting that the referendum results had obviated the NLD's 1990 election victory appeared soon after the official confirmation of the outcome, thereby further undermining the opposition's claim for legitimacy through the people's mandate.

18 See, e.g., *Burma Bulletin* 17 (May 2008), pp. 8–11.

[19] See, e.g., Htet Aung Kyaw, "NLD Ordered to withdraw Statement", Democratic Voice of Burma, 25 September 2008, in BurmaNet News, 25 September 2008.

[20] See "Is NLD's future really dim and indistinct?" (in Myanamr language), a news analysis by the *New Era Journal*, 18 December 2008, at <http://www.khitpyaing. org/news/December_08/18-12-08e.php> (accessed 2 January 2009).

[21] See, e.g., Taylor, op. cit., pp. 505–06.

[22] See, e.g., Saw Yan Naing, "most ceasefire groups undecided on 2010 election", *Irrawaddy*, 8 July 2008, in BurmaNet News, 8 July 2008. The constitution stipulates that six townships in the current Shan State would be grouped into two districts which together constitute the Wa "Self-Administered Division", one of the six self-administered zones or divisions each of which would be one level lower (in the overall administrative hierarchy) than the relevant state or region, while seven states and seven regions constitute the Union of Myanmar (article 56).

[23] There were reportedly 300 detainees who were tried or sentenced during the year. See, e.g., the list posted by the Assistance Association for Political Prisoners (Burma) at <www.aappb.org/prisonrs1.html>.

[24] See, e.g., Mizzima News, "Nine arrested in rare protest in Rangoon", 30 December 2008 at <www.mizzima.com/news/inside-burma/1493-nine-arrested-in-rare-protest-in-rangoon.html>; and *Burma Bulletin* 13 to 16 (January to April 2008), 20 to 22 (August to October 2008).

[25] For example, in November, Thura popularly known by his stage name Zaganar (tweezers) a prominent satirist cum comedian as well as activist who was arrested while doing cyclone relief work got 59 years while Min Ko Naing and Ko Ko Gyi, leaders of the "88 Generation" student movement (arrested in August 2007) together with 21 of their associates were each sentenced to 65 years imprisonment. A blogger and NLD member Nay Phone Latt was sentenced to over 20 years and U Gambira a leading figure in the September 2007 monks-led protest received a sentence of 68 years. It was reported that over 180 dissidents were tried and sentenced between 4 and 28 November. See *Burma Bulletin* 22 (October 2008) and 23 (November 2008), Appendix 1.

[26] See *Irrawaddy* (December 2008), p. 26.

[27] During his visit in March, Gambari was told by the junta spokesperson that the UN call for revisiting the constitutional drafting process to make it all inclusive was impossible and substantial dialogue with DASSK would be possible only if she gave up her confrontational stance and revoke her call for punitive sanctions. Gambari's role as an "impartial mediator" was also questioned and he was accused of breaching the trust by releasing DASSK's statement after visiting her during his last trip in November. See "Junta Rejects UN Calls to Amend Draft Constitution", Associated Press, 8 March 2008, in BurmaNet News, 8 March 2008.

[28] See *Burma Bulletin* 21 (September 2008).

29   See "Secretary-General not to visit Myanmar without substantive progress by
      Government", UNSG office of the Spokesperson, 3 December 2008, in BurmaNet
      News, 3 December 2008.

30   See, e.g., "Ban urges "groups of friends", corporates to influence Burma", Mizzima,
      9 December 2008, in BurmaNet News, 9 December 2008.

31   There are currently five BSOs. See *Burma Bulletin* 18 (June 2008), p. 6.

32   See, e.g., *Living Color* (January 2009), pp. 30–31; and *Burma Bulletin* 19 (July 2008),
      p. 4; and ibid., 22 (October 2008), p. 4.

33   For examples of explosions in other towns and the countryside see, e.g., ibid., 13
      (January 2008), pp. 4-5; ibid., 14 (February 2008), p. 5; ibid., 19 (July 2008), p. 5;
      and ibid., 21 (September 2008), pp. 4, 10.

34   See, e.g., "Junta commander: Thailand violating Burmese sovereignty", Shan Herald
      Agency for News, 19 August 2008, in BurmanEt News, 19 August 2008.

35   The KNLA was weakened when its 7th brigade commander Major General Htain
      Maung defected with most of his troops to the government side and set up the Karen
      Peace Council in his base area. See, e.g., Saw Yan Naing, "The New KNU-Let's
      Wait and See", *Irrawaddy*, 28 October 2008, online edition at <http://www.irrawaddy.
      org/print_article.php?art_id=14516> (accessed 16 February 2009).

36   See "Opium Poppy Cultivation in Southeast Asia: Lao PDR, Myanmar, Thailand",
      UNODC Report (December 2008), pp. 1, 45. For an in-depth analysis of the
      government's relationship with ceasefire groups, see Mary Callahan, *Political Authority
      in Burma's Ethnic Minority States: Devolution, Occupation, and Coexistence*, Policy
      Studies 31 (Southeast Asia) (Singapore and Washington, D.C.: Institute of Southeast
      Asian Studies/East West Center, 2007).

37   See *Living Color* (January 2009), pp. 30/48.

38   The following is based on various news agency reports and the "Year in Review"
      section in *Living Color* (January 2009).

39   See paragraph 40 of the declaration at the conclusion of the 15th SAARC Summit
      available at <www.saarc-sec.org//data/summit15/summit15declaration.htm> (accessed
      17 February 2009).

40   See, e.g., "Bangladesh diplomats head to Myanmar for energy row talks", Associated
      Press, 5 November 2008, in BurmaNet News, 5 November 2009; and *The Voice*
      (Myanmar language journal) 10–16 November 2008 (special supplement).

41   See White House Press Release, Office of the Press Secretary, 16 September 2008,
      "Memorandum for the Secretary of State: Major Drug Transit or Major Illicit drug
      Producing Countries for Fiscal Year 2009", Presidential Determination no. 208–28,
      available at <www.state.gov/p/inl/rls/prsrl/ps/109777.htm> (accessed 9 December 2008).

42   For elaboration on U.S.-Myanmar relations over the drugs issue see the article by
      Paul Sarno in this volume.

43   For details, see *Burma Bulletin* 14 (February 2008), p. 8.

44   For details, see ibid., 17 (May 2008), p. 14.

45 See ibid., 19 (July 2008), p. 7.

46 See ibid, 23 (November 2008), p. 10.

47 See ibid., 21 (September 2008), p. 11; and ibid., 22 (October 2008), p. 10.

48 See ibid., 21 (September 2008), p. 8. Interestingly, this credentials challenge by the MPU was not endorsed by the NCGUB (National Coalition Government of the Union of Burma) the self-styled exiled government led by DASSK's cousin Dr Sein Win.

49 See "PRESIDENCY CONCLUSIONS, Brussels European Council 19/20 June 2008", 11018/08 CONCL.2, Brussels, Council of the European Union, 20 June 2008, p. 21.

50 See "Council Conclusions on Burma/Myanmar", Council of the European Union, 2092nd GENERAL AFFAIRS Council meeting, Brussels, 10 November 2008, Press Release.

51 See "Statement by the President of the Security Council", UNSC, S/PRST/2008/13, 2 May 2008.

52 See "Draft Resolution II, Situation of human rights in Myanmar", in Report of the 3rd Committee to the 63rd Session of the UNGA, A/63/430/Add.3, 5 December 2008.

53 See "Statement by H. E. U Nyan Win, Minister for Foreign Affairs and the Chairman of the Delegation of the Union of Myanmar", New York, Permanent Mission of the Union of Myanmar to the U.N., 29 September 2008.

54 Unless otherwise stated, all statistical data for this section are derived from the information posted at the website of the Myanmar government's Central Statistical Organization, available at <http://www.csostat.gov.mm/sIndicators.asp>.

55 It was also observed that "official statistics are constrained by weaknesses in resources and institutions, making objective assessment of economic performance difficult". See "Myanmar", in Asian Development Outlook 2008: Workers in Asia, available at <www.adb.org/Documents/Books/ADO/2008/MYA.asp> (accessed 8 December 2008).

56 See IMF-World Economic Outlook Database, October 2007, available at <www.networkmyanmar.org/index.php?option=com_content&task=view&id=35&itemid=45> (accessed 2 February 2009); and "Myanmar (Burma) Country Report", (London: Economist Intelligence Unit, November 2008), p. 25.

57 See PoNJA, op. cit., p. 21.

58 The actual cumulative influx of FDI could be much less and nearer to 50–60 per cent of the approved figure.

59 This drastic increase was probably due to the custom fees levied on some 900,000 (illegally imported) motorcycles that were allowed to be registered during the second half of the year.

60 See "Special Report", FAO/WFP Crop and Food Security Assessment mission to Myanmar, 22 January 2009, p. 15.

61   It is interesting to note that Singapore foreign minister as the standing ASEAN chair remarked that the grouping as a whole "could give" itself a "C-grading" for its performance in helping Myanmar cope with Nargis (see "ASEAN Report Card, 'C' for group's effort after Cyclone Nargis", *Today*, 18 July 2008, p. 10.

62   See "Burma/Myanmar after Nargis: Time to normalize aid relations?" Asia Report no. 161, Brussels International Crisis Group, 20 October 2008.

63   The remittances from up to two million overseas workers in Southeast Asia and beyond could be substantial but remained undocumented. Many could lose their jobs as the host countries' economies shrink. Prices of rice, rubber, beans and pulses, marine products and even natural gas were negatively affected by the global downturn (personal communications and observation in Myanmar, May, July and November 2008).

THE WAR ON DRUGS

Paul Sarno

Introduction

This article demonstrates the inadequate response of the international community to the suppression of drugs in Myanmar[1] and the lost opportunity by the United States to reverse its policy toward interdiction since 2002. First, it provides a brief history of drug production in Myanmar and examines the reliability of surveys conducted by the United Nations Office of Drugs and Crime (UNODC) and the United States, both together with Myanmar, on opium cultivation and of estimates of amphetamine type stimulants (ATS) production. Second, it sheds light on international and domestic efforts to halt the production and distribution of opium, heroin and ATS, and discusses the roots of the dramatic decline in opium cultivation and production over the twelve years preceding 2007. Third, it evaluates the alleged involvement of authorities under the State Peace and Development Council (SPDC), the governing body of Myanmar, in the drug trade. Fourth, it concludes that extensive assistance by the international community and local authorities is vital to avoid a humanitarian disaster in the opium cultivation areas and consequent reversal of the favourable progression.

An Historical Overview

For centuries farmers have grown the opium poppy plant mostly in the far reaches of northern Myanmar for medicine and to raise cash. The British commercialized the cultivation in colonial times. After Independence in 1948, Myanmar nationals, often minority groups in the growing areas, have became the wholesalers, while ethnic Chinese merchants and international syndicates located in Thailand and, later, China have been the ultimate major purchasers of the poppy crop. Since

PAUL SARNO is a graduate of the University of Pennsylvania and the Columbia University Law School.

the completion of ceasefire agreements between the Myanmar government and various ethnic armed resistance groups starting in 1989, the latter have been given varying degrees of autonomy in their fiefdoms and are permitted to tax the poppy farmers, opium manufacturers and distributors.

Beginning in 1999, Myanmar and these local ethnic minorities agreed to eliminate poppy growing by 2014 and the former increased its suppression efforts after a period of lethargy. Thereafter, poppy growing and production were largely confined to the Shan State and to the Kokang and Wa ethnic minorities in whose areas most of the crop was being cultivated, until they banned such planting.

In 2000, production of amphetamine type stimulants (ATS) was commenced, largely in the Wa regions. Most was sold in Thailand and China.

Measuring Drug Production in Myanmar

There is controversy about the reliability of the surveys of poppy cultivation and yield. First, farmers have developed a proclivity for planting further and further from the roads in already remote areas to escape detection and possible eradication. Second, they have established other strategies to evade periodic ground and satellite photographic detection and eradication, such as broadcasting seeds twice in the same field in one or two month intervals or in different fields at different times. Thus the poppy yield is harvested at disparate times. Third, other planters pour iodized salt on a field to accelerate rot of plant residue left after eradication and then re-broadcast using urea fertilizer to bring a poppy crop to fruition. There is also early cultivation in the hopes of harvesting before the surveying begins. Fourth, the personal on-site inspection portion of the UNDOC surveys are conducted principally by Myanmar government officials, including the police, albeit overseen by visits from UN personnel, and farmers and headmen are reluctant to admit income from poppy cultivation where the state policy is opium extermination. Fifth, much of the farmed areas are under the control of ethnic groups, and the surveyors cannot live amongst the thousands of cultivators throughout the usual growing season, much less the entire year. Therefore the surveyors' assessment cannot be as accurate as that of the farmers who reside there or the traffickers who visit often.

Any relatively precise quantification of the production of amphetamine tablets is much more nettlesome as their manufacture is more difficult to detect. Unlike opium production, virtually no acreage or extensive manpower or expertise is required in order to produce these pills in small mobile laboratories. No such manpower is needed to transport them on routes which are altered constantly and they can be conveyed utilizing much less effort than the caravans of mules necessary for the passage of heroin. Satellite imagery is of little or no assistance in discovery or measurement of the effectiveness of suppression of the producing laboratories. Moreover, unlike the refining of opium to produce heroin, there is no emission of smoke or revelatory smell during the production of these pills. Because of these obstacles, Myanmar, the United States and the UNODC have not even attempted to survey, much less publish, any precise numbers on the annual production and distribution of such pills. The last two, and some others, have offered only estimates.

Survey Methodology and Results

Despite these challenges, the United States and the UNODC have attempted to calculate the poppy cultivated and the yield produced in Myanmar. Usually, the Myanmar government has assisted in those surveys. Over the last decade and until early 2005, the United States, through visual inspections conducted by Myanmar government personnel accompanied by Americans, has conducted on-site surveys of land where opium poppy is likely to be grown based on extensive satellite photography. Myanmar has not approved a U.S.-led Opium-Yield Survey since before 2005. However, in 2006 and 2007, Myanmar officials expressed an interest in conducting the survey, but did not communicate their desire in time to conduct the survey.

Beginning in 2002, UNODC has also surveyed by utilizing a lesser quantity of such photography. It has also relied more on visual inspections by Myanmar government observers (supervised and coordinated by experienced UN personnel) of a sampling of villages randomly selected from a database provided by the Myanmar Forest Department.[2] Such inspections are more extensive than those employed in order to issue the United States reports.

All such surveys demonstrate a striking diminution in the total area under poppy cultivation of between 75 and 80 per cent within a decade since 1996. The decrease in total yield is equally dramatic. Over the ten year period ending in 2005, metric tonnage produced declined by over 85 per cent (between 2180 and 2248 metric tonnes).[3] The trend was only reversed in both categories in the 2007 growing season and in cultivated area in the 2008 season for reasons which will be explained later.

Table 1 sets forth the calculation by the United States sponsored annual inspections of the area under opium cultivation and the yields of that crop.

TABLE 1
United States Sponsored Inspections

Date of Survey	Opium Cultivation (number of hectares)*	Potential Production (metric tonnes)
1996	163,100	2,560
1997	155,150	2,365
1998	146,494	1,750
1999	99,300	1,090
2000	108,700	1,085
2001	114,317	865
2002	77,700	630
2003	47,130	484
2004	30,900	292
2005	40,000	380

Note: *A hectare is equal to about 2.471 acres.
Sources: International Narcotics Control Strategy Reports of the United States Department of State Bureau for International Narcotics and Law Enforcement Affairs (the "INCSR"), issued March 2004, p. 9; and 2005, Southeast Asia Section, pp. 3, 6; and INCSR vol. 1, Drug and Chemical Control issued March 2006, p. 244.

The United States publishes no specifics of its methodology. It employs many more satellite images than the UNDOC and, until the 2005 survey, fewer on-site inspections; at least some of which included the participation of DEA personnel.[4]

Table 2 states the results of the UNODC annual surveys of such hectares and yield.

As the poppy growing season generally lasts from October through February, the on-site portion of the 2006 UNODC survey was conducted by 153 three-person teams of Myanmar government employees from December 2005 through March 2006. They inspected three states, Shan, Kachin and Kayah, where almost all the poppy is grown. Preceding that ground survey, the UNDOC analysed the 2005 survey and concluded that with the confirmation of the cessation of cultivation in the Wa Special Region no. 2 by 2006, most of the crop was probably now being grown in the southern and eastern areas of the Shan State. It refined that judgment by further considering land cover, slope, altitude and previous opium free territories within those areas of the Shan State as detected in the 2005 survey. Based on all those factors, high resolution satellite photographs then were taken over two five-week intervals covering eleven and nine territories in those two areas. A digest of that 2006 photography led to the creation of a map where poppy was likely to be growing in that year.

TABLE 2
UMODC Surveys

Date of Survey	Opium Cultivation (number of hectares)	Potential Production (metric tonnes)
2002	81,400	828
2003	62,200	810
2004	44,200	370
2005	32,800	312
2006	21,500	315
2007	27,700	460
2008	28,500	410

Sources: UNODC Opium Poppy Cultivation in Southeast Asia January 2009 ("Opium Survey 2008"), pp. 46, 50.

That map and analysis of the 2005 survey were the foundation for the selection and visits to 632 villages in those areas: 450, 99 and 83 in the Shan, Kachin and Kayah States, respectively.[5] This represented an area inhabited by about 252,000 people, a five per cent sampling of the population in those three states. The teams actually conducted three on-site surveys, a planted area estimation survey of only 291 villages, a rapid assessment inspection undertaken by two UNODC employees over two weeks to verify the ground survey in certain locations and a socio-economic survey which questioned headmen and heads of households.[6]

Based on the photography and surveys, the estimates of 2006 cultivation and metric tonnages are stated in Tables 3 and 4.

Importantly, the socio-economic survey of 2006 found that the decrease in poppy field cultivation, an insignificant increase in tonnage and an increase in yields per hectare caused the price of opium charged by the farmer to increase by 22 per cent to an average of US$230 per kilogramme. That, together with a decrease of 34 per cent in the number of households growing opium in 2006 compared with the year before, resulted in those households earning in 2006 an average of US$437 (a 49 per cent increase over 2005). This was US$119 more on the average than those who have ceased growing opium. Thus, there was concern that this disparity would cause a resumption of cultivation by the poorest of the former planters. Apparently, these fears were realized when the 2007 Opium Survey found that the annual average income of opium growers progressed to US$501 as the price per kilogramme paid to them rose to US$265.

Those households that have ceased growing opium are now cultivating maize and more rice and are raising livestock and poultry, but as will be discussed later

TABLE 3
Areas of Poppy Cultivation — 2006

Admin Unit	Hectares	Variation from 2005 (%)	Metric Tonnage
East Shan	4,550	+15	40.5
North Shan	240	−91	2.7
South Shan	15.660	+39	260.0
Spec Reg 2 (Wa)	0	100	0
Kachin	1,020		11.9
Kayah	15		0.2
Totals	21,500 (rounded)		315 (rounded)

Source: Opium Survey 2006, p. 68.

TABLE 4
Percentage of Townships surveyed
where Opium Cultivation was found — 2006

East Shan	8 of 10 (14 per cent of all villages)
South Shan	17 of 21 (10 per cent of all villages)
North Shan	6 of 19 (2 per cent of all villages)
Kachin	2 of 4 (30 per cent of villages in 2 twps)*

Note: * One year later, the surveyors found that cultivation in 40 per cent and 30 per cent of villages in the Southern and Eastern Shan State, respectively. The percentage of villages with cultivation in the Northern Shan State remained unchanged from the previous year and the poppy crop was found in only 7 per cent of villages in five townships in the Kachin State, Opium Survey 2007, p. 66.
Source: Opium Survey 2006, pp. 71, 107, 110 and 113.

in this article, it is extremely difficult for these farmers to replace the income formerly earned from poppy cultivation without financial assistance and as of now, such aid has not been forthcoming in any amount deemed necessary.

Over the twelve year period of the surveys, not all of this reduction is attributable to direct actions of the Myanmar government and ethnic minorities' leadership. Bad weather and public awareness campaigns have also contributed to the decline.

There has not been any survey of production for the ATS. However, there is a consensus based on anecdotal observation of widespread use of the pills, principally in Thailand and China, and the seizures reported in those countries and Myanmar that several hundreds of millions of amphetamine pills were manufactured in and distributed from Myanmar in both 2006 and 2007. The UNODC made attempts to estimate the magnitude (but not quantify) such production from the origin of ATS seized by authorities.[7]

For example, Myanmar reported the seizure of 18.92 million tablets in the sixteen months from 1 January 2005 to 30 May 2006 followed by an additional one million in June 2006 and 200,000 in August of that year, contributing to the confiscation that year of a reported 2.821 kilogrammes of ATS, the greatest annual quantity ever measured. Naypitaw also seized 325, 1288 and 530 kilogrammes of precursor chemicals in 2005, 2006 and 2007, respectively.[8] The United Nations and the United States substantially concur that these interdictions occurred. Apprehensions and destruction by the government of Myanmar continued in 2008. Additionally, the UNODC stated that Thailand and China had reported widespread seizures of amphetamines manufactured in Myanmar.[9]

To What Extent is the Myanmar Authorities Involved in the Drug Trade?

There is a dispute whether, at what level, and to what extent the Myanmar military is facilitating the drug trade. The UNODC surveys do not discuss this. Several commentators assert that the very top echelon of the armed forces is involved actively while others claim the participation is limited to the Military Intelligence, led until 2004 by General Khin Nyunt, who had extensive connections to drug entrepreneurs, and to numerous battalion commanders at the Lieutenant Colonel rank.[10] In 1999, they allegedly lent moneys to cultivators to finance the crop, taxed it on harvest, owned shares in heroin and amphetamine refineries and their troops guarded those fields and factories. One narrative of a man personally reported that a Regional Commander was best friends with a high level trafficker. Another interviewee witnessed Myanmar intelligence officers accompanying a Ya-ba shipment into the Karen State.[11]

In contradistinction to some of these conclusions, the United States government, hardly favourably disposed toward the Myanmar government, has consistently maintained that there is no or little credible evidence that senior officials in the Myanmar government are directly involved in the drug trade. However, it believes that lower level government officials, particularly army and police personnel posted in border areas, are involved in enabling the narcotics traffic. Some of these have been prosecuted and received lengthy prison terms. But, no army officer above the rank of full colonel has ever been prosecuted for a drug offence. Two other authoritative sources concluded that as late as 2003 lower ranking military may have been enmeshed in the drug trade. However there was no proof of the involvement in it of top SLORC leaders.[12] Many of the claims of cooperation at the highest levels of the SLORC/SPDC were written or are based on events witnessed in the late 1990s or very early years of the twenty-first century. For example, the person, identified by Phil Thornton's informant as a close friend of a major drug trafficker, has not been a Regional Commander in a position to directly facilitate drug cultivation and distribution since November 2001 when he was moved out of operational command to serve as a member of the SPDC.[13]

The most reasonable assessment therefore is that the vast majority of the drug cultivation and production occurred before 2006 in the areas controlled by ethnic minorities, e.g. Wa, Kokang and Pa-O, who reached ceasefire agreements with the SPDC over a decade ago. Those pacts give the minorities control in varying degrees over what transpires in their regions. The SPDC could not halt much of the drug cultivation, production, manufacture and distribution within them without major altercations with the minority groups. Furthermore, that trade itself is controlled by Chinese syndicates headquartered outside Myanmar. While local government troops stationed in the areas may be assisting in those activities for their profit (especially now that the army has been ordered by the SPDC to largely self-finance its own food and shelter), the overwhelming evidence over at least the last five years is that the members of the SPDC and the high levels of the commands are not part of the drug trade.

Three general factual circumstances support this conclusion. First, there were widespread seizures and eradication of drugs by the Myanmar government in that period. For example, the United States wrote in its 2006 Report that heroin seizures by Myanmar doubled over 2002–05; in eleven months of 2005, 1.6 million amphetamine tablets and 1,000 kilogrammes of raw opium were interdicted. In the same year, the Myanmar authorities, in cooperation with American and Australian agents, intercepted 102 kilogrammes of ICE, crystal amphetamine, and disrupted a drug smuggling syndicate.[14] Eleven heroin laboratories in northern and southern Shan State were destroyed from January 2005 through May 2006.[15] Seizures have continued through at least July 2008.[16]

While the UNODC's annual survey does not monitor or confirm the results of eradication performed by the Myanmar government, it reports that 3,907 hectares of poppy were exterminated during the 2004–05 growing season, an increase of 39 per cent above the 2,820 hectares of such fields destroyed by Myanmar during the previous similar span. Moreover, according to it, 3,970 and 3,598 hectares of poppy were annihilated in the 2005–06 and 2006–07 seasons, respectively.[17]

Some disbelief has been expressed concerning the drug burning disclosed by Naypitaw. On one occasion in 1991, the heroin burnt allegedly had been purchased by the SLORC from leading Kokang traffickers. Another claim is that the SPDC burns mostly sugar and Tamarind paste together with a little opium.[18] While the Myanmar government officials may have been able to engage in such deception in the past, the consensus among diplomats whose drug representatives witnessed the destructions over the last five years is that they are genuine.[19] And, United States, Chinese, Thai and Australian narcotics agents now assist in the arrests and seizures which precede the conflagrations.

Second, the Myanmar government concluded and implemented agreements during this time with Thailand, Laos, China and India to cooperate with those countries in drug suppression. Third, the SPDC's efforts to eradicate drugs by 2014 have resulted in the surrender of several leading drug traffickers who were a counter-force, albeit limited, to it in some ethnic minority areas.

The Policy Responses to Suppression of the Poppy Cultivation

The cessation of most poppy cultivation caused farmers' income to plummet by between 25 and 90 per cent. In some areas, 89 per cent of the villages faced food insecurity with 45 per cent suffering such deficiency between 3 and 12 months of a year. After the ban, one-third of villages in areas surveyed were evaluated as economically poor. Literacy rate was only 33 per cent and food cost consumed 75 per cent of the budget of poor and moderate households representing 82 per cent of the total populace sampled.[20] Thus, it is not difficult to comprehend why most Wa oppose the prohibition.

As stated above, the encouraging long-term decline in Myanmar poppy cultivation and production did not continue for the main growing season of 2006–07. The decreasing acreage and tonnage through 2005–06 increased the per kilogramme price for the opium actually harvested from US$187 in 2005 to US$230 a year later. By early 2007, that price had risen to US$265.[21] This, together with the lack of adequate assistance to farmers who terminated cultivation and suffered diminished income, prompted a minority of them to re-locate, especially to the Kayah and Kachin states, and to resume poppy growing. Farmers in other areas, such as the Shan State, recommended or increased their crop and production given the price incentive and lack of assistance to act otherwise.[22] Only additional assistance to these farmers and their families will persuade them not to resume sowing.

At the present time, there are at least six projects which attempt to assuage loss of revenue. Among them are a modest UNODC/Wa project financed by the United States (US$8 million), Japan, Italy, Germany and the U.K., Australia and a UN (Human Security Funds) contribution to UNODC-supervised activities which parallel that project. The project, which began in 1998, had an initial five-year duration and was a US$12.1 million supply-reduction programme to encourage the growing of improved varieties of rice and winter crops, the application of fertilizers, the raising of livestock and the use of veterinary services in areas of the Wa State controlled by the United Wa State Army. The project was extended to 2007 and the budget increased to US$16.8 million. Despite that extension, a Wa representative complained that, "...we are getting a tenth of what we need". The UNODC representative in 2003 apparently agreed as he termed the project "too limited to make a big difference".[23]

In January 2005, the U.S. unsealed indictments against seven United Wa State Army leaders for conspiracy to manufacture or distribute heroin and methamphetamines. This, along with subsequent death threats by the Wa against Drug Enforcement Administration agents, led to the United States' reallocation of unspent funds from the Wa project to those outside the Wa territory. The United States reportedly is reluctant to authorize any further funding in that territory unless the Wa authorities appropriate significant funds for amelioration of the farmer's plight. Perhaps the Wa would be so willing especially if a third party with funding were ready to offer other aid.[24] In November 2008, the United States prevented the withdrawal of assets under its control of 43 individuals and firms with ties to the United Wa State Army, alleging they are or are linked to, producing and exporting synthetic drugs.[25]

The UNODC also established a project in the Wa and Kokang areas of the Shan State in 2003. The goal is to prevent a return to the growing of poppy. Eighteen partner organizations, including the World Food Program (WFP), the FAO and certain international non-governmental organizations are coordinating these activities. As part of that programme, the World Food Program is providing 382,000 ex-poppy farmers and their families, who face the loss of a major source of income, with food for public work or education and demonstration plots for the growing of higher altitude replacement crops. In February 2007, the WFP announced it was expanding the programme to feed 726,000 people. The project is now supported by the UNODC and nine countries, plus the funds diverted by the United States to non-Wa areas. While the latter's participation was scheduled to be phased out by 2007, there are reports that it will confer with the WFP to discuss increasing such aid. Non-governmental organizations (NGOs) implement many of these projects.[26]

Additionally, China revealed that over ten years it had delivered food and crop substitution aid valued at US$101.9 million and another US$22.5 million in 2006 to plant rubber, tea and other cash crops in Northern Myanmar and Laos. It also reported that over one hundred of its private companies invested millions of dollars in the substitution of sugarcane and rubber for opium in the Shan State with China allowing their importation free of tariffs. Some of this aid has allowed the Wa leaders to initiate the hiring of impoverished farmers on such rubber plantations at low wages.[27] That hardly benefits the farmers.

Thailand reportedly had contributed over US$1.6 million to support opium crop substitution in eastern Shan State as part of eight other such projects. It also initiated the Yongkha crop substitution project in the Wa area but received no financial support from other agencies or countries. Myanmar has some projects of its own, such as one to exchange opium seeds for those of other crops which allegedly yielded 141 tonnes of the former.

On the other hand, the Japanese effort to support the growth of buckwheat as a cash crop in the Kokang and Mong Ko regions of the northeastern Shan State largely failed because the difficulty of transport to markets in Japan multiplied the costs and caused much of the product to spoil. What reached Japan in edible form was too expensive for the market or unappetizing.[28] Thus, crops appealing to the local markets are much more likely to be successful. Japan has accomplished more in the region with distribution of rice and corn seeds and rubber and tea plants for crop sales to Kokang markets and by assisting with irrigation, fertilizer and a warehouse to store substitute crops in new agricultural development for 117,000 people.

From at least December 2003, the UNODC has warned that all this assistance is inadequate to aid these cultivators and their families who have abandoned planting their major cash crop. For example, in the Wa Special Region 2 less than US$20 million has been spent on development aid since 1998, less than US$3 per person. Now that poppy cultivation has decreased by at least 82 per cent and the Kokang and Wa Special Regions 2 and 4 are reportedly virtually free of opium, there is even greater need for such humanitarian aid. Shariq Bin Raza, the UNODC Representative in Myanmar, wrote:

> The Government [of Myanmar) and its development assistance partners
> have to ensure that food security and alternative livelihood programmes
> are strengthened and expanded to support those farmers who decided to

> abandon opium poppy cultivation. It is necessary to create an appropriate
> environment to encourage those who have not yet made this decision in
> combination with measures to reduce and eradicate opium cultivation in
> a sustainable way. Failing to do so may lead to a humanitarian disaster
> and human misery in Myanmar.[29]

The United States' encouragement of drug extermination and of income and crop substitution is important to the success of each. As a donor with more resources than others and the leader in the attempt to encourage change in attitudes of the government of Myanmar, decrease in worldwide opium production and an improvement in economic conditions in largely agricultural Myanmar, an increase in Washington's participation in these programmes is essential.

Replication of the United States' neglect to assist Myanmar in improving the lot of farmers adversely affected by suppression of poppy cultivation is not desirable.

The opportunity to recognize Myanmar's efforts on opium abolition and to certify Myanmar as cooperating in the reduction of narcotics improved on 10 January 2002, when Congress enacted changes to the primary governing statute. Section 489 of that Statute mandates that the President submit a report annually to Congress identifying each country which is a major illicit drug producing, drug-transit or major money laundering country.[30] Bilateral assistance[31] and American support for multilateral assistance must be denied to such a country unless the President makes a further certification in that report that in the previous year such country has cooperated fully with the United States or has taken adequate steps on its own to achieve full compliance with the United Nations Convention Against Illicit Traffic in Narcotic Drugs and Psychotropic Substances. The President is also required in it to identify on that "majors list" any country that has "failed demonstrably ... to make substantial efforts" during the previous twelve months to adhere to international counter-narcotics agreements and to take certain counter-narcotics measures set forth in United States law".[32]

At the same time, Congress gave the President additional flexibility in reaching a decision relative to such a certification by enacting a new provision. That change mandated that such United States aid may not be furnished for fiscal year 2002 to any such country if it has been certified previously by the President as a major pursuant to said Section 490 and it had, during the past 12 months, so "failed demonstrably", unless, he determines that at any time after the President's initial report to Congress, such country has made "substantial efforts" to adhere to its obligations under international counter-narcotics agreements, and has taken counter-narcotics measures as required under said Section 489.

Thus, these January 2002 provisions ameliorated the requisite pre-conditions for the renewal of foreign assistance to Myanmar although it had previously been certified as a "major". Before the amendment provisions, Section 489 of the Foreign Assistance Act of 1961, as amended, required that the State Department affirmatively report that a country had "met the goals and objectives of the United Nations convention against illicit traffic in narcotic drugs and psychotropic substances" in order to obtain such aid.

In May 2002, the SPDC released Aung San Suu Kyi from house arrest and the State Department invited Colonel Kyaw Thein of the branch of the Military Intelligence deeply involved in anti-narcotics strategy to Washington for a discussion of what Myanmar needed to accomplish to obtain the support of that Department toward certification. He met with Rand Beers, then Assistant Secretary of State for International Narcotics and Law Enforcement. The Myanmar government then agreed to the United States conditions.[33]

One month later, Deputy Assistant Secretary of State Matthew P. Daly testified before a Congressional Committee that the enactment of anti-money laundering laws, the designation of high level drug traffickers for prosecution as well as the continuing reduction of poppy in the area under cultivation and production would qualify Myanmar for serious consideration concerning certification of its anti-drug programme. Daly made it clear that the United States could pursue better communication and cooperation with the SPDC on narcotics enforcement without diminishing American support for political reform and reconciliation between the regime, the ethnic minority movements and the opposition National League for Democracy.

Such compliance and certification were important enough to Yangon that it retained a high powered Washington lobbying firm, one of whose members involved in the particular account was a friend of President Bush, to support its efforts.[34]

The State Department was aware (as it later reported in March 2003) that for the 2002 growing season, Myanmar poppy cultivation had decreased from 114,317 hectares in the previous year to 103,862. And perhaps more significantly, the Department stated that potential yield diminished from 865 to 630 metric tonnes during that year. In late 2002, as the time for the President's report relative to certification approached, it appeared that the State Department believed that Myanmar had met the requirements set forth in Daly's testimony to Congress. As such, it might very well have its name removed from the list of non-complying nations, having made "substantial efforts" during 2002 to adhere to international narcotics agreements and had taken the requisite counter-narcotics measures.

That possibility apparently dismayed those who both oppose the military regime and lobby extensively for the application of maximum sanctions. While Assistant Secretary of State James Kelly and the American charge in Yangon, its highest ranking representative there, were praising the improvement in Myanmar cooperation with the international community on narcotics issues, the anti-Myanmar regime lobbyists were issuing statements opposing any change in certification and so influencing the United States media.[35] Their position was enhanced when in December 2002, the State Department released a report of its investigation, conducted in late July, of an earlier account by an NGO documenting widespread rape of Shan and other minority women by members of the Myanmar armed forces, including its officers, in minority areas and the absence of any punishment meted out to them.[36] Moreover, in the November 2002 elections, control of the United States Senate shifted from the Democrats to the Republicans, albeit by a narrow margin.

Finally, in March 2003, the State Department reported that once again, Myanmar had failed demonstrably to meet its international counter-narcotics obligations while also finding that:

> Although still a major producer of illicit opium, Burma's overall production in 2002 declined substantially for the sixth straight year. ... Over the past several years, the Burmese government has significantly extended its counter-narcotics cooperation with other states....
>
> In 2002, Burma also responded to rising international concerns regarding the quality of its anti-money laundering regime by enacting a powerful new money-laundering law that criminalizes money laundering in connection with virtually every type of major criminal activity. The first investigations under this law began in July, resulting in the seizure of several hundred thousand dollars in assets.[37]

Despite such favourable findings, on both 30 January and 15 September 2003, President Bush certified that Myanmar had failed demonstrably during the previous twelve months to adhere to its obligations under the international counter-narcotics agreements and to take measures set forth in Section 489 (A)(1) of the FAA. Accordingly, under the law, the United States could not furnish any bilateral, or vote for any multilateral foreign assistance to Myanmar.[38] That unfavourable certification has been attributed to opposition lobbying efforts, the report on rape and/or the shift of control in the Senate from Democrat to Republican.[39]

On the other hand, excoriation of many of the Myanmar government's policies and practices seems clearly justified. Among other indictments, the refusal to honour the results of the 1990 elections, the harsh repression of monks, who demonstrated in October 2007 for lower fuel prices, and of political and ethnic adversaries, the use of forced labour and the draconian persecution of the few ethnic minorities, including civilians, who continue to oppose the regime militarily are all well documented. Continuously and especially each time there is a suggestion by others, including recognized scholars in the field of Myanmar studies, that the United States policy of isolating Myanmar by continuing severe economic sanctions has not accomplished any of the major goals intended, these opposition groups insure that those in the executive and Congress do not deviate from the policies in effect with increasing fervor since the coup of 1988. The continued stream of illicit drugs from Myanmar is included in the litany of wrongs committed by its rulers.

This resistance to any change in the existing policies, including favourable certification recognizing Myanmar's drug suppression efforts, avoids correction of the dire straits in which these agricultural families now find themselves, having abandoned poppy farming. Ignoring the continuing decline in poppy cultivation and tonnage, the removal of Myanmar from the list of those countries failing to cooperate in the fight against money-laundering (associated with the conversion of illegal drug profits into investments in legitimate businesses),[40] and its increased efforts to interdict ATS production and distribution, that adverse finding by the State Department has been repeated every year since then. Thus the United States has supplied no meaningful aid to eliminate or reduce poppy or to alleviate the plight of the cultivators who have ceased growing it.[41]

The Way Forward

By reason of the performance of the government of Myanmar in these areas after 2003, the United States might well consider alteration of its narcotics policy in order to certify that the country has made sufficient efforts to adhere to international narcotics agreements and to take counter-narcotics measures as required by United States law. The previous certifications to the contrary need not be repeated. Myanmar then could be given the opportunity to receive multilateral as well as United States bilateral aid.

The United States could promise to increase its funding of the crop substitution projects, initiate new aid projects and encourage the construction of roads which will allow substitute crops to reach local markets more inexpensively. It is anticipated (and necessary) that the other nations now furnishing such aid, including Myanmar itself, would increase their contributions and ethnic minority authorities involved, to the extent able, would render assistance. The furnishing of United States aid could be calibrated commensurate with future results by Myanmar in the opium and ATS suppression areas and an agreement to join with the United States in resumption of annual joint poppy surveys. The latter could resume its cooperation with Myanmar in the suppression efforts, reportedly withdrawn when Myanmar suppressed forcibly the September 2007 demonstrations led largely by the monks.[42]

Massive sustenance and infrastructure improvements are necessary if the trend toward continued poppy reduction, if not virtual elimination in Myanmar, is to be sustained. Only such assistance will persuade cultivators to continue to desist from growing poppy or if they have not yet ceased such farming, to do so and grow other crops.

While the Myanmar government has made efforts to interdict the manufacture and shipment of ATS, this has proven more difficult to bring to reasonable levels for logistical reasons as well as because the primary beneficiaries of the trade are well organized Chinese syndicates outside Myanmar, not the Myanmar government. Here, law enforcement assistance to the SPDC appears to be the only solution.

Notes

Paul Sarno is a member of New York State Bar (ret) and the Burma Studies Group. He lectures on Southeast Asia in Sarasota, Florida and at various locations in Connecticut. The views expressed here do not necessarily represent those of any organizations with which he is affiliated. E-mail: Plsarno@yahoo.com.

[1]   The author wishes to extend his appreciation to the interviewees who must remain unnamed in this article. In it, "Myanmar" is used to identify the former Burma and but no political significance should be attributed to such use.

[2]   The first comprehensive survey was conducted by the Government's Central Committee for Drug Abuse Control (CCDAC) in cooperation with the United Nations International Drug Control Program (UNDCP). The UNDOC performed a greater supervisory role starting with the 2003 survey.

[3]   In arriving at this conclusion, the United States survey figures for 1996 and the UNODC totals for 2005 are utilized to calculate the latter's recordation of the ten year decrease because the UNODC has surveyed for only the last five years of that decade. If such United States figures for 1996 and the UNODC totals for 2007 are utilized, hectares under cultivation and tonnage decreased by about 82 per cent over the twelve years ending with the latter year.

[4]   Interview with American Embassy representative in Yangon in June 2007.

[5]   The villages were selected presumably by the UNDOC and Myanmar government's CCDAC from a comprehensive list compiled by the CCDAC, the organization responsible in Myanmar for ending all drug production by 2014, Opium Survey 2006, pp. 101–03, interview with UNODC personnel in Yangon in June 2007.

[6]   The UNODC utilized substantially similar survey procedures as a basis for the 2007 Opium Survey and supplemented them with an off-season survey in September 2006 in the South Shan State to detect any planting in the rainy season, Opium Survey 2007, pp. 67, 98–104.

[7]   UNODC, World Drug Report 2007, p. 128; INSCR 2007, vol. 1, pp. 267, 273.

[8]   UNODC, *Amphetamines and Ecstasy: 2008 global ATS Assessment*, dated 9 September 2008, p. 29.

[9]   Interviews in Yangon, 14 and 15 June 2007 and for example, "Myanmar seizes more stimulants in June", Xinhua General News Service, in Burmanet News, 20 July 2006; "Myanmar announces hundreds of drug arrests", Agence France-Presse, in Burmanet News, 15 September 2006; Report of the International Narcotics Control Board for 2006 ("the INCSR"), pp. 62–63, 243; INCSR 2007, vol. 1 (March 2007): 268, 270.

[10] Catherine Brown, "Burma: The Political Economy of Violence", *Disasters*, vol. 23, no. 3 (1999): 246, 251.

[11] Ya-ba is a Thai name of a form of ATS tablet. Desmond Ball, "Burma and drugs: The Regime's Complicity in the Global Drug Trade", pp. 5–7; Bertil Lintner, "Drugs and Economic Growth in Burma Today", pp. 185, 187; Phil Thornton, *Restless Souls Rebels, Refugees, Medics and Misfits on the Thai-Burma Border* (Bangkok: Asia Books, 2006), pp. 174–77; Steve Hirsh, "Officials, critics clash over Myanmar Opium Questions", UN Wire, in Burmanet News, 18 December 2003.

[12] INCSR 2006, p. 244; INCSR 2007, vol. 1, p. 271; see also Plan for Implementation of Section 570 of Public Law 104–208, Conditions in Burma and U.S. Policy Toward Burma for the Period 28 September 2000 to 27 March 2001, FR Doc 01-10260, p. 16; Interview with UNDOC Myanmar Representative Jean-Luc Lemahieu by Steve Hirsch, UN Wire, in Burmanet News, 19 December 2003; Ronald D. Renard, *The Burmese Connection. Illegal Drugs and the Making of the Golden Triangle* (Boulder: L. Rienner, 1996), p. 106.

[13] However, in June 2008, State Peace and Development Council member Lieutenant General Ye Myint was reportedly retired from his position as Chief of the Bureau of Special Operations Number 1 shortly after his son was alleged to have been arrested on drug trafficking charges.

[14] INCSR 2006, p. 243.

[15] "Myanmar seizes more stimulant tablets in June", Xinhua in Burmanet News, 2 July 2006.

16 For example, "Myanmar arrests 385 drug traffickers in July: State Media", Agence France-Presse, in Burmanet News, 13 August 2008; the United States describes seven such seizures, INSCR 2007, vol. 1, p. 270.

17 Khun Sam, "Burma claims it's winning the war on drugs", *Irrawaddy*, in Burmanet News, 26 June 2006 (this article reports 4,149 hectares, as converted from the 10,249.85 acres stated, eradicated in 2005–06).

18 Bertil Lintner, "Cross-Border Drug Trade in the Golden Triangle", p. 33; Thornton, *supra*, p. 179.

19 Interviews in Yangon on 12, 14 and 15 June 2007.

20 Interviews in Yangon on 11 and 12 June 2007.

21 Opium Survey 2007, p. 53.

22 Ibid, pp. 62, 66.

23 "Opium ban seen spurring humanitarian crisis in Myanmar Region", UN Wire, in Burmanet News, 15 December 2003.

24 Interviews in Yangon on 15 and 19 June 2007.

25 United States Treasury Department, Office of Foreign Assets Control, "Treasury Action Targets Burmese Drug Cartel", HP-1268, dated 13 November 2008 found at <http://www.ustreas.gov/press/releases/hp1268.htm>.

26 In February 2006, the Myanmar government issued guidelines for UN Agencies and NGOs active in Myanmar. While there was initial dissatisfaction about the amount of supervision sought by that government over the providers of aid and several prominent NGOs withdrew from the country, many of those who remain comply with some of the rules, such as advance notification to the government of visits to the project site and accompaniment at it by its representative. Other strictures, e.g. prior approval of staff hires and registration of offices, are observed in the breach.

27 Interviews in Yangon on 12, 15 and 18 June 2007; Ben Blanchard, "China offers rare praise for Myanmar's drug fight", *Reuters*, in Burmanet News, 25 June 2008; "China develops more substitute crops for opium poppy in bordering countries", Xinhua General News Service, in Burmanet News, 20 February 2007; "Agency views Chinese role in replacement planting scheme in 'Golden Triangle'," Xinhua via BBC, in Burmanet News, 27 June 2005.

28 Interviews in Yangon on 11, 15, 19 and 20 June.

29 Opium Survey 2006, p. 59.

30 See Sections 489 and 490 of the Foreign Assistance Act of 1961, as amended and in force in 2002 (the "FAA", 22 U.S.C.A. 2291) and, in particular, 22 U.S.C.A. Sec 2291h(a)3.

31 While the statute requires the withholding of only 50 per cent of bilateral aid, the reality in Congress was that no such aid would be appropriated while such a determination is in place.

32   22 U.S.C.A. Sec 2291j(a),(b) and (e).

33   "Myanmar to stop more opium growth", Associated Press, 20 May 2002; Burmnet News 22 May 2002, interview with a former State Department employee, October 2004.

34   *Washington Post*, 22 November 2002, in Burmanet News; Fielding, Kimberly and Thet Khaing, "US Envoy Congratulates Government on Narcotics Control Works", *Myanmar Times*, 9–15 December 2002, p. 3.

35   E.g. Aung Zaw, "Saying No to Burma's Druglords", *Irrawaddy*, in Burmanet News, 30 November – 2 December 2002; "Speed Precursors coming from outside Burma a lame excuse, retorts Shan exile", Shan Herald Agency for News, in Burmanet News, 13 December 2002; Al Kamen, "Close Shave on Burma", *Washington Post* (column), 23 December 2002; "A blunder on Burma", *Washington Times*, 2 December 2002 (editorial).

36   Investigation of Burmese Military Rape of Ethnic Women Trip Report, 1–4 August 2002, Bureau of Democracy, Human Rights and Labor, U.S. Department of State, in Burmanet News, 9–11 December 2002.

37   INCSR 2002, released March 2003, Burma Section, Summary.

38   68 FR 5787, 68 FR 54973. Humanitarian aid could be furnished despite such prohibition but, as a practical political matter it was and remains unlikely that any will be approved in any magnitude by Congress absent such certification.

39   Written communication to the author from Matthew P. Daly and David I. Steinberg, *Turmoil in Burma Contested Legitimacies in Myanmar* (Norwalk, Conn: EastBridge, 2006), p. 116.

40   INCSR 2007, vol. 2, pp. 119–20. Myanmar enacted The Control of Money Laundering Law in June 2002 and issued The Control of Money Laundering Rules in December 2003. It has closed three banks for money laundering and arrested the Chairman of one and some of his associates, INCSR 2006, p. 244.

41   The latest finding was made on 16 September 2008, Presidential Determination no. 2008-28 found at <http://www.state.gov/p/inl/rls/prsrl/ps/109777.htm>.

42   Jacob Bayman, "Burma's largest rebel army battles increase in opium production", *San Francisco Chronicle*, in Burmnet News, 15 January 2008.

Philippines

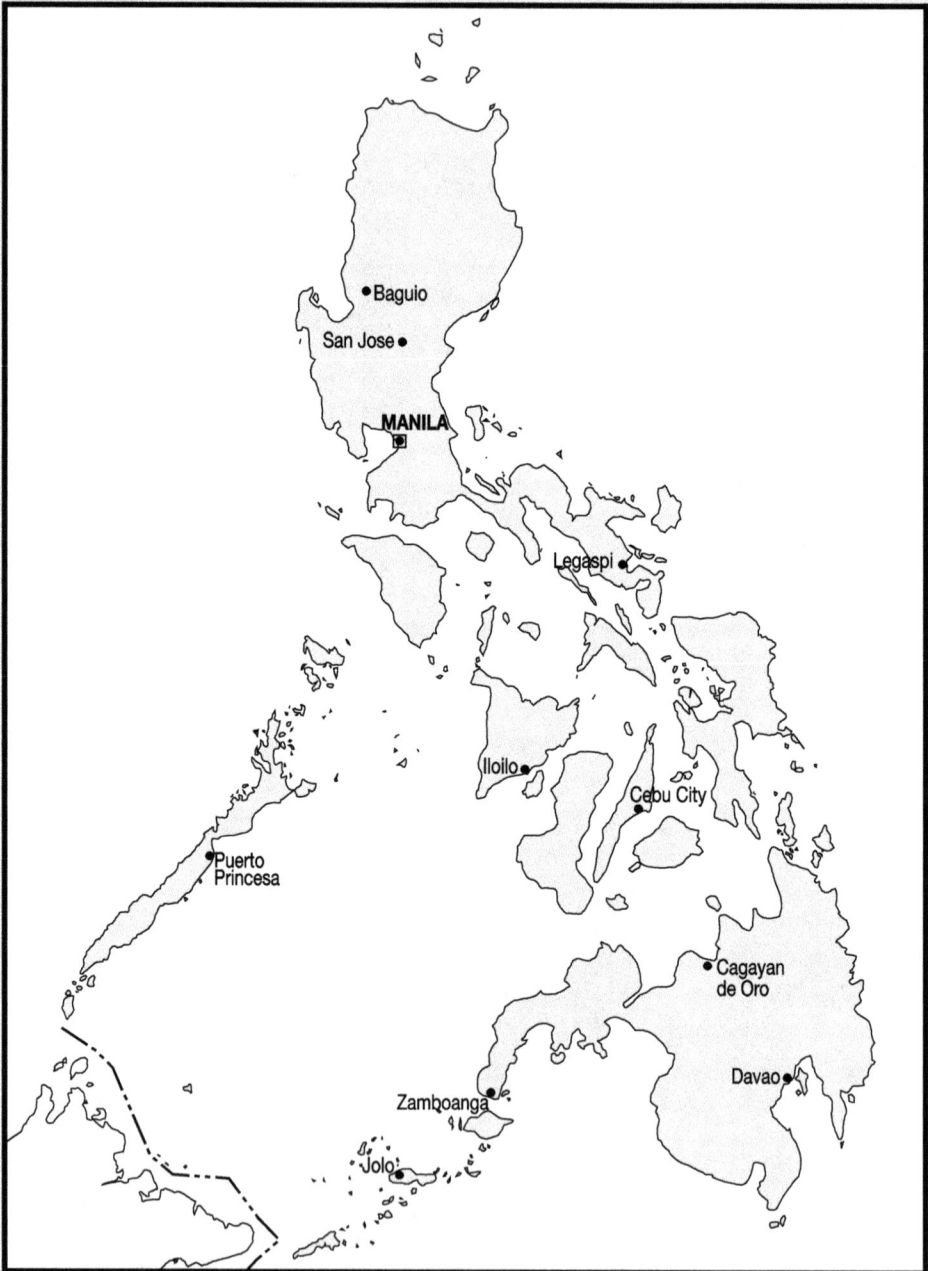

- Baguio
- San Jose
- **MANILA**
- Legaspi
- Iloilo
- Cebu City
- Puerto Princesa
- Cagayan de Oro
- Davao
- Zamboanga
- Jolo

PHILIPPINES IN 2008
A Decoupling of Economics and Politics?

Melanie S. Milo

The Philippine economy started 2008 on a high note — it had just registered its highest real GDP growth rate in three decades of 7.2 per cent in 2007, which was significantly higher than the 6.1–6.7 per cent target set by the government. This was attributed to spending related to the May elections, which typically bolsters consumption expenditure; government expenditure on infrastructure projects; and personal consumption expenditure, supported by overseas Filipinos' remittances.[1] This despite a weakening external environment, particularly as a result of instability in U.S. and global financial markets.

As in previous years of inordinately strong economic performance, the question was whether it could be sustained in 2008 and beyond. But given the domestic factors that drove growth in 2007, and the real fallout from the U.S. and eventual global financial crises, some economic slowdown was to be expected in 2008. The question was how well the Philippine economy would cope with the impending U.S. and global recession.

In contrast, political controversies and disturbances that began in 2007 were carried over into 2008, in addition to those that began in earlier years. The continued strong performance of the economy despite continuing political instability has raised the question of whether economic performance has decoupled from political developments in the Philippines.

The article first discusses economic performance and trends in the Philippines in 2008, followed by a discussion of key political developments that could have had the most negative impact on the economy.

MELANIE S. MILO is a Fellow at the Institute of Southeast Asian Studies (ISEAS), Singapore.

The Philippine Economy in 2008

Economic Growth and Sectoral Performance

Table 1 shows real GDP growth rate by type of expenditure for 2005–08. The period from 2002 was a period of steady, moderate growth, ranging from 4.4 per cent in 2002 to a high of 7.2 per cent in 2007 for real GDP, and from 4.2 per cent to 8 per cent for real GNP. Real GDP growth slowed down significantly to 4.6 per cent in the first three quarters of 2008, compared to 7.5 per cent during the same period in 2007. However, it has also been argued that weaknesses of the Philippines' national income accounting system are very likely to have led to an overstatement of GDP growth from 2000.[2]

On the demand side, growth of personal consumption expenditure, which has consistently accounted for almost 80 per cent of real GDP since the early 1990s, slowed down in the first three quarters of 2008 as a result of increasing oil and food prices. On the other hand, the continued strong inflow of overseas Filipino workers' (OFWs) remittances kept consumer spending fairly robust. Because of the significant increase in the number and employment quality of OFWs in the first three quarters of 2008, remittances grew at a higher rate of 17.1 per cent over the same period in 2007. This drove the 19 per cent growth of net factor income from abroad, which in turn contributed to the 5.9 per cent real growth of GNP.

Government consumption expenditure, which accounts for around 7 per cent of real GDP, accelerated in 2006–07 with the disbursement of funds for the government's infrastructure programme, the 2007 elections, and the salary adjustment of government employees. It then declined in the first two quarters of 2008 compared to the same period in 2007. It picked up only in the third quarter due to a significant increase in the maintenance and other operating expenses of the government.

The share of capital formation to GDP has steadily declined from around 22 per cent in 2001 to 18 per cent in 2007. The year 2007 was a banner year for the Philippine economy not just in terms of overall GDP growth, but also in the significant growth of capital formation. But this was driven by real construction expenditures, which grew by over 21 per cent in 2007 and was largely accounted for by public spending. On the other hand, investment in durable equipment grew at a slower rate of 4.5 per cent. In 2008, investment in fixed capital formation in the first quarter of 2008 grew by just 2.9 per cent from 10.3 per cent in the same period last year. Higher investments in residential assets sustained the double-digit growth of private construction, but this was more than offset by the decline in public construction, which resulted in an overall contraction of over 3 per cent. In contrast, investment in durable equipment grew faster. In the third quarter of 2008, the trend was reversed. Fixed capital formation grew by 4.8 per cent. In

TABLE 1
Growth of Real GDP by Type of Expenditure, 2005–08
(per cent)

Growth	2005	2006	2007 (year on year)				2008 (year on year)		
			Q1	Q2	Q3	Q4	Q1	Q2	Q3
By type of expenditure:									
Personal consumption	4.8	5.5	5.9	5.6	5.7	6.2	5.2	4.1	4.6
Government consumption	2.3	10.4	9.5	11.9	6.4	4.6	1.9	–1.5	12.5
Capital formation	–8.8	5.0	8.7	17.6	7.6	11.0	4.0	15.3	4.8
Exports	4.8	13.4	10.8	4.9	3.7	3.9	–6.1	7.6	4.7
Imports	2.4	1.9	–1.8	–10.5	–5.0	0.2	–5.8	–0.7	5.1
Gross Domestic Product	5.0	5.4	7.0	8.3	7.1	6.4	4.7	4.4	4.6
Net factor income from abroad	10.7	6.1	11.3	25.3	31.9	0.6	18.3	14.8	24.7
Gross National Product	5.4	5.5	7.3	9.8	9.1	6.0	5.8	5.5	6.5

Source: National Statistical Coordination Board.

particular increased public expenditures on capital outlay for priority projects led
to a 20 per cent real growth in public construction, as the government tried to
pump-prime the economy. Private construction also sustained its growth, leading
to an overall growth of 15.8 per cent which is comparable to the 16.8 per cent
real growth rate of construction in the same period in 2007.

With the economic slowdown in the industrialized countries, total merchandise
exports fell by 11 per cent in the first quarter of 2008. In particular, the country's
primary exports of semiconductors and electronic microcircuits, and finished
electrical machinery fell dramatically. Total merchandise imports likewise fell by
7.3 per cent in the same period. They were somewhat offset by the growth of
non-factor services exports and imports. Merchandise exports began to recover
in the second quarter, and merchandise imports in the third quarter.

In terms of distribution of GDP by industrial origin, the share of agriculture,
fishery and forestry has been gradually declining over the past three decades, and
was around 18 per cent in 2008. Industry's share, has likewise slowly declined
from around 40 per cent of GDP in the early 1980s to just 33 per cent in 2008.
In particular, GDP share of manufacturing declined from around 28 per cent to
23 per cent over the same period. Manufacturing accounted for around 70 per
cent of industrial output in 2008, followed by construction with around 15 per
cent share. Finally, the services sector, which has been the dominant sector since
the mid-1980s, further increased its share to almost half of GDP in 2008. Around
a third of services output is accounted for by wholesale and retail trade.

Table 2 shows real GDP growth rate by industrial origin. All three major
economic sectors contributed to the economy's strong performance in 2007.
Under industry, mining/quarrying and construction, which accounted for 2 per
cent and 5 per cent of GDP, grew by almost 26 per cent and 23 per cent in real
terms, respectively. Services continued to drive the economy, though, with all
subsectors performing well in 2007. Sectoral growth then decelerated in the first
three quarters of 2008. And in contrast to previous years, industry grew slightly
faster than services, with manufacturing growing at a faster rate of 4.5 per cent,
compared to 3.7 per cent in the first three quarters of 2007. In particular, the leading
contributor to manufacturing growth was food manufacturing, which accounted
for around 38 per cent of total manufacturing. Sharp declines, on the other hand,
were recorded in electrical machinery, textiles, furniture and fixtures.

A key weakness that has been noted in the robust economic growth in 2007
was the manufacturing sector, which only grew by 3.4 per cent in real terms. It also
marked the third year of consecutive decline in manufacturing growth rate which,
it has been argued, is a "clear manifestation of the 'Dutch disease' phenomenon:

TABLE 2
Growth of Real GDP by Industrial Origin, 2005–08
(per cent)

Growth	2005	2006	2007 (year on year)				2008 (year on year)		
			Q1	Q2	Q3	Q4	Q1	Q2	Q3
1. Agriculture, fishery & forestry	2.0	3.7	4.0	4.2	5.7	5.7	2.7	5.0	2.5
a. Agriculture & fishery	2.0	3.7	4.0	4.3	5.9	5.7	2.7	5.0	2.5
b. Forestry	4.2	7.0	-6.1	-8.3	-17.7	-5.4	2.2	-3.7	7.2
2. Industry sector	3.8	4.8	6.6	10.3	6.6	4.9	3.0	4.5	7.1
a. Mining & quarrying	9.3	-6.1	14.7	38.9	24.0	21.5	14.1	-12.4	-4.1
b. Manufacturing	5.3	4.6	4.1	3.4	3.7	2.6	2.4	6.2	4.7
c. Construction	-5.9	9.6	21.7	37.0	17.8	13.4	-3.4	3.7	21.3
d. Electricity ,gas & water	2.5	6.4	4.4	5.4	8.4	8.3	9.5	6.7	9.7
3. Service sector	7.0	6.5	8.4	8.4	8.0	7.8	6.6	4.2	3.8
a. Transport., comm'n, storage	7.3	6.3	10.5	9.6	5.8	7.4	5.6	3.9	1.5
b. Trade	5.6	6.1	7.2	7.6	9.1	8.8	5.8	4.2	4.2
c. Finance	13.5	11.3	16.3	14.2	11.4	10.4	12.2	1.0	1.3
d. Dwellings & real estate	5.3	5.7	5.5	6.0	6.8	5.0	7.3	7.6	6.6
e. Private services	7.5	6.9	8.4	9.1	8.7	7.6	5.7	6.0	5.2
f. Government services	5.0	2.3	1.7	2.4	3.4	2.9	4.0	2.5	3.3

Source: National Statistical Coordination Board.

a booming economy accompanied by a slowdown in the manufacturing sector". It is considered a worrying trend because of the critical role that a dynamic manufacturing sector plays in the sustainability of the country's economic growth and development.[3]

Growth of construction slowed down significantly in the first three quarters of 2008 compared to the previous year. In particular, public construction contracted in the first two quarters, although this was more than offset by private construction. Public construction rebounded in the third quarter as the government implemented its priority infrastructure projects.

The dramatic growth of financial services in 2004–07, and its deceleration in 2008, is noteworthy in the context of the prevailing global financial crisis. Although as a percentage of GDP, financial services only accounted for 5–6 per cent. Continued growth of financial services in 2008 was due to the strong performance of the banking sector. In contrast, the non-banking sector, which includes insurance, investment companies, security dealers and brokers contracted in the first three quarters of 2008.

When the U.S. subprime crisis broke out in mid-2007, the *Bangko Sentral ng Pilipinas* (BSP) Governor Tetangco assured the public in various speeches that the Philippine banking system would not be significantly affected because of the limited exposure of Philippine banks to sophisticated structured products such as derivatives and collateralized debt obligations (CDOs). The CDO market was only 0.2 per cent of total bank assets in mid-2007, and had no subprime mortgages as underlying assets. In a more recent speech made during a public hearing of the Senate Committee on Banks in late September 2008, he then reported that Philippine based banks' exposure to Lehman Brothers was 0.3 to 0.4 per cent of total assets, which is around US$320 to 430 million. This involved a limited number of banks, and transactions arising from Special Purpose Vehicles as well as the direct investment in Lehman-issued financial instruments. The limited exposure has been attributed to the combination of prudent regulation and Filipino investors' lack of financial sophistication. And Philippine banks are deemed as well positioned to cope with the ongoing financial crisis because of the reforms that were undertaken in the aftermath of the 1997 Asian financial crisis; banks are well capitalized; and there is ample liquidity in the system. However, it has been noted that most disclosures were only on the amount of provisions set aside to cover the exposures, and not the amount of exposures themselves. Thus, the figures could be higher than what BSP reported.[4] And although the figures appear miniscule in terms of percentage, they are not insubstantial particularly in the context of a still credit-constrained economy.

As the country's estimated population reached 90.68 million in 2008, the economy seems to have kept pace with population growth. Per capita GDP grew by 5.1 per cent in 2007; per capita GNP by 5.9 per cent; and per capita personal consumption expenditure by 3.8 per cent. Growth of per capita GDP, GNP and personal consumption expenditure in the first three quarters of 2008 then decelerated to 2.8, 4.4, and 2.3 per cent, respectively.

However, questions have been raised on whether economic growth has truly trickled down. In particular, there has been a decline in real average family income from 2003 to 2006 based on the 2006 Family and Income Expenditure Survey (FIES) despite the rise in per capita GDP. This discrepancy is due to some extent to the steady increase in corporate profits, which is not captured by the FIES, and the persistent decline in wages as components of GDP. This phenomenon of declining share of GDP going to labour and increasing share of GDP going to capital has also been observed in other economies, including China and the U.S. But the trend is found worrisome for the Philippines because the rising share of capital was not accompanied by a comparable trend in investment level, which also explains why the benefits of higher economic growth have not been shared more equitably.[5] It should be noted that poverty incidence among families increased from 24.4 per cent in 2003 to 26.9 per cent in 2006, while poverty incidence among the population rose from 30 per cent to 32.9 per cent. Thus, a group called Former Senior Government Officials issued a statement in mid-March slamming the President's economic reports of steady growth and poverty reduction as a "PowerPoint mirage". Members of the group included former director generals of the National Economic and Development Authority (NEDA), and budget and finance secretaries.

Employment

The unemployment rate was redefined beginning in April 2005 to coincide more with the ILO's definition. Previously, the unemployed consisted of those without work and seeking work. The criterion "available for work" was then added, which caused the number of unemployed to decrease by 1.5 million. Out of the estimated 58.2 million population 15 years old and above in October 2008, 37.1 million persons were estimated to be in the labour force. This labour force participation rate of 63.7 per cent is slightly higher than the 63.2 per cent recorded in October 2007. Overall, the period of steady, moderate economic growth that began in 2002 is not perceptible in Figure 1. The unemployment rate has been fairly stable. It went down to 6.3 per cent in October 2007, from 7.4 per cent in October 2005, but again rose to 6.8 per cent in October 2008. There was an improvement in the rate of underemployment, which fell from around 21 per cent in October 2005 to

17.5 in October 2008. Most of the underemployed were working in the agriculture sector (48.8 per cent) and services sector (36 per cent). Underemployment rate in the industry sector was significantly lower at 15.2 per cent.

Similar to the distribution of real GDP by industrial origin, employment share by industry has been very stable over the years. Of the total 34.5 million employed persons in October 2008, almost half (49.6 per cent) worked in the services sector. Workers in the agriculture sector accounted for 35.7 per cent of the total employed, while only 14.7 per cent of the total employed was in the industry sector. In the latter sector, manufacturing accounted for the biggest percentage (8.4 per cent of total employed), followed by construction (5.4 per cent of total employed). Employment in services has been growing the fastest, as shown in Figure 2. Growth of employment in industry was largely in construction, while overall employment in manufacturing has contracted including a 5.2 contraction in October 2008.

Because job creation continues to be insufficient even after several years of sustained, moderate economic growth, deployment of OFWs remains a government priority (see Figure 3). Total deployment grew by just 1.4 per cent in 2007. In the

FIGURE 1
Labour Force Participation Rate, Unemployment[a]
and Underemployment Rates, 2002–08
(year-on-year, per cent)

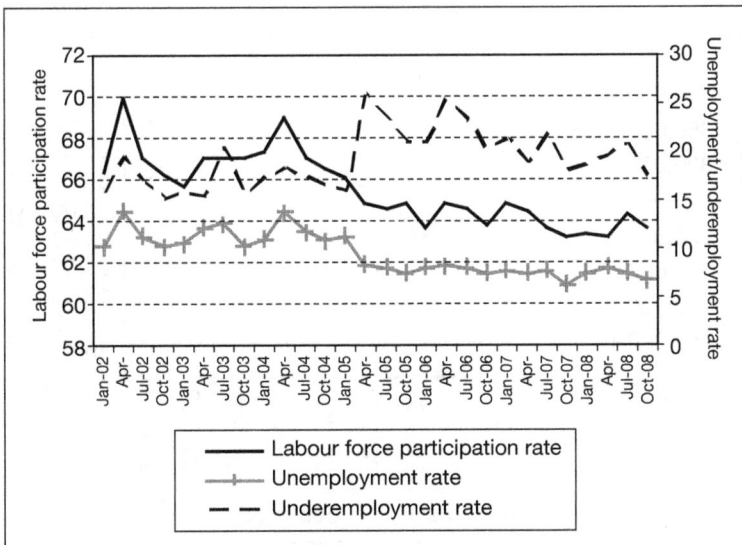

Note: [a] Starting April 2005, a new unemployment definition was adopted. In particular, another criterion, namely "available for work" was added, which resulted in a downward bias.
Source: National Statistics Office.

FIGURE 2
Growth of Employment, by Major Industry Group, 2003–08
(year-on-year, per cent)

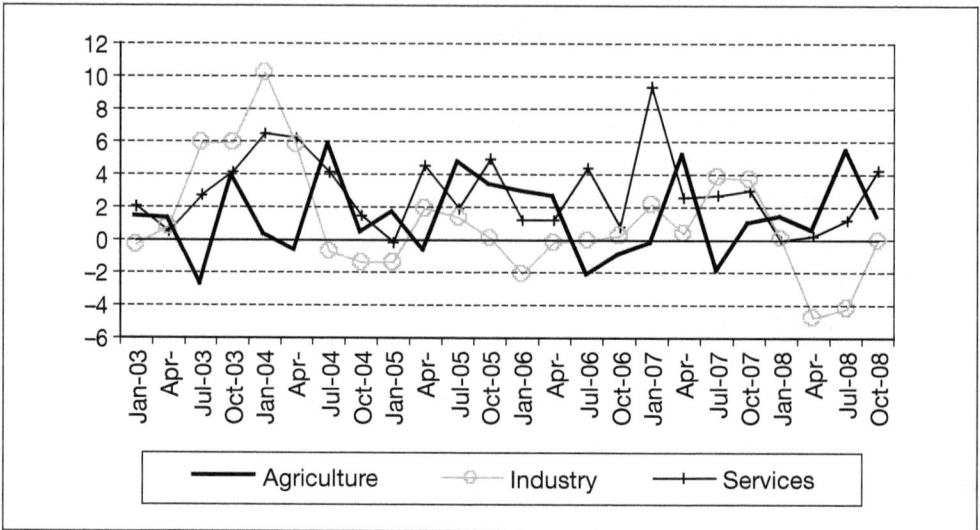

Source: National Statistics Office.

FIGURE 3
Quarterly Deployment and Remittances of OFWs, 2006–08

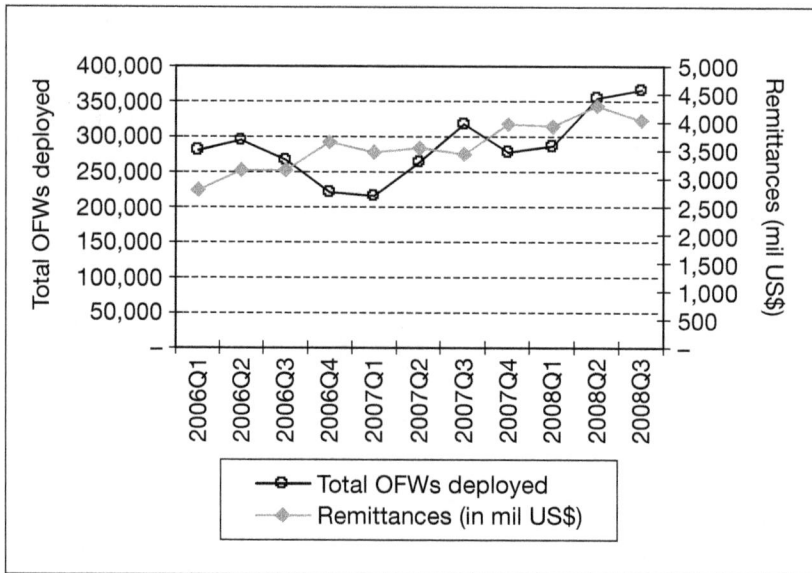

Source: Bangko Sentral ng Pilipinas, Philippine Overseas Employment Administration.

first three quarters of 2008, deployment of OFWs grew by 26 per cent compared to the same period in 2007. The number of OFWs deployed in the first three quarters of 2008 already reached more than a million (1,005,767). Most of the newly-hired OFWs were deployed in the Middle East.

Although retrenchments of OFWs are already being reported, for instance those in Taiwan, government officials are optimistic about future deployment of OFWs, particularly to the Middle East. Thus, remittances are expected to continue to support economic growth in the Philippines. But it has also been argued that what the Philippines should instead focus on is how to use the OFW windfall to develop an exit strategy from the "remittance-driven economy",[6] including using OFW remittances to address the country's infrastructure needs.[7]

Prices and Fiscal Position

From a low of 2.8 per cent average inflation in 2007, the monthly headline inflation rate shot up to as high as 12.5 per cent in August 2008 year-on-year (see Figure 4), as world food and oil prices significantly increased. Expenses for food account for over 50 per cent of total personal consumption expenditure, and the Philippines has become the world's largest importer of rice. The appreciation of the peso by 18.7 per cent in 2007 helped temper the inflation rate, although it also adversely affected the income of families of OFWs. Headline inflation began to moderate in September, falling to 8 per cent in December. Excluding food and energy, monthly core inflation steadily increased from 3.4 per cent in January to 7.9 per cent in November, which is well beyond the target of 3–5 per cent and indicates that the source of inflationary pressure had widened. Thus the Bangko Sentral ng Pilipinas (BSP) raised its key policy interest rates by a total of 100 basis points in June, July and August 2008. The rates were then reduced by 50 basis points in December 2008 to 5.5 per cent for the overnight borrowing or reverse repurchase (RRP) facility and 7.5 per cent for the overnight lending or repurchase (RP) facility.

In May 2008, the government postponed its targeted 2008 balanced budget to 2010 as it prepared to pump-prime the economy. Figure 5 shows various indicators of the government's fiscal position. From a high of 5.3 in 2002, the national government fiscal deficit fell to just 0.2 per cent in 2007. It rose to around 1 per cent of GDP during the first three quarters of 2008. And from a deficit of 5.6 per cent in 2002, the consolidated public sector fiscal position (CPSFP) posted a small surplus beginning in 2006. Thus, the government's stronger fiscal position augured well for its capacity to pump-prime the economy as the external

FIGURE 4
Monthly Headline and Core Inflation Rates, 2001–08
(year-on-year, per cent)

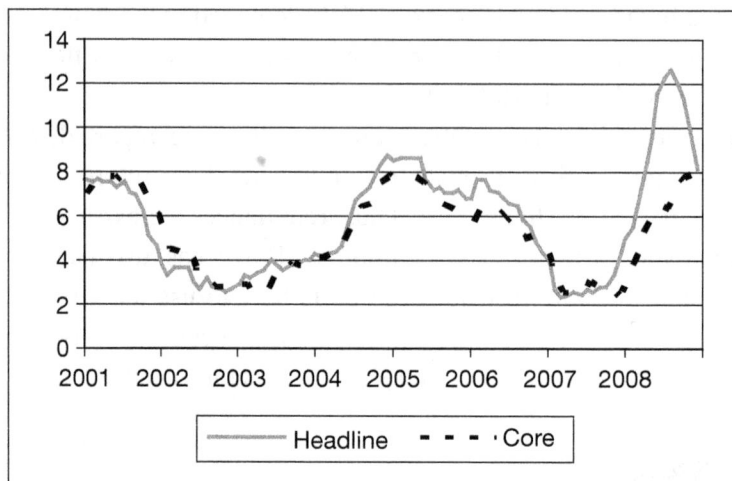

Source: Bangko Sentral ng Pilipinas.

FIGURE 5
Indicators of Fiscal Position, 2001–08[a]
(per cent of GDP)

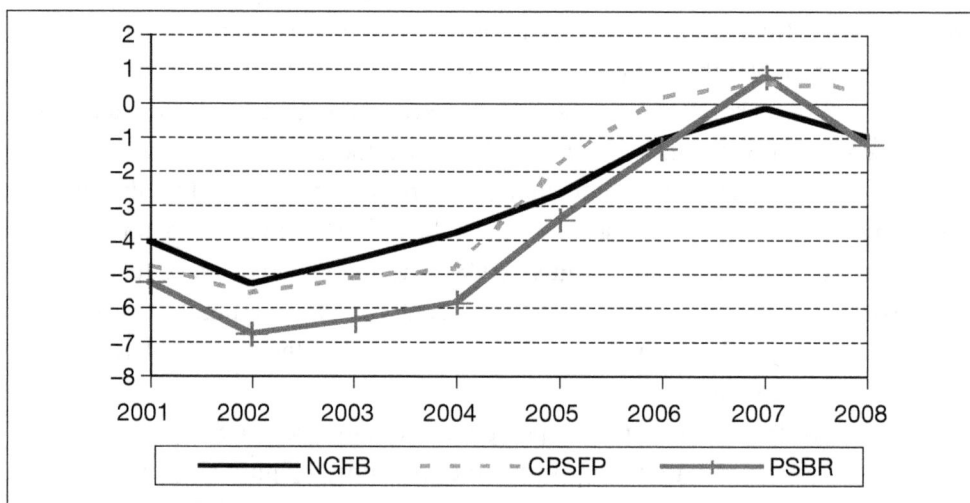

Notes: [a]As of 3rd quarter 2008.
NGFB – National government fiscal balance
CPSFP – Consolidated public sector fiscal position (NGFB plus monitored government-owned and controlled corporations, government financial institutions, local governments, and other public sector entities).
PSBR – Public sector borrowing requirement
Sources: Bureau of Treasury; National Statistical Coordination Board.

environment continued to worsen in 2008. However, it should be noted that the improvement in the national government and consolidated public sector fiscal positions in 2007 and 2008 was largely due to privatization proceeds, which are non-recurring income.

Also, the still fairly high level of public debt does not allow for significant fiscal expansion. Outstanding public sector debt in March 2008 was around 5 trillion pesos or 73 per cent of GDP, of which around 54 per cent was owed to foreign creditors.

For a long time, the Philippines has been an exception in the region in the worst sense of the word, especially when compared to the more dynamic economies in Southeast Asia — be it in terms of economic performance, poverty alleviation and overall human development, corruption, etc. Apparently, this is not the case in 2008. While some economies in Southeast Asia experienced significant downturns, the Philippines continued to pose a very respectable growth rate. Even better, some have argued that the Philippines would fare better in the midst of the current global financial crises and economic slowdown, compared to other economies in the region.

But there are caveats to the story. The economies least vulnerable to the global slowdown would be those that are less reliant on external trade and foreign financing, and have more room for counter-cyclical policy. In the case of the Philippines, "the principal reason for the benign (*direct*) impact of a global economic slowdown is the weak linkage between Philippine manufactured exports and the domestic manufacturing sector".[8] But, as what happened in the aftermath of the 1997 Asian financial crisis, the indirect economic effects could be more costly and damaging.

In addition to economic consequences, there will be broader social effects of which the government needs to be mindful. These include the need for some social protection for the vulnerable groups. In early January, the Department of Social Welfare and Development launched a new poverty reduction strategy called the "*Ahon Pamilyang Pilipino*" (APP) programme. APP is a five-year, five billion pesos cash assistance programme to the poorest of the poor, and is aimed to benefit 300,000 families in the country's 20 poorest provinces. Initially, a total of 6,000 families identified by social workers from six pilot areas — Pasay and Caloocan cities in Metro Manila, Esperanza and Sibagat towns in Agusan del Sur province, and the towns of Lopez Jaena and Bonifacio in Ozamis City — received an ATM card which would be credited with a maximum monthly government dole-out of 1,400 pesos. In exchange, the families agree to keep the children in school and bring them to health centres regularly, among other conditions.

However, there were already almost 4.68 million poor families in 2006. And as a result of the dramatic increase in food prices in 2008 alone, the still high incidence of poverty among the population has been projected to rise further to around 35 per cent in 2008, from 33 per cent in 2006.[9]

There are also the long standing institutional issues that hamper Philippine economic development, particularly the Philippines' political system that has not kept pace with the requirements of economic development.[10] That being said, it is highly doubtable whether the renewed push in 2008 for charter change by the current administration, which is primarily seen as a way to circumvent constitutional term limits, is the way to address the issue. This is discussed further in the next section, together with other key political controversies in 2008.

Political Developments in 2008[11]

Cha-Cha, Con-Con, and Con-Ass[12]

A total of 31 measures have been filed and are pending before the Committee on Constitutional Amendments of the House of Representatives since the 14th Congress opened in July 2007. Of these, 8 are bills, 9 are concurrent resolutions, 2 are joint resolutions, and 12 are House resolutions.[13] Expectedly, all except one propose either to amend the 1987 Constitution or revise some of its provisions "in order to make it more responsive to the demands of the times". In particular, 21 measures argue for charter change (or more commonly referred to as "cha-cha") either by constitutional convention or "con-con" (10 measures), constituent assembly or "con-ass" (9), either con-con or con-ass (1), or people's initiative (1). The others call for revisions of specific provisions, or relate to issues concerning the amendment of the Constitution.

In the Senate, 5 measures have been filed before the Senate committee on constitutional amendments — 2 bills to amend the constitution, one via a people's initiative and the other via constitutional convention; 2 joint resolutions to amend the constitution, one via a constituent assembly and the other via constitutional convention; and a Senate resolution filed in December 2008 by Senator Benigno Aquino III, son of former President Corazon Aquino, which called for an inquiry into "the need for Congress to submit to the electorate, through the May 2010 national elections, the question of calling a constitutional convention, or, to legislate the holding of a constitutional convention and the election of delegates simultaneous with the May 2010 national elections".

There are three modes provided under Article XVII of the 1987 Constitution by which it could be amended. Congress may, by a vote of two-thirds of all its Members, call a constitutional convention, or by a majority vote of all its Members, submit to the electorate the question of calling such a convention. Another way is for the Philippine Congress to sit as a constituent assembly, with the Senate and the House convening as one to propose amendments to the Charter; and upon a vote of three-fourths of all its members. Finally, Section 2 states that "Amendments to this Constitution may likewise be directly proposed by the people through initiative upon a petition of at least twelve per centum of the total number of registered voters, of which every legislative district must be represented by at least three per centum of the registered votes therein". Any proposed amendment or revision to the 1987 Constitution then needs to be ratified by the majority of Filipinos in a plebiscite.

Among the proposed changes are the shift from the presidential and unitary form of government to a parliamentary and federal form of government; the lifting of the term limits of elected officials; and more recently the removal of limits on foreign investments. Transitory provisions would also extend the terms of currently sitting officials. Thus, the move is widely seen as a bid to keep President Arroyo and her cohorts in power after the end of her term in 2010. Not surprisingly, majority of the measures were filed by members of the pro-administration party, Lakas-Christian Muslim Democrats or Lakas-CMD (14), and President Arroyo's own political party, the *Kabalikat ng Malayang Pilipino* or Kampi (7).

Several administration congressmen already began hinting of fresh moves to push for charter change when Congress reconvened in late January. The House committee was set to resume hearings on eight resolutions, mostly calling for charter change through a constitutional convention. According to administration lawmakers, they had the numbers to get the proposed amendments approved. However, attempts by previous governments to change the constitution were met with strong public protests because of deep mistrust that the sitting president would use it primarily to change the provision limiting the presidency to a single six-year term. This held especially true for the current administration.

In April, Press Secretary Bunye informed the press that President Arroyo believes she does not have enough time left in her term to undertake charter change. That being said, he also said the President would not stop her allies in Congress from pursuing it.

Also in April, Senator Aquilino Pimentel, Jr managed to form a bipartisan group of 11 senators to sign Senate Joint Resolution No. 10, "to convene the Congress into a constituent assembly for the purpose of revising the Constitution to establish a federal system of government". Five days later, 5 additional senators were made co-authors of the resolution. This is a significant turnaround to the

Senate's opposition to a similar initiative by the President and the House of Representatives in 2007. In particular, Senator Pimentel proposed the creation of 11 federal states and one federal administrative region, Metro Manila.

This resolution then became President Arroyo's basis for renewing talks of charter change in August, particularly in connection with the proposed Muslim homeland accord. That is, she was advocating federalism as a way to resolve the conflict in Mindanao. The government had negotiated a Memorandum of Agreement on Ancestral Domain (MOA-AD) with the Moro Islamic Liberation Front (MILF), which Malaysia brokered. MOA-AD seeks to establish an expanded Bangsamoro homeland in Mindanao, the ultimate objective of which was "to secure their identity and posterity, to protect their property rights and resources as well as to establish a system of governance suitable and acceptable to them as distinct dominant people". It was supposed to be signed in early August in Malaysia. However, the Supreme Court issued a temporary restraining order on the signing of MOA-AD, and later declared it "contrary to law and the Constitution" with a vote of 8–7 in mid-October.

President Arroyo's endorsement cast doubts on the Senate resolution, with some senators threatening to withdraw their signatures. Later that month, the House committee on constitutional amendments voted to call for nationwide consultations until the end of November, before deciding on whether there should be charter change. However, the resolution was recalled in the following week.

Instead, House Speaker Prospero Nograles filed a resolution in September that sought to lift foreign equity and land ownership limits in the Constitution. It was intended to test if Congress could amend specific provisions without having to go through the mandated processes. Although he acknowledged that the resolution cannot progress into law even if it receives majority support, it could then serve as the basis for a constitutional inquiry before the Supreme Court.

The push to amend the Constitution via a constituent assembly gained ground in the House of Representatives in November, when Congressman and the President's eldest son Mikey Arroyo embarked on a signature drive on an unreleased resolution calling on the Senate and the House to amend the Constitution by voting jointly instead of separately. Such a voting scheme would clearly be disadvantageous to the Senate's 23 members, who then strongly opposed the move. The Supreme Court was then seen as the next battleground, should the majority in the House of Representatives succeed in bringing the resolution to the Supreme Court.

Only one measure filed before the House committee on constitutional amendments — House Resolution No. 888 (HR888) — which was filed in December 2008, called for "rejecting any and all moves to amend the 1987 Constitution before the 2010 elections including the proposed convening of Congress into a constituent assembly". It is perhaps not surprising that the principal author of HR888 is Satur Ocampo, one of the party list representatives of the militant group *Bayan Muna*. In particular, the resolution condemned some proposals as "patently self-serving and abhorred by the people", and aimed at circumventing term limits of incumbent officials by postponing the May 2010 presidential elections.

Public sentiment against charter change also remained very strong. A series of protest actions was called for by business, religious, labour, civic society, and opposition leaders in November and December. This culminated in what political analyst Amando Doronila referred to as "the most broadly based civil society mass protest in Makati City since the declaration of a national emergency by President Macapagal-Arroyo in 2006".[14] Although the estimated 10,000 crowd did not come close to the number that joined the people power demonstrations in 1986 and 2001, it was enough to derail the administration's push for charter change. Clearly, the Arroyo administration misread the public's reluctance to participate in another people power movement to overthrow the President as apathy toward such "high-handed bureaucratic solutions".[15]

It was also argued that the renewed push for charter change early in the year was a ploy to divert the public's attention from the NBN-ZTE scandal, which was a carry-over from 2007.

NBN-ZTE Scandal and the Political Fallouts

The National Broadband Network (NBN) — Zhong Xing Telecommunications Equipment Company Limited (ZTE) deal involved a US$329.5 million contract between the Philippine government and ZTE, a Chinese firm based in Shenzhen and reportedly the biggest telecommunications enterprise in China, to set up a national broadband network for the Philippine government. The project was to be financed by a loan from China. The contract was signed in April 2007 by Philippine Department of Transportation and Communications Secretary, Leandro Mendoza, and ZTE Corporate Vice President Yu Yong in Boao province, with the attendance of President Arroyo. It was one of five economic and trade agreements signed between the Philippines and China, which President Arroyo witnessed.

Rumours of overpricing, bribery, and illegality in the awarding of the contract to ZTE immediately followed the signing of the contract. The deal turned into a full-blown scandal in August 2007 when then Commission on Elections (COMELEC) Chairman Benjamin Abalos was identified as having "brokered" the deal. A Senate resolution was then filed in early September for the Blue Ribbon Committee to investigate the deal. Two other Senate committees joined in the investigation — trade and investment, and national defense and security. The testimony of three witnesses at the Senate hearings served to solidify the allegations.

First to testify was Jose "Joey" de Venecia III, son of then House Speaker Jose de Venecia, Jr., who claimed he was present at a meeting in China where Abalos demanded money from ZTE officials. He also testified that Abalos offered him a US$10 million bribe to stop him from bidding for the NBN project, and that First Gentleman Mike Arroyo also pushed for the ZTE contract. Joey de Venecia headed Amsterdam Holdings, Inc. (AHI), a company that made a bid for the NBN project with a build-operate-transfer (BOT) scheme.

Next to testify was then NEDA Director General Romulo Neri, who claimed that Abalos offered him 200 million pesos to approve the ZTE contract. He also testified that he mentioned the bribery attempt to President Arroyo, who told him not to accept it. When further questioned about the President's direct involvement in the matter, he invoked the doctrine of "executive privilege".[16] This also became Neri's excuse for refusing to further testify at the Senate hearings, which carried over into 2008. To compel him to testify, the Senate issued an arrest warrant against him in late January 2008, although several attempts to serve the warrant failed. Neri then turned to the Supreme Court, which issued a temporary restraining order against the arrest warrant. In March 2008, the Supreme Court voted 9–6 in favour of Neri's petition to invoke executive privilege.

Just a few days after Joey de Venecia's testimony and before Neri's testimony in September 2007, President Arroyo suspended the NBN project. In early October 2007, Abalos resigned as chair of COMELEC, and the President cancelled the ZTE contract while on a state visit to China.

After four months, the three committees involved in the investigation were set to end the proceedings since the key witnesses had already refused to speak further on the matter. But a third witness was identified and summoned in late January 2008 — Jun Lozada, who was a close associate of Neri and acted as his technical consultant in the NBN project. But Lozada left the country just hours before the Senate hearing. The committee likewise issued a warrant of arrest against him. Upon his return to the country a few days later, he claimed he was taken into policy custody against his will. Upon his release, he sought refuge with the religious community. His testimony corroborated that of Neri's regarding the involvement of Abalos, and he also explicitly linked Abalos to the First Gentleman. He further claimed that Neri knew more than what he had revealed at the Senate inquiry. At one point, Neri even asked for some kind of a "kitty" in exchange for his testimony, claiming that doing so would seriously jeopardize his future career. In mid-February, Lozada and Abalos confronted each other in a TV interview. Lozada's candor, even about his own misdemeanors, strongly appealed to the general public and he received widespread support including from the influential Catholic Bishop's Conference of the Philippines (CBCP) and former President Corazon Aquino.

After almost a year of hearings and testimonies, the three committees involved in the investigation announced in late August 2008 that they would soon submit a preliminary report and conduct a final hearing in September. The report is supposed to contain recommendations on what laws to enact to prevent the recurrence of such deals. However, no report has been released, much less bills filed, which is not unusual in such Senate "inquiries in aid of legislation". The Senate Blue Ribbon Committee has since turned to other inquiries.

As a result of his son's testimony, Congressman Jose de Venecia, Jr., was removed as Speaker of the House in early February 2008, which was described as "the most gruesome political assassination in Philippine legislative history".[17] The President's party, *Kampi*, under the leadership of her two congressmen sons, spearheaded the campaign to unseat de Venecia. Just before the vote was called, de Venecia made an impassioned privilege speech, in which he recounted his role in the President's successful bid for public office, and charged her, and her family members and cohorts with various acts of corruption. The most damning admission in his speech was his supposed knowledge of attempts to tamper with the results of the presidential elections in 2004, including the "Hello Garci" controversy.[18] He resigned as Lakas-CMD president in March that year. But despite affirming his intimate knowledge of the details of the NBN-ZTE project and assurances of his "commitment to the public's search for truth", he did not testify at the Senate hearings. In December, he released his authorized biography entitled *Global Filipino: The Authorized Biography of Jose de Venecia Jr. the Visionary-Five-Time Speaker of the House of Representatives*. The book contained several chapters on alleged corruption under the Arroyo administration, including the cancelled NBN-ZTE project.

Following the key testimonies, calls for President Arroyo's resignation were thus renewed and a series of protest activities were held. This included another major Friday night rally in Makati City on 15 February, with an estimated crowd of around 10,000. More "indignation rallies" and protest actions were held later that month in commemoration of the 22th anniversary of Edsa I on 25 February. In contrast, the by then cynical public largely ignored the 7th anniversary of Edsa II in January, which deposed former President Joseph Estrada who was then replaced by then Vice-President Arroyo.

Foremost among the key personalities who called on President Arroyo to resign was former President Cory Aquino, who was the uniting force in Edsa I and a key player in Edsa II. She first called on President Arroyo to resign in the aftermath of the "Hello Garci" controversy in 2005, and rued her participation in Edsa II. While speaking at the launch of de Venecia's authorized biography in December, she even went as far as apologizing to former President Estrada, who had spoken earlier, for her role in Edsa II. She later explained that the apology was made tongue-in-cheek, in response to Estrada's statement of having forgiven those who helped oust him in 2001, although she did not take back the apology. Perhaps that is the reason why she did not advocate another people power movement.

In contrast, because of differing views among the 120 Catholic bishops, CBCP did not call for President Arroyo's resignation. Instead, the group called for "communal action" in search for truth, and urged President Arroyo and all branches of government "to take the lead in combating corruption", in a statement released in February following an emergency meeting.[19] However, the president of CBCP, Jaro Archbishop Angel Lagdameo, acting in his personal capacity together with four other bishops, issued a separate statement in October, which declared that: "The time to start radical reforms is now. The time for moral regeneration is now. The time to conquer complacency, cynicism and apathy and to prove that we have matured from our political disappointments is now. The time to prepare a new government is now."[20] However, despite the strong wording, the five bishops fell short of calling for another people power uprising. Because the statement was not fully backed by the Catholic Church and was not definitive enough, it did not resonate with the public. Instead, the statement was strongly criticized by the business community.

As a staunch ally of the President, former Speaker de Venecia had led the administration coalition in the House of Representatives to defeat impeachment complaints filed against President Arroyo in 2005, 2006, and 2007, which the Philippine Constitution limits to one a year. Thus, it was ironic that he became an endorser of the fourth impeachment complaint filed in October, when the one-year ban on filing a new complaint ended. He then testified at the start of deliberations on the substance of the fourth impeachment complaint in late November, detailing the President's role in the botched NBN-ZTE deal and other acts of corruption. But after only three days of hearings, the House Committee on Justice voted 42–8 to declare the fourth impeachment complaint also insufficient in substance. The committee decision was then taken up on the floor, with the dominant administration bloc expectedly voting in favour of the committee decision. Simply put, this was the expected outcome all along.

With the administration majority in the House and the President's defiance of calls for her resignation, the only other approach to remove her from office was people power. But as the government and political analysts have observed, the people seemed tired of people power. Also, there was no clear, undoubtedly better alternative. Thus, public outrage over revelations of corruption and attempts to change the Constitution, while remaining strong, has not reached that "critical mass". But this should not be interpreted as a rejection of people power per se, but as a more realistic assessment and recognition of what it can and cannot achieve. That is why most people are patient to wait for the 2010 presidential elections. As Doronila pointed out,

> Filipinos have been beguiled by the bloodless 1986 People Power Revolution as a broadly based populist movement. They have regarded people power as a painless panacea for political change, causing them to fall back to it as a quick-fix and convenient solution to political deadlocks … But the magic of people power has waned and is no longer available to re-ignite the mass movement of 1986 … The luster of EDSA as a quick-fix, painless decision to resolve the stalemates of the increasingly ungovernable, electorally founded Philippine democracy has faded over the past two decades.[21]

In an interview given during the 22nd anniversary of Edsa I, President Arroyo was quoted as saying that, "the world will not forgive an Edsa III".[22] But if she and her allies continue to devise such brazen schemes in 2009 to extend their term, as evidenced in 2008, the Filipino people are highly likely to continue to be unforgiving of such schemes. It should be noted that quarterly public opinion surveys conducted by the Social Weather Station since 1986 have shown that President Arroyo is more unpopular than any of the three preceding presidents.[23] Net satisfaction rating of her performance has been consistently negative since October 2004. And her annual average net rating of –30 per cent for 2008 was even worse than the –25 per cent she received in 2005, when she experienced the worst crisis of her presidency. The trend in her public satisfaction rating seems irreversible.

The argument has been made that the Philippine economy seems to have insulated itself against political disturbances, or has already factored in continuing political instability. But this view is disputed in a 2007 study conducted by the Asian Development Bank.[24] And even if it were true, the question is how well the economy can cope if adverse external developments are added into the equation.

Without a doubt, political maneuverings in 2008 significantly compromised the government's capacity to steer the economy through the deepening global economic slowdown. This is very much evident in the fact that the government has not come up with a clear-cut, well-defined, well-thought out plan of action, despite announcing a 330 billion pesos stimulus package in early 2009. The next logical question is, how much of this amount will also be lost to corruption?

Notes

[1] J. Yap, "What's in store for the Philippine economy in 2008?", *Development Research News* **26**, no. 1 (2008): 1–8 (Makati City: Philippine Institute for Development Studies, 2008).

[2] F. Medalla and K. Jandoc, "Philippine GDP growth after the Asian financial crisis: Resilient economy or weak statistical system?", Discussion Paper no. 0802 (Quezon City: University of the Philippines, School of Economics, 2008).

[3] Yap 2008.

[4] R. Bernardo and C. Tang, "Okay so far", Global Source Market Brief — Philippines, 18 September 2008.

[5] Yap 2008.

[6] E. De Dios, R. Fabella, and F. Medalla, "The Remittance Driven Economy", a paper written for the Center for National Policy and Strategy (CNaPS), Quezon City, 2007.

[7] R. Fabella, "The Peso appreciation and the sustainability of Philippine growth: Need we worry?", Discussion Paper no. 0803 (Quezon City: University of the Philippines, School of Economics, 2008).

[8] Yap 2008, p. 4.

[9] R. Briones and A. Balisacan, "Dealing with the soaring price of rice", *Policy Notes* no. 2008–05, Philippine Institute for Development Studies, Makati City, 2008.

[10] E. De Dios and P. Hutchcroft, "Political economy", in *The Philippine Economy: Development, Policies and Challenges*, edited by A. Balisacan and H. Hill (Quezon City: Ateneo University Press, 2003).

[11] This section draws on numerous articles from the *Philippine Daily Inquirer's* website <www.inquirer.net>.

[12] The discussion of measures filed in the House of Representatives draws on Ilagan, "A torrent of cha-cha measures", Online article, Philippine Center for Investigative Journalism <http://www.pcij.org/blog/?p=3263>, 2008.

[13] A concurrent resolution is a legislative measure, which binds both the Senate and the House of Representatives. Passed by both Houses, concurrent resolutions are not presented to the President and do not have the force of law. House resolutions are written motions often adopted to express approval or disapproval of a particular issue, but cannot progress into a law (Ilagan 2008).

14   A. Doronila, "Con-ass bid in House derailed", *Philippine Daily Inquirer*, 15 December 2008.

15   A. Doronila, "Frustrations over coups, people power", *Philippine Daily Inquirer*, 14 April 2008.

16   Executive privilege relates to the President's power to withhold certain types of information from the courts, the Congress and ultimately the public. Typically, the types of information covered include "those which are of a nature that disclosure would subvert military or diplomatic objectives, or information about identity of persons who furnish information of violations of law, or information about internal deliberations comprising the process by which government decisions are reached" (from Joaquin G. Bernas, quoted in Doronila 2008, "Battle arena over NBN shifts to SC", *Philippine Daily Inquirer*, 3 March 2008).

17   A. Doronila, "Night of a hundred knives", *Philippine Daily Inquirer*, 6 February 2008.

18   The controversy was triggered by the release in June 2005 of audio recordings of a phone conversation between President Arroyo and then COMELEC Commissioner Virgilio Garcillano, in which they allegedly discussed the rigging of the 2004 national election results. It culminated in the filing of an impeachment complaint against President Arroyo by the minority bloc of the House of Representatives, which was successfully defeated by the majority bloc led by then Speaker Jose de Venecia.

19   "Seeking the Truth, Restoring Integrity", Catholic Bishops' Conference of the Philippines statement dated 26 February 2008.

20   "5 Bishops: 'Time to prepare a new government is now'", CBCP News, 28 October 2008.

21   A. Doronila, "Stalemate benefits general", *Philippine Daily Inquirer*, 25 February 2008.

22   "'World won't forgive another Edsa' — Arroyo", *Philippine Daily Inquirer*, 24 February 2008.

23   "Fourth Quarter 2008 Social Weather Survey: PGMA's net satisfaction rating at –24", Media Release, Social Weather Station, 15 December 2008.

24   Asian Development Bank, *Philippines: Critical Development Constraints* (Manila: Asian Development Bank, 2007).

PHILIPPINE ECONOMIC DEVELOPMENT
A Turning Point?

Kelly Bird and Hal Hill

Introduction

Notwithstanding its sometimes negative international image, the Philippine economy has been performing well in recent years, better than is commonly recognized. Until the global financial crisis in 2008, the country experienced its longest period — five years — of uninterrupted positive per capita economic growth since the 1970s. It seems to have moved on from the "two lost decades", 1983–2003, when there was no net increase in per capita incomes. Business is beginning to insulate itself from the seemingly perennial curse of political machinations souring the commercial environment. That is, business and politics are apparently "decoupling".

The Philippines has an unenviable history of politics nipping promising economic growth trends in the bud, resulting in a volatile development trajectory around a low average growth rate.[1] The country grew quite strongly in the 1970s under Ferdinand Marcos. But this was debt-driven growth, which became unsustainable when the debts came due and political instability set in in the early 1980s. One of Marcos's enduring contributions to international polemics was the phrase "crony capitalism".

Then, under arguably the country's most successful president, Fidel Ramos, growth accelerated in the 1990s, until the onset of the Asian economic crisis.

KELLY BIRD is Senior Economist, SEFM at the Asian Development Bank.

HAL HILL is H.W. Arndt Professor of Southeast Asian Economies, Research School of Pacific and Asian Studies at the Australian National University.

This was of course an event outside of Ramos's control. It had the effect of slowing the economy but, unlike its high-growth neighbours, the Philippines did not experience a deep economic crisis. Ramos was then succeeded by Joseph Estrada — under the 1987 Constitution, the president is not permitted to serve more than one consecutive term — and political instability and backsliding again set in. Estrada had been under house arrest since his removal in early 2001, but in late 2007 he was pardoned and set free by his successor, the current president, Gloria Macapagal-Arroyo.

The key to the recent success is that, since the deep economic and political crisis of 1985–86, the reformers have been able to enact and institutionalize enough major policy victories to satisfy the business community that they are a more or less permanent feature of the political economy architecture. Two in particular stand out: an independent and high quality central bank, BSP, ensuring that monetary and exchange rate policy continue to function effectively, and trade policy reform that has resulted in a much more open economy. For some of this period, fiscal policy has become more prudent, although it remains hostage to Congressional intrigues. These reforms capitalize on what has always been one of the country's greatest strengths, its educational advantage. Philippine professional and technical labour, well educated and English-speaking, has always been highly competitive.

The purpose of this article is to examine the country's recent economic performance, and to relate these outcomes to the policy environment. Unless one believes in good luck or exceptionally favourable international circumstances as the explanators — and neither appears plausible — in recent years, this improved economic performance must be the result of domestic factors that propel economic growth. We examine these factors, focusing on macroeconomic management followed by trade policy, microeconomic reform and governance. Section 2 reviews recent economic performance, including the macroeconomic record. Next in section 3 we investigate microeconomic reform and governance, traditionally the most difficult areas of policy reform. Section 4 presents recent social trends, while in section 5 we summarize our main arguments.

Growth and Macroeconomic Policy

Philippine economic growth in 2007 was 7.3 per cent, the highest for almost 30 years and not far off Asia's high-growth economies. Most major sectors performed well, with services, growing at 8.2 per cent, contributing 56 per cent of the increase. On the demand side, consumption as always was the major engine of growth, contributing 65 per cent of the total. But, encouragingly, investment grew strongly for the first time in a decade, at 9.5 per cent, compared to the anaemic average for 1997–2006 of just 0.8 per cent. Owing to slower global growth, and sharply higher energy and food prices, growth is likely to be more subdued in 2008, perhaps around 5.5 per cent. The economy slowed to around 4.6 per cent in 2008 on the back of a surge in commodity prices and later a sharp slow down in the global economy. Despite these external shocks, the macroeconomic framework remains sound.

Four features of this recent growth performance deserve comment. First, the economic expansion has been the longest in three decades (see Figure 1). Since 2000, growth has averaged 5.1 per cent per annum, superior to both the two preceding decades. The comparison of average per capita growth rates underlines this point: 2.5 per cent since 2000, compared to 0.3 per cent in the 1990s and –0.8 per cent in the 1980s. There is also evidence to suggest that the underlying "potential growth rate" is rising, consistent with structural change in the economy.

Second, this decade's growth is historically unusual, in that it has not been accompanied by either a fortuitous but temporary improvement in the terms of trade, or by unsustainable macroeconomic imbalances that would presage a

FIGURE 1
Philippine Economic Growth, 1970–2007
(per cent)

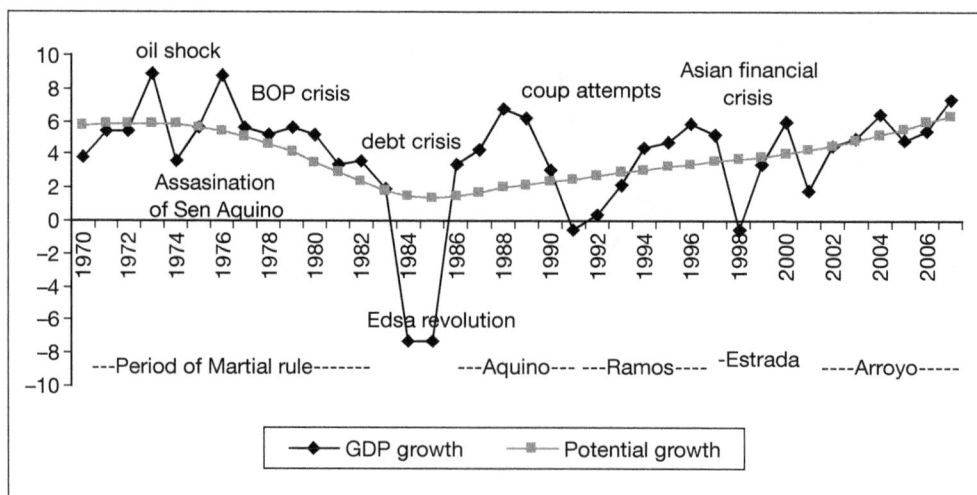

Source: National Statistics Office.

balance of payments of crisis. That is, unlike for example in the Marcos period, the current growth is occurring against a backdrop of monetary policy stability, relatively strong balance of payments (with remittances playing a major role) and the recently recovered fiscal prudence. Moreover, the growth is being achieved in spite of the continuing decline in the country's terms of trade, as its energy and food import bills mount.

The reform of the central bank, and the monetary policy regime set in place and progressively refined since the early 1990s, is a key factor in this outcome.[2] A strategy of inflation targeting combined with a considerably more flexible exchange rate regime has guided Philippine macroeconomic policy through some major domestic and international shocks, with consistently moderate inflation (see Figure 2). In the past decade, these challenges have included the Asian economic crisis and its aftermath, an extra-legislative replacement of a president, a contentious general election, several near coup attempts, terrorist attacks, a major fiscal crisis, a severe loss of international investor confidence, protracted insurgency in the country's south, and a substantial increase in oil and food prices. On each occasion, exchange rate flexibility has essentially provided the shock absorber that has accommodated these events, without derailing growth or triggering a major bout of inflation. This is a key explanation for the Philippines having graduated from its earlier record of boom and bust economic growth. In these earlier periods,

FIGURE 2
Central Bank Independence and Inflation, 1976–2007

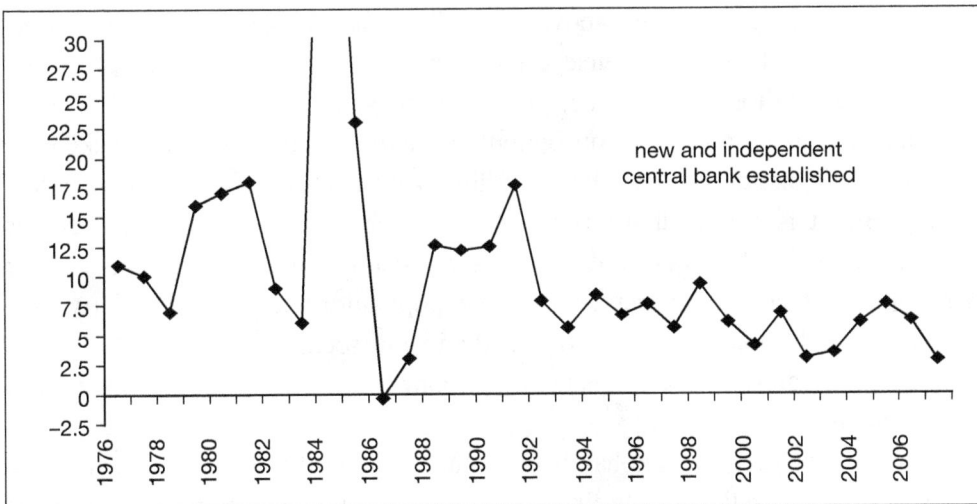

Sources: Bangko Sentral ng Pilipinas (BSP); CEIC.

balance of payments crises typically resulted from the monetization of large fiscal deficits and an attempt to adhere to an uncompetitive exchange rate, precipitating a general economic slowdown.

Third, in contrast to previous growth spurts, the past decade has witnessed positive total factor productivity growth.[3] This marks a turning point from the long history of negligible or negative growth. The intuition for this outcome is obvious: GDP growth has accelerated, but investment and labour force growth have not. TFP has increased across the major sectors, the fastest growth being recorded in services, reflecting the importance of new internationally oriented services. For example, the Philippines is the second most successful operator of BPO (business process outsourcing) facilities in Asia after India, from call centres to a range of IT services. More generally, the increased TFP growth constitutes the reform dividend from the 1990s: trade liberalization and greater competition in non-tradables sectors (e.g. telecommunications, financial services).

Fourth, international remittances have made a significant contribution to the recent growth performance. These hit record levels in 2007, about US$17 billion (including an estimated US$3 billion of informal remittances), increasing by 50 per cent since just 2004. Remittances have kept the current account in strong surplus (about 5 per cent of GDP), they partly explain the strength of the peso in 2007, and they now account for approximately 10 per cent of household income, in the process pushing some above the poverty line. International remittances to the Philippines are the fourth highest in the developing world, after China, India and Mexico, all much larger economies. They are explained by the country's education advantage as noted above, as well as increasingly open international labour markets. There is of course a vigorous debate about the merits of such a large overseas Filipino workforce, OFW's as they are referred to locally. With international employment a ready option for many Filipinos, it may weaken the resolve of the nation's political leadership to push ahead with difficult policy reform. But it is a critical determinant of household welfare, and the benefits are reasonably widely distributed across all decile groups, allowing at least 4 million Filipinos (or 5 per cent of the population) to escape poverty (see Figure 3). In the longer term, a key factor in the social cost-benefit analysis is whether the migration is permanent or temporary, and here the evidence is thus far inconclusive.

Investment performance has been a puzzle since the Asian financial crisis. After rapidly expanding in the first half of the 1990s, investment growth in the Philippines slumped following the Asian crisis and has been slow to recover,

FIGURE 3
**Number of Persons Who Have Escaped Poverty and Moved into a
Higher Income Group as a Result of Remittances in 2006**

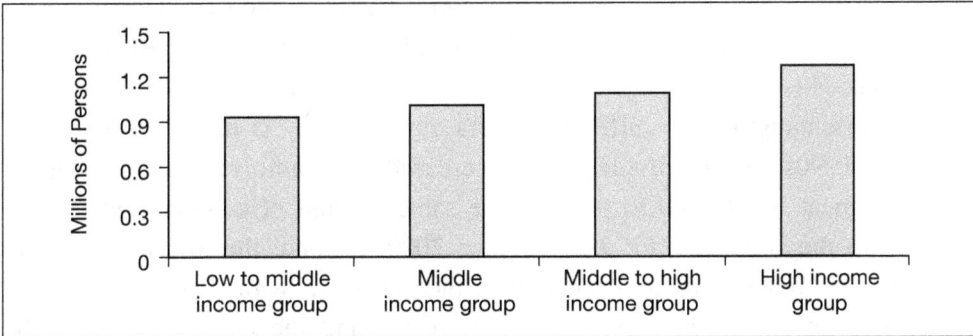

Source: FIES 2006.

FIGURE 4
Trends in Investment Rates — Regional Comparison
(indexed to 100 in 1996)

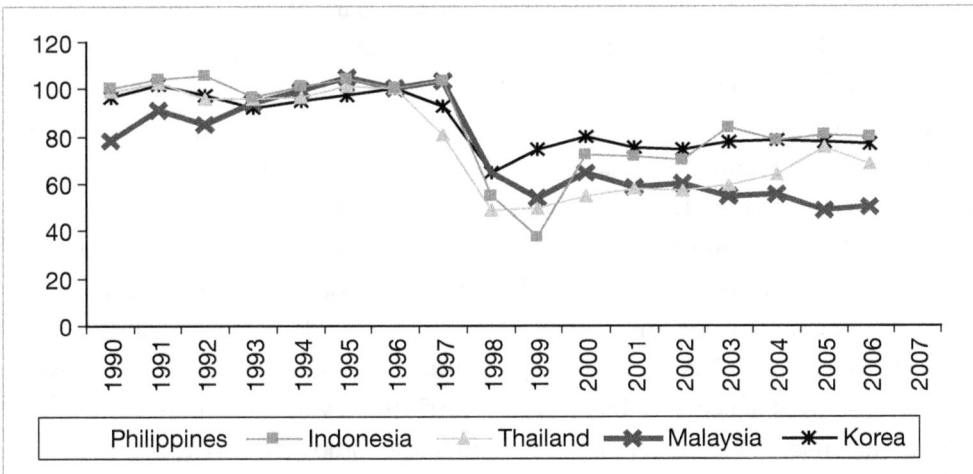

Note: Investment rates refer to capital formation to GDP (nominal values).
Source: Central Statistics Agencies of the countries.

a characteristic shared with all the other crisis-hit countries since 1998 (see
Figure 4). The Philippines was investing the equivalent of 23 per cent of its GDP
before the crisis but this had declined to 14.5 per cent in 2006. The decline in
investment covered both private and public investments. Investment spending

however picked up strongly in 2007 for the first time in ten years growing by 11.8 per cent well above its average annual growth rate of 0.8 per cent from 1997 to 2006. Overall, the gross investment to GDP ratio improved from 14.5 per cent in 2006 to 15.3 per cent in 2007. The slow recovery in investment has occurred at the same time the Philippines has enjoyed its longest economic expansion. There are several factors that may help to explain this puzzle, although disentangling the different factors quantitatively is much harder to do. First, the 1990s reform dividend has increased economic efficiency meaning less investment is required to produce the same amount of economic growth as reflected in the surge in TFP growth since 2000. Second, the lower investment rate may also reflect structural change in the economy, with a shift away from heavy investments in industry, the export sector and the energy sector in the early 1990s towards smaller-scale investments in the services sector. Third, the surge in remittances since the crisis complicates the measurement of investment, as some portion of remittances go to investments that may not be recorded in the national income accounts. Fourth, poor economic governance has hurt investor confidence and this is also reflected in slow recovery in investment (see below).

Fiscal policy has always been the weakest part of the Philippine macro-economic policy framework. This reflects the political economy reality that it may be possible to insulate monetary policy from politics, but it is much more difficult to do so for revenue and expenditure, both in aggregate and in their composition. As Figure 5 shows, in most years fiscal deficits have been contained to 2–3 per cent of GDP. During the mid-1990s the Ramos administration achieved a rare feat in the country's history by handing down three consecutive fiscal surpluses. There have been two really serious episodes of large fiscal deficits in recent memory: in the mid-1980s, when then president Marcos attempted to unsuccessfully spend his way out of a political crisis, and in the 2000s, when Congress blocked successive budgets. By 2005, there was general agreement that near fiscal crises were damaging, and that fiscal prudence has to be the order of the day. Hence, the budget is now very nearly balanced, at 0.2 per cent in 2007. In view of the economic slowdown in 2008, the government allowed an expansion in the budget deficit to 1 per cent of GDP and expects to run a deficit of 1.5 per cent in 2009 in line with neighbouring countries' announcements to run fiscal stimulus in a global recessionary environment. In any case, the country will therefore be able to grow its way out of what looked like an alarming public debt scenario just a few years ago. Nevertheless, the fiscal position remains weak. First, national government debt is still high at over 50 per cent

FIGURE 5
The Philippines: National Government Fiscal Balance, 1970–2007
(per cent GDP)

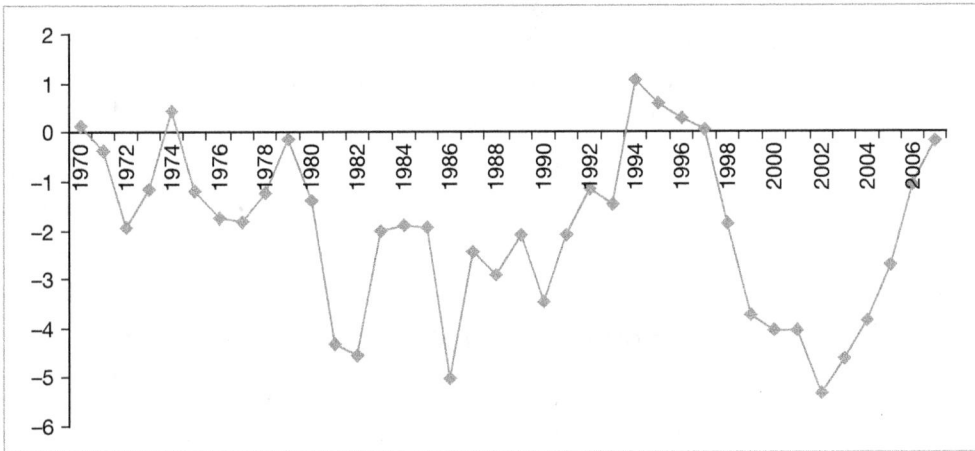

Source: Department of Finance.

of GDP, and non-financial public debt about 15 percentage points higher. There has been temporary relief from the recent peso appreciation (about 40 per cent of national government debt is external) and improved credit ratings. However, any global increase in interest rates will place further pressure on debt service. Second, the revenue effort remains weak, and 'tax buoyancy' (the responsiveness of tax revenue to GDP growth) is low. Third, there is a large contingent liability problem in the broader public sector, particularly with regard to the unfunded pension liability.

On the external environment, much has changed in the last five months. The turmoil in financial markets intensified in September 2008 following the failure of important financial institutions in the U.S. that froze interbank and credit markets around the world and triggered a global liquidity shortage. The negative impacts on the Philippines economy emerged in October 2008 due to significant foreign participation of the country's bond and stock markets. These impacts manifested in a number of forms: (i) the stock market declined by about 30 per cent by the end of the year; (ii) yields on dollar bonds increased by nearly 400 basis points; and (iii) the peso depreciated by 20 per cent against the U.S. dollar on a year-on-year basis. However, gross reserves remained essentially intact at around US$36 billion as outflows were offset by inflows of remittances. The direct effect of the global crisis on the banking system in the Philippines has been minor due to lack of direct investment in the troubled U.S. assets. Liquidity in the banking system had tightened since September but only modestly compared to other countries in the region such as Indonesia. The soundness of the banking system measured by capital adequacy ratios and non-performing loans has so far remained stable. Exports have contracted and this will place some pressure on the balance of payments and exchange rate. Going forward, the economy is expected to remain at a low growth rate of about 4 per cent in 2009. Inflation which peaked at 12 per cent in the third quarter of 2008 has decelerated to 8 per cent by December 2008 on a year-on-year basis and is expected to continue to fall back to its 4–5 per cent range in the next quarter.

Trade Policy, Microeconomic Reform and Governance

Microeconomic reform is generally politically more difficult to enact than the key macro reforms such as establishing an independent central bank or even imposing legislative restrictions on fiscal deficits. This is because the range of actors and vested interests opposed to reform is typically broader and more complex. While the Philippine record in this area has been patchy, there have been some notable achievements. We discuss the issues with reference to trade reform and governance.

The Philippines is now a durably open economy. It was the first ASEAN economy to adopt an import substitution strategy, in the late 1940s, and it got stuck in this inward-looking regime for the next 40 years. Beginning in the late 1970s, however, reformers — principally academics from the University of the Philippines — have become increasingly influential, and they have had major intellectual and policy victories. As Figure 6 shows, average tariff rates have fallen significantly, from over 30 per cent to about 7 per cent, and there seems very little likelihood of a reversal. As credible and gradual reforms, there can be little doubt that the lower tariffs have contributed to the observed increase in the country's total factor productivity growth. The Philippine average tariff compares favourably with that of its neighbours, including Indonesia (8 per cent) and Thailand (16 per cent). Importantly, the dispersion in its tariff rates has also fallen significantly, and thus there is not the distortion in resource flows that existed historically. The reforms have also been accompanied by other major liberalizations, for example in telecommunications, finance and transport, and they have been underpinned by a supportive exchange rate regime for most of the period. Moreover, export-oriented firms have been effectively placed on a free-trade footing, through the operation of various drawback and export zone arrangements,

FIGURE 6
Nominal Average Tariffs, 1985–2007
(in per cent)

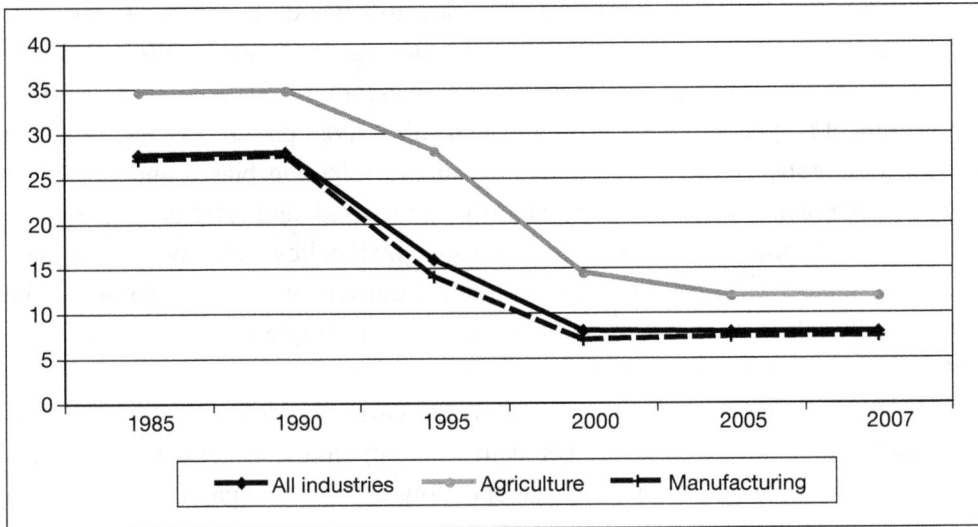

Source: Tariff Commission.

principally under the auspices of the Philippine Export Zone Authority. These reforms were implemented in a gradual, consensual manner, under the auspices of the Philippine Tariff Commission, which provides a forum for both expert technical information and public presentations by interested parties.

Three features of the reforms warrant emphasis. First, they were almost entirely unilateral in nature. The Philippines is a founding member of the Association of Southeast Asian Nations, and has participated fully in ASEAN trade policy initiatives, including those with its major trading partners. But until very recently, the government largely eschewed preferential trading arrangements, including Bilateral Trade Agreements. Secondly, in contrast to the historical pattern of a strong bias towards manufacturing protection, the trade regime now favours agriculture. The political economy reasons for this switch are complex, but three appear to be important: the major analytical work on reform was directed at dismantling manufacturing protection, while work on agriculture was somewhat neglected; the advent of democracy meant that the rural areas, and therefore rural voters, were empowered; and there are more opportunities to circumvent WTO and other restraints on trade in agriculture (e.g. quarantine and other requirements). Third, the major trade issues now relate to the prevalence of non-tariff barriers. These remain principally in agriculture and related activities, such as rice, corn, coffee, hogs and processed meats. Although reform here has been slower, one advantage of the sweeping tariff reductions has been to put political pressure on these 'unreformed sectors'.

Unlike the indicators discussed thus far, governance is inherently difficult to measure. There is no widely agreed upon summary indicator, while composite indicators suffer from the usual calibration, weighting and aggregation issues. Measurement is typically undertaken through subjective opinion surveys, and even the most rigorous of these are subject to sample selection biases and sentiment swings. Governance indicators are generally input-based, and there is no guarantee that good institutions will necessarily ensure good policy outcomes. Moreover, history is replete with examples of economies introducing major reforms in the context of weak institutions formally defined (for example Indonesia in the late 1960s, Vietnam in the mid-1980s).

Nevertheless, as with investor surveys, carefully defined and measured governance indicators can be of some use in pinpointing a country's strengths and weaknesses. They can be useful in shedding light on the processes by which governments are selected, held accountable, monitored and replaced; on the capacity of governments to manage resources efficiently and to formulate, implement and enforce sound policies and regulations; and the respect of citizens and the state for the institutions that govern a society. These exercises are particularly useful for comparative surveys, where several countries are included according to a standard methodology and measurement techniques. Table 1 reports one widely used set of indicators, from the World Bank's Worldwide Governance Indicators released in June 2008. Countries are assessed according to six political, institutional and economic policy indicators, based on 276 variables measuring different dimensions of governance. The results are presented as percentile rankings, in which a higher score indicates a higher ranking relative to the 212 countries in the study. The results are presented here for seven Southeast Asian countries, that is, excluding the special cases of Brunei, Myanmar and Singapore. Very high rankings would not be expected since the survey includes the high income OECD group of economies.

The results for the Philippines broadly accord with a priori expectations. It scores quite well for 'voice and accountability', where it is the highest in the sample, reflecting the country's media freedom and the scope for democratic participation. Regulatory quality is generally adequate, although below that of Malaysia and Thailand. Perhaps surprisingly, government effectiveness has a similar ranking. The country's weak points are political stability (the lowest in the sample), control of corruption (above only the emerging economies of

TABLE 1
Southeast Asian Governance Indicators, 2007

Country	Voice and Accountability	Political Stability	Government Effectiveness	Regulatory Quality	Rule of Law	Control of Corruption
1. Philippines	43.3	10.1	56.4	50.5	33.8	22.2
2. Indonesia	42.8	14.9	41.7	43.7	27.1	27.1
3. Malaysia	31.3	52.4	82.9	67.0	65.2	62.3
4. Thailand	29.8	16.8	61.6	56.3	52.9	44.0
5. Vietnam	6.7	56.3	41.2	35.9	38.6	28.0
6. Cambodia	24.0	28.8	20.9	30.6	13.8	8.2
7. Lao PDR	6.3	42.8	21.3	15.0	17.1	13.0

Note: Percentile ranking is interpreted as follows: The Philippines has a rank of 43.3 per cent for voice and accountability. This means that the Philippine score for this category is higher than 43.3 per cent of the 212 countries included in the indicator, or conversely about 56.7 per cent of the 212 countries have a higher score.
Source: World Bank, *Governance Matters 1996–2007: Worldwide Governance Indicators*, Washington, D.C., 2008.

Cambodia and Laos) and rule of law. Some of these results may not appear to be internally consistent: for example, can reasonably adequate government effectiveness and regulatory quality co-exist alongside perceived high levels of corruption? Nevertheless, the general picture to emerge is one of government performing moderately well, albeit in the context of widespread corruption, high levels of political instability and weak rule of law. Separately, the study presented estimates of governance quality over time. The Philippine rankings declined for most indicators over the period 1998–2004; thereafter there has been some improvement, except for those related to corruption and political stability.

These quantitative indicators need to be supplemented with detailed case studies of policy and institutional reform. It is beyond the scope of this article to examine cases of reform, but it will be useful to briefly mention some salient Philippine examples since the 1990s. The outstanding case, as mentioned earlier, is the central bank, BSP. Under the Central Bank Act of June 1993, BSP was assigned an explicit policy objective, the maintenance of price stability, and it was guaranteed fiscal and administrative autonomy, including that related to staffing and salaries. The BSP has established an enviable record of technical competence and fiscal probity, unlike its predecessor institution. It has also been very successful with regard to inflation outcomes, as noted above.

Reforms since 2000 have been more difficult to identify owing to the constant political uncertainty and the sharp reduction in civil service salaries. But one reform that has been introduced over this period is the Government Procurement Reform Act of 2003. This consolidated all rules of public procurement, mandated the use of an electronic procurement system (known as PhilGEPS), and required the participation of private and NGO observers in the procurement process. This reform is still in the implementation stages. Benchmarking exercises indicate that it performs very well with regard to its legislative and regulatory framework, well on integrity and transparency, but less well with regard to operations, monitoring and enforcement.

Social Indicators

Philippine social indicators have always displayed mixed outcomes, reflecting on the one hand the country's educational strengths and on the other its deeply entrenched poverty. We focus here on two dimensions of the poverty challenge, the relationship between poverty and growth, and sub-national variations in poverty incidence.

First, the Philippines shows the usual inverse relationship between economic growth and poverty incidence. As Figure 7 indicates, for the comparable Family Income and Expenditure Series from 1985 onwards, the percentage of the population below the nationally defined poverty line almost halved in the next two decades. The decline in poverty appears to be almost linear but it is generally faster in periods of higher economic growth.[4]

There are two somewhat unusual aspects of the country's poverty story. The first is that poverty is less responsive to growth than in most other East Asian countries.[5] Growth is always a necessary but not sufficient condition for poverty reduction, but in the Philippines the complementary policy inputs are more important. That is, additional strategies are needed to ensure that the poor can participate in the opportunities created by growth. One obstacle has been labour market policies that discourage a labour-intensive growth path. The country's minimum wage regulations have discouraged employment growth: in 2006, for example, Manila's minimum wage was equivalent to 153 per cent of the country's per capita GDP. In contrast, those for Bangkok and Jakarta were 44 per cent and 68 per cent respectively. Minimum wages in the Philippines are now set locally, and some local governments have endeavoured to create

FIGURE 7
The Philippines Long Term Poverty Rate and Per Capita Incomes
(% of Population)

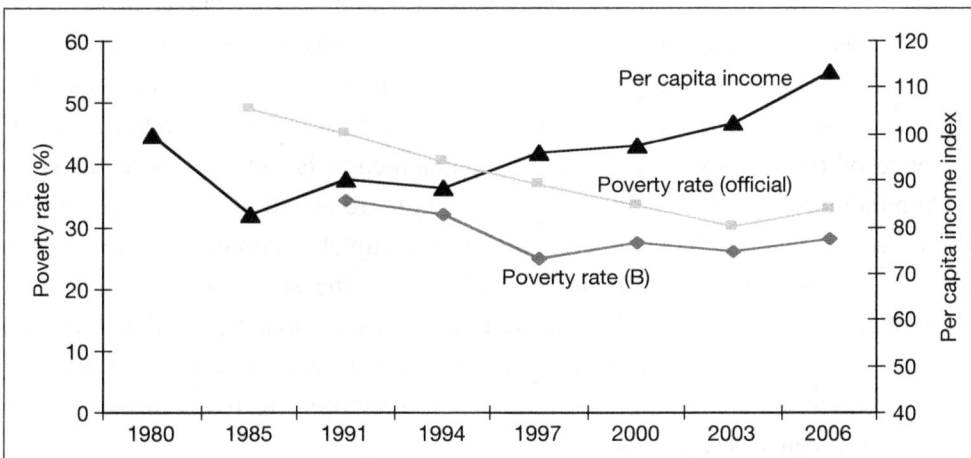

Note: Per capita income adjusted to inflation and indexed to 100 in 1980. Poverty rate (B) refers to the rate calculated based on the methodology of Balisacan (2003).
Sources: The Family Income and Expenditure Survey (FIES); CIEC.

more employment-friendly environments. But greater Manila accounts for about 55 per cent of the national output, and therefore employment opportunities elsewhere are limited. Another factor explaining the lower poverty elasticities is the country's slow growth of output and productivity in agriculture, still the major sector of employment, since the 1980s. This slower growth reflects the under-investment in rural infrastructure (roads, irrigation, extension services) over this period, together with tenancy uncertainty created by the agrarian reform programme. An additional factor is the limited targeting of educational subsidies, with the result that the quality of public schooling is skewed towards more affluent urban dwellers.

The other unusual aspect of poverty outcomes, as revealed in Figure 7, is that between the last two Family Income and Expenditure Surveys (FIESs), in 2003 and 2006, poverty actually increased marginally, even as growth was quite strong. What could explain such a puzzling outcome? One factor could be a sharp increase in inequality, but inequality typically does not move significantly over short periods, and anyway the gini appears to be relatively stable between the two years and the calculated Lorenz curves are essentially identical for the two years suggesting no structural change in the distribution of income between the two years. A more plausible explanation is the increase in energy costs in 2006 due to the hike in electricity tariffs, the increase in VAT rate by 2 percentage points, and its extension to petroleum products. Family expenditure data from the FIES show that the share of household spending on energy and transport increased for both poor and non-poor groups.[6] Note, however, that this period predates the very rapid increase in food prices, and so this latter factor could not have been the explanation. Moreover, inflation was anyway quite moderate. Yet another possible explanation is that the rapid increase in remittances over this period disproportionately benefited the rich. There is some, albeit limited, evidence of this occurrence, but such a phenomenon is anyway more likely to explain increased inequality rather than pushing more people into poverty. Finally, it may just be that the 2006 FIES results are incomplete. Income and expenditure have always been substantially under-estimated in the series, but in the past it is thought that the degree of understatement was reasonably predictable, and therefore could be adjusted. Unfortunately, there is no independent means of checking these results. It is arguably therefore premature to reach any definitive conclusion about poverty trends.

The second important feature of Philippine poverty is the very large differences across administrative regions (see Figure 8). Such an outcome reflects mainly the very large differences in regional per capita income. The country's richest region,

FIGURE 8
The Philippines: Sub-National Poverty Rates and
Per Capita Incomes, 2006

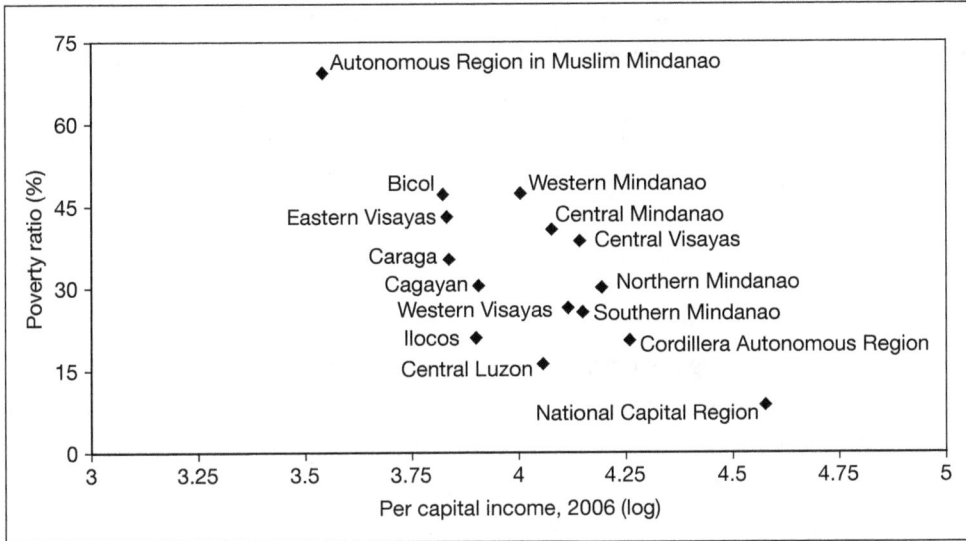

Sources: FIES 2006; CIEC.

Metro Manila, has a per capita income of about 12 times that of the poorest, the ARMM (Autonomous Region of Muslim Mindanao). The differences in poverty incidence are of a similar order of magnitude. More generally, the regional poverty picture highlights the skewed nature of development in the Philippines, in particular between the more affluent regions of Manila and its surrounds, alongside the deprivation in the south of the country.[7] Very high poverty (in excess of 40 per cent) is found in Bicol (the most southerly region of the main island of Luzon), in nearby Eastern Visayas (principally Samar), and in the ARMM together with Western and Central Mindanao. The ARMM is by far the most serious, with a poverty incidence approaching 70 per cent. This region also lags well behind the national average on other social indicators, with the lowest life expectancy and adult literacy rates.[8] Such outcomes reflect a complex mix of factors, including historically entrenched deprivation, decades of conflict, and low quality local governance. It is difficult to see how these problems can be addressed without a comprehensive programme of peace, security and development. In its absence, the region will continue to be a source of regional discontent and low-scale terrorism.

The Government has a wide range of social protection programmes including health insurance, education scholarships for the poor, school feeding programmes, subsidized rice through the National Food Authority, public employment schemes, and the community development programme known as the Kalahi programme. These programmes are thought to be fragmented and the overall results in terms of net welfare benefits to recipient groups are mixed. An ADB study on social protection coverage shows that such programmes only cover one third of the poor compared with an average of one half of the poor in Southeast and East Asia.[9]

Conclusion

It is too early to judge whether the Philippines has decisively turned away from years of underperformance. Economic growth of 5–7 per cent is not yet comparable to that of China, India or Vietnam, not to mention historically that of the other Asian tigers during their high growth phases. Nor is it yet durable enough to be having a major, broad-based impact on living standards. Recent turmoil in global markets will put back growth in 2009 below its long run potential.

More reform is needed. The agenda is a long one, comprising at least six core elements. First, fiscal prudence has been achieved in part by starving the public sector of much needed investments in schools, hospitals and other amenities. The public revenue effort needs to be intensified. Second, broad-ranging civil service reform is badly needed. The old adage about halving the number of civil servants while doubling their pay has more than a ring of truth about it. Third, infrastructure is inadequate. The country invests about half the East Asian average (as a per cent of GDP) in this sector. Both public and private sector investment is needed, and each has distinct, complex constraints. Fourth, the government's social expenditures need to be better targeted, as well as increased. Social indicators for the poor, particularly in the Muslim majority region of the country's southwest, are slipping further behind the national average. Fifth, there needs to be a durable peace settlement in Mindanao, which remains the most important and protracted theatre of conflict in Southeast Asia. Although the conflict is confined to a relatively small area of the country, its broader repercussions are considerably larger. It tarnishes the country's international image, it distracts the government from other pressing reforms, and it diverts large flows of domestic and international resources from other very needy regions in the country.[10] Sixth, the microeconomic and governance reform agenda, aimed at supporting a simple, de-politicized, business-friendly, transparent, and non-corrupt environment, is a large one.

It is true that the growth is heavily reliant on just a few sectors, notably remittances, some new international services (especially the so-called 'call-back centres'), and (for periods) export-oriented electronics. Additionally, there are distributional concerns related to how widely the benefits are being spread, both across households and regions. Poverty in the Philippines is falling less slowly than in almost any other East Asian economy, owing to its slower growth and to the fact that its poverty is less growth-responsive than elsewhere.

Moreover, there is little evidence of a consensus among the political, bureaucratic and business elite that rapid, broad-based growth is the nation's overwhelming policy priority, in the way that such a commitment drove economic success in much of East Asia since the 1960s. The 1987 Constitution has bequeathed an institutionally weakened government structure with many checks and balances, thus making reform a slow and difficult process. The election supervision process remains highly contentious. Political scandals and corruption allegations, big and small, continue apace, and allegedly reach up to the highest levels of the administration. Opinion polls (e.g. those conducted by the respected Social Weather Station) consistently report that the public has a very low opinion of its political leaders.[11]

But it is important not to overlook the achievements to date. Achieving durable policy reform is never easy, the more so in a country like the Philippines with its unpredictable politics. The lesson is that "Econ 101" — getting a few key policies "right" — combined with "Politics 101" — convincing the business community that they are here to stay — gets countries a long way. It is possible to be cautiously optimistic about the country's future, as it was in the 1950s and 1960s, and again in the 1990s during the reforming Ramos administration.

Notes

1   For general overviews, see A. Balisacan and H. Hill, eds., *The Philippine Economy: Development, Policies, and Challenges* (New York: Oxford University Press and Manila: Ateneo University Press, 2003); and G.P. Sicat, *Philippine Economic and Development Issues* (Manila: Anvil, 2003).

2   The most sophisticated analysis of the current exchange rate and monetary policy regime is provided by M.S. Gochoco-Bautista and D. Canlas, "Monetary and Exchange Rate Policy", in *The Philippine Economy: Development, Policies, and Challenges*, edited by H. Hill and A. Balisacan (New York: Oxford University Press and Manila: Ateneo Univesity Press, 2003), pp. 77–105.

[3] That is, the residual of GDP growth, after deducting the growth of capital and labour inputs. "Philippines: Critical Development Constraints", *Country Diagnostic Studies* (Manila: Asian Development Bank, 2007).

[4] See A. Balisacan, "Poverty and Inequality", in *The Philippine Economy: Development, Policies and Challenges*, edited by H. Hill and A. Balisacan (New York: Oxford University Press and Manila: Ateneo University Press, 2003), pp. 311–41.

[5] See A.M. Balisacan, "Local Growth and Poverty Reduction", in *The Dynamics of Regional Development: The Philippines in East Asia*, edited by A. Balisacan and H. Hill (Northampton: Edward Elgar Publishing and Asian Development Bank Institute, 2007), pp. 417–18, for discussion of a range of estimates. He concludes that the elasticity for the Philippines is in the range 1.3–1.6, compared to the developing country average of about 2.5, and with several East Asian countries higher still.

[6] In 2006 there was an increase in the value added tax, its extension to petroleum products, and increases in fuel and electricity prices.

[7] A. Balisacan and H. Hill, eds., *The Dynamics of Regional Development: The Philippines in East Asia* (Cheltenham: Edward Elgar, 2007).

[8] For a detailed examination of development issues in Mindanao, see HDN and UNDP (Human Development Network and United Nations Development Program), *Philippine Human Development Report: Peace, Human Security and Human Development in the Philippines* (Manila: HDN and UNDP, 2005).

[9] See ADB, "Scaling Up the Social Protection Index for Committed Poverty Reduction", Philippines Country Report (Manila: Asian Development Bank, 2007*b*).

[10] More generally, the level of criminality remains high. Recently, the Philippines was ranked the second most dangerous country in the world for journalists, although the country enjoys an open and vibrant media. Election-related fatalities are high.

[11] Although note that, even though the national government may be slow to reform, some local governments are able to move more quickly. The Philippines was the first case of "democratic decentralization" in East Asia, commencing in 1991, and the country is slowly beginning to reap the benefits of this programme, at least in some of its better governed localities (see Balisacan and Hill, eds., 2007).

Singapore

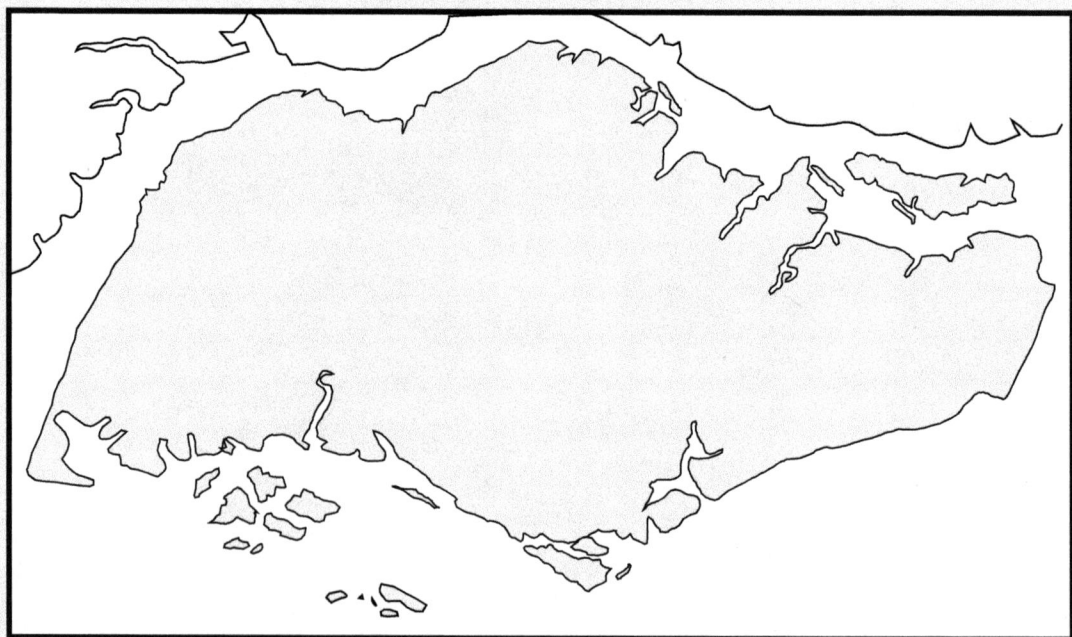

SINGAPORE IN 2008
Negotiating Domestic Issues, Confrontations and Global Challenges

Terence Chong

The Escape

Singapore began 2008 in high drama. On the early evening of 27 February, Singaporeans were told of a breakout from the Whitley Road Detention Centre (WRDC). Mas Selamat bin Kastari, an Indonesian-born Singaporean, held under the Internal Security Act, sparked the largest manhunt ever launched in Singapore. He was allegedly the head of the Singapore branch of militant group *Jemaah Islamiah* (JI) and, according to the Singapore government, was suspected of plotting to attack Singapore Changi Airport in 2002 by crashing a plane into it. Arrested in January 2006 by Indonesian anti-terror squads in Java, Mas Selamat was then deported to Singapore. He was never formally charged with any terrorism-related offences but was held by the state under the Internal Security Act. A nation-wide search involving the Singapore Police Force, the Gurkha Contingent, the Police Tactical Unit and the Police National Service Key Installation Protection Unit was conducted. They were later joined by the Singapore Guards and the Singapore Armed Forces Military Police Command.

Response from the public ranged from mild alarm to anger, the latter of which was manifested largely on Internet blogs and forums. Public criticism was directed at several levels. Many were critical of the way a supposedly dangerous terrorist suspect could have so easily slipped out of a high security detention centre and at the misinformation given out to the public by the police. Initial news alerts informed the public that Mas Selamat walked with a limp; later alerts noted that the limp was only visible when he ran. Critics also accused the pro-government

---

Terence Chong is a Fellow at the Institute of Southeast Asian Studies (ISEAS), Singapore.

media of trying to play down the incident and skirting key issues. One political commentator, observed "The mainstream media did its job of trying to play down the most shameful part of the incident", while a media academic wrote about the mainstream media not asking the most immediate question of "how" Mas Selamat escaped: "The question is so natural and so obvious that you'd think anyone barely paying attention would ask it. Unless, apparently, one worked for the national news media."[1] Lastly, criticism was also directed at Wong Kan Seng, the Minister for Home Affairs over the fact that news of Mas Selamat's escape was not disseminated to the public until four hours after it happened. Singaporeans were only provided some details at a parliamentary session the next day.

A Committee of Inquiry (COI) was duly set up. But even the choice of individuals appointed to the committee aroused disapproval in some quarters. The three members of the COI, announced on 2 March 2008, were retired judge Goh Joon Seng, ex-police commissioner Tee Tua Ba, and deputy secretary at the Home Affairs Ministry, Choong May Ling. Some questioned the inclusion of Choong, a high ranking officer within the Home Affairs Ministry, to an inquiry that was investigating a department under the very ministry she belonged to. The opposition Workers' Party also suggested that President S.R. Nathan appoint a Commission of Inquiry under the Prisons Act instead so that investigations could be made public. The COI, nevertheless, proceeded with its task and produced a report that was made partially public by Wong Kan Seng in a ministerial statement in parliament on 21 April. The COI identified three critical factors that allowed Mat Selamat to escape. Firstly, there was a physical security breach because the ventilation window in the toilet from which Mas Selamat escaped did not have grilles; secondly, the guards watching him allowed him to close the door of the urinal cubicle when they should not have done so; and thirdly, there was a physical weakness in the perimeter fencing outside the Family Visitation Block, where the toilet was located, which made it easier for Mas Selamat to get out of the detention centre's premises.[2]

The incident led to questions over government complacency and accountability. Famed for its efficiency and readiness, the government and its agencies were now described as being complacent by members of the public. To make matters worse, on 11 June, in a separate case, two detainees awaiting their court appearance made an escape bid because the police had failed to observe "standard operating procedures".[3] Meanwhile public outcry for government accountability was also loud. Home Minister Wong apologized publicly for the escape but this did not appease many who wanted to see the resignation of those responsible. In the end, the superintendent of the WRDC was sacked for the security lapse while his deputy was demoted. The two Gurkha officers guarding Mas Selamat were also charged and demoted while the Special Duty Operative handling the detainee's family visit when the incident happened was also fired. Letters of warning were served to three others — the Special Duty Operative's supervisor, the Chief Warder as well as the Technical Officer responsible for the CCTV upgrading at the detention centre.[4] The Prime Minister resisted calls for resignation of the head of the Internal Security Department, which had oversight of WRDC and that of Home Minister Wong, arguing that "Singapore should not encourage a culture where officials and ministers resign whenever something goes wrong on their watch, regardless of whether or not they are actually to blame".[5] While some Singaporeans seemed satisfied with the way the punishment was apportioned, for others this only reinforced deep-set cynicism over notions of accountability.[6]

The Economy: A Weak End to a Strong Start

The high drama of the escape almost eclipsed an arguably more profound revelation — Singapore's annual inflation rate hit a 25-year high of 6.6 per cent in January.[7] According to the Department of Statistics, the inflation rate, as indicated by the Consumer Price Index (CPI), was the highest since the 7.5 per cent level in March 1982. The Ministry of Trade and Industry (MTI) noted that the January rise in inflation was due to one-off factors such as a housing value revision. Housing costs, which account for 21 per cent of the CPI, have the third-largest weighting after food and transport and communication costs. More pertinently, food prices, which carried the largest weighting in the CPI, rose 5.8 per cent in January from a year earlier while transport and communication costs rose 6.9 per cent between January 2007 and January 2008, driven by soaring global fuel prices and higher taxi fares.

Inflation rates came against the backdrop of Singapore's continued economic growth. The economy grew by 6.7 per cent in the first quarter of 2008, compared to 5.4 per cent in the last quarter of 2007. This prompted the National Wage Council (NWC) to recommend a one-off special payment to help rank-and-file workers, particularly low wage workers, better cope with the impact of inflation. The government set the example by giving civil servants a mid-year bonus of 0.5 month. On top of this was the one-off special payment where Division III and IV officers received S$250 and S$300 respectively, while Division I and II officers received S$100.

Meanwhile the globalizing of the local job market continued at an unrelenting pace. In January it was reported that six out of every 10 jobs created in 2007 went to foreigners. This was the first time in at least six years that their share was larger than locals'. Although this came at a time when job creation was at a record high and when unemployment and retrenchment were at record lows, the Manpower Ministry (MOM) hastened to add that Singapore residents (citizens and permanent residents) had benefited from overall job creation. MOM noted that although the local share of total new jobs dropped from 52 per cent in 2006 to 39 per cent in 2007, this was because of "the limits to the growth of Singapore's indigenous workforce and the larger base of jobs created".[8] It was reported that local employment grew by 92,100 in 2007, up from 90,900 in 2006 while the booming economy, with the buoyant service and construction sectors, created 236,600 jobs, up from 176,000 in 2006, an 11-year high.

The services sector contributed 144,100 more jobs, boosted by the increase in hiring across a wide range of industries, especially by financial and professional services. In addition, the construction sector added 49,000 workers, double that of 2006 while manufacturing employment also rose, by 49,900, spurred by strong demand in marine and offshore engineering. As a result, overall unemployment averaged 2.1 per cent, down from 2.7 per cent in 2006, with resident unemployment at a decade-low of 3 per cent. Such news characterized the strong economic growth in the beginning of 2008. And then, the global financial crisis came.

After years of easy mortgage, the housing bubble in the U.S. finally burst in 2007. What became known as the subprime mortgage crisis quickly resulted in mortgage companies going out of business. Unfortunately for many U.S. and international investors — both individuals and institutions — who had bought AAA rated mortgage securities from banks and financial institutions, such securities were severely devalued, with many losing a great deal of money. Singapore, closely tied to the global economy, could not escape the impact. Although local banks emerged largely unscathed because of limited exposure to the so-called 'toxic assets', segments of the financial services sector more sensitive to market trends were affected such as the trading of stocks, shares and bonds, foreign exchange trading activities, and fund management activities. The local stock-market index has dropped by over 40 per cent from the peak in October 2007.

A significant number of Singaporeans who had invested in structured products like Lehman Brothers minibonds, Pinnacle Notes, Jubilee Series Notes and DBS's High Notes saw their life savings wiped out. These local investors, many of them retirees, claimed that banks had aggressively sold such structured products to them without explaining the inherent risks and dangers involved. In response, Senior Minister and Monetary Authority of Singapore (MAS) chairman Goh Chok Tong was quoted as saying, "That's life, if you want good rewards, you have to take risks. Otherwise, leave your money with the CPF [Central Provident Fund]."[9] These investors began to organize themselves and gathered regularly at the Speakers' Corner at Hong Lim Park to listen to financial advice from experts and to ascertain their options. After large crowds thronged the Speakers Corner on a regular basis MAS announced that it would help local investors with their complaints, with most of them expected to be resolved by early 2009.

The crisis also hit the local property market. Residential property sales transactions saw a sharp drop. In the third quarter of 2008, the private property price index registered the first quarter-on-quarter decline since the first quarter of 2004. The crisis also weakened consumer demand around the world, thus impacting Singapore's manufacturing and domestic exports. Singapore's non-oil domestic exports fell by 8.5 per cent in the third quarter of 2008, with the biggest declines in electronics and pharmaceuticals. The tourism sector was also hit with visitor arrivals falling by about 6 per cent in July and August 2008. Previously strong growth in retail sales also slowed down. Not counting motor vehicles, real retail sales grew by a mere 2.5 per cent in the first eight months of 2008, compared to 8 per cent last year.

Singapore fell into a technical recession in the third quarter of 2008. Year-on-year, the city-state's economy declined 0.6 per cent for that period, with pundits predicting that the economy may shrink by as much as 1 per cent in 2009, the first time since 2001. The manufacturing industry, which accounts for a quarter of the economy, shrank 11.4 per cent from a year earlier, resulting escalating losses at companies such as Chartered Semiconductor. An estimated 1,500 of the 2,000 workers retrenched in Singapore in the third quarter were from manufacturing and more are expected to be retrenched in manufacturing and finance, with DBS leading the way by firing 900 of its staff.[10] On the flip-side, the country's inflation rate fell in November to an 11 month low to 5.5 per cent due to plunging oil prices. In response to the recession and to tackle the economic challenges, the Singapore government has brought forward the budget in 2009 from February to 22 January.

Population Matters

In response to the strong economic growth in the previous years, Singapore saw a big spike in population.[11] The city-state's population grew by a record 5.5 per cent in 2007, the highest annual increase since records were collected in 1871. As of June 2008, there were 4.84 million people living in Singapore, up from 4.59 million last year. Given the country's open-door immigration policy and its low birth rates, it is no surprise that this growth was due to the jump in foreigners. Their numbers expanded by a whopping 19 per cent, translating to about 1.2 million of them. In contrast, the number of citizens grew by a mere 1 per cent, while the number of permanent residents climbed 6.5 per cent. Together, they make up the 3.64 million residents.

According to the National Population Secretariat (NPS), under the Prime Minister's Office, which released the figures, the country's total fertility rate (TFR) was still low but more births were registered. TFR inched upwards from 1.28 in 2006 to 1.29 in 2007. There were 18,032 resident births registered in the first six months of 2008, compared with 17,325 births in 2007; with the increase primarily due to more first-order births. In order to encourage more Singaporeans to have children, the government recently enhanced the Marriage and Parenthood (M&P) Package. This enhancement meant that Singaporean couples would be able to claim the higher Parenthood Tax Rebate (PTR) if their children were born on or after 1 Jan 2008. Together with other Singaporean couples whose children were born before 2008, these parents could also claim the enhanced tax reliefs for income earned in 2008.

Singapore also saw an increase in new permanent residents and new citizens. 34,800 applicants were granted PR status while 9,600 applicants were granted citizenship in the first six months of 2008, compared to 28,500 and 7,300, respectively, in the same period in 2007. Singaporeans were also going global. NPS observed that more Singaporeans are also going overseas for work and study. As of June 2008, there were about 153,500 overseas Singaporeans (OS) compared with 147,500 a year ago. The most popular destinations with Singaporeans were Australia, the UK, the U.S. and China.

Cabinet Reshuffle 2008

The first major political event of the year was the Cabinet reshuffle on 29 March. New ministers were appointed for the ministries of law, education and manpower, together with the promotion of some junior ministers. S. Jayakumar made way for K. Shanmugam, Senior Counsel and Member of Parliament (MP) for Sembawang group representation constituency (GRC), as Law Minister. Shanmugam is also concurrently Second Minister for Home Affairs. Jayakumar continues as Deputy Prime Minister and Coordinating Minister for National Security. Manpower Minister Ng Eng Hen became Minister for Education, taking over from Tharman Shanmugaratnam who assumed the post of Finance Minister in December 2007. Gan Kim Yong, who was previously Minister of State for Manpower, became

Acting Manpower Minister. Vivian Balakrishnan gave up his post as Second Minister for Information, Communication and the Arts, but continues as Minister for Community Development, Youth and Sports.

Meanwhile, four Ministers of State were promoted. Lim Hwee Hua became Senior Minister of State, keeping her appointments in the Finance and Transport Ministries. S. Iswaran was promoted to Senior Minister of State with the Trade and Industry Ministry. Grace Fu similarly became Senior Minister of State, receiving a new appointment in the Education Ministry, while serving her present appointment in the National Development Ministry. Lastly, Lui Tuck Yew was also promoted to Senior Minister of State. He will be newly appointed to the Ministry of Information, Communications and the Arts (MICA), while continuing with his present appointment in the Education Ministry. Those expecting Singapore's first woman full minister to be announced this year were disappointed although several candidates have the potential to make the step up.

Pedra Branca

May 2008 saw the end of a long standing squabble between Singapore and Malaysia over the sovereignty of Pedra Branca and its outcrops. The dispute arose in February 1980, when Singapore protested against a 1979 Malaysian map that placed Pedra Branca within its territorial waters. After years of diplomatic tussles the matter was referred to the International Court of Justice (ICJ) which awarded the main island to Singapore, and two smaller outcrops nearby to Malaysia. The ICJ however did not make a definitive ruling on the third rock of contention, South Ledge, which is visible only at low tide. According to the ICJ, it belongs to whoever owns the territorial waters it sits in. Deputy Prime Minister S. Jayakumar, part of Singapore's legal team at The Hague noted that "We are pleased with the judgment because the court has awarded sovereignty over Pedra Branca, which is the main feature in dispute, to Singapore" while Malaysia's Foreign Minister Rais Yatim hailed it as a "win-win" judgment and that both countries would "forge ahead" in their bilateral relationship.[12]

Interestingly, the ICJ had rejected Singapore's argument that Pedra Branca was *terra nullius* (no man's land) in 1847 when the British took ownership of it and built Horsburgh Lighthouse there. The court took into account various historical writings, treaties and letters relevant to the case, and decided that these showed that the Sultanate of Johor possessed original title to the island, dating back to the sixteenth century. However, the ICJ noted that Singapore had carried out certain crucial activities on the island in the latter half of the twentieth century.

These included its investigation into marine accidents in the waters around Pedra Branca, control of visits to the island, plans to reclaim it and installation of military communications equipment there. The ICJ found that these activities carried out by Singapore were an indication of *a titre de souverain* (acts consistent with sovereignty), while noting that Malaysia had failed to protest against any of these activities even though it was aware of them.

Lastly, the ICJ observed that a 1953 letter from the Johor Acting State Secretary informing the colonial authorities in Singapore that Johor did not claim ownership over Pedra Branca was of major significance. The letter made clear that Johor acknowledged that it did not have sovereignty over Pedra Branca. The ICJ thus judged that although Johor had initially possessed the original title to Pedra Branca, that title subsequently passed to Singapore. In the end the 16 judges of the ICJ voted 12 to four in Singapore's favour. With regard to the Middle Rocks, the ICJ ruled that Malaysia's claim of original title still stood because there were no activities on Singapore's side to claim it as Singapore's. Nevertheless, while the ICJ ruling has settled sovereignty issues, other issues remain. For one, Singapore and Malaysia have to decide how to delimit the territorial waters in the Pedra Branca and Middle Rocks area. A joint technical committee is already in place to discuss these and related issues.

The Two Lawsuits

Singaporeans witnessed a rare piece of political drama with the lawsuit filed by Lee Kuan Yew and Lee Hsien Loong against the Singapore Democratic Party (SDP). Although such lawsuits are not seen as unusual in Singapore, the novelty lay in the Minister Mentor's willingness to be cross-examined by opposition politician Chee Soon Juan in open court, the first time this has happened. The two People's Action Party leaders were suing Chee and the SDP leadership for repeating remarks published in the SDP newsletter *New Democrat* alleging that they were corrupt and had covered up wrongdoings at the National Kidney Foundation. MM Lee and PM Lee were seeking aggravated damages. Six of the SDP's leaders apologised, leaving six others who refused.

The SDP did not file a defence but Chee and his sister, Chee Siok Chin, did. The Chees denied any responsibility for any alleged offending remarks and said their remarks over the government's handling of the NKF were "substantially true".[13] The Chees offered three arguments: the subject — the National Kidney Foundation scandal — was a matter of public interest; their remarks were fair comment; and they had "qualified privilege" as members of a political party.

Lawyers for MM Lee and PM Lee rejected the arguments and argued that the Chees knew that the articles in the newsletter were untrue. They pointed out that Chee Soon Juan had apologised to MM Lee earlier; an apology the SDP leader later retracted. They also argued that the articles could not be construed as being comment but that the Chees were making a statement of fact, and were driven by malice.

Time limits were set by the court on the cross-examination of Prime Minister Lee Hsien Loong and Minister Mentor Lee Kuan Yew by Chee Siok Chin and Chee Soon Juan. Nevertheless, when PM Lee took the stand, there was little opportunity to reply, as objections were raised by his lawyer repeatedly against Chee Soon Juan's line of questioning. When MM Lee took to the stand, Chee Soon Juan took the opportunity to question him over a range of issues, many of them not directly related to the case at hand. From perennial complaints like an uneven playing field for opposition parties, the absence of human rights, press freedom, freedom of speech to MM Lee's counsel reading out a letter of citation from Transparency International, an international NGO, the exchange between the two men played out like a piece of political theatre that kept Singaporeans entranced. However, the court found this line of questions to be irrelevant to the defamation case and later held the Chees in contempt for persisting with them. In the end, the court awarded damages of S$500,000 to PM Lee and S$450,000 to MM Lee. After taking into account the S$170,000 which each plaintiff had earlier received in settlement from six other defendants, damages of S$330,000 were ordered to be paid to PM Lee and S$280,000 to MM Lee.

This was followed by a lawsuit in November brought against the *Wall Street Journal Asia* (WSJA) and its editors by Singapore's Attorney-General Chamber (AGC) for contempt of court. The AGC alleged that three articles the WSJA published in June and July had "impugn the impartiality, integrity and independence of the Singapore Judiciary".[14] The articles in question were two of the newspaper's editorials, with the third a letter from SDP leader Chee Soon Juan. One editorial examined the lack of democracy in Singapore and included an account of the exchange in court between MM Lee and Chee, while the other focused on the Singapore Judiciary, based on a report by the International Bar Association's Human Rights Institute in July which alleged executive interference in the Judiciary.

According to Attorney-General Walter Woon, the articles suggested that the Singapore courts did not dispense justice fairly in cases involving critics of senior government figures, and that they helped suppress political dissent through the award of damages in libel suits. AG Woon pointed to cases involving the same paper in 1985 and 1991 and surmised that this demonstrated a long-running campaign of the paper against the Singapore government. Such a campaign was part of a broader argument between segments of the Western press and the government over the definition of democracy and how it is practised in Singapore. The AG disparaged WSJA's claim that it was merely criticising the law of libel in Singapore and had no intention of undermining the judiciary as "disingenuous and intellectually dishonest", and added that there was a right to free speech in Singapore but subject to restrictions like libel, the law of contempt, sedition and public order concerns.[15]

WSJA's lawyer Philip Jeyaretnam, in turn, argued that publishing the comments of other people did not mean that the paper endorsed them. He also rejected the suggestion that the WSJA was campaigning to reform the political system here. Instead, the published articles were just responding to events which were unfolding in the Singapore courts. Furthermore, the WSJA had carried rebuttals from Singapore officials to its editorials in full, and that there was also no real risk of the articles undermining public confidence in the administration of justice here. However, if the court did find WSJA guilty of contempt, Jeyaretnam urged that the penalty be in keeping with past fines for similar cases. In the end, High Court Judge Tay Yong Kwan fined the paper S$25,000, the highest ever in such a case, and ordered its publisher Dow Jones Publishing Co. (Asia) Inc. to pay S$30,000 in legal costs.

Death of JBJ

A low point in 2008 was the passing of Joshua Benjamin Jeyaretnam, Singapore's best-known opposition politician, on 30 September. Of Sri Lankan Tamil descent, Jeyaretnam was an Anglican Christian who attended Saint Andrew's School in Singapore. He later read law at University College London and went on to be the leader of the opposition Workers' Party (WP) of Singapore. Although Jeyaretnam's place in national history was secured in 1981 when he became the first opposition politician to be elected to parliament since Singapore's independence in 1965, he will also be known for the number of legal battles he fought and lost with the Peoples' Action party (PAP). He served as a member of parliament from 1981 to 1986, and again as non-constituency member of parliament (NCMP) 1997–2001.

At the historic Anson by-election in 1981, Jeyaretnam defeated the PAP's Pang Kim Him with 51.9 to 47.1 per cent of the vote. He was re-elected to the same seat in 1984 with 56.8 per cent of the votes, and became, along with

Chiam See Tong, one of only two opposition politicians to win in that election. However, only months after his 1984 re-election, he was charged for allegedly mis-stating party accounts. In 1986, he was found innocent in a district court of all charges but one. The prosecution appealed and a retrial was ordered. At the retrial, Jeyaretnam was found guilty on all counts and was sentenced to three months imprisonment (later commuted to one month), and fined S$5,000. This was enough to disqualify him from standing for election for a period of five years. In addition, he was also disbarred.

However, because the trial had been held in a district court, and not the High Court, Jeyaretnam was able to appeal against his disbarment to the Privy Council in the UK. The Privy Council reversed the district court's judgment. In the light of the Privy Council's decision, Jeyaretnam requested that the President remove the convictions. The President, on the advice of the cabinet, declined to do so. This however, did not stop Jeyaretnam from persisting with his style of firebrand politics. At an election rally in 1988, even though he was not contesting, he took to the stage and alleged that then PM Lee Kuan Yew had committed a criminal offence by aiding and abetting former Minister of National Development Teh Cheang Wan to commit suicide, and had covered up on corruption. The PM filed a lawsuit against him. Justice Lai Kew Chai presided over the case and found Jeyaretnam guilty of slander, ordering him to pay Lee damages of S$260,000. Because of the fines and convictions, Jeyaretnam was unable to stand for office until 1997. In 1997, immediately after Jeyaretnam became NCMP, he was met with eleven defamation suits. During one of the election rallies he was alleged to have injured PM Goh Chok Tong's reputation by saying, "Mr Tang Liang Hong has just placed before me, two reports he has made to the police against, you know, Mr Goh Chok Tong and his people."[16] The trial judge Rajendran found Jeyaretnam liable and ordered him to pay damages of S$20,000. The plaintiff appealed and damages were raised to S$100,000 plus S$20,000 in court costs.

Jeyaretnam not only tested the boundaries of political discourse; he was also the subject of a documentary that went on to question the definition of "political films" in Singapore. On 4 January 2002, a documentary — A Vision of Persistence — that captured Jeyaretnam selling his books in public places and meeting with his supporters was withdrawn from the Singapore International Film Festival. It was feared that it could have violated Section 33 of the Films Act that bans the import, production, distribution, and exhibition of a "party political film". This resulted in public debates, especially over Internet forums, over the nature of political discourse and the definition of 'politics' in Singapore with the general consensus being that such bans were blunt instruments of censorship and had very little place in a global city aspiring to be culturally vibrant. There is little doubt that this documentary was crucial in highlighting this anachronistic regulation, which resulted in the government's re-think of the Films Act in 2008.

Upon his death, it became clear how the local mainstream media sought to remember him. Jeyaretnam was posthumously reconstructed as a fighter, a man of idealism and passion; one who never gave up no matter how insurmountable the obstacles or opponents. Comments in the national broadsheet, The *Straits Times*, included quotes from PAP lawmakers observing that "He was like the Chinese doll, the *bu dao weng* — you knock him down, he comes back, you knock him down, he comes back up again." Another PAP parliamentarian noted, "I have admiration for people like him, a person who never gives up, a person who suffered for his convictions, and who goes down fighting all the way." Why he needed to be knocked down over and over again, or go down fighting, was expediently left out. A columnist of the same newspaper noted that "when both your friends and political enemies use the same descriptions of you, you can be sure they are true. In Mr Jeyaretnam's case, sincerity, tenacity and courage are words many have used to describe him."

Now, after his death, Jeyaretnam's embodiment of idealism and passion can be fashioned for the purpose of nation-building. It was never the case that Jeyaretnam was politically irrelevant, rather he was politically inconvenient. With his passing, the man can now be rehabilitated by the local press for national memory. It can now co-opt his idealism and passion for the state's own agenda. It speaks of him as a fighter, but not what he fought for — pluralist democracy, human rights and press freedom. It speaks of his great struggles, but not what he struggled against — PAP hegemony, authoritarianism, the use of punitive lawsuits in politics and so on. He was a fighter in a vacuum; he struggled against the unspoken. Jeyaretnam is well on the way to becoming a museum artifact in the halls of our national memory.

Slow Liberalization: The Easing of Regulations

2008 will also be remembered for the incremental liberalization of certain regulations. PM Lee Hsien Loong used the annual National Day Rally Speech on 17 August to make an important announcement regarding three forms of political restrictions in Singapore. The first is that the 10-year-old ban on "political films" will be eased. Currently, under the Films Act, a party political film is defined as that "(a) which is an advertisement made by or on behalf of any political party in Singapore or any body whose objects relate wholly or mainly to politics in

Singapore, or any branch of such party or body; or (b) which is made by any person and directed towards any political end in Singapore".[17] According to Minister for Information, Communications and the Arts Lee Boon Yang, his ministry (MICA) plans to table a Bill in parliament to amend the Films Act in early 2009. Lee noted that "films which are factual documentaries or recordings of live events held in accordance with the law ought to be allowed" because "such films are less likely to turn politics into an emotional and irrational debate with all the dangerous consequences".[18]

The second concerns podcasts and vodcasts. These new forms of communication were banned in the lead-up to the 2006 general elections. Political parties and citizens were not allowed to make and disseminate podcasts and vodcasts during political campaigns for fear of stirring up popular emotions which the government felt would distract from the issues at hand. Thirdly, the longstanding ban on outdoor protests and demonstrations would be lifted within the confines of Speakers' Corner in Hong Lim Park. For the first time in decades, Singaporeans will be allowed to stage outdoor protests without the need for police permits. Furthermore, instead of the Singapore police, the National Parks Board will be in charge of managing Speakers Corner, although it has the option of referring cases to the police as it sees fit.

These moves to liberalize regulations to encourage greater political participation is largely in keeping with the Lee Hsien Loong administration's promise of working towards a more open and accommodative society. The government itself acknowledges that public policies must evolve to remain relevant to both the current political and media landscape. Given the changing expectations and technological literacy of younger Singaporeans, the government has little choice but to make policy moves, albeit incremental, towards the more liberal end of the ideological spectrum. Such moves are not merely the result of playing catch-up with the aspirations of young liberal Singaporeans but also to offer avenues to apathetic and politically disinterested Singaporeans to articulate their concerns. This is because despite the country's economic growth and material affluence, the one nagging concern amongst citizens and politicians alike has been the price of that success. Political apathy, ignorance of national history, and over-dependence on the state are perennial complaints in Singapore. The flight of talented Singaporeans overseas, adding to the estimated 150,000 already abroad, is another side-effect of economic success. The move to liberalize modes of political expressions may be seen as way to engage and stimulate otherwise materially sedated Singaporeans who see no need to articulate themselves beyond the five Cs.

The report made to the government by Advisory Council on the Impact of New Media on Society (AIMS) is part of this liberalization process. AIMS was appointed in April 2007 to study the implications and impact of new media on society and to make recommendations to the government on how to address the social, ethical, legal and regulatory issues arising from new media. The council submitted its report — *Engaging New Media: Challenging Old Assumptions* — to MICA Minister Lee Boon Yang on 1 December after conducting a six-week public consultation. Chaired by veteran editor Cheong Yip Seng, the 13-member council consulted a wide range of stakeholders including media and telecommunications industry players, educators, bloggers, academics, non-government and government agencies, as well as a cross-section of Singapore society, such as parents and students. On 9 January 2009, the government accepted 17 out of 26 of AIMS' recommendations including the permitting of "factual" and "objective" party political films, the setting up of an independent advisory panel to review such party political films and greater e-engagement.[19] Among those recommendations it rejected were call to remove registration need for individuals, groups and political parties that provide online political content; spelling out clearly why a film is banned (under Section 35); and obliging a Minister to give reasons for a ban on films.

Conclusion

Finally, Singapore made its mark on the international stage with the first ever Formula 1 night race held on 26 September. The staging of this event went some way in boosting the nation's global city credentials. Won by Renault's Fernando Alonso, the race was watched by millions around the world and offered valuable global exposure for the city-state. Such mega-events are no longer a luxury but necessities for Singapore as it entrenches itself in the ongoing competition for global city status. Besides the Formula 1 in 2008, mega-events in Singapore include the hosting of the IMF and World Bank in 2006 and the up-coming Youth Olympics in 2010. Rather than being seen as indulgences, they are a process of building up allure and glamour in the Singapore brand. The mega-events act as magnets for international attention thus keeping the city-state in the consciousness of journalists, feature writers, international magazines and opinion-makers.

Such mega-events, however, must be complemented by the steady and persistent nurturing of local talent, practices and culture. Such local talent and practices will make up the essence of a national identity that will distinguish the city-state from dozens of other equally glamorous global cities. This is why the

National Arts Council (NAC) deserves credit for announcing that it will not cut funding for the arts in 2009 despite the dire economic situation. At a time when corporate funding for the arts has fallen significantly, NAC will not deny support to the major annual arts events and festivals that dot the national calendar such as The M1 Fringe Festival, the MOP, ARTSingapore and the Sun Festival. It will also be going on with its biennial Singapore Art Show and Singapore Writers Festival, the Singapore Arts Festival and Noise Singapore. Meanwhile the Design Singapore Council will still host its Singapore Design Festival and the National Museum its Night Festival. NAC has also recently launched the Arts Creation Fund to support the creation of homegrown or Asian works and the Arts For All plan with the aim of bringing arts to the community. Such efforts will ensure that the local arts and culture will not be ignored because of more glamorous mega-events. Over a longer period of time, they will contribute towards the identity-building process of the global city.

Notes

[1]   *Reuters*, "Singapore faces blogging ire over militant escape", by Melanie Lee, 6 March 2008 <http://www.reuters.com/article/technologyNews/idUSSP29412620080306> (accessed 20 November 2008).

[2]   *Channelnews Asia*, "Three critical factors led to Mas Selamat's Escape", 21 April 2008 <http://www.channelnewsasia.com/stories/singaporelocalnews/view/342715/1/.html> (accessed 20 November 2008).

[3]   *Straits Times*, "Escape bid from court: SOPs not followed", 12 June 2008 <http://www.asiaone.com/News/AsiaOne%2BNews/Singapore/Story/A1Story20080612-70418.html> (accessed 20 November 2008).

[4]   *Channelnews Asia*, "Superintendent of detention centre sacked over Mas Selamat's escape", by Wong Siew Ying, 26 May 2008 <http://www.channelnewsasia.com/stories/singaporelocalnews/view/350057/1/.html> (accessed 20 November 2008).

[5]   *Straits Times*, "Don't overreact, go overboard over one bad incident: PM Lee", 22 April 2008.

[6]   One good example was the cynical but prescient observation by a popular blog on 29 February 2008: "Mas Selamat has managed to run away. But in the end, it will be Wong Kan Seng who makes the really Great Escape", Mr Wang Says So (29 February 2008), "The Great Escape" <http://mrwangsaysso.blogspot.com/2008/02/great-escape.html> (accessed 20 November 2008).

[7]   *Channelnews Asia*, "Singapore's inflation rate hits 25-year high of 6.6%", by Margaret Perry, 25 February 2008 <http://www.channelnewsasia.com/stories/singaporelocalnews/view/330959/1/.html> (accessed 22 November 2008).

8   *Straits Times*, "6 in 10 jobs go to foreigners", by Goh Chin Lian, 31 January 2008.

9   *TODAY*, "No high returns without risk", by Lin Yanqin, 29 September 2008.

10 *Straits Times*, "DBS slammed for layoffs", by Sue-Ann Chia, 14 November 2008.

11 *Straits Times*, "Population hits 4.84m", by Li Xueyi, 26 September 2008.

12 *Straits Times*, "Pedra Branca belongs to Singapore", by Lydia Lim, 24 May 2008.

13 *Straits Times*, "MM, PM reject Chees' defence arguments", by Sue-An Chia, 29 May 2008.

14 *Straits Times*, "Wall St. Journal Asia sued", by Sue-Ann Chia, 12 September 2008.

15 *Straits Times*, "AG asks for deterrent fine", by Zakir Hussain, 5 November 2008.

16 *Asian Wall Street Journal*, "Jeyaretnam: A Worthy Legacy", (Editorial), 31 July 2001.

17 Films Act (Chapter 107) <http://statutes.agc.gov.sg/non_version/cgi-bin/cgi_retrieve. pl?&actno=Reved-107&date=latest&method=part> (accessed 25 November 2008).

18 *Straits Times*, "Ban on political films to be eased", by Jeremy Au Yong, 23 August 2008.

19 Ministry of Information, Communication and the Arts, Remarks by Dr Lee Boon Yang, Minister for Information, Communications and the Arts, at the media conference on the Government's response to the recommendations made by the Advisory Council on the Impact of New Media on Society (AIMS) in the report "Engaging New Media: Challenging Old Assumptions" <http://app.mica.gov.sg/Default.aspx?tabid=36&ctl=D etails&mid=539&ItemID=934> (accessed 14 January 2009).

THE SINGAPORE OF MY DREAMS

Tommy Koh

This essay is on the Singapore of my dreams. My dreams have obviously changed over the years. I will begin with my school boy's dreams.

A School Boy's Dreams

I grew up in colonial Singapore. After the Second World War, my parents sent me to a Chinese primary school. After a few years, because of my unsatisfactory progress, my parents decided to switch me to the English stream. I spent a bridging year in a Catholic school and then joined the Outram School, which was then a government primary school. I completed my secondary education at Raffles Institution (RI).

What were my school boy's dreams for Singapore?

First, I dreamt that one day Singapore would be independent and we would be able to rule ourselves. I was greatly influenced by the anti-colonial struggles and nationalist movements then taking place in Asia and Africa. I remember debating the merits and demerits of colonialism with one of my expatriate teachers in RI.

Second, I dreamt that one day Singapore would be without slums and all Singaporeans would have access to good housing, clean water and modern sanitation. I had relatives living in Bukit Ho Swee[1] and they lacked all three. I used to accompany my mother and aunt to visit them. I am very glad that this dream of mine has come true.

Third, I dreamt that all families would earn enough income to enable them to live decently. After the war, there were a lot of poor people in Singapore.

TOMMY KOH is Chairman, Institute of Policy Studies (IPS), Singapore. He has written this article in his personal capacity in response to an invitation from the editor of *Southeast Asian Affairs*.

Today, the situation is vastly different. If we use the internationally accepted criteria of US$1 per day or US$2 per day, there are no poor people in Singapore. However, the reality is that for the bottom 30 per cent of our population, life is very tough. We should do more to help our poor and disadvantaged families without undermining our work ethic and our culture of self-reliance.

Fourth, I dreamt that one day we would live in a society in which the law would be just and people did not fear either the gangsters or the police. In those days the rule of law was weak and the people lived in fear of both the gangsters and the colonial police. I was angered by the sight of the police going around arresting the hawkers. I wrote an article for my school magazine, *The Rafflesian*, protesting against such arrests and pleading that the government should create places for the hawkers to ply their trade. I suffered my first experience of censorship by the British Director of Education and was told that my article could not be published. Today, the rule of law in Singapore is strong, with good law and order, an honest and competent police force, and an independent and non-corrupt judiciary.

A Young Man's Dreams

I was one of the lucky students who, in 1957, was admitted to study law at the University of Malaya, in Singapore. I graduated in 1961 and spent a year as David Marshall's law pupil. In 1962, I was admitted to the legal profession and hired by the Faculty of Law as an Assistant Lecturer, joining my classmates, Thio Su Mien and Koh Kheng Lian. I then spent a year at Harvard Law School and another year at Cambridge University. I came home in 1965 when Singapore unexpectedly became independent, fulfilling one of my schoolboy dreams. Singapore was, however, faced with an uncertain future because the conventional wisdom at that time was that an independent Singapore was not viable. Singapore's independence was therefore greeted by both cheers and tears. I was one of the minority who believed that an independent Singapore would succeed.

What were my dreams for Singapore as a young man?

First, I wanted independent Singapore to survive and to be accepted by the international community as a new member state. Three years after our independence, I was sent to the United Nations, in New York, as Singapore's Permanent Representative to help secure this agenda.

Second, I wanted Singapore to succeed economically, to create enough jobs for our unemployed and the young people entering the workforce each year. Our economic achievements in the past forty-three years have surpassed my dream.

Third, I had hoped that we would find a socio-economic model which would achieve growth with equity. We have achieved growth but we have not done as well with equity. The disparities of wealth and income have become wider, not narrower. I find it shocking that our gini index is worse than that of the United States.[2] In addition, as our sociologist, Tan Ern Ser,[3] has warned us, we are beginning to see the stratification of our society by social class. We should not abandon our dream of achieving both prosperity and equity. We should combat all forms of social snobbery and never allow an underclass to form in Singapore.

Fourth, I wanted a better balance in our early years of nation building between the new and the old. I belonged to a group of idealistic young men called Singapore Planning and Urban Research group or SPUR in short. We lobbied the government to conserve some of our landmark buildings, historic neighbourhoods and streets. We did not want to lose our built heritage as we plunge head long into the planning and building of a new Singapore. We were ahead of our time and the conservation movement did not enjoy strong support until the 1980s. I am, however, very pleased to say that, in recent decades, due to the good work of our Preservation of Monuments Board and the Urban Redevelopment Authority, we have done well in conserving our built heritage compared to other Asian cities.

Fifth, I dreamt that mutual understanding, peace and harmony would continue to prevail among Singaporeans of different races, religions, languages and cultures. In this respect, Singapore has done well. The two books[4] on ethnicity and religious diversity, edited by Dr Lai Ah Eng, confirm this impression. The Inter-Religious Organization, Singapore (IRO), a non-governmental organization, has made a major contribution to religious harmony in Singapore. We have developed a culture of tolerance, acceptance and respect for the faiths of others. Denigrating the faiths of others is both ethically and legally unacceptable in Singapore. I am also cheered by the growing percentage of inter-racial marriages in Singapore. Singapore should aspire to become a global centre for inter-ethnic, inter-religious and inter-cultural dialogue.

Sixth, I dreamt that Singaporeans would enjoy good governance and the rule of law. In 1960–61, when I was the President of the University of Malaya Students Law Society, I had advocated the setting up of an ombudsman in Singapore. I did so because in Singapore, the exercise of discretionary power by the government is not subject to judicial review. Although we have an honest government and one of the best bureaucracies in the world, mistakes can and do occur. An ombudsman would be empowered to investigate and report on complaints by citizens of maladministration. I still hope that one day Singapore would have an ombudsman although the need for one is not as great now as it was 47 years ago.

My Dreams Now

I have not stopped dreaming for Singapore. What are my dreams in my old age?

First, I dream that Singaporeans would be less obsessed with money and that we would grow in kindness and graciousness. I have always heeded my mentor, S. Rajaratnam's[5] warning that Singaporeans should not become a people who know the price of everything and the value of nothing. I think we are in such danger. We seem to calculate everything in terms of money. We seem to think that a person's worth is measured by the amount of money he or she makes. We have imitated one of the worst aspects of American capitalism by paying our senior executives inflated salaries while, at the same time, stagnating the salaries of our middle and lower strata.[6] I am glad that the President recognizes annually members of some of the professions which do not pay well but which make enormous contributions to our society, such as, teachers, nurses, social workers, librarians, etc. I also thank the media for showcasing selfless Singaporeans who help the poor and the disadvantaged, both at home and abroad. Money is important. We all need enough money to live in reasonable comfort and with material sufficiency. Money cannot, however, buy you good health, a happy family, good friends, peace of mind and joy. I hope that one day, Singapore's favourite film-maker, Jack Neo[7] will make a new movie, entitled "Money Enough Lah".

Are Singaporeans a kind people? I am inclined to say, yes, when I remember the generosity with which Singaporeans responded to the Boxing Day tsunami, cyclone Nargis, the earthquake in Szechuan, etc. I am constantly impressed by the letters written to the forum page of the *Straits Times*, thanking certain Singaporeans for the kindness they had shown to strangers. At the same time, I am shocked by the unkindness and even cruelty shown by some Singaporeans towards their foreign domestic workers and foreign workers more generally. Some of our foreign domestic workers are denied a decent place to sleep in, adequate food and rest and are treated as less than fellow human beings. As for the reports of wanton cruelty towards animals, I often wonder who these monsters are who commit such evil deeds. The record is therefore a mixed one. There are many kind Singaporeans but there are also many unkind Singaporeans. My good friend, Koh Poh Tiong, the Chairman of the Kindness Movement, therefore has a challenging job to do.

Are Singaporeans a gracious people? One area in which we are definitely not a gracious people is our driving manners or lack of them. From our driving practices and habits, one can infer that Singaporeans are aggressive, self-centred, inconsiderate and ungenerous. Is this an accurate portrait of ourselves? Let us hope that our driving manners, our selfish behaviour on our buses and trains, and in our elevators, do not reflect the kind of people we really are. The Minister Mentor is probably right when he said recently that we still have a long way to go to become a gracious and cultured people.

Second, I would like Singapore to become the Geneva of the East and the Venice of the twenty-first century. I think Singapore is a welcoming, efficient and secure meeting place for representatives of adversaries. We have already hosted some such meetings, for example, between the People's Republic of China and Taiwan in 1993, and between the United States and North Korea, more recently. Venice existed for almost 800 years as an independent city-state. One of the reasons for its success and longevity was that it welcomed the merchants, artists, and other talented people of different countries and civilizations to live and work in Venice. In the same way, Singapore should continue to welcome the talented people of all nations and civilizations to live and work here. We can become the Venice of the twenty-first century.

Third, Singapore can be the cultural hub of Southeast Asia and the home city of the Asian cultural renaissance. Singapore already has the best cultural infrastructure in Southeast Asia. We have the best museums of the region. The Esplanade is the region's best centre for the performing arts. Singapore has turned necessity into a virtue. Because of our small size and short history, we have no choice but to collect the history, heritage and visual arts of the region. As a result, we have the best and most comprehensive collection in the world of the nineteenth century and twentieth century visual arts of Southeast Asia. It was fitting that the world premiere of Robert Wilson's staging of the Buginese epic, I La Galigo, took place in Singapore. Beginning in 2008, the National Heritage Board will organize annually a festival to celebrate the civilization of an ASEAN country. The inaugural festival on Vietnam in 2008 was a great success. In 2009, we will showcase the Philippines. We have also taken the initiative to organize the first conference of ASEAN's museum directors. Singapore can however serve an even larger region. Because of our ethnic composition and our vision, Singapore can bring together the civilizations of Southeast Asia, China, South Asia and even Islam. The Asian Civilization Museum is a living example of our aspiration to be the home city of the Asian cultural renaissance. The recent initiative by the Arts House to organize the conference and festival, "Asia on Edge", should be applauded. I also welcome the proposal of the new President of the National University of Singapore, Tan Chorh Chuan, to set up a new Global Asia Institute at the University.

Fourth, Singapore can be Asia's "greenest" city. Singapore is already Asia's greenest city in the physical sense. Recently, some friends from Hong Kong, France and UK told me how impressed they were by our trees. Our Botanic Gardens have been awarded three stars by Guide Michelin, putting it in the same category as the iconic Eiffel Tower of Paris. We will soon open two new gardens in Marina Bay. But, Singapore is green not just physically but in its policies towards water, sanitation, air pollution, land use, sewage treatment, etc. The book, "Clean, Green and Blue"[8] by Tan Yong Soon, Lee Tung Jean and Karen Tan, tells the remarkable story of Singapore's journey in reconciling rapid economic growth with care for the environment. Singapore should also be "green" in the protection of its nature reserves and biological diversity, in the more efficient use of energy and the reduction of carbon dioxide emission, in the recycling of waste, and in the promotion of clean and renewable energy. I would like to see Singapore becoming a centre for the financing of green business and technology, a preferred venue for test-bedding new green technologies, products and services and for the trading of carbon credit. I am glad that a major Norwegian company has opened a plant to manufacture solar panels in Singapore. I am also encouraged by the seed money which the National Research Council has invested in research and development in solar energy. In the twenty-first century, with more than half of humanity living in cities, one of our greatest challenges is to make our cities as sustainable as possible. Singapore can be a role model for Asia and for the world.

Fifth, I think Singapore can become an important intellectual centre of the world. Our two leading universities, National University of Singapore and Nanyang Technological University, have been recognized as world class universities. I am confident that the Singapore Management University will soon join them. Our polytechnics, institutes of technical education, primary and secondary schools are much admired in the region. As a result, Singapore is beginning to attract a large number of foreign students to study here. There has also been a quantum leap in the percentage of our GDP invested in research and development.[9] The culture of respect for learning and research is growing and more and more young people are taking careers in research and scholarship. Our think-tanks are expanding in number and ascending in quality. Our Japanese friends have sometimes referred to Singapore as "a think-tank country". What more can we do? We can invest more money in research in the social sciences and humanities. At the moment, the Ministry of Education is the only source of such funding. The National Research

Council does not make grants to support such research and there is no local equivalent of the U.S. Social Science Research Council. We can be more open in releasing data to researchers. We also need to grow the culture of tolerance for alternative and dissenting views. Without such a culture, scholarship, especially in the social sciences and humanities, will not flourish.

Conclusion

Singapore is a microcosm of the world of the twenty-first century. It is globalized and multicultural. It is both urban and green. It is situated at the confluence of the civilizations of Southeast Asia, China and India. Because of its colonial heritage, Singapore is part East and part West. It is a leading candidate for Asia's most global city. Let us make Singapore one of the most liveable cities in the world.

Notes

[1]   Bukit Ho Swee was a densely populated area which had thousands of squatter homes built with combustible materials such as attap and wooden boards. Between 1934 and 1968 this squatter area experienced three big fires. The second fire which occurred in 1961 was the biggest fire in Singapore (adapted from Singapore Encyclopedia).

[2]   The 2007/08 United Nations Human Development Report's Gini Index ranks the United States as number 12 (with gini index of 40.8) and Singapore as number 25 (42.5) in the world. A gini index of "0" represents perfect income equality whereas a gini index of "100" represents perfect income inequality.

[3]   Tan Ern Ser, *Does Class Matter? Social Stratification and Orientations in Singapore* (Singapore: World Scientific, 2004).

[4]   Lai Ah Eng, ed. *Beyond Rituals and Riots: Ethnic Pluralism and Social Cohesion in Singapore* (Singapore: Eastern Universities Press, 2004); Lai Ah Eng, ed. *Religious Diversity in Singapore (*Singapore: Institute of Southeast Asian Studies, 2008).

[5]   The late S. Rajaratnam was a founding member of the People's Action Party. Together with Lee Kuan Yew, Goh Keng Swee and Toh Chin Chye, he led the struggles for Singapore's independence. He was the first Foreign Minister of independent Singapore, and later deputy Prime Minister.

[6]   See Chua Hak Bin, "Singapore Economy: The New and the Dual Economy", in *Singapore Perspectives 2007: A New Singapore*, edited by Tan Tarn How (Singapore: World Scientific Press, 2007); and Yeoh Lam Keong, "A New Social Compact for Singapore", *Straits Times*, 23 November 2007.

[7]   Comedian, actor and film director, Jack Neo Chee Keong first became a household name by being a comedian. His wrote and starred in the film *Money No Enough*, a

film about the lives of working class Singaporeans who were trying to make ends meet. Neo was awarded Singapore's Public Service Medal in 2004 and the Cultural Medallion in 2005 (adapted from Singapore Encyclopedia).

8   Singapore: Institute of Southeast Asian Studies, 2008.

9   The gross domestic expenditure on R&D (GERD) increased from S$5,010 million in 2006 to S$6,339 million in 2007. The unprecedented year-on-year increase by 26.5 per cent is a significant jump from the 9.3 per cent year-on-year increase in 2006. As a percentage of GDP, GERD rose from 2.31 per cent in 2006 to 2.61 per cent in 2007 (Source: A*Star Press Release, 23 December 2008).

Thailand

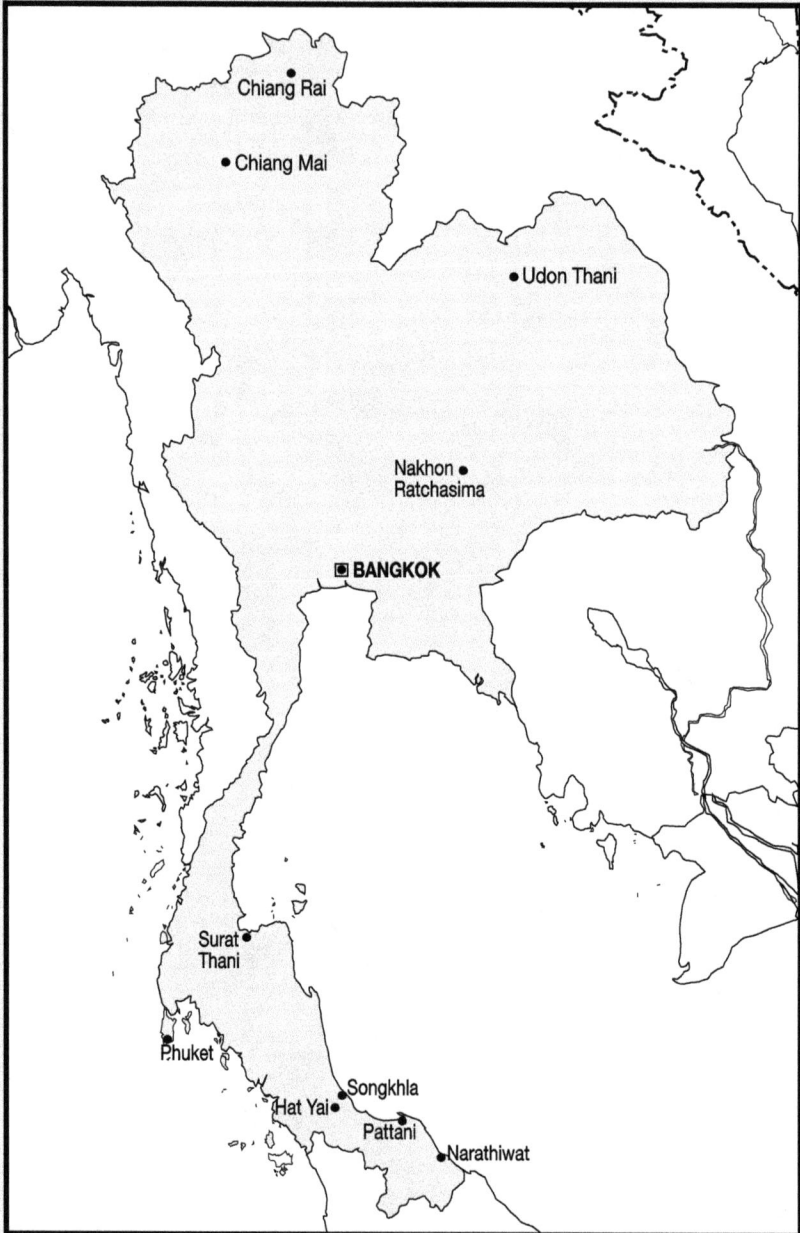

- Chiang Rai
- Chiang Mai
- Udon Thani
- Nakhon Ratchasima
- BANGKOK
- Surat Thani
- Phuket
- Hat Yai
- Songkhla
- Pattani
- Narathiwat

THAILAND IN 2008:
Democracy and Street Politics

James Ockey

The UDD protesters are Thais like us, but they are just misled. For this reason, please just beat them until they are unable to walk, not beat them to death.

> Captain Songklod Chuenchupol
> PAD weapons trainer
> *Bangkok Post*, 7 September 2008

Now my daughter asks me what happened to make the formerly peaceful PAD protests turn so disgusting and ugly...Thailand is wrecked, brought down by those who claim to love their nation and their King. When will Thailand become a peaceful country again...?

> Letter to the Editor
> *Bangkok Post*, 30 November 2008

Let's imagine that the government failed — What would become of Thailand? The politics on the street will follow for years to come. What will we teach our children? How can we look the foreigners in the eyes and say we are a civilized country? We will get poorer and poorer by the day and ordinary crimes will increase. And able people will shun politics as a career — leave it to mad dogs. People will come to our land and look at us not with admiration but pity. Is this what we want?

> Internet comment on a *Bangkok Post* story, 27 August 2008

The year 2008 was yet another eventful year for Thai democracy. With yet another new constitution and more new institutions, to go along with a deeply

---

JAMES OCKEY is Associate Professor at the Department of Political Science, University of Canterbury, Christchurch, New Zealand.

divided society, it was certain to prove a challenging time. Red shirt and yellow shirt demonstrators came into confrontation on several occasions, culminating in a takeover of both of Bangkok's airports by the yellow shirts, leaving hundreds of thousands of tourists stranded. While the protestors eventually left peacefully, there can be no doubt that the year saw a weakening of all major institutions. Thailand also faces a difficult period for the economy, and some challenges in foreign relations. We begin by outlining the divisions in society, with a brief look backward, to clarify the origins and the depth of the divide in Thai society. We then turn to the political events of the year, followed by a brief discussion of the economy and foreign relations.

The Divide in Thai Society

While it is fairly simple to classify the divide in Thai society as regional, with the North and Northeast on one side, the South and Bangkok on the other, or as class-based, with the middle classes on one side, the poor on the other, and the rich divided, it is worth keeping in mind the divide is not so simply structural, and is of fairly recent origin. The election of 2001 delivered a large plurality of seats to one political party, Thai Rak Thai, both nationally and in Bangkok, drawing on voters from all classes. Only in the South, where the Democrat party has a strong foundation, did Thai Rak Thai, the party of billionaire Thaksin Shinawatra, struggle to make inroads. Furthermore, at that time, Thaksin was fairly new to Thai politics, having received his first cabinet position from political ally Chamlong Srimuang. Media tycoon Sondhi Limthongkul was also an ally during these years. By the end of its first four-year term, Thai Rak Thai had been successful enough that it won re-election in the largest landslide in modern Thai political history, again performing well in Bangkok, and struggling only in the South. The division that has emerged in Thai society, while it certainly has roots in regional and class differences, began shortly after that landslide victory.

The opposition to Thaksin came about in no small part through the efforts of Sondhi Limthongkul, who not only provided leadership, but also provided a large amount of the funding for the anti-Thaksin efforts. Especially at the beginning, Sondhi also took full advantage of his media empire to develop support. He began by decrying the corruption of the Thaksin government in weekly broadcasts, which soon turned into open air rallies. Corruption, however, is nothing new in Thailand, and while it certainly can still provoke a certain level of outrage, to develop the depth of commitment he would require to overthrow such a popular government, Sondhi needed a more emotive issue. He found that issue in Thai nationalism, and in particular in one of the main pillars of Thai nationalism, the monarchy. With the highly revered king having reached an advanced age, and with many concerned for him and for what might come after, Sondhi began to claim that Thaksin was a closet republican, and that he was seeking to usurp the power and authority of the king.[1] This marked a dual appeal to nationalism and royalism that provided the depth of commitment that Sondhi required. At the same time, accusing the hugely popular Thaksin of anti-royalism provoked a strong reaction from his supporters, so that charges of loyalty and disloyalty to Thailand's most beloved institution lie at the heart of the division in Thai society. Sondhi's movement later combined with other anti-Thaksin forces to form the People's Alliance for Democracy (PAD), and added the charismatic but uncompromising Chamlong Srimuang to its leadership. As the PAD increasingly turned to undemocratic methods, including calls for a royally appointed government and calls for a military coup, they began to depict themselves as defenders of the monarchy, rather than defenders of democracy, so that the institution and symbol of the monarchy was drawn into the dispute. While the king and the royal family carefully avoided comment, some were quick to interpret any statement or act, no matter how small, in the light of the conflict. Charges of lese majeste proliferated on both sides, in an indication of the way that claims of loyalty to the monarchy had become so central to the political dispute.

After the coup of September 2006, the coup leaders set out to end the division in Thai society by eliminating the influence of Thaksin.[2] Thaksin was charged with corruption, and both he and members of his family had assets confiscated. His Thai Rak Thai party was dissolved and 105 of its leaders were barred from political participation for five years. A new constitution was promulgated with provisions to decentralize power, and to advantage Thaksin's political opponents in the ensuing election. The coup group also seems to have interfered in the electoral process in support of some political parties.[3] Ultimately, all these attempts to eliminate the influence of Thaksin came to nought, as he and his policies had won the loyalty of many voters, especially in the north and the northeast, and among the poor more generally. We can see how deeply entrenched the division had become by looking briefly at the results of the December 2007 election. Although the election system has changed quite frequently in Thailand, in 1986, 1996, and 2007, a multiple member election district system was in place, where each district would have one, two, or three winning candidates. To win all three seats in a three member district would indicate strong support for a party in

TABLE 1

	1986	1996	2007
Three Seat Districts	77	93	90
Swept	22	40	60
Split	55	53	30
Per cent Swept	28.6	43.0	66.7
Two Seat Districts	52	56	63
Swept	20	25	40
Split	32	31	23
Per cent Swept	38.5	44.6	63.5

that area. This provides a good way to look at party and societal divisions by examining the numbers of districts where voters lined up behind a single party rather than dividing their votes between parties. The results of the three elections for the multiple member election districts can be seen in Table 1.

In 1986, a single party was able to capture all seats in an election district only about one third of the time. Even in 1996, before the rise of the Thai Rak Thai party, only about 44 per cent of election districts were swept by a single party. By 2007, some two thirds of all districts were swept by one party. Thus we can see the deepening of the divide in Thai society. Since these election districts are also geographically based, of course the divide is also geographical in nature. As noted previously, the Democrat party swept districts in the South, while the Phalang Prachachon party, a successor to Thaksin's dissolved Thai Rak Thai party, swept many of the districts in the North and Northeast. Of course such divisions are neither unusual nor dangerous in a democracy under normal circumstances, but with protest leaders' insistence on making the issue one of loyalty, rather than difference over policy, and strong uncompromising egoists involved on both sides (Sondhi, Chamlong, Thaksin and Samak, in particular), the circumstances became anything but normal.

The Societal Divide and the Samak Suntharavej Government

When the election results emerged for the 23 December 2007 election, the Phalang Prachachon party won 233 of the 480 seats, to just 165 for the Democrat party. And while the Election Commission (ECT) disqualified a number of Phalang

Prachachon candidates (and a much smaller number of Democrat party candidates), the Democrat party total was much too low for a Democrat-led coalition to be feasible; even if all the small parties joined, it would have only a very slim majority. The Election Commission, widely criticized for its perceived lack of neutrality during and after the election, also set out to investigate charges that could lead to the dissolution of virtually every party, though few expected that to eventuate. In the meantime, Phalang Prachachon rushed to put together a coalition and announce a government, hoping to make any manoeuvring by the ECT or other non-elected bodies irrelevant. In early January, a coalition was announced, and Phalang Prachachon party leader Samak Suntharavej became the new prime minister.

Samak's ascendance to the position of prime minister came as something of a surprise. Samak began his political career in the 1970s as a member of parliament for the Democrat party, splitting away to form his own party after the 1976 massacre. A long-time bitter rival of both PAD leader Chamlong Srimuang and the Democrat party, an ultra-rightist and a royalist well known for his aggressive political style, he had seemingly accepted that he would have no chance at the premiership after the early successes of Thai Rak Thai, as he shifted his focus to Bangkok politics, winning election as the mayor of the city. However, when Thai Rak Thai was dissolved and all of its executives were barred from participation, Phalang Prachachon turned to Samak. His royalist credentials were beyond reproach, and his aggressive political style seemed suitable given the party's problems with coup leaders. As a campaign leader, he seemed the ideal choice; however, many Phalang Prachachon party members were not entirely comfortable with the thought of Samak as a leader. Nor was Samak content to remain a mere proxy for Thaksin, so that tensions arose quickly when Samak became prime minister, both within the party, between rival factions, and through the efforts of his political opponents.

While the factional structure in the Phalang Prachachon party was quite complex, we can roughly group it into three: MPs from the North, who supported Thaksin; MPs from the upper Northeast, including the Isan Phattana faction, who also supported Thaksin; and the Newin Chidchob faction, made up of MPs from the central and lower northeast regions, with a core group of around 30 members and perhaps another 70 loosely affiliated MPs who supported Samak. The Thaksin supporters expected that the main goals of the new government would be to amend the constitution, and prepare the way for the return of Thaksin, followed by a relatively quick call for new elections, while Samak and his supporters wished to govern for a longer period. The split between factions was further complicated by the struggle to gain seats in the cabinet, with Newin's faction gaining a proportionally greater share than Isan Phattana. These differences within Phalang Prachachon left the government, despite its large majority, in a somewhat precarious position. Samak also faced two court cases brought by his opponents, and the Phalang Prachachon party faced a third charge of vote-buying by one of its executives, which could result in its dissolution.

One of the first goals of the Phalang Prachachon party was to arrange for Thaksin to return. This was quickly achieved, as he returned to Bangkok on 28 February 2008. Although he was arrested at the airport on an outstanding corruption charge, he was immediately granted bail while the case proceeded in the courts. This quick success did not ease tensions, however, as Thaksin supporters sought to move ahead rapidly on constitutional amendments, which could then lead to a dissolution of parliament and a new election, and, they hoped, a return to politics for Thaksin. Samak, on the other hand, had finally achieved his lifelong ambition of becoming prime minister, and he was not in any hurry to give it up. Phalang Prachachon's opponents also wished to prevent the amendment of the constitution, similarly fearing that it might allow Thaksin to return to politics.

As the government continued to push to amend the constitution, the PAD again took to the streets in what would be another prolonged protest. Although the protests were well-funded by donations, mainly from Sondhi's business empire, as with the previous effort, it quickly became clear that resisting constitutional amendments would not invoke the level of commitment necessary to sustain the protests, particularly since all parties supported some amendments, with the debate being over which amendments should be made. Just as before, the PAD turned to nationalism to shore up support.[4] While the defense of the monarchy remained a key tenant of this appeal to nationalism, this time the PAD also tried a new tactic. Cambodia had been seeking to gain World Heritage Site status for Phreah Vihar temple, located on a remote mountain along the Thai-Cambodia border. The temple had been the subject of a bitter dispute between Cambodia and Thailand in the post-World War Two era, with the dispute resolved in Cambodia's favour by a 1962 World Court decision. That decision was never fully accepted by many in Thailand, though over the years, the two nations developed a cooperative relationship to develop the site for tourism. As the most convenient route to the temple — until recently, the only route to the temple — ran through Thailand, both sides benefitted, and eventually border posts were established in a convenient location, with some 4.6 square kilometres of disputed territory between the border posts and the temple. This *de facto* border, which facilitated tourism, was a cause of concern to some in the security community, but not an irritant in Thai-Cambodian relations, until the PAD decided to take up the issue to gain nationalist support for its cause. As we shall see, not only did this evoke a rather chauvinistic form of nationalism, but it eventually resulted in armed clashes between Thai and Cambodian troops in the area.

The border problems grew out of what had been quite cordial relations between the Samak government and the Hun Sen government in Cambodia. The Samak government placed early priority in foreign relations on reinforcing positive relations with its neighbours. The government decided to support the Cambodian application for World Heritage Site status, as long as the disputed territory was not included in the application, and after negotiations, Foreign Minister Noppadon Pattama signed a joint communiqué. While security officials were satisfied with the result of the negotiations,[5] the Democrat party decided to submit a censure motion in parliament. Declaring, "Our sacred mission is to protect our motherland and take back Thai territory", PAD leader Sondhi Limthongkul turned out protestors both in Bangkok and along the border as he turned to nationalism to strengthen commitment to the anti-Thaksin cause.[6] The PAD also claimed that the attempt to improve relations with Cambodia was aimed at easing the way for Thaksin's business dealings in the region. While the Democrat censure motion failed, in an indication of the interplay between different segments of the anti-PPP groups, the constitutional court then took up the case, ultimately ruling that the joint communiqué amounted to a treaty and that Noppadon had thus violated the constitutional requirement that treaties be approved by the parliament. Noppadon was forced to resign and the PAD had both its new nationalist cause and an early victory, of a sort, to buoy its supporters. Despite the withdrawal of Thai support, UNESCO approved the application for World Heritage Site status.

The border dispute not only solidified the commitment of the PAD's core supporters, taken together with a weak economy and a spate of court decisions against Thaksin and the government, it also contributed to rising discontent within the coalition.[7] Consequently, Samak sought to reinforce government legitimacy by taking advantage of the resignation of Noppadon to reshuffle the cabinet. He also announced a number of new programmes, designed to stimulate the economy by injecting money at the grassroots level, programmes that were immediately deemed "populist" by his opponents. At the same time, the call for constitutional amendments was renewed, further displeasing the PAD. The reshuffle failed to generate additional support, and Samak ran out of time before he had the opportunity to implement the new programmes. Indeed, the reshuffle widened factional divisions within the PPP. The struggle for seats in the new cabinet further divided those factions that supported Thaksin and those that supported Samak. Newin Chidchob again played a prominent role in support of Samak, and his faction was rewarded accordingly. According to reports, Newin at this time also began advising members of the PPP to solicit donations to form a new party, in case the PPP were to be dissolved, and suggested a coalition government with the opposition Democrat party as a possible alternative to the existing coalition.[8] This suggestion proved unpopular with the factions that were close to Thaksin, so that the party continued to weaken internally, even as it faced increasing challenges from parliamentary, extra-parliamentary, and institutional opponents.

Despite the divisions within the party, and the long-running protests, the greatest threat to the PPP coalition government, to the parties within the government, and to individual government leaders came from the increasingly politically activist courts.[9] While the military continued to refuse PAD calls for a coup, a series of cases against the government were underway in the courts, cases that could be used to bring the government down. On the advice of some of their confidantes, Thaksin and Potchaman, out on bail while their tax evasion case was on appeal, applied for permission to leave the country to attend the Beijing Olympic games. At the end of July, they jumped bail, claiming it was impossible for them to get a fair trial, and returned to London, though they promised to return at some time in the future. Rather than declare victory, the PAD sought to step up demonstrations, stating that it would not quit until Thaksin was made to pay for his crimes, and the government was replaced by one not allied to him. Although the British government later bowed to pressure, and revoked Thaksin's visa, he remained in exile through the end of the year.

The success in forcing Thaksin into exile again raised the possibility that PAD demonstrators would simply melt away; PAD leaders thus needed to find a new way to reaffirm the commitment of their supporters, or risk losing the power and influence they had worked so hard to gain. In a sign of its new aggressiveness, the PAD had been training security guards who could also serve as shock troops when they chose to take the offensive. The United Front of Democracy Against Dictatorship (UDD), composed of Thaksin supporters also established security units, and fears of a clash between the two sides grew. Concerned at the fading support, PAD leader Sondhi called on all supporters to join a rally on 26 August which he deemed "the last whistleblow", where PAD would seek to take over government house to block a cabinet meeting. They also planned to block government buildings and major roads in Bangkok and around the country, as well as the airports at Hat Yai and Phuket. "If we fail this time, we'll quit and surrender the country to them. When people don't care about us, we won't have to care about them. Let others take over the country", vowed Sondhi.[10] The PAD, rather optimistically, hoped to turn out 300,000 people, a bit under one half of one per cent of the total population. Actual numbers were much smaller, perhaps 30,000. Meanwhile, even in Bangkok, where the PAD's support was strongest, according to one poll, some 70 per cent were opposed to the attempts to overthrow the government while another poll found nearly 90 per cent were opposed.[11] When PAD demonstrators, some armed with guns and knives, attacked a government television broadcasting station, many in the press turned against the PAD as well. Nevertheless, the seizure of Government House did succeed in galvanizing core supporters, as intended.

Samak responded to the takeover of government house and other government buildings by calling an emergency session of parliament, and then flying to Hua Hin to meet the King.[12] When violence broke out between the UDD and PAD demonstrators, leading to the death of one UDD supporter, he also declared emergency law in Bangkok, to little effect. The coalition then decided to hold a referendum to let the people decide whether the government should resign, a move immediately rejected by the PAD. Arrest warrants were also issued for PAD leaders. Reluctant to disperse the PAD demonstrators by force, yet no longer able to simply ignore them, the government became increasingly paralysed, unable to act on other matters with the situation still unresolved. Meanwhile, PAD refused to enter into any negotiations unless Samak and the cabinet resigned.

The impasse was finally broken on 9 September, when the constitutional court, in a 9-0 decision, decided that due to his participation in two television cooking shows, Samak had violated the constitutional ban against outside employment. It declared that due to the violation, he and the cabinet had to leave office immediately. The courts thus again took on a political role at a time of crisis, and again gave the PAD what it had demanded, with its decision based on what many government supporters considered frivolous grounds.[13] The constitutional court did leave the way open for Samak to be reappointed, however, and his coalition partners immediately declared support for his return.

PAD vs Somchai Wongsawat

In the ensuing days, coalition partners and faction leaders within the PPP came under heavy pressure to withdraw support from Samak in an attempt to end the political crisis. The divisions within the PPP played an important role, as those who had lost out in earlier cabinet reshuffles agitated to have Samak replaced. Samak and his allies moved quickly to forestall opposition; however, he proved unsuccessful. When parliament met on 12 September to vote on the appointment of the prime minister, coalition partners and some 70 members of the PPP absented themselves from the meeting, so that the parliament lacked a quorum. Ultimately, it was the divisions within the PPP that prevented the return of Samak. Coalition partners claimed that they had stayed away to allow the PPP the necessary time to resolve its internal conflict, and certainly without the 70 PPP votes, Samak could not have succeeded. Abandoned by all but his closest supporters, Samak chose to withdraw from the contest. Among the losers were Newin Chidchop and his faction, which had consistently supported Samak and had led the move to bring him back as prime minister.

When it became clear that Samak would not return, competition developed over other candidates within the government. After considerable manoeuvring, which included participation by phone for Thaksin, Somchai Wongsawat emerged as the preferred choice. Somchai was the former permanent secretary of the justice department, and was married to Thaksin's younger sister Yaowapha, a former MP who had long controlled the family's faction in the parliament. As a long time bureaucrat, Somchai enjoyed a certain amount of respect. At the same time, he was heavily dependent on his sister's faction for his position, so that his ascension indicated a greater role for Thaksin's core supporters in the new government. The PAD chose to continue its demonstrations, reiterating its determination to oppose constitutional amendments, change the form of government to a less democratic model, and root out all Thaksin influence in the government. They also insisted that the government had to bring Thaksin to trail, a demand that no government could meet, given that Thaksin had chosen exile overseas. In addition, while Somchai did not face the personal legal challenges of his predecessor, the case for dissolution of the PPP was still pending in the activist courts.

At this juncture, the PAD, now victorious in its battle against Samak, again found itself in danger of losing support. Drawing on the same tactics employed when Thaksin went into exile, PAD leaders decided to go on the offensive. When the parliament met to hear the policy speech of the new government, and to formally inaugurate it, PAD demonstrators marched to the parliament and surrounded it, disrupting the session and keeping the MPs trapped inside. Many, including the new prime minister, were forced to climb over the fence to get past the demonstrators. When police arrived to clear a path, violence broke out, quelled by the use of tear gas. Two protestors were killed, and well over 400 were injured, including eight police officers.[14] Police were blamed for the deaths, as popular sentiment swung against the government, and in favour of the protestors. When the Queen established a medical aid fund for those injured, and later attended the funeral of one of the protestors,[15] PAD members interpreted her actions as indicating royal support for their cause, further strengthening their resolve.

While the PAD remained ensconced at Government House, and continued to hold rallies, it did, for a time, back away from its more aggressive tactics, due perhaps in part to the violence and in part to the funeral of Princess Galyani, which included a series of religious rites culminating in mid-November. The PAD also celebrated another victory when Thaksin was convicted of corruption in a 5-4 Supreme Court decision, and sentenced, in absentia, to serve two years in prison. His wife Potchaman was acquitted. But if Prime Minister Somchai gained something of a respite from the demonstrators, he faced increased pressure from the military as Army Commander Anupong Paochinda suggested that he should resign to show responsibility for the violence used against protestors. To many, this pressure from a military that had carried out a coup just two years earlier seemed irresistible, and rumours of a coup proliferated. However Somchai insisted that the Anupong had only offered advice, and instead appointed an independent panel to investigate the incident.[16] With little to gain from taking power directly, the military chose not to intervene forcefully.

The conviction of Thaksin led to some concerns among his supporters that his support might erode. Consequently, even as PAD temporarily backed away from its more aggressive tactics, the UDD and Thaksin ramped up their own rallies. Thaksin arranged to talk to his supporters by phone from overseas. Originally intended for live broadcast, organizers eventually decided to hold the event at a large stadium in Bangkok. While this was not the first such event, it was widely promoted as a show of support for the government at a time of military pressure, as well as a show of support for Thaksin personally. More than 80,000 people turned out for the rally and the phone call.[17] Demonstrations also took place in several provinces around the country, and another rally was planned for December. Unhappy with the show of support, the military subsequently accused Thaksin of involving the monarchy in politics since he told his supporters that only a royal pardon or people's power could bring him home,[18] thus again making loyalty to the crown central to the political divisions.

After the conclusion of funeral ceremonies, tension increased between UDD and PAD demonstrators. One Thaksin supporter, Maj-General Kattiya Sawadiphol, issued an ultimatum for PAD to leave Government House or face the consequences. Shortly after the ultimatum, a bomb was tossed into the compound, one of several bombings since demonstrations had begun. More violence between the two groups followed. The situation was further exacerbated when Thaksin said he would name his enemies at the upcoming rally, followed by a PPP member of parliament claiming that either Thaksin or his wife would return to Thailand on 25 December.[19] Although there was no confirmation or denial from Thaksin, many PAD supporters were determined not to let their victory slip away. Consequently, the PAD began to prepare for what its leaders called "the last battle".

On 22 November, final preparations were put in place for this last battle. Speaking to PAD supporters, Sondhi again appealed directly to royalist nationalism to buttress support for the difficult and dangerous demonstrations to come:

> I would like to invite people to join the last battle. We know what we are doing and we believe that what we are doing and will do has same objective which are to protect the country [nation], religion and monarchy [king].[20]

On 23 November, PAD supporters thus gathered at Government House to implement what they called "King Taksin Operation".[21] The plan called for seizure of the parliament, to prevent any attempt to amend the constitution, seizure of the Finance Ministry and some other financial centres, and seizure of Don Muang airport, the smaller of the two Bangkok airports, where cabinet meetings had been held after the occupation of Government House. In this way they hoped to place enough pressure on the government to force the unconditional resignation of Prime Minister Somchai. The plan was put in motion on 24 November, as the PAD expanded its original plan, marching first to the parliament, where the speaker simply cancelled the session, then to a variety of other sites around Bangkok, including Don Muang airport, where the cabinet gave way without resistance, the Supreme Command, and Chat Thai party headquarters. The police watched passively throughout, and it soon appeared that the last battle would never take place.

Determined to provoke a confrontation, Chamlong announced the PAD decision to seize Suvarnabhumi airport to fellow demonstrators.[22] Somchai was scheduled to return from the APEC summit in Peru, and by taking the airport they hoped to prevent his return. At the same time, it was clear that closing down the airport would be an act impossible to ignore. They followed through by taking control of the airport on 25 November, shutting down all flights and stranding hundreds of thousands of tourists in Thailand and Thais seeking to return from overseas. Despite the takeover, Prime Minister Somchai was able to return, landing at Chiang Mai airport.

Even in the face of the tremendous damage done to the economy, the government was paralyzed by the seizure of the airports. The military refused to intervene, perhaps because it had nothing to gain and everything to lose, perhaps because it too was so divided internally that it could not act. The police also failed to intervene, even when Prime Minister Somchai replaced the commander of the national police force. Perhaps most surprisingly of all, even as public support for the PAD slipped to 11 per cent,[23] even as the PAD was heavily criticized by diplomats and international investors, the palace remained silent, despite PAD claims that its highly unpopular actions were for the sake of the monarchy.[24]

In the end, the activist constitutional court again intervened to end the impasse. Although the trials regarding the dissolution of the PPP and two other coalition parties for alleged vote-buying were still in their early stages, the court decided not to listen to any witnesses, choosing instead to move directly to closing statements and an immediate decision.[25] Given such an unusual procedure, the ruling was inevitable as the constitutional court again ruled against the supporters of Thaksin, dissolving all three parties and banning their executives, including the prime minister, from political participation for the next five years. With the PPP dissolved and the prime minister removed from office, the PAD claimed victory, although it insisted that if the new government was not to its liking, it would again take control of the airports, deeming the heavy economic cost as a small price to pay in defense of nation and king.

The members of the PPP had prepared for the dissolution of their party, which, given the past decisions of the court, seemed inevitable, if premature. The Phuea Thai party had been prepared as an alternative party, which all PPP members of parliament were meant to join. A new prime minister would be chosen and the government coalition would remain largely unchanged. Again, however, intense pressure was placed upon coalition members and PPP factions to defect, in order to allow the Democrat party to govern. At this juncture, disaffected faction leader Newin Chidchop found himself in the position of kingmaker, a position he clearly relished, as each side lobbied him for support during the ensuing week. By agreeing to support a Democrat-led coalition, he was able to secure favourable cabinet positions for his faction. The Democrat party also chose to appoint as foreign minister the highly controversial Kasit Piromya, who had supported the occupation of the airport, perhaps hoping to pacify the PAD, perhaps simply confirming a long-standing alliance.[26] Democrat party leader Abbhisit Vejjachiwat became the fourth Thai prime minister within the space of a year.

Foreign Relations

Throughout the year, Thailand's foreign relations were deeply affected by the political turmoil. Upon coming to office, Prime Minister Samak, adhering to a Thai tradition, set out to visit neighbouring countries first, to solidify relations within the region. That effort was soon eroded when the PAD accused the government of treason in supporting the designation of Phreah Vihear as a World Heritage site, discussed above. With Cambodia in the midst of an election, and the PAD using the issue to promote nationalism, tensions rose between the two countries. Each side deployed additional troops to the area, culminating in two clashes between the sides in October. Two Cambodian soldiers were killed, and a number of others were wounded on each side. Following the clashes, the Thai foreign minister called on Thai civilians to leave Cambodia. Thus PAD politicization led to an erosion of ties with neighbouring Cambodia, though some attempt had been made to mend those ties and demarcate the border by the end of the year. The PAD takeover of Bangkok's airports further eroded relations with Thailand's neighbours, as Bangkok is a major hub for flights into Laos, Cambodia, Burma, and Vietnam. The seizure of the airports thus had a major impact on neighbouring countries, and may undermine the status of Bangkok as a regional hub over the longer term as those countries seek to limit their dependence on Suvarnabhumi airport. In addition, the seizure of the airports led to the postponement of the ASEAN summit meeting scheduled for Bangkok in December, and left Thailand behind in the signing of free trade pacts underway within ASEAN.

Thailand's relations with the West were also undermined by the political instability. Britain was placed in a difficult position as the PAD protested Thaksin's presence there. Britain eventually took the unusual step of cancelling Thaksin's visa while he was travelling in Asia. It was the seizure of the airports, however, that had the most impact on ties with the West. Australia and European countries were forced to take action to get their citizens home through other airports. EU ambassadors together with the United States, Australia, Canada, Japan, South Korea, and New Zealand ambassadors issued a joint statement noting that the seizure was dangerous, inappropriate, and damaging to Thailand's international image. They called for problems to be resolved democratically.[27] The United States separately declared that the seizure of the airports was not an acceptable means of protest, and called on the PAD to withdraw.[28] The U.S. State Department also issued a travel advisory. The greatest impact, however, was at the people-to-people level, as thousands of stranded visitors left disillusioned, and thousands more cancelled their plans to visit Thailand.

The Economy

Thailand has seen growth constrained in recent years by a lack of excess production capacity, and by political instability. To solve the constraint in production capacity, more investment, foreign and domestic, is necessary, yet the political instability has served to constrain that investment. The political instability, with the consequent frequent changes in government, including twice changing the entire regime, leaves potential investors feeling uncertain about the direction of economic policy, a sentiment perhaps exacerbated for foreign investors by the stirring up of nationalist fervour.[29] Thailand had thus experienced slower growth than the region as a whole since the beginning of the political unrest in 2006, with little likelihood of turning that around until the investment climate improves. Nevertheless, in the first quarter of 2008, the Thai economy exceeded expectations, growing at a 6.1 per cent pace year-on-year, led by strong export numbers.[30] For the economy that was the high point of the year; in the second quarter growth slowed dramatically, as a result of high inflation, and political uncertainty as the PAD demonstrations began. The second half of the year, the impact of the global slowdown began to be felt. Although this moderated inflation, it also undermined the export sector, which had led the strong growth in the first quarter. This, together with the political uncertainty, meant difficult times in the second half of the year for the Thai economy.

As the effects of the global downturn expanded, the political uncertainty also increased. When the PAD took over the airports in November, cutting off air cargo out of Bangkok temporarily, exports, which had carried the economy in the first quarter, declined 18.6 per cent year-on-year, the first drop since 2002, and the largest drop in recent history.[31] Thai economists predicted that the airport seizures would lead to a 40 per cent decline in tourist arrivals — a much larger decline than that caused by SARS or the tsunami of 2004. The cost to the Thai economy was estimated at some 140 billion baht, and some 1 million jobs. The business confidence index declined to 34.4 per cent, the lowest level in the last decade, indeed the lowest level by some five per cent.[32] When the year ended, the Stock Exchange of Thailand composite index had declined from 858.10 to 449.96, a decline of nearly 48 per cent,[33] in line with the rest of the region, and even with the announcement of a large stimulus package, the government, rather optimistically, was hoping to manage zero to two per cent growth rate for 2009.[34] Under the circumstances, solving the underlying problem, the need for more investment to overcome the lack of surplus capacity necessary for further growth, will almost certainly continue for some time, albeit with less urgency, given that growth will be constrained anyway due to the global economic downturn.

Thailand in 2008

The year 2008 was a difficult year for Thailand. The Thai economy, Thailand's international image, and virtually every major political institution suffered, as the democratic political system was undermined. Divisions in Thai society deepened. If we consider briefly some of the key institutions in Thai society, we can see some of the damage done. The police force, in breaking up the demonstrations on 7 October, found themselves at the centre of a controversy, due to the death of a protestor hit by a tear gas canister. They also proved incapable of controlling the demonstrations, allowing the situation to burgeon out of control. The military, from one point of view, distinguished itself by staying out of politics, and perhaps emerged with relatively little damage. From another point of view, the military did intervene in politics, by placing pressure on the government to quit. Yet the government simply ignored the military, leaving it impotent. The political party system was undermined, with a number of parties dissolved, to be replaced by new parties with different names, but the same people. Developing a stable party system became more difficult. As for the monarchy, the palace and its bureaucrats have consistently expressed a desire to remain above politics, and the monarchy has not taken any public stance. Yet the PAD and other political actors, by insisting that the reason for their political actions is their loyalty to the monarchy, have made the monarchy central to the political divisions in society. We can see the extent to which the monarchy has been made a subject of contention by the PAD and its opponents in the expansion of lese majeste cases, which are currently being used both to attack rivals and to demonstrate loyalty to the king. There are currently some 40 cases of lese majeste underway; in addition, over 2,300 Internet sites deemed offensive have been banned.[35] Drawing the monarchy into politics in this way has created problems for both the political system and the palace. As for the courts, and especially the constitutional court, in taking on an explicitly political role and intervening consistently on one side, they appear to have undermined their credibility. As the respected economist Pridiyathorn Devakula, formerly a finance minister and governor of the Bank of Thailand, has noted,

> The judgments in a few cases affected the confidence of people in the justice system. I do understand that such judgments did help in easing up political tension. But it is not worth trading it with the confidence of people — local and international — in the justice system as a whole. Political problems should be solved by political means....[36]

And yet the greatest damage was done to the democratic system itself. In refusing to accept democratic outcomes, in refusing to compromise, and in advocating a coup and a new non-democratic system, the PAD has damaged the foundations of democracy in Thailand. Most troubling is the PAD insistence that, because it believes its cause is just, because it is defending the nation, it has the right to overthrow the government, using any means at its disposal. In effect, it has claimed veto power over any government, even a democratically elected highly popular one. Of course if the PAD has this right, other groups will claim it as well, and at year's end, UDD demonstrators were preparing to take the same kind of stand, using tactics similar to those the PAD used in the early stages of its demonstrations. Politics in the streets thus parallels, even rivals, politics in the parliament, and may become more important. Unless the government can find some way to change this new culture, Thailand will become very difficult to govern. Since the Democrat party is effectively a minority government of a sort, in that it was chosen by a minority of voters, this task is made even more difficult, and political stability may prove elusive.

NOTES

[1]   See Duncan McCargo, "Populism and Reformism in Contemporary Thailand", *South East Asia Research* 9 (March 2001): 89–107; "Network monarchy and legitimacy crises in Thailand", *Pacific Review* 18 (December 2005): 499–515; and "Toxic Thaksin", *Foreign Affairs*, 27 September 2006, online at <http://www.foreignaffairs.org>.

[2]   These events are further described in James Ockey, "Thailand in 2007: The Struggle to Control Democracy", *Asian Survey* 48 (January-February 2008): 20–28.

[3]   In observing the election in the Northeast, I noticed quite open vote-buying by two different small parties with rumoured military support. In one case, a candidate bragged to me that his party was sure to win because it had the support of security forces. On the other hand, it was often difficult to even locate an office for the Phalang Prachachon party, as candidates chose to keep exposure to corruption charges to a minimum.

[4]   Demonstrators seem to have comprised PAD supporters, Democrat party loyalists bussed up from the South, and some paid demonstrators, with the combination varying over time. Note that paid demonstrators may or may not believe in the cause for which they demonstrate.

[5]   *Nation*, 18 June 2008.

[6]   Nopporn Wong-Anan, "Temple Tantrums Stalk Thai-Cambodia Relations", *Reuters*, 20 July 2008. Note that Noppadon had previously been Thaksin's lawyer.

7   In addition to the disqualification of PPP MPs due to alleged election irregularities, three cabinet members had been disqualified, a party deputy leader was convicted of electoral fraud, automatically initiating proceedings to consider dissolution of the party, and court cases against Samak were still pending. Thaksin's wife Potchaman was found guilty of tax evasion, even as things began to look bad for Thaksin and Potchaman in a real estate fraud case. Additional cases were still pending against Thaksin as well.

8   See Pradit Ruangdit, "PPP Rifts Expose 'Gang of Four'", *Bangkok Post*, 8 August 2008.

9   In speaking to supreme court judges in April 2006, the king advised the courts that it was their duty to resolve the political crisis at the time, as the king did not have the right to interfere. Although the king was speaking of a specific crisis, and rejecting PAD calls for royal intervention, since that time, the courts have been much more politically active, in ways that have generally benefitted the PAD and its allies. For a translation of the speech, see *Nation*, 27 April 2006 <http://nationmultimedia. com/2006/04/27/headlines/headlines_30002592.php>.

10   *Bangkok Post*, Breaking News, 25 August 2008.

11   Bangkok University poll, "Khon Krung Thep khit yangrai kap khwamkhluanwai khong klum phantamit" [What Do Bangkokians Think About the Actions of the PAD], online at <http://research.bu.ac.th/>; Suan Dusit Poll, "Khwamkhithen khong prachachon to hetkan mop phantamit" [People's Opinions Regarding the Events of the PAD "Mob"], online at <http://dusitpoll.dusit.ac.th/polldata/2551/2551_048.html>. The low level of support also tells us that the majority of the middle class opposed PAD tactics, and perhaps its cause as well, so that any depiction of events as class warfare is much oversimplified.

12   *Nation*, 4 September 2008.

13   With Thaksin claiming he could not get a fair trial, many of his supporters came to distrust the courts. Subsequent decisions against the PPP were seen in that light.

14   "Thai Protesters Vow to Press On", *BBC News*, Internet edition, 8 October 2008.

15   *Bangkok Post*, 8 October 2008; 14 October 2008.

16   *Bangkok Post*, 18 October 2008.

17   *Bangkok Post*, 2 November 2008. While we should be cautious about comparing attendance at a rally with attendance at a demonstration, this appears to be larger than any crowd turned out by the PAD during the year.

18   *Bangkok Post*, 4 November 2008.

19   *Bangkok Post*, 13 November 2008. He provided the first initial of each of those enemies. Two of those first initials matched up with retired soldiers on the privy council.

20   *Nation*, 23 November 2008.

21   *Nation*, 24 November 2008. King Taksin was the king who reorganized Thai forces after the fall of Ayuthaya in 1767. He famously ordered his troops to break their rice

bowls before one battle, sending the message that victory must come before their next meal.

22   *Thairath*, 26 November 2008.

23   Bangkok University poll 403 <http://research.bu.ac.th>, 27 November 2008, "Khwamkhithen khong prachachon to kankratham lae kansadaeng khong klum tang tang" [The Opinions of the People to the Actions and Demonstrations of Various Groups].

24   The palace bureaucracy is very conscious of the public image of the monarchy, and must have been aware of the risk of being associated with such unpopular actions. The King was too ill to give his traditional birthday address just a few days later, perhaps partially explaining the silence. Some, including PAD supporters, took the silence as signifying support for the movement.

25   *Bangkok Post*, 29 November 2008.

26   At least three other leading members of the PAD were named as advisors to cabinet ministers. As noted, the PAD drew heavily on Democrat party supporters from the South during the course of its movement. Although the Democrat party leadership had distanced itself from some of the more controversial tactics, it nevertheless worked toward common goals.

27   *Nation*, 4 December 2008.

28   *Bangkok Post*, 30 November 2008.

29   Compulsory licensing of some pharmaceuticals and attempts to change foreign investment and retail business laws are examples of the impact of nationalism on economic policy debates during the last few years. All created uncertainty for foreign investors. For more details, see Ockey 2008, p. 27.

30   *International Herald Tribune*, 25 August 2008.

31   "Thai Exports Shrink Most in 17 Years on Global Slump", *Bloomberg*, 22 December 2008.

32   See Bank of Thailand <http://www.bot.or.th>, Economic Indices, Table EC_EI_005.

33   Stock Exchange of Thailand, Market Statistics <http://www.set.or.th/en/market/market_statistics.html>.

34   "Three Top Agencies See 0–2 per cent Growth for 2009", *MCOT English News*, 5 February 2009.

35   *Nation*, 29 January 2009.

36   *Nation*, 5 January 2009.

THAILAND'S CRISIS OVERLOAD

PETER WARR

Introduction

Thailand has endured a succession of recent crises: the Asian financial crisis of 1997–99, originating with the collapse of its own currency and reducing investor confidence for the entire decade since; the terrible tsunami of December 2004; outbreaks of SARS and Avian Influenza; rural drought; an interminable insurrection in its southernmost Muslim provinces, producing more than 4,000 deaths; and growing concern about the consequences for Thailand of global climate change. As if all that were not enough, in 2008 an additional double crisis overwhelmed the country: a self-inflicted internal political crisis deepening social divisions within the country and culminating in the closure of Bangkok's international airport in late 2008; and the repercussions of the most serious global financial crisis since the Great Depression of the 1930s.

Thailand's immediate prospects are somber, along with the rest of East Asia. In contemplating this depressing story it is easy to lose long-term perspective. Despite the serious problems, the quality of everyday life in Thailand has continued to improve over several decades and poverty incidence has maintained its long-term decline. Thailand has already achieved essentially all of its Millennium Development Goals, well ahead of the target date of 2015, while most developing countries lag far behind schedule. The current crisis will undoubtedly produce a pronounced economic contraction and some worsening of poverty incidence. No one knows how long-lasting this episode of deglobalization will be, but it will be temporary. It should be seen in the context of long term economic improvement which can be expected to continue once the global crisis subsides.

PETER WARR is John Crawford Professor of Agricultural Economics at the Australian National University (ANU). He is also Convener of the Arndt-Corden Division of Economics and Director of the National Thai Studies Centre at ANU.

Accordingly, this chapter turns first to Thailand's current twin crises: the internal political crisis and the worldwide financial crisis. It then places these events in longer term perspective by reviewing Thailand's long term economic experience and in particular the impact of the last serious economic crisis to affect Thailand — the Asian financial crisis of 1997–99. To see what is likely to happen as a result of the present contraction it is helpful to look at what happened during previous economic downturns.

The Internal Political Crisis

Thailand's ongoing political conflict is about a challenge to the social dominance of the country's traditional elite — the educated Bangkok middle class, including the civil service, the military, and the aristocracy. The challenge arose from a group of political entrepreneurs who had successfully appealed to the massive rural electorate.

The most important of these political entrepreneurs was Thaksin Shinawatra, a clever business tycoon elected Prime Minister by large majorities in 2001 and again in 2005. Thaksin was elected by offering populist policies to the rural majority. But he was deposed by a military coup in September 2006, allegedly because of corruption and because his government was said (by the generals) to be disloyal to the monarchy. Thaksin denied any such disloyalty, but while he remained in exile after the coup, a court decision banned him from political activity in Thailand and disbanded his *Thai Rak Thai* political party for alleged electoral fraud. In addition, Thaksin was convicted *in absentia* for misusing his powers while Prime Minister in support of his wife's business interests.

In the subsequent elections of January 2008 the People's Power Party (PPP), a successor to Thaksin's banned *Thai Rak Thai*, won office with right-wing veteran politician Samak Sundaravej as its leader. Opponents of Thaksin and his allies were enraged. They now identified themselves by wearing yellow shirts, the royal colour, and ironically called themselves the People's Alliance for Democracy (PAD). They clashed openly and violently with Thaksin's supporters, now identified at their rallies by red shirts. In late 2008 the PAD's protests against the PPP government became increasingly strident, justified mainly by the claim that Samak and the PPP were mere proxies for the fugitive Thaksin.

While in office, Samak had continued to host a television cooking programme and received payment for doing so. In September, the full bench of the Constitutional Court ruled that it was unconstitutional for Samak to maintain his television career while Prime Minister, and disqualified him from office. The ruling PPP promptly replaced him as Prime Minister with Thaksin's brother-in-law, Somchai Wongsawat. The PAD were even further enraged.

On 25 November the PAD occupied Bangkok's Suvarnabhumi International Airport, causing its closure and demanding that Somchai step down. The ensuing chaos caused great damage to Thailand's tourist industry and to commerce dependent on air freight. The airport siege ended after eight days, on 2 December, when the Constitutional Court voted to disband the three government coalition parties, including PPP, again for electoral fraud.

To the amazement of almost everyone, some former members of the disbanded PPP agreed to ally themselves with the opposition Democrat Party, allowing its leader Abhisit Vejjajiva to become Prime Minister. The PAD had previously said it would accept no other premier than Abhisit. They were thus able to claim the political outcome as a victory for their tactics and the banning of PPP as a vindication of their opposition to the government on the grounds of its electoral corruption.

Behind the political soap opera lies something basic: a dispute about the meaning of democracy, or at least the form that democracy should take in Thailand. The essence of the PAD's objections to Thaksin and his 'proxies' was not just that they had acquired power through corrupt electoral practices, a claim that was seemingly vindicated by the court decisions against *Thai Rak Thai* and PPP. More fundamentally, it was a challenge to the principle of one-person-one-vote.

Thaksin had demonstrated a capacity first to enrich himself massively by manipulating government telecommunications regulators and then to use this wealth to advance himself politically. He was then able to use this new political power to enrich himself, his family and his closest supporters, even further. But he could not attain political power without mass support. His political discovery was to find a way to harness the power of the rural electorate. The secret was to promise them handouts at the expense of the public purse and then to deliver on those promises. He did both of those things. Thaksin remains greatly admired by the rural masses, the basis of his political support. These groups recognize the economic benefits that Thaksin brought to them while in power and could not care less about his alleged corruption or his personal greed.

Thaksin frightens the traditional elite and is despised by them. Contrary to their name, the PAD is essentially a conservative middle class movement who desire a return, at least partially, towards Thailand's more authoritarian past. They perceived the electoral successes of Thaksin, Samak and their allies as having demonstrated the failure of electoral democracy because it threatened the dominant position of the elite: the army, the civil service and the aristocracy. They have seen what electoral democracy can deliver and they do not like it. They would have opposed Thaksin's right to govern whether there had really been electoral fraud, as claimed, or not.

During their opposition to Samak's government, the PAD leaders demanded that Samak step down and two basic changes be made. First, the proportion of the Parliament that is elected should be limited to 30 per cent, the rest appointed by the elite. Second, they demanded the possibility of a Prime Minister who was not an elected member of Parliament. The PAD pointed out that the two most respected Prime Ministers of recent decades, Prem Tinsulanonda and Anand Panyarachun, were not elected but appointed by the King. The position of the PAD was thus a rejection of one-person-one-vote electoral democracy. Beneath this is a long-standing urban disdain for the competence of the poorly educated rural people who elected Thaksin and Samak. Thaksin was seen as the cunning politician who had learned how to manipulate them. It is revealing that the PAD website includes a statement employing the term 'low class' to describe their red-shirted opponents. There is an undeniable social class dimension to the conflict. Crudely put, for many of the PAD leaders and supporters, Thaksin's rural voters were ignorant buffaloes who should not be permitted to determine the leadership and direction of the country. That role rightfully belonged to the elite.

Since Abhisit's rise to power the global financial crisis has dominated public attention and the underlying domestic political conflict has rightly been sidelined. But when new elections are eventually held, Thaksin's allies — 'proxies' or not — may well win again. Such is the magnitude of their rural support. Once that happens, the crisis resumes. Thailand is groping, sometimes stumbling, towards a form of democracy that suits its own circumstances. The underlying conflict is deep and will not be resolved easily.

The Global Financial Crisis

The financial crisis is proving to be more serious than almost anyone imagined. Credit is the lubricant facilitating the operation of the global trading system. The supply of credit rests on the existence of trust, especially among financial institutions, that debts can and will be honoured. The crisis has destroyed that trust. Everyone is afraid of lending, for fear that the borrower will turn out to be unable to repay. The global supply of credit has thus evaporated and international trade has severely contracted. Export dependent economies such as Thailand are already suffering and the prospects are for worse problems to follow. *Deglobalization* is the latest grim addition to economic jargon. The recent economic forecasts of

Asian governments have proven to be uniformly too optimistic and, as we will see, Thailand is no exception. As the global crisis deepens there is a continuing danger of a protectionist response which could greatly deepen the economic contraction, as it did in the 1930s with disastrous consequences.

The mode of transmission of the crisis to Thailand is primarily not through its financial institutions. Fortunately, their direct exposure to the failing U.S. and European financial institutions is small. The problem similarly does not arise from bottlenecks on the supply side of the Thai economy. The transmission is through a contraction in the demand for Thailand's output, particularly its exports. Along with many of its Southeast Asian neighbours, Thailand has benefited from globalization through expansion of its exports. The downside is vulnerability to a contraction in export demand, and this is what has occurred. Export demand corresponds to an extraordinary 75 per cent of Thailand's output. In January 2009, the year-on-year contraction in Thailand's exports was 26.5 per cent, accounting by itself for a 20 per cent contraction in aggregate demand. Consumption and especially private investment demand have also been negatively affected, but export demand is the main story.

Why is the contraction in exports so large? The contractions of GDP in the U.S. and Europe are currently of the order of 2 to 4 per cent. How does this become a decline in demand for imports from developing countries of up to ten times that magnitude? The reason is that the financing of working capital in the advanced economies has become very expensive and in some cases it is unobtainable. Monetary authorities in the advanced countries are pumping funds into the financial system as rapidly as they can, but the deterioration of the intermediation function of the financial system means that this does not yet translate into availability of credit to business enterprises that need it. Financial institutions are afraid to lend to them. Retail and wholesale businesses respond to expensive or unobtainable working capital by cutting the size of their inventories. While they attempt to achieve lower levels of inventories their demand for new product may contract to zero.

The bad news is that a radical cut in the desired level of inventories magnifies the contraction in the demand for new product. But the good news is that this very large inventory component of the contraction of demand is temporary. Inventories will not contract to zero. When they have reached their lower desired levels, the contraction in the demand for new product will abate. The new level of demand may be lower than the previous level, taking into account the lower level of consumer and investor spending in the advanced economies, but it will be larger than the level temporarily observed during a period of radical inventory downsizing.

What can Thailand do about it? So far as the contraction in export demand is concerned, not much; all that can be done is to ride out the storm as well as possible. But there is the scope to expand other components of aggregate demand. The candidates are: increasing private consumer spending (57 per cent of GDP); increasing private investment spending (19 per cent of GDP); reducing import spending (75 per cent of GDP); and increasing government spending (24 per cent of GDP). Consumers and investors are rattled by the economic news and there is limited scope to induce them to spend more in such an uncertain environment. Both consumer spending and investment spending are declining, not increasing, and there is very little the government can do about it.

If import demand could be reduced, that would leave more scope for domestic producers to take up the resulting slack in demand and this is why protection is so attractive politically in times of economic downturns. But that would be a great mistake. Protectionism is like cocaine. It provides an immediate stimulus, but this short-run boost is achieved only at the expense of undermining the determinants of long-term economic performance. And is addictive; once rates of import protection increase it is very difficult to get rid of them later.

During the Great Depression of the 1930s increasing protectionism worldwide worsened the magnitude of the global contraction. In this, the Congress of the United States was an ignominious leader. The Smoot-Hawley Tariff Act of 1930 set in train an increase in global protection that contributed to the depth of the Depression and the circumstances leading to World War II. Through its "Buy American" clause inserted into President Obama's current financial bailout package, the United States Congress has revealed to the world how little it has absorbed from its own history. It is imperative that the rest of the world not follow suit and succumb to the temptation to increase protection. Fortunately, the Thai government of Abhisit Vejjajiva shows every sign of being a constructive regional leader in this respect. Prime Minister Abhisit's remarks at the February 2009 summit of ASEAN leaders were encouraging in their recognition of the dangers of a resort to protectionism. But if the contraction proves to be long-lasting, can this resolve be maintained? The question arises as much for Thailand as for any other country.

That leaves government spending. The arithmetic is simple. Export demand is three times the size of government spending. If export demand contracts by 10 per cent, then to make up the slack in aggregate demand, government spending has to expand by 30 per cent, and so forth. To make up for a 26 per cent contraction in export demand, government spending would need to expand by 78 per cent. Nothing like that is possible.

There is scope for public debt to be increased and inflation is not currently a serious concern. These are not the immediate problems. The problem is the logistics of expanding public expenditure so quickly and by such a large amount. There is said to be a portfolio of infrastructure projects waiting on the shelf for government approval, but this cannot be sufficient to expand spending enough to avert a contraction of output. This is a particular problem in an environment where corruption in public spending is a matter of great scrutiny. The same issue arises in Indonesia. Public officials are understandably reluctant to expand procurement quickly, for fear of making mistakes that could render them liable later to criminal charges of corruption or malfeasance.

The government has announced its intention to expand public spending to mitigate the impact of the contraction in aggregate demand resulting from the crisis. That is desirable and it will reduce the magnitude of the recession that results. But there seems no possibility that it will be sufficient to prevent negative economic growth during 2009 and possibly 2010.

Unfortunately, the government's own economic projections do not convey this point because they are based on unduly optimistic assumptions about almost all components of aggregate demand, especially export demand. A report from the government's economic planning agency, the National Economic and Social Development Board (NESDB), released on 23 February 2009, revealed that during the fourth quarter of 2008 real GDP had declined by 4.3 per cent, leading to growth for the full year of 2008 of 2.6 per cent.[1] The report also projects growth for 2009 in the major categories of aggregate demand: private consumption (2.2 per cent), private investment (–3.0 per cent), exports (–6.2 per cent) and imports (–5.4 per cent). The implications of these projections are summarized in Table 1.

Table 1 shows, in column (1), various illustrative target growth rates for real GDP constructed by the present author. Columns (2) to (5) show, respectively, the real growth rates of private consumption, public investment, exports and imports projected by the NESDB. The final column (column (6)) shows the present author's calculation of the change in public spending that would be required to achieve the target growth rate of GDP (column (1)) given the NESDB assumptions in columns (2) to (5). According to these calculations, to achieve zero growth of real GDP virtually no expansion of public expenditure would be needed. Growth of 5 per cent could be achieved with an expansion of public spending of only 20 per cent.

The problem is that almost all of the NESDB assumptions seem overly optimistic. Table 2 varies these assumptions in only one respect. The projected

TABLE 1
Thailand: Required Growth in Government Expenditure to Maintain Target GDP Growth Rates (%) with Export Growth as Forecast

Target GDP growth rate	Forecast change in private consumption	Forecast change in private investment	Forecast change in export	Forecast change in import	Required change in public expenditure
(1)	(2)	(3)	(4)	(5)	(6)
0.0	2.2	-3.0	-6.2	-5.4	0.4
2.0	2.2	-3.0	-6.2	-5.4	7.9
3.5	2.2	-3.0	-6.2	-5.4	14.2
5.0	2.2	-3.0	-6.2	-5.4	20.5

Note: Assumed GDP shares: private consumption 57 per cent; private investment 19 per cent; exports 75 per cent; imports 75 per cent; public expenditure 24 per cent.
Source: Author's calculations, based on projections from National Economic and Social Development Board 2009.

TABLE 2
Thailand: Required Growth in Government Expenditure to Maintain Target
GDP Growth Rates (%) with Export Growth as in January 2008 to January 2009

Target GDP growth rate	Forecast change in private consumption	Forecast change in private investment	Forecast change in export	Forecast change in import	Required change in public expenditure
(1)	(2)	(3)	(4)	(5)	(6)
-2.0	2.2	-3.0	-26.5	-5.4	54.8
0.0	2.2	-3.0	-26.5	-5.4	63.1
2.0	2.2	-3.0	-26.5	-5.4	71.4
3.5	2.2	-3.0	-26.5	-5.4	77.7
5.0	2.2	-3.0	-26.5	-5.4	83.9

Note: Assumed GDP shares: as in Table 1.
Source: Author's calculations, based on projections from National Economic and Social Development Board 2009.

growth rate of exports actually observed between January 2008 and January 2009, –26.5 per cent, is substituted for the NESDB's projection, –6.2 per cent. The impact is dramatic. To achieve zero growth of aggregate demand, an impossible expansion of public spending of 63 per cent would be required. To keep the decline of real GDP to no more than 2 per cent a 55 per cent expansion of public spending would still be needed. These growth rates of public spending are not feasible, so if the actual contraction of exports during 2009 turns out to be anything like the January 2008 to January 2009 contraction, a large contraction in GDP is inevitable. The Thai government's assumptions seem unduly optimistic, wrongly implying that it is possible for Thailand to avoid a recession during 2009.

In any case, maintaining aggregate demand is not the same thing as maintaining employment. The export industries releasing employees are more labour-intensive than the average, meaning that more workers are laid off per million baht of output contraction in these industries than would be the case for a uniform contraction of all industries of the same money value. In other words, the proportional contraction in formal sector employment resulting from the export contraction will be substantially greater than the proportional contraction in GDP.[2] But public investment tends to be more capital-intensive than the average, especially the large infrastructure projects sitting on the government's shelf waiting for implementation. One million baht's worth of this kind of spending generates far fewer jobs than are lost through a million baht contraction in export demand. To maintain employment, the expansion in public investment would thus have to be even larger than the above calculations indicate.

A Longer Term Perspective

Long Term Growth and the Asian Financial Crisis

Thailand's long-term growth performance is described in Figure 1, showing the level of real GDP per capita in each year (vertical bars) and its growth rate (solid line) for the period 1951 to 2008. The figure identifies four periods of Thailand's recent economic history: I — Pre-boom (until 1986); II — boom (1987 to 1996); III — crisis (1997 to 1999); and IV — recovery (2000 to 2008). Over the period 1968 to 1986, the average annual growth rate of Thailand's real GNP was 6.7 per cent (almost 5 per cent per person), compared with an average of 2.4 per cent for low and middle-income countries.[3] Then, over the decade 1987 to 1996, the Thai economy boomed, growing at 9.5 per cent in real terms. Over this decade, the Thai economy was the fastest growing in the world.

FIGURE 1
Thailand: Real GDP Per Capita and Growth of Real GDP Per Capita,
1951–2008

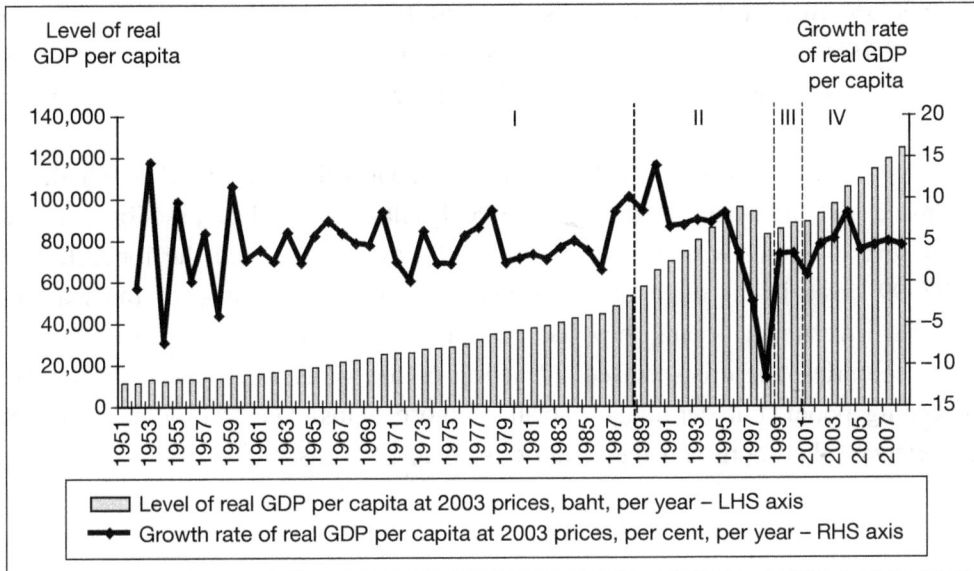

Source: Author's calculations, using data from NESDB, Bangkok.

The crisis of 1997–99 rudely interrupted this boom. The economic damage done and the hardship that resulted were both substantial. The crisis eroded some of the gains from the economic growth that had been achieved during the long period of economic expansion, but it did not erase them. At the low point of the crisis in 1998, the level of GDP per capita was almost 14 per cent below its level only two years earlier, in 1996. Nevertheless, because of the sustained growth that had preceded the crisis, this reduced level of 1998 was still higher than it had been only five years before that, in 1993, and was seven times its level in 1951.

Since the crisis, Thailand's economic recovery has been moderate. The rate of growth of real GDP has been somewhat below its long-term trend rate and it was not until 2003 that the level of real GDP per capita had recovered to its pre-crisis level of 1996. Foreign direct investment has declined dramatically since 1998 and private domestic investment has remained sluggish. Despite the slower than expected recovery, in 2006 the level of real economic output per person was 19 per cent above its 1996 pre-crisis level and almost 10 times its level 55 years earlier. The average annual rate of growth of real GDP per person over this entire period of five-and-a-half decades was 4.2 per cent.

Figure 2 places this experience in a comparative Southeast Asian perspective. Data on real GDP are presented for Thailand, Indonesia, Malaysia and the Philippines. All data are indexed such that GDP per capita in 1970 = 100. Booms occurred in Thailand, Malaysia, and Indonesia from the mid-1980s to the mid-1990s, interrupted by the Asian financial crisis. Thailand's boom was the largest, but most other East Asian countries (except the Philippines) were not far behind.

As Figure 2 shows, in 1997–99 serious contractions occurred in Thailand, Malaysia and Indonesia. Relative to 1996, Thailand's initial contraction was the most severe. Along with Indonesia, its contraction also lasted the longest. The 1997–99 crisis in all three of these countries was the collapse of the export–oriented investment booms they had shared over the preceding decade.[4] For all these countries, the crisis erased a fraction of the gains experienced during the preceding boom, but definitely not all of those gains. The Philippines had not experienced the boom and the Asian crisis had little discernable impact.

FIGURE 2
Indonesia, Malaysia, the Philippines and Thailand:
Real GDP Per Capita, 1960–2008
(Indexed to 1970 = 100)

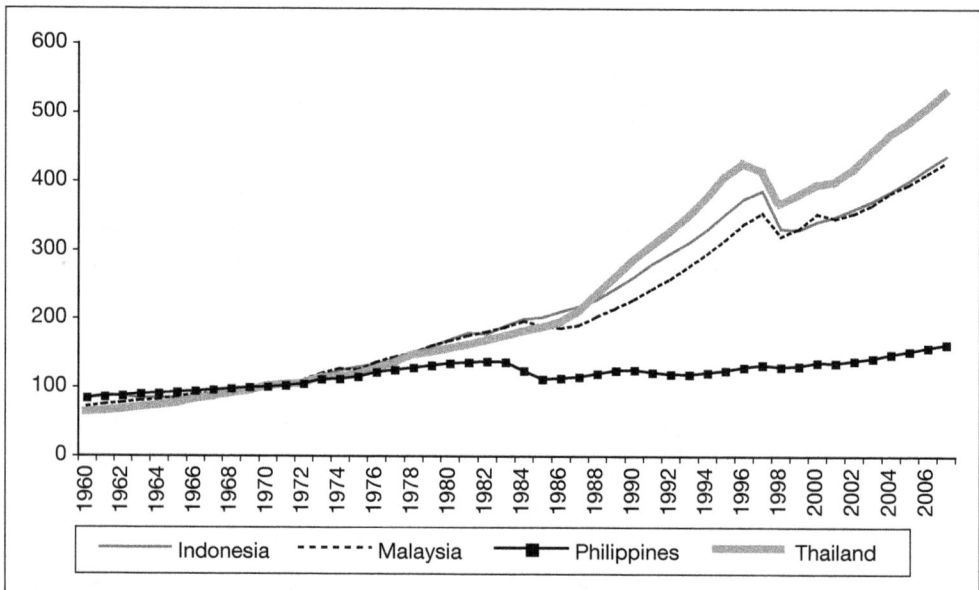

Note: Real GDP per capita is calculated using US$ at constant 2000 prices.
Source: Calculated from World Bank, World Development Indicators, various issues.

TABLE 3
Thailand, Indonesia and Malaysia: Contributions to Expenditure on GDP,
1987–2007

Country/Period	Consumption	Investment	Government	Net exports	Total
Thailand					
Pre-crisis (1987–96)	54.8	38.9	9.9	–5.0	100
Crisis (1997–99)	54.0	27.0	10.5	8.5	100
Post-crisis (2000–07)	57.6	26.0	11.3	5.3	100
Indonesia					
Pre-crisis (1987–96)	55.0	27.8	9.1	0.4	100
Crisis (1997–99)	65.0	24.5	6.5	5.0	100
Post-crisis (2000–07)	62.1	23.7	7.7	6.6	100
Malaysia					
Pre-crisis (1987–96)	48.8	37.2	12.8	1.2	100
Crisis (1997–99)	43.5	35.0	10.5	11.5	100
Post-crisis (2000–07)	46.1	23.0	12.6	18.3	100

Source: Author's calculations, using data from World Bank, World Development Indicators, various issues.

Why has Thailand's recovery been so slow? The crisis was a contraction in aggregate demand, rather than a contraction in productive capacity. Labour and capital were underutilized because there was insufficient demand for Thai output. Where did this contraction in demand come from? Table 3 shows that it came from private investment demand. The upper section of the table shows the composition of expenditure on GDP in Thailand during the pre-crisis boom

FIGURE 3
East Asia: Investment Shares of GDP, 1993–2007

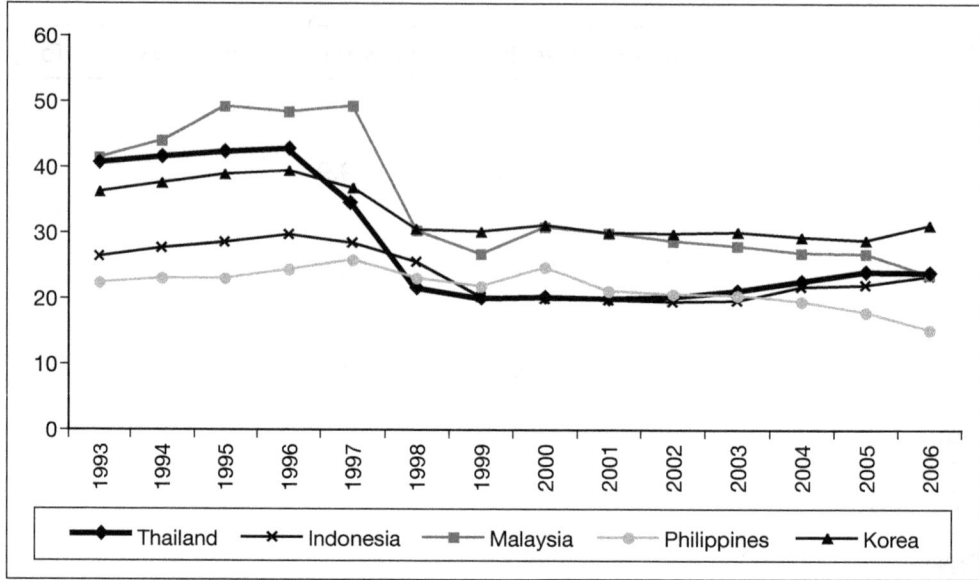

Source: Author's calculations, using data from World Bank, *World Development Indicators*, various issues.

(1987 to 1996), the crisis (1997 to 1999) and the post-crisis recovery period (2000 to 2007). During the crisis, the share of investment in GDP collapsed by 13 percentage points. Investor confidence was severely damaged by the events surrounding the crisis and during the post-crisis recovery period, this share did not recover sufficiently to restore Thailand's long-term rate of growth.

This problem of reduced investor confidence following the Asian financial crisis was not unique to Thailand. Table 3 shows similar calculations for two other crisis-affected Southeast Asian economies, Indonesia and Malaysia. The pattern is similar. Finally, Figure 3 shows annual data on the share of investment in GDP in five crisis-affected East Asian economies: Thailand, Indonesia, Malaysia, the Philippines, and Korea. Although the contraction of private investment in Thailand is at least as large as any other (Malaysia is similar), the figure shows that the problem of sluggish post-crisis recovery of investment was shared by several East Asian economies. It would not seem appropriate to look for country-specific causes. The decline of investor confidence was region-wide, at least among the countries seriously affected by the crisis. The crisis showed the possibility that investors could be bankrupted by macroeconomic events over which they have no control and where they have little or no forewarning. The main point is that a collapse of private investment was the means by which the crisis impacted on each of these countries and that once investor confidence had been damaged restoring it was a difficult and slow process.

Poverty Incidence and Inequality

Is economic growth really so important? Do the poor actually benefit from it, or only the rich? If it is the latter, does a contraction in growth really matter? The following discussion draws upon the official poverty estimates produced by the Thai government's National Economic and Social Development Board (NESDB), which, like all other available poverty estimates, are based upon the household incomes collected in the National Statistical Office's Socio-Economic Survey (SES) household survey data. Despite their imperfections, these are the only data available covering a long time period. These survey data have been collected since 1962. The early data were based on small samples, but their reliability has improved steadily, and since 1988 the raw data have been available in electronic form. A difficulty in comparing these data over time is that the poverty line has been revised several times, changing upwards the real purchasing power that it represents. Figure 4 summarizes the author's attempts to compile a long-term series on poverty incidence, based on a consistent poverty line — one held constant in real purchasing power — from 1962 to 2007.

Figure 4 focuses on the familiar headcount measure of poverty incidence: the percentage of a particular population whose household incomes per person fall below the poverty line. Until recently, the SES data were classified according to residential location in the categories municipal areas, sanitary districts, and villages. These correspond to inner urban (historical urban boundaries), outer urban (newly established urban areas), and rural areas, respectively. Poverty incidence is highest in the rural areas, followed by outer urban, and lowest in the inner urban areas. When these data are recalculated in terms of the share of each of these residential areas in the total number of poor people and then the share of the total population, as in the last two rows of the table, respectively, a striking point emerges. In 2006, rural areas accounted for 86 per cent of the total number of poor people but only 64 per cent of the total population.

Figure 4 also shows the Gini coefficient of inequality. This index potentially takes values between zero and one, with higher values indicating greater inequality. The index for Thailand rose significantly over the 45 years shown. Combined with the reduction in absolute poverty, which occurred at the same time, this

FIGURE 4
Thailand: Poverty Incidence and Inequality, 1962–2007

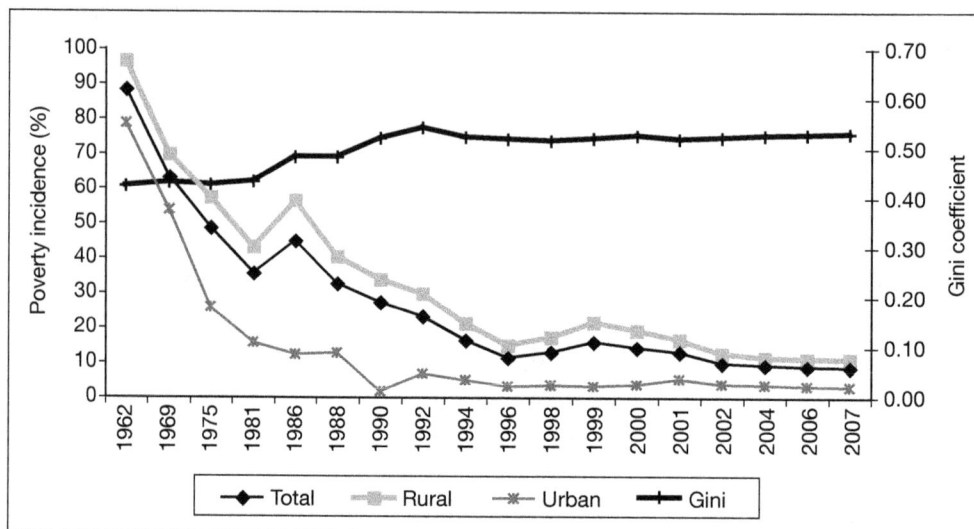

Notes: Poverty incidence means the number of poor within a reference population group expressed as a proportion of the total population of that group. The headcount measure of aggregate poverty incidence is the percentage of the total population whose incomes fall below a poverty line held constant over time in real terms; rural poverty is the percentage of the rural population whose incomes fall below a poverty line held constant over time in real terms, and so forth. Poverty share means the number of poor within a reference population group expressed as a proportion of the total number of poor within the whole population. Population share means the population of a reference group expressed as a proportion of the total population of that group. The data shown are identical to data published by the National Economic and Social Development Board (NESDB) for the years 1988 to 2006, except that the published data for Municipal Areas and Sanitary Districts have been aggregated to an 'urban' category using their respective population shares in the total for urban areas (the sum of the two) as weights. The data for the earlier years have been spliced together with this series from published sources so that the resulting series matches the NESDB series for the year 1988. In accordance with the practice of the Thai government statisticians, both poverty incidence and inequality are based on incomes rather than expenditures in these data. Higher values of the Gini coefficient indicate greater inequality.

Source: Author's calculations, using data provided by the NESDB, Bangkok.

means that the real incomes of the poor increased with economic growth, but the incomes of the rich increased even faster. The data reveal a considerable decline in poverty incidence up to 1996, a moderate increase to 1998, and a further increase over the following two years. Over the eight years from 1988 to 1996, measured poverty incidence declined by an enormous 21.4 per cent of the population, an average rate of decline in poverty incidence of 2.7 percentage points per year.

That is, each year, on average 2.7 per cent of the population moved from incomes below the poverty line to incomes above it. Over the ensuing two years ending in 1998 poverty incidence increased by 1.5 per cent of the population. Alternatively, over the eight years ending in 1996 the absolute number of persons in poverty declined by 11.1 million (from 17.9 to 6.8 million); over the following two years the number increased by 1 million (from 6.8 to 7.9 million). Thus, according to the official data, measured in terms of absolute numbers of people in poverty, the crisis reversed 9 per cent of the poverty reduction that had occurred during the eight-year period of economic boom immediately preceding the crisis.

Poverty Reduction and Economic Growth

What caused the long-term decline in poverty incidence? It is obvious that over the long term, sustained economic growth is a necessary condition for large-scale poverty alleviation. No amount of redistribution could turn a poor country into a rich one. Long term improvements in education have undoubtedly been important, but despite the limitations of the underlying SES data, a reasonably clear statistical picture also emerges on the short-term relationship between poverty reductions and the rate of economic growth. The data are summarized in Figure 5, which plots the relationship between changes in poverty incidence, calculated from the data used in Figure 4, above, and the real rate of growth of GDP over the corresponding period.

Periods of more rapid economic growth were associated with more rapid reductions in the level of absolute poverty incidence. Moderately rapid growth from 1962 to 1981 coincided with steadily declining poverty incidence. Reduced growth in Thailand caused by the world recession in the early to mid-1980s coincided with worsening poverty incidence in the years 1981 to 1986. Then, Thailand's economic boom of the late 1980s and early 1990s coincided with dramatically reduced poverty incidence. Finally, the contraction following the crisis of 1997–99 led to increased poverty incidence. The recovery since the crisis has been associated with significant poverty reduction. Economic growth matters for the poor, as well as the rich.

As shown in Figure 5, the correlation between these two variables is unmistakable. However, one pair of observations is a clear outlier — the data point corresponding to the period 1996–98, which captures the major impact of the Asian financial crisis. It should be noted that poverty data are not available for the years 1997 to 1999. The correlation between poverty reduction and growth, based on data for the periods before and after the crisis period, would predict

FIGURE 5
Thailand: Poverty Incidence and Economic Growth, 1962–2007

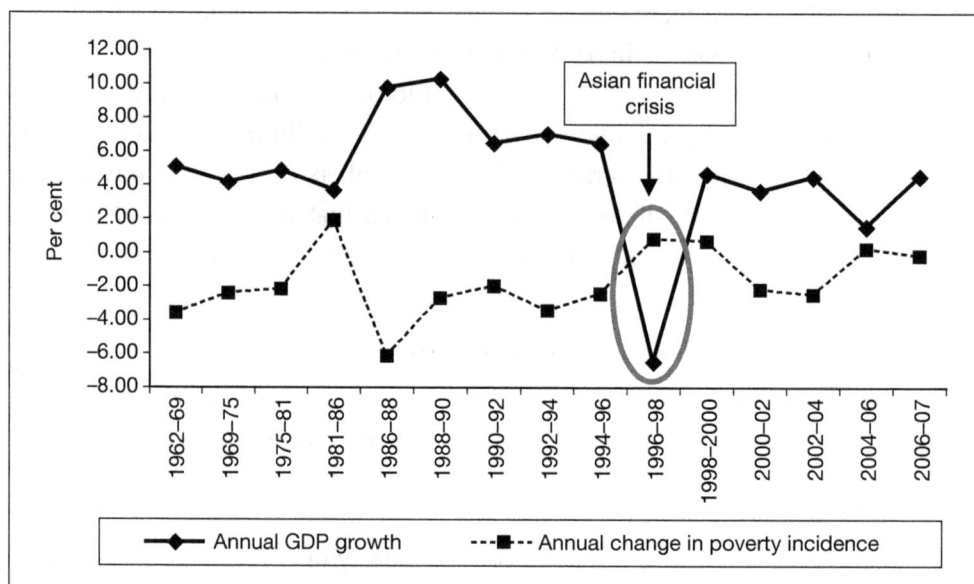

Source: Author's calculations using poverty data as in Figure 4 and GDP data from NESDB, Bangkok.

that a large decline in GDP such as one that occurred during the crisis period would produce a larger decline in poverty incidence than the one that actually occurred. This point is examined more systematically in Table 4 and Figure 6. Table 4 reports two regressions on the relationship between the rate of change of poverty incidence (negative values mean a decline in poverty incidence), the dependent variable, and the rate of GDP growth over the corresponding period, the independent variable. The first regression includes all data points. The estimated coefficient is negative as expected (the faster the growth, the greater the poverty reduction) and significant at the 5 per cent level.

The second regression equation is the same except that the data point for the Asian financial crisis period, 1996–98, is omitted. The estimated coefficient is somewhat larger and again significant at the 5 per cent level. This second equation is then used to predict the change in poverty incidence that would be expected to result from the reduction in real GDP observed in the crisis. The results are summarized in Figure 6. An annual rate of GDP growth of –6.5 per cent (the one that actually occurred) would be expected to result in an annual increase in poverty incidence of 4.52 per cent. The 95 per cent confidence interval

TABLE 4
Thailand: Poverty — Growth Regressions

Independent variable	Coefficient	t-statistic	p-value
1. Dependent variable dP; all observations			
Intercept	−0.247	−0.35	0.729
Real GDP growth	−0.346	−3.01	0.011
$R^2 = 0.430$; adj $R^2 = 0.383$; $F = 9.07$; $p = 0.0108$			
2. Dependent variable dP; all observations except 1996–98.			
Intercept	0.960	0.85	0.416
Real GDP growth	−0.548	−2.90	0.014
$R^2 = 0.433$; adj $R^2 = 0.381$; $F = 8.40$; $p = 0.0145$			

Note: Regression equation: $dP = a + by$, where dP is the annual rate of change of poverty incidence between data points, y is the average annual rate of growth of real GDP between data points and a and b are the estimated coefficients.

Source: Author's calculations, using data from the NESDB, Bangkok.

FIGURE 6
Thailand: The Growth/Poverty Nexus and the Asian Financial Crisis

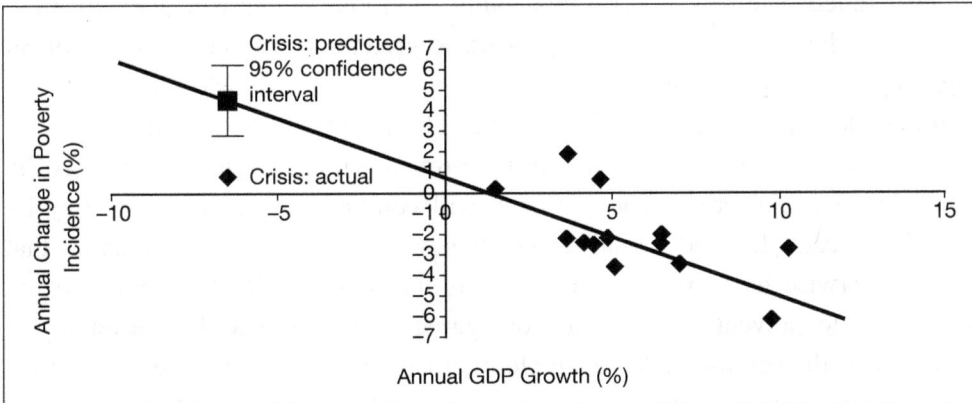

Source: Author's calculations, using data as in Table 4 and Figure 5.

around this prediction is [2.92, 6.12], meaning that given the estimated regression equation we can be 95 per cent confident that the level of poverty incidence that would result from a growth rate of real GDP of −6.5 per cent will lie within the range of 2.92 to 6.12 per cent. However, the observed annual increase in poverty incidence ("Crisis: actual" in the figure) was only 0.8 per cent, well outside this 95 per cent confidence interval. Poverty did not increase nearly as much as would be predicted on the basis of the contraction in real GDP.

Several hypotheses can be advanced for this seeming anomaly. One is that the dramatic depreciation of the baht that immediately followed the crisis raised the prices of exported commodities, including most major agricultural goods. This benefited the rural poor but harmed the urban poor. The net effect may have been a reduction in poverty incidence. Another hypothesis, supported by extensive anecdotal evidence, is that Thai people assisted one another to an unusual extent during the crisis. Urban workers, laid off from construction and manufacturing employment returned to their extended family base in the provinces. There they were absorbed into the business activities of the extended family and the loss of household income (on which the poverty calculations are based) was much less than would have otherwise occurred.

Conclusion: Thailand's Twin Crises

The conclusion seems inescapable that hard economic times lie ahead for the Thai people. Two crises will continue to bite: the country's unresolved internal political conflict and the global financial crisis. Political conflict will resurface when elections are next called. The precise form this conflict will take is unpredictable but it too may have adverse economic consequences. Regrettably, Thailand's rival political support groups have learned that holding the public to ransom by occupying public facilities like airports is an effective tactic. There may be more of it.

Both export demand and private investment will be negatively affected by the global financial crisis. The economy will contract during 2009, possibly by 4 to 5 per cent. Expanded public spending will moderate the contraction that would otherwise have occurred but there is no possibility that it could expand sufficiently to prevent a contraction of aggregate output. The Thai economy is resilient and the central bank has ample international reserves to ride out a crisis. The country is as well-placed as any to emerge from the current crisis rapidly when global economic conditions improve. Regrettably, no one knows how soon that will happen.

Changes in poverty incidence are sensitive to the rate of growth and poverty incidence will be impacted by the coming economic slowdown.[5] Nevertheless, an examination of the experience of the Asian financial crisis of 1997–99 shows that poverty incidence did not increase nearly as much during that period as would have been predicted from the statistical relationship between poverty incidence and economic growth. Thai people assisted one another to an unusual extent during this period and this moderated the increase in poverty incidence that would otherwise have occurred. If the impact of the global financial crisis proves to be as pronounced as is feared, this 'shock-absorber' capacity of Thai society may be called upon again.

Notes

The research assistance of Razib Tuhin is gratefully acknowledged. The author is responsible for all defects.

[1] The sectoral composition of this reported 2.6 per cent annual growth was agriculture 5.1 per cent, industry 3.4 per cent and services 1.2 per cent. The unusually high reported growth in agriculture arose from reported agricultural growth of 8.6 per cent and 9.6 per cent in the second and third quarters, respectively. These data warrant closer examination.

[2] This is presumably why a contraction in exports from China is causing a decline in total employment within China even though reported GDP growth is still 6 per cent. China's export industries are highly labour-intensive.

[3] World Bank, *World Development Report* 1998 (New York: Oxford University Press, 1998).

[4] Peter Warr, ed., "Boom, Bust and Beyond", in Thailand Beyond the Crisis (London: Routledge, 2005), pp. 3–65.

[5] World Bank, *Thailand Economic Monitor*, December 2008, World Bank Office, Bangkok, available at <www.worldbank.or.th>.

Timor-Leste

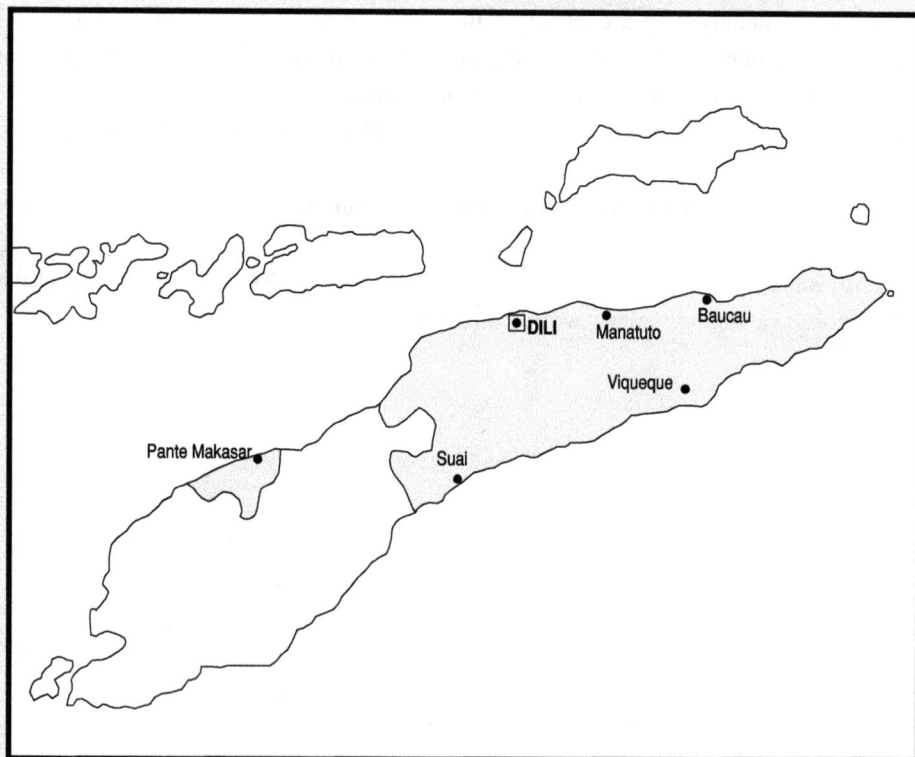

EAST TIMOR IN 2008
Year of Reconstruction

Damien Kingsbury

The near-fatal shooting of East Timor's president, Jose Ramos-Horta, on 11 February 2008, by members of renegade Major Alfredo Reinado's gang, and the death of Reinado himself, broke a deadlock in East Timorese politics that had threatened to keep the country in a state of perpetual crisis. Prior to this incident, most observers had noted that the recently elected Parliamentary Majority Alliance government of Xanana Gusmao needed to address two critical issues. The first issue was returning the remaining tens of thousands of internally displaced persons to their homes. The second, which allowed the first to happen, was resolving the issue of the "petitioners", soldiers who had deserted the army in 2006, sparking an internal conflict that almost led to state collapse. Without having the "petitioners" problem resolved, the country's internally displaced persons (IDPs) claimed they felt too insecure to return to their homes.

Resolving Inherited Problems

At the beginning of 2008, East Timor remained unsettled, by Reinado's gang and the petitioners still on the loose, by the IDPs who were largely Fretilin supporters, and by Fretilin itself refusing to accept the legitimacy of the outcome of the 2007 elections, which saw its vote cut in half to just under 30 per cent and a coalition of parties led by Xanana Gusmao's Timorese Council for National Reconstruction (CNRT) form government. Fretilin embarked on a campaign of protest that continued well into 2008 which, set against the still fragile backdrop of IDPs and military mutineers, could have pushed the country back into chaos at any time. The presence of the Internal Stabilization Force and

DAMIEN KINGSBURY is Director, Masters of International and Community Development, School of International and Political Studies, Deakin University, Australia.

UN police helped ensure the country did not again divide, as it had two years previously.

All of this changed just after dawn on Monday 11 February 2008. As the sun was rising out of the Banda Sea behind the Indonesian-built Christo Rei statue on Fatucama Hill at the eastern point of Dili's sweeping harbour, East Timor's President Jose Ramos-Horta was out in the morning coolness for his daily walk along the Areia Branca with two members of the F-FDTL, not far from his home at Meti-hau. A few minutes after six a.m., a foreign diplomat driving by stopped and told the exercising Ramos-Horta that he had heard gunshots. The diplomat asked if Ramos-Horta wanted a lift. Ramos-Horta declined. Ramos-Horta also received a telephone call from the Senior Legal Advisor to the President, Paulo Dos Remedios who lived in the area, advising him of shootings at his home. A group of ten armed men in two cars, led by fugitive Major Alfreido Reinado, had occupied the president's home, and a few minutes later, the early arriving morning shift of the presidential guard confronted the invaders, shooting dead Reinado and another of his gang. Despite the shooting, Ramos-Horta pressed on but, approaching the gates of his home, was himself shot twice and critically wounded. Ramos-Horta dragged himself inside and telephoned for help. One of the East Timor Defence Force (F-FDTL) guards with him was also shot and critically wounded. 18 minutes later, members of the Portuguese paramilitary Republican National Guard (GNR) special operations sub-group Bravo arrived, calling an ambulance to take Ramos-Horta to the Australian army hospital.

A further telephone call was made from Ramos-Horta's home to the home of the prime minister, Xanana Gusmao, spurring him to leave his house at Balibar to go to Ramos-Horta's aid. However, at about 7:45 a.m., shortly after leaving his house, it was surrounded by a group of armed men, under Reinado's second in command, Lieutenant Gastao Salsinha. Gusmao's wife, Kirsty Sword Gusmao, telephoned Gusmao to let him know of the situation, just at the moment his two cars were also attacked. Gusmao's guard in a second car returned fire, and Gusmao and his guards escaped unharmed into the bushes, making their way into Dili on foot.[1] Ramos-Horta, meanwhile, was treated for serious gunshot wounds and then evacuated to Darwin for further life-saving surgery, where he spent the next two months recuperating.

While on the run in the weeks prior to this event, Reinado had undertaken an interview on Metro TV, broadcast from Jakarta, raising speculation that Reinado had assistance from across the border. While Metro TV staff denied that Reinado had been to Jakarta, some of his men were later arrested there, and months after the event it was shown that Reinado had an Indonesian identity card on him at his time of death. Possession of the card did not indicate high level Indonesian support — such "KTP" cards had long been available from local immigration offices for a price.

Indonesian President Susilo Bambang Yudhoyono told President Ramos-Horta that he would not tolerate any support for the East Timorese rebels in Indonesia and had Indonesian authorities quickly supply information about telephone intercepts between Reinado's men and their supporters. However, he also warned East Timor's leaders against making public comments about Indonesian involvement in support for the rebels. However, three of Reinado's men were arrested at the Kupang, West Timor home of Joao Tavarres, who had a long and close association with the Indonesian army, including organizing the East Timor militias, in business and in cross-border smuggling following East Timor's independence. Reinado, too, had close links to border patrol police, including receiving weapons from them, who had been involved in cross-border smuggling in concert with former militia and TNI members. The indication was, therefore, that if the attack against Horta and Gusmao had not been directed by TNI officers in West Timor, they were at least active in supporting Reinado and his men and were aware that this contributed to the destabilization of East Timor.

One of those arrested at Tavarres' house, Ismail Moniz Soares (known as Asanco), had telephoned one of the security guards at Ramos-Horta's home at 6:04 a.m. on the morning of the attack, suggesting that Reinado's team could have had inside help in occupying the house. Soares was among those who, after the attack on Ramos-Horta, ambushed Gusmao as he left his own home. Two of the other rebels arrested at Tavarres' house were Jose Gomez and Egidio Carvalho, who had been involved in the attack on Ramos-Horta's house.

After some days, Reinado's second in command, Lieutenant Gastao Salsinha, surrendered to East Timorese and UN police in the Emera district capital of Gleno, along with the remaining 11 of his armed supporters. They were finally transferred into formal custody in Dili on 29 April 2008. In a ceremonial surrender, the 12 men handed over their weapons at the government offices in Dili, where President Ramos-Horta shook their hands and offered his personal forgiveness. The rebels formally surrendered to Deputy Prime Minister Jose Luis Guterres, who said the surrender offered a new beginning for East Timor: "It's a historic moment for the country and historic moment for the people of East Timor. We believe that from now on the Timorese development will start and we will have a better future."[2]

These events and those that followed, including the imposition of a "state of siege",[3] highlighted East Timor's continuing political fragility. Paradoxically, this event also broke a critical stalemate in East Timor's political life and could be seen to have many more positive than negative consequences. It was, in many respects, the end of a series of critical political events that had threatened to destroy East Timor's young democracy and to turn this child of the United Nations and the international community into a failed state.

The state of emergency that had been declared after the shooting of Ramos-Horta and the attempt against Xanana Gusmao was lifted on 22 April, 10 weeks after its imposition and two days after Ramos-Horta returned to East Timor, although it was retained in Ermera, where Reinado had been based. If there was one benefit from the state of emergency, it was that as the F-FDTL took primary responsibility for security, the relationship between it and the East Timor National Police (PNTL) appeared to markedly improve.[4] More negatively, however, it had directly inserted the F-FDTL into the issue of internal security which, under the constitution, was the purview of the PNTL. Ramos-Horta returned to Dili to a hero's welcome, with several crowds deep lining the roads between the airport and his home.

The question was raised at this time as to how Reinado could enter Indonesia so easily and who was paying for his travel, as well as funding his ability to remain on the run in East Timor. According to respected Australian journalist and long-time Timor watcher, Lindsey Murdoch, Reinado had entered Indonesia via the island of Batam near Singapore on a false passport, under the name of Simlisio de la Crus — the same name as on his Indonesian identification card. Reinado had also been in contact, on 19 January, with East Timor born Jakarta gangster "Hercules" Rosario Marcal, and had 21 Indonesian telephone numbers listed in his mobile phone when he was killed.[5] Hercules was known to have close associations with the TNI in Jakarta. Two of Reinado's men were later arrested at Hercules' house in Jakarta.[6] Reinado also had A\$800,000 in a Commonwealth Bank account in Australia, held jointly with his lover Angelita Pires, at his time of death, from which around A\$200,000 had been withdrawn. Reinado had A\$30,000 is cash on him when he was killed, and had been well resourced with weapons and communications equipment, which had helped him evade capture. There was considerable speculation about the origins of these funds, with an intelligence source[7] saying that mobile telephone intercepts had identified the funding agent as being an East Timorese politician.[8]

Most importantly, however, the death of Reinado broke a deadlock in East Timorese politics. It allowed the government to begin its programme of relocating IDPs from the camps back to their homes, it removed a key bargaining chip from the Petitioners and hence allowed a resolution of their claims, it distanced both the prime minister and the president from the taint of association with Reinado which had dogged them until that point, and it enhanced their legitimacy, particularly that of Ramos-Horta who was, in an all too real sense, "blooded".

In assessing why Reinado and his gang had attacked Ramos-Horta and Gusmao, it appeared that the attack was originally intended as a kidnapping or an attempt to force a final decision of Reinado's situation in his favour, but which went wrong. The motivation for the kidnapping was that Reinado believed that his discussions with Ramos-Horta aimed at finding a resolution to the issue were being undermined by the government's dealings with the Petitioners and that he was, in effect, being double-crossed. After the shooting, it was revealed that Ramos-Horta had put to Reinado the proposal of accepting being convicted and jailed, but then released under a general amnesty for all parties convicted of offences during the 2006 troubles. However, as noted by one observer, few involved in the 2006 violence had been prosecuted and after Lobato's release and escape, no one was actually in custody, which only reaffirmed East Timor's culture of impunity.[9] This sense of impunity was compounded in July, with the long-awaited release of the report of the Commission on Truth and Friendship. When Indonesia told the United Nations that it would assume responsibility for the prosecution of those involved in the killing of more than 1,500 people in East Timor in 1999, most observers understood this meant that few if any of those responsible for the crimes would spend time in jail. Few events could have been as predictable. The Indonesian legal system had a long history of protecting the military from meaningful sentencing, especially given that the military must be tried in its own, usually sympathetic courts. Further, the "nationalist" fervour whipped up by the military over the "loss" of East Timor meant that any negative decision against the army or police would be construed as tantamount to subversion. In this environment, the outcome of the few trials that were held did not bode well for an independent judgment.

If the shooting of Ramos-Horta was the most important political event of 2008, it was so because not only did it almost end the life of the president, but because as noted it broke a political deadlock. The process of relocating the IDPs and closing down their camps occurred over several months, and in cases where the IDPs had a more overt political agenda there was some resistance. However, the government paid families up to US$4,000 to return to their places of origin, which was enough to rebuild or otherwise start afresh. This amount of money was the equivalent of around eight or so years' average income, and represented a significant incentive to most of the IDPs.

Similarly, negotiations with the Petitioners continued well into the year and, without Reinado's shadow over the proceedings, there was eventually progress in resolving their claims, even if not through returning them to the military. Indeed, while these negotiations were continuing, the F-FDTL went through a new round of recruitment, indicating that the Petitioners were beginning to slip into history. In July, the petitioners were declared to be civilians and hence no longer members of the F-FDTL.[10] They then accepted what appeared to be a generous pay-out offer of US$8,000 each and began their lives anew.

Opposition

Despite being in office for a relatively short period of time, there were a number of allegations of corruption levelled against the then still relatively new Parliamentary Majority Alliance (AMP) government, most notable of which were those in relation to the government purchase of cars and the letting of an emergency food aid contract. In the first instance, Fretilin had been highly critical of the government for pursuing what it claimed was a policy of buying 65 new "luxury" cars for parliamentarians. Fretilin claimed the cars would be allocated individually and used for private purposes In June 2008, this led to student demonstrations at the University of Timor Leste opposite the parliament building.[11]. Under a law enacted by the previous Fretilin government on demonstrations being at least 100 metres from parliament, the police used tear gas and arrested more than three dozen protesters. For a moment, it appeared as though the AMP government was heading down the same authoritarian path as the previous Fretilin government.

However, the protesters were released and the government went to some lengths to explain that it was not buying "luxury" cars for the private use of parliamentarians. Rather, the Finance Minister, Emilia Pires, said that the purchase order was for 26 four wheel drive base model Toyota Prado cars to be allocated for parliamentary committee work, particularly involving travel to the districts. A 27th car was to be given to the government by Toyota as part of the package. Pires said that the cost of maintaining older vehicles and renting cars had amounted to just over US$13 million in the four years to 2008, which was the equivalent of buying 389 new Toyota Prado cars. She added that of all the cars allocated to government departments, the number requiring high maintenance was 1,736, a further 707 were not working and not repairable, 109 were "lost" at handover, 21 were not registered to the government and 69 cars were under dispute.

She also noted that of vehicles donated to the previous government, many had not been registered with the government assets department. In particular, Pires noted that of 50 Land Cruisers donated by one aid agency, only five were registered to the government,[12] (the assumption being that the rest were being used for private purposes only). At one level this was a relatively trivial issue, but the energy that was put into it by Fretilin, and the way the student demonstrations could have turned more serious, indicated that the political environment remained fraught, and that Fretilin in particular was not shy about pushing to the limit issues that, upon examination, often lacked substance or upon which it itself might have been found wanting. However, concern about police corruption that had existed under the previous government resurfaced, finally being brought to a head with an joint investigation leading to the suspension and proposed charging of eight mid-ranking and senior officers.[13]

Fretilin continued its campaign of sniping and political harassment. But in a substantive sense, and especially given that it did return to sit in the parliament, this was more or less the activity of a conventional if not entirely "loyal" opposition. Most of Fretilin's criticisms of the government were strident,[14] which was unhelpful to the broader state of affairs given a continuing sense of fragility and deep-seated uncertainty that permeated much of East Timorese society. But as the political game continued, as the "opposition" attacked and the government responded, it appeared that East Timor was beginning to settle into a pattern of behaviour familiar in many more developed and historically embedded parliamentary democracies. There was no doubt that East Timor remained vulnerable to fracturing as a political society. But the longer it did not do so, the better chance it had of not doing so.

Even when the Timorese Social Democratic Association-Social Democratic Party (ASDT-PSD) partner in the AMP coalition said in May that it would quit the coalition because of alleged government corruption, this appeared more as an internal party matter over the allocation of ministries rather than any external issue. This sense was compounded, too, when soon after that threat, it said that it would not leave the coalition for another 12 months. One might have thought that if the issues over which it was concerned were so pressing that it had to announce its departure from the government then it would have done so immediately. But regardless of how this issue resolved, it lacked a sense of sincerity of intention, and was more a part of a political game. It might have been that the ASDT contemplated being in opposition, not in government, with Fretilin, as it was quickly deduced that the ASDT's coalition with PSD had fractured and that the AMP government could survive without ASDT support.

Moreover, ASDT and Fretilin were not comfortable political bedfellows, and the thought of working together as a coherent opposition was less attractive than the reality of access to government.

In any case, the concern that this fairly clearly Fretilin-inspired manoeuvre was supposed to have caused the AMP government was quashed when it was realized that not only could the AMP government maintain a majority without ASDT but that it had quickly done a deal with the National Union of Timorese Resistance (Undertim) to shore up its parliamentary numbers. There is a view that it is not what politicians say that counts, but what they do. ASDT said much but did little, and appeared to be paying the price of its disloyalty on one hand and its incapacity on the other. Fretilin, meanwhile, was reduced to returning to its tactics of sniping, if with less effect.

While the AMP government's legislative programme for 2008 focused primarily on economic development and food security, it was remarkable for the introduction of legislation that, given the country's problems, seemed unnecessary. Perhaps most puzzling in a country that had recently been wracked by internecine violence was the government proposed legislation on the right of citizens to acquire firearms. This bill was initially defeated in June when the coalition broke ranks over it, but was again proposed later in the year. A similarly unnecessary bill gave special recognition to the Catholic Church. Although the country is predominantly Catholic, this "accord" offered little material advantage to the state or the people, but privileged the Catholic Church as a moral arbiter in state affairs. Related to this was the introduction of anti-abortion legislation, which was passed, establishing abortion as murder.

Economic Policy

The AMP government's economic policies, which were the centrepiece of its legislative programme, were also hotly debated. Prime Minister Gusmao's economic policy was based on addressing the needs of the people as soon as possible with capital that was available, rather than allowing the people to suffer while waiting until interest on the capital had accrued. Fretilin was highly critical of the AMP government over its pursuit of this policy, manifested as tapping into the capital of the country's interest-based Petroleum Fund. The Petroleum Fund Consultative Council and the Economy, Finance and Anti-corruption parliamentary committee also opposed the government's plan to withdraw US$290 million from the Petroleum Fund. This was in excess of the benchmark for sustainable income (US$396.1 million in 2008), and was opposed on the grounds that the government had not justified the need for the additional funds.

The AMP government's proposal was to more than double its income, from US$347.7 million to US$773.3 million, or an increase of 122 per cent, even though between January and March it had only spent 10 per cent of the proposed budget total. That amount was predicted to increase soon after, however, to 45 per cent by the middle of the year and to rise to 55 per cent by the end of the year. However, a constitutional court ruling later in the year raised doubts over the legality of accessing the extra funds,[15] a claim rejected by the government.

Based on June 2008 prices, East Timor's oil revenue had doubled over the previous year, to US$200 million a month, and boasted the Petroleum Fund from US$2 billion in 2007 to US$5 billion in 2008. This pushed East Timor's per capita gross domestic product (GDP) to a nominal US$4,500, meaning that it was quickly approaching the status of a "middle income" country (per capita GDP US$6,000). Yet in 2008, most East Timorese were unaware, or at least not recipients, of their country's increasing economic status. There was concern, however, that having access to large amounts of direct income, rather than using earned interest, could lead to fiscal irresponsibility, with money being thrown at programmes that produced little if any concrete outcomes. However, there was a sense that, should the political and economic situation remain fairly stable, East Timor's economic future looked much brighter than its economic past. This in turn boded well for retaining political stability. It was wiser, though, to retain a strong sense of circumspection about such rose-tinted optimism, especially given that, as this was being written, malnutrition remained a serious and in some parts of the country a seemingly intractable problem.

Although East Timor's people had a long history of malnutrition and chronic food shortages, this problem continued unabated and, indeed, worsened by the continuing drought that affected the region, becoming critical by the "hungry season" — the first part of the calendar year in which Timorese traditionally have little food left and new crops are not yet available. In response to this, Gusmao authorized the increased government purchase of rice, doubling its quantity from 8,000 tonnes to 16,000 tonnes but, at a time of escalating world food prices, increasing the purchase order price from US$4 million to US$12 million. The contract was let to Tres Amigos, a company directed by CNRT member Germano da Silva, apparently without an open tender process. In its second major allegation of corruption, Gusmao was immediately attacked by Fretilin, with some media raising similar concerns.

However, Gusmao responded by saying that the country only held 7,900 tonnes of rice in reserve and that its required balance for food security for a three months period was 24,000 tonnes. He added that the process of tendering for the bid had gone to a selective tender process on 1 February 2008, in which seven companies were asked if they could meet the government's requirements of purchasing and warehousing the rice. Only Tres Amigos was able to comply with both aspects of the requirements and so received the contract.

Fretilin was also highly critical of the AMP government replacing the Timor Sea Designated Authority (TSDA) with a National Petroleum Authority (NPA). The NPA was responsible for regulating all petroleum exploration, production, processing and sales both onshore and offshore in East Timor. The creation of the NPA was under a decree passed by the Council of Ministers, which Fretilin criticized for lacking in public consultation and transparency.

The other major aspect of the AMP government's economic policy was the introduction of sweeping tax changes, including no income tax for income below US$500 a year and at a flat 10 per cent a year for income above US$500 a year. Services tax was capped at five per cent, while withholding taxes were at between two and 10 per cent. Import duty and sales tax was capped at 2.5 per cent, while excise tax was increased on alcohol and tobacco but reduced on petrol, a basic and expensive commodity. Interestingly, the tax on guns and ammunition was set at 200 per cent, even though the parliament had rejected the proposal put by Xanana Gusmao that would have made it possible for private individuals to register and own guns. This policy was not explained by Gusmao, and was roundly criticized as being unhelpful and potentially dangerous in a country already traumatised by violence.

While East Timor's economy stabilized somewhat due to increased oil revenues, distribution of the country's wealth remained problematic. Average mean income, as opposed to per capita GDP, remained low, at around US$500–600 per person, while those outside the main towns continued to survive in an often largely cashless economy. Especially in light of continued drought conditions and the global increase in the price of rice, 70 per cent of Timorese households remained moderately to severely "food insecure", rising to over 80 per cent in Cova Lima and Oecusse districts.[16]

In large part, the gap between per capita GDP and actual income reflected the government's difficulty in distributing available funds, especially beyond Dili. However, the government was aware of the need to get funds out of the centre to the districts, in order to promote regional development and, especially, to increase the level of financial liquidity in the districts and sub-districts.[17]

In order to promote local development projects, however, the government needed to put in place a mechanism to achieve this.

To help ensure there would be a mechanism in place to promote local development, and through which funds could be channelled to the districts, throughout 2008 the government worked on a plan for political and economic decentralization, following from the previous Fretilin government's plan for an even more localised political system. This AMP government's decentralization programme was to be based upon holding district council elections, and devolving administrative responsibility to the district level. Planning for this process was slow, however, and the first such steps were not intended to be taken until 2009, initially in only four districts.[18]

Late in the year, the government also announced that it had let a tender to a Chinese government-owned company to build two power plants to provide electricity to the whole country for a full 24 hours per day. This follows intermittent electricity to most of the country and no electricity to some parts. The plan was for a 120 megawatt plant in Manatuto, and a 60 megawatt plant on the south coast, being enough electricity for East Timor's current and projected power needs. This infrastructure project was to be East Timor's largest to date, although was criticized for being reliant on expensive fuel oil. Another large infrastructure project — an LNG processing plant on East Timor's south coast — seemed a less likely prospect, as the parent company, Woodside Petroleum, preferred to build a floating plant or a plant at Darwin, Australia (the latter option compromised by Australia's new carbon tax). Woodside's reasons for not building in East Timor included greater project cost in East Timor, including sending a pipeline from the Greater Sunrise field across a deep sea trench, a lack of local staff or infrastructure support, and potential political instability. Wanting the development, technology transfer and related industries, the East Timor government strongly protested this decision, and could have deferred the project to the longer term future,[19] or at least sought some recompense.

Stability?

East Timor continued to have many problems which dogged its future. But towards the end of 2008 it was showing real signs of internal stabilization. To this end, the Australian Defence Force drew down 100 of its 700 personnel contribution to the International Stabilization Force that had been sent to quell the troubles of 2006. Australia, however, retained a long and perhaps open-ended commitment to East Timor and its stability, and was expected to retain a military presence there for as long as was deemed necessary by the East Timor government.

In all, East Timor ended 2008 much better than it had started it, and the prospects for the future were brighter rather than dimmer than in 2007. But coming off such a low base, and with so many continuing problems, East Timor's future continued to be one beset by struggle. Any success, though, was a positive over its previous existence.

Notes

1   C. Banz, *Report: UNMIT Internal Review Panel on the UN Response to the Attacks on the President and the Prime Minister on 11 February 2008* (Dili: UNMIT, 2008).

2   A. Barker, A "Ramos-Horta personally forgives rebels", ABC News On-line, 29 April 2008.

3   The term "declaracao de estado de sitio" means "state of place", but translated as "state of siege or emergency, or martial law", involving a night curfew, increased powers of arrest and detention, and the inclusion of the F-FDTL as part of the active security forces.

4   J. Virgoe, "Timor's predicament", *The Age*, 23 April 2008.

5   L. Murdoch, "Rebels accuse Alkatiri of engineering massacre", *The Age*, 8 June 2008.

6   L. Murdoch, "Dili gangs turn on Australian forces", *The Age*, 27 October 2008.

7   In personal communication with the author, Dili, 12 June 2008.

8   The name of the funding agent remains confidential until or unless charges are laid. It was not, however, either the president or the prime minister.

9   J. Virgoe, "Timor's predicament", *The Age*, 23 April 2008.

10 UNMIT, "The State declares petitioners to be civilians: Timor Post", UNMIT Media Review, 14 July 2008.

11 AFP, "Timor Leste students protest against cars for lawmakers", Dili, 11 June 2008.

12 E. Pires, "Minister of Finance addresses parliamentary vehicle purchases", Media Release, Ministry of Finance, Dili, 16 June 2008.

13 X. Gusmao, "Dispatch No: 023/IVGC/PM", Office of the Prime Minister, Democratic Republic of Timor-Leste, Dili, 18 August 2008.

14 J. Hand, "East Timor opposition plans rally", *Canberra Times*, 26 October 2008.

15 La'o Hamutuk, "Timor-Leste Appeals Court Invalidates State Budget", 14 November 2008 <http://www.laohamutuk.org/econ/MYBU08/BudgetRuledUncons titutional08.htm> (accessed 15 November 2008).

[16] Oxfam, "Timor-Leste food security baseline survey report", Dili, 16 October 2008.

[17] This observation is based on discussions with government ministers and advisers.

[18] According to the Minister for State Administration, Archangelo Leite, personal conversation, 15 October 2008.

[19] RDTL, "Timor-Leste empenhado no oleoduto" (East Timor committed to the pipeline), Press Release, Democratic Republic of East Timor, Dili, 2008.

Vietnam

VIETNAM IN 2008
Foreign Policy Successes but Daunting Domestic Problems

Joern Dosch

In 2008 the ruling Vietnamese Communist Party (VCP) maintained its firm grip on power, rejecting domestic and international calls for political reform and pluralism. In one of the most controversial demonstrations of government power, two reporters of the state sponsored Thanh Nien and Tuoi Tre newspapers were arrested in May for their coverage of a major corruption scandal in the country. In October the People's Court found both journalists guilty of "abusing democratic freedoms to infringe upon the interests of the state".[1] On the economic front, Vietnam has been severely affected by soaring inflation and downward pressure on the country's currency, the dong, raising international concerns about the country's economic stability. The economic turbulences provided a fertile ground for the revival of conservative politicians whose strengthened influence poses a challenge for Prime Minister Nguyen Tan Dung. A champion of economic reform, Dung has emphasized the importance of anti-corruption efforts and sought to increase ministerial responsibility in place of close party control. Despite some high profile anti-graft cases, corruption and abuse of office remain serious problems and continue to test the VCP's legitimacy.

In foreign affairs, Sino-Vietnamese relations seemingly improved after the low point in December 2007, when the Vietnamese government tolerated anti-Chinese demonstrations outside the Chinese embassy in Hanoi and consulate in Ho Chi Minh City. Hanoi and Beijing announced a "comprehensive strategic partnership" and agreed to set up a "hot link" between the two countries. However, beneath the surface the bilateral relationship is more sour than sweet and several

JOERN DOSCH is Professor of Asia Pacific Studies, Department of East Asian Studies, University of Leeds, United Kingdom.

new disturbances emerged during the year. While economic relations between Vietnam and the United States have gone from strength to strength — in June, Vietnam and the U.S. agreed to launch negotiations on a bilateral investment treaty — diverging views on human rights continue to be a persistent thorn in the side of Hanoi's relations with Washington.

Growing Societal Demands for Change but Slow Progress on Political Liberalization

Advocates of faster reform for Vietnam essentially saw the years between the 9th Party National Congress in 2001 and the 10th Congress in 2006 as lost time. In spite of impressive economic growth and government successes in reducing poverty, the reformers increasingly perceived "the incremental and slow changes in politics as key impediments holding the country back, well behind faster-paced developments in China and elsewhere".[2] While some modest moves towards political reforms have taken place since 2006, the fault lines between reformers and conservatives remain largely unaffected. At the same time Vietnam's policy-making has more and more been influenced by inputs, including demands, from newly emerging social groups and shifting structures of influence within the state-party apparatus. Vietnam is still a unitary state, where a bureaucratic elite shapes policy-making.[3] Recent developments nevertheless suggest that the spectrum of groups that try to affect policy has widened, notwithstanding the retention of an effective monopoly over political discussion and policy formulation by the government and the VCP.

As part of the process towards more pluralism and the related changing decision-making dynamics *within* the state-party system, decisions made by the CPV politburo that once had the power of law are today authoritative only to a great extent, that is, not absolutely. The influence of Vietnam's Quoc Hoi or National Assembly (NA) in the policy-making process has grown. During its third session (6 May–7 June), the NA demonstrated its new assertiveness with regard to the Hanoi expansion plan. The plan envisages expanding the capital to 3.6 times its current size of 920 square kilometres by entirely incorporating Ha Tay province and parts of Vinh Phuc and Hoa Binh provinces. Although the NA eventually ratified the plan, several members had criticized "its poor planning and unclear implementation roadmap". A report by the NA's Legal Affairs Committee stated that while the government advocated the expansion to ensure Hanoi's social and economic development, it failed "to address the social and cultural impacts, especially on Ha Tay Province which would become part of the expanded Hanoi".

The report also noted that the government had not spelled out the financial outlay for the expansion.[4] However, the legislature's increasing proactiveness does not yet translate into support of pro-democracy reforms. Shortly before the closing of the fourth session in November, the NA rejected a trial plan that would have allowed direct local elections in April 2009. According to the proposal, which had been discussed by NA members and outlined in a detailed assembly paper, citizens in 385 communes nationwide would have directly elected their people's committee chairperson. Comparisons have been drawn with the village-level elections introduced by China some two decades years ago. The National Assembly instead voted to extend by two years until 2011 the terms of commune and district leaders who were indirectly elected in a process vetted by the VCP.[5]

While maintaining the pace of economic liberalization, the government has continued to clamp down on oppositional civil society actors in an attempt to retain its monopoly on power. In trials throughout the year several members of the Bloc 8406 movement — named after the date (8 April 2006) when its founding members posted an online manifesto calling for democratization and civil liberties in Vietnam — and other pro-democracy activists were sentenced to prison terms. With the death of Hoang Minh Chinh in February, the pro-democracy movement lost one of its most prominent figures. The veteran activist had been among the first signatories of the 8406 manifesto and relaunched the still-banned Democratic Party of Vietnam (DPV). Hundreds of Vietnamese relatives and supporters attended his funeral, a politically charged event held under heavy policy scrutiny.[6] According to two outlawed dissident groups, the People's Democracy Party (PDP) and the California-based Viet Tan, several pro-democracy campaigners were arrested in September during demonstrations by Catholics against the government. In December, eight Vietnamese Catholics went on trial charged with disturbing public order and destroying property. Since January — with a peak of activity in August and September — hundreds of Catholics have protested the seizure of 14 acres of land by the Vietnamese government which they claim belongs to the Church. The protest took the form of mass prayer vigils on the disputed land which was part of the capital's Thai Ha parish until 1954 when the communist forces took power from the French in North Vietnam and seized most church land.[7]

However, on several other occasions the government demonstrated that it was willing to listen to societal demands. In March the government extended the number of religious organizations that enjoy freedom to practice their faith as long as they do not oppose the Party and existing political structure. Operating licenses were granted to 13 additional religious groups, including the Baha'is, the Theravada Buddhist sect, and the Vietnam Mennonite Church. To date the government has recognized 106 Protestant Christian groups, licensed 1,156 groups and granted land-use certificates to around 30 religious establishments. Senior government officials now praise the positive contribution of religion to society, though they still insist on vetting senior clerical appointments.[8] Even the 2008 update of the traditionally rather critical Congressional Research Service Report on U.S.-Vietnam relations concludes that "most Vietnamese now are able to observe the religion of their choice".[9]

Ethnic minorities also benefitted. Protest related to ethnicity emerged as a new phenomenon in Vietnam's modern history in 2001 and was the result of a decade-long quasi-neglect of ethnic minorities. Violence in the Central Highlands that first gripped the country in 2001 intensified in 2004, when some 10,000 Montagnards (also referred to as Degars and thuong/highlanders) in Dak Lak and Gia Lai provinces protested against government repression of their religion (many are Christian) and against the confiscation of their land. The government has subsequently worked towards improving the basic infrastructure in the Central Highlands and providing more protection for the rights of minorities. An EU delegation that visited Dak Lak province (which is home to 44 ethnic minority groups) in November 2008 stated that the province had made "socio-economic and cultural achievements".[10] According to the Chairman of the provincial People's Committee Lu Ngoc Cu, over the past few years Dak Lak recorded an average economic growth rate of 11.2 per cent, the highest among Central Highlands provinces.[11] During a visit to three Central Highlands provinces in the same month, a group of four Western states, Canada, Norway, Switzerland and New Zealand, noted "demonstrable progress" and "some positive trends towards greater religious freedom" in the remote region. At the same time the delegation found that the Montagnards remain under-represented in local government while "ethnic minority poverty is increasing".[12]

The Struggle between Reformers and Conservatives Continues

The far-reaching economic and modest political reform process is spearheaded by Prime Minister Nguyen Tan Dung who relies on a heterogeneous group of progressive members among the political elite, tied together by ideological affinity and interest convergence. The conservative-reformer cleavage is not identical with the generation gap in the Politburo's Central Committee — still the centre of political power in Vietnam. Some prominent reformers are too old for re-election, such as former NA Chairman Nguyen Van An, while some younger members of the Central

Committee are ardent conservatives, for example Information Minister Le Doan Hop. Dung has established strong progressive and pro-globalization credentials since taking office in 2006 by masterminding several trade and investment liberalization policies. In 2008 Vietnam concluded a free trade agreement (FTA) with Japan, is currently acting as the coordinator for EU-ASEAN FTA negotiations (the EU and Vietnam currently also considering the feasibility of a bilateral FTA), expressed interest in joining a trans-Pacific free trade deal and started bilateral investment treaty negotiations with the U.S. and Canada.[13]

The current economic turbulence has strengthened the reform-critical voices — centred on VCP secretary general Nong Duc Manh — who have tried to exploit Dung's difficulties in stabilizing the market forces and finding effective policy responses to counter increased pollution and congestion as well as the continued prevalence of corruption. The main criticism was directed at the Premier's handling of inflation which reached a 17-year high of 28.3 per cent in August before slightly easing for three consecutive months.[14] High inflation has been among the main causes for a proliferation of labour strikes. Industrial action reflects the anger of the tens of thousands of Vietnamese who have left rural farming communities to seek work at foreign-invested factories in the new industrial zones around Hanoi and Ho Chi Minh City, only to see the buying power of their wages decrease amid rising food and fuel costs. By mid-year food costs had risen by an estimated 44 per cent, while transport and housing had increased by around 25 per cent. According to government statistics, about 300 strikes took place in the first quarter alone, a three-fold increase compared to the first quarter of 2007 when 103 strikes were recorded. The sharp rise in industrial action happened despite new labour rules that make workers liable to compensate their employers if they walk off the job illegally.[15] The economic downturn appears to have triggered "a growing discontent about the country's economy, leading to private discussions about the effectiveness of government solutions and its leaders' ability".[16] According to the Far Eastern Economic Review, in a closed meeting in September experts from semi-independent economic think-tanks "raised fundamental questions about the issues underlying the troubled economy, including inadequate measures to ensure quality of economic growth, the lack of good governance, and the shortage of unskilled workers".[17]

Yet, given that the entire political elite has benefitted greatly from ongoing economic liberalization and the economy grew by 6.2 per cent in 2008, Dung's position is not likely to face any direct challenge from the conservative quarter. Still, the tensions within the VCP are believed to be the most intense in over a decade. Dung's individualistic and non-consensual leadership style has irritated, if not angered, the conservative camp led by party chief Manh. The divergence between Dung's focus on economic growth and Manh's emphasis on economic stability is growing. Furthermore, the progressive camp in the VCP was weakened with the death of former prime minister Vo Van Kiet in June. A champion of liberalization, he maintained influence as a powerful behind-the-scenes patron over a group of party officials, including to some extent Dung, and continued to promote his reform ideals after retiring as an advisor to the party's Central Committee in 2001, Kiet's last official position. In the first half of the year speculation was growing about the possibility of a mid-term party conference — the first of its kind since 1994 — to address internal party divisions.[18] The conference, which book place eventually, confirmed the rifts within the VCP and the existing discontent with Dung's performance.

The Media as a Key Battleground

In addition to the economy the media has emerged as a key battleground between reformers and conservatives. While reformers do not necessarily support the concept of unrestricted press freedom, they do view a freer media as a potentially useful tool for policing corruption and thus minimising potential sources of popular discontent with party rule. Conservatives perceive even limited press freedom as a serious challenge to the VCP.[19] The latter group had the upper hand in 2008 despite a promising signal for more press freedom early in the year.

In February, Manh praised the press for unmasking graft and thereby fulfilling "the people's desires". The most notable case was a scandal at the transport ministry in 2006 in which newspapers revealed how officials had gambled around US$750,000 of public money on the outcomes of football matches and then paid bribes to cover up the crime (the so-called PMU18 case). In the clean-up that followed, the head of a road-building department at the ministry was jailed, along with seven others.[20] However, the arrest and sentencing of two journalists who reported on this high-level graft case, called into question the government's intention to loosen its tight grip on the press. Nguyen Viet Chien (Thanh Nien newspaper) and Nguyen Van Hai (Tuoi Tre newspaper) were arrested in May and charged with "abusing their position and power while discharging public duty".[21] Under a 2006 decree, journalists face large fines for transgressions of censorship laws, including denying revolutionary achievements, spreading "harmful" information, or exhibiting "reactionary ideology".[22] Along with the journalists two police investigators who provided the press with information about the case were accused of "deliberately revealing work secrets". After a day-and-a-half long trial, on 15 October the court handed out the sentences. Viet Chien, who pleaded not guilty throughout, was given a 24-month custodial sentence, while Van Hai, who pleaded guilty and asked for leniency, was given two years of re-education without detention.[23]

The government rejected widespread criticism of the trial from the two newspapers themselves as well as human rights organizations, foreign donors, the U.S. and the EU, noting that it was held in accordance with international standards and had been attended by representatives of foreign missions and a number of foreign journalists. Foreign Ministry spokesman Le Dung was quoted as saying, "Vietnam is fully aware of the threat of corruption, and considers corruption as a national disaster and the fight against corruption as a very important task." He also encouraged the "the press to take an active part in the fight against corruption in a comprehensive, thorough and lawful manner".[24]

While the government maintains tight control over the media, comprising around 11 daily newspapers and more than 50 provincial television stations, Catherine McKinley's comprehensive study of Vietnam's press confirms that generally the freedom for Vietnamese journalists to report and investigate cases of corruption is growing.[25] Although Nguyen Tan Dung has made reform and anti-corruption efforts a priority, neither press freedom nor corruption or indeed political change were addressed by the 7th Plenum of the VCP Central Committee in July. Topping the agenda was a discussion of the country's current domestic economic challenges. Broad resolutions on youth, intellectuals and rural areas were also put forward.[26]

Corruption: The Main Challenge to the VCP's Legitimacy

Corruption and abuse of office remain the VCP's most serious problem and both the conservative and the reform camps are full of corrupt officials. Citizens' complaints about official corruption, governmental inefficiency and untransparent bureaucratic procedures have increased in recent years. Although senior party and government officials have publicly acknowledged growing public discontent, the government has so far mainly responded with a few high-profile prosecutions of officials and private individuals rather than comprehensive reforms.[27] Ongoing crackdowns on corrupt officials and state-owned enterprises are a good indication that the government takes graft seriously, but they are equally an indicator of the pervasiveness of the problem. In the first six months of 2008 government auditors uncovered fraud worth D970 billion (US$61 million) and "misdeeds in economic management" of approximately D400 billion. By May almost 400 people had been charged with corruption-related offences. In addition, the General Department of State Audit found that D2.8 trillion (US$170 million) in taxes had been evaded in 2007, especially in the construction sector, of which authorities have recovered less than 10 per cent.[28] Vietnam was ranked 121 out of 180 countries surveyed in Transparency International's 2008 Corruption Perceptions Index (two positions higher than in the previous year).[29]

In November, chief government inspector Tran Van Truyen unveiled a long-term national strategy for the fight against corruption (until 2020). This very ambitious strategy is intended to eliminate the conditions from which corruption arises and build a transparent government apparatus with incorruptible civil servants. The corruption prevention plan comprises five measures: improving the transparency of authorities and agencies; completing the economic management regime; building a fair competitive business environment; improving supervision, surveillance, investigation and prosecutions; and raising society's awareness of its role in the fight against corruption. The government also considers legislative measures to publicize the income of government officials. In an interview Tryuen announced that in the first phase of the strategy's implementation the government will look into public assets, followed by an investigation of the private sector and the extent to which firms were involved in the bribery of state employees. In the near future inspectors would focus on land management, finance and banking, credit and the equitization of economic groups and corporations.[30] As a related significant measure to create international confidence in Vietnam's anti-corruption roadmap the government decided to sign the UN Convention against Corruption.

In a particularly image-damaging case, which is under investigation, a Ho Chi Minh City official allegedly received more than US$2 million bribes from executives of the Japanese consulting firm Pacific Consultants International (PCI), in exchange for helping the firm win contracts in the East-West Highway project. The World Bank (WB) warned it would stop lending money to Vietnam if it discovered any wrongdoings regarding official development assistance (ODA) funding. Vietnam will receive WB preferential loans of US$1.5 billion per annum over the next three years.[31] The issue of corruption ranked high on the agenda of the Consultative Group (CG) Meeting of Vietnam's international donors and the government in early December. At the sidelines of the meeting the Head of the EU delegation to Vietnam, Sean Doyle, commented, "Donors and investors may not help as much as they have in the past if they don't see more transparency, receive more economic information and so on, and also receive strong signals that the government is doing something about corruption."[32] The total donor commitment to Vietnam for 2009 reached just over US$5 billion, a decrease of

US$400 million as compared to 2008.[33] The drop was mainly due to Japan's decision to freeze ODA (expected to be more than 1 US$ billion) until Vietnam took effective measures against corruption. This is the first time Japan held back ODA and Tokyo did so with substantial support from domestic reformists outside the Vietnamese government. Both the EU and the U.S. also addressed human rights concerns in their statements to the CG meeting.[34]

Human Rights: A Thorn in the Side of Vietnam's Otherwise Prosperous International Relations

Although Vietnam was removed from the U.S. State Department's CPC ("country of particular concern") list that names states "engaged in or tolerated particularly severe violations of religious freedom" in November 2006, human rights issues have regularly resurfaced on the bilateral agenda.[35] Washington and Hanoi conduct a twice yearly human rights dialogue, in which the U.S. raises questions on religious freedom and democratic reforms in Vietnam. Driven by what some American policy-makers see as a breach of promise by Hanoi to embrace reforms towards greater political freedom and substantial improvements in human rights when it joined the WTO, the U.S. House of Representatives passed binding legislation in September 2007 that ties U.S. foreign aid to Vietnam to its human rights record while serving the purpose of promoting the "development of freedom, human rights, and the rule of law" in the country.[36] The Vietnam Human Rights Act of 2008 confirmed the provision by linking the expansion of U.S.-Vietnam relations to "significant improvement in human rights for Vietnamese citizens, particularly those enshrined in the International Covenant on Civil and Political Rights, of which Vietnam is a signatory". [37] In a similar vein, the 2008 edition of the U.S. State Department's Human Rights Report on Vietnam (which covers the year 2007) found that Vietnam's "human rights record remained unsatisfactory".[38] The Vietnamese Foreign Ministry claimed that the report did "not give objective observations on the real situation in Vietnam and [was] based on false and prejudiced information".[39] Vietnamese Americans, a growing political force in the United States, have been trying to convince U.S. lawmakers to exert more pressure on Hanoi to improve human rights. As in the case of Sino-American relations, the U.S. human rights agenda towards Vietnam is largely driven by the domestic dynamics of foreign policy-making in Washington that allows for the significant leverage of pressure groups on the conduct of foreign affairs.

Economic relations between the two states have not been affected by human rights concerns. Since the implementation of the Vietnam-U.S. Bilateral Trade

Agreement (BTA) in 2001, two-way trade has increased from US$1.5 billion to about US$10 billion in 2007.[40] Following the state visit of Dung to Washington in June, the two countries launched bilateral investment treaty (BIT) talks and the Bush Administration announced that it would explore whether to add Vietnam to the Generalized System of Payments (GSP) programme. The programme extends duty-free treatment to certain products that are imported from designated developing countries. Since 2005, the U.S. and Vietnam have held annual visits between President Bush and either the Vietnamese President or the Prime Minister. In June Dung also became the highest level Vietnamese official since the Vietnam War to visit the Pentagon, where he met with Secretary of Defense Robert Gates. The two states also announced the commencement of a formal "Security Dialogue" on political-military issues, a process that the United States has with four other Southeast Asian countries. The June summit was a clear indication of an ongoing deepening of U.S.-Vietnam relations. President Bush went so far as to vow to support Vietnam's security, sovereignty, and territorial integrity — a hint at China's assertiveness in the South China Sea.[41] As Mark Beeson correctly points out, Washington's relations "with Vietnam have become increasingly cordial. … [T]here is no small irony in the way in which history has developed; the USA has ultimately achieved the very result it wanted through the indirect use of 'soft' rather than 'hard power'".[42]

No two sets of bilateral relationships are more important to Vietnam than its relations with the United States and China. Maintaining the best possible balance in its relations with the two powers has emerged as the cornerstone of Vietnam's foreign relations in the post-Cold War era. A low point in diplomatic relations with Beijing was reached in December 2007 when thousands of Vietnamese took to the streets of Hanoi and Ho Chi Minh City to protest against what they viewed as China's incursions into Vietnamese territory in the South China Sea (the first public rally in half a century in communist Vietnam).[43] Anti-China protests resurfaced in December 2008 but were quickly overwhelmed by the Vietnamese government forces. In late May and early June 2008 Party General Secretary Manh paid an official visit to China where he met Chinese Premier Wen Jiabao, and President Hu Jintao. It was Manh's fourth trip to China since he was elected for the post in 2001. Among other issues the two sides agreed to set up hotlines between the leaders, and to make greater use of the Steering Committee on Vietnam-China Bilateral Cooperation. Consensus was also reached to finish demarcating the land border between Vietnam and China by the end of 2008.[44] In October, during further talks in Beijing, this time between Wen Jiabao and Nguyen Tan Dung, the two governments agreed to implement the Gulf of

Tonkin Border Delimitation Agreement (ratified in 2004) to avert conflicts over oil and gas exploitation. However, in the dispute concerning the sovereignty of the Spratly Islands a sustainable solution has yet to be found. In July, China reportedly pressed the American oil firm Exxon Mobil to cancel an exploration deal with Petro Vietnam in areas of the South China Sea off Vietnam's south and central coasts, claiming the acreage lay in Chinese territorial waters.[45] A statement issued by the Foreign Ministry made it clear that Vietnam was prepared to stand its ground in the dispute: "Vietnam possesses sufficient historical evidence and a legal basis to confirm its indisputable sovereignty and sovereignty rights over the Hoang Sa and Truong Sa archipelagos, as well as Vietnam's waters and continental shelf."[46] A sense of resentment towards China, emanating from historical legacies, persists within much of Vietnam's political elite, as remained the case with a proportion of the wider Vietnamese population.[47] The prevailing distrust between the two nations once again became an issue in August 2008, when "four Chinese-language websites carried an alleged Chinese plan to invade Vietnam". In response, the government in Hanoi "twice summoned senior Chinese diplomats to its Foreign Ministry to voice concerns about the possible negative impact on bilateral relations and to request the removal of the offending document from Chinese web sites".[48] Despite strong diplomatic efforts to strengthen Sino-Vietnamese relations and the rhetoric about a strategic partnership, China's assertiveness against Vietnam was such an irritant among the Vietnamese elite and the populace at large that even party boss Manh — who favours close relations with China — had to emphasize the need to defend Vietnam's sovereignty and territorial integrity in his speech before the All-Army Political-Military Convention in December 2008.

In multilateral settings Vietnam was able to put its mark on international organizations and cooperation schemes. As a non-permanent member of the UN Security Council (SC) for the 2008–09 term Vietnam took over the chairmanship during the month of July. After the devastation caused by Cyclone Nargis in Myanmar in early May, Vietnam reportedly joined fellow SC members China, Russia, and South Africa in opposing calls for the Council to invoke a "responsibility to protect" that would have permitted the international community to bypass Myanmar's ruling junta in providing humanitarian assistance.[49] As for regional cooperation, Vietnam was among the group of five member states that ratified the ASEAN Charter early — Vietnam handed over its ratification document on 4 April — paving the way for the Charter to take effect from 1 January 2009. As the unofficial leader of the "CLMV" group (Cambodia, Laos, Myanmar, Vietnam) representing the least developed of the ASEAN countries,

Vietnam hosted a summit meeting of the four prime ministers in November in Hanoi. The four countries are also members of the Mekong River Commission and the Greater Mekong Subregion (GMS). Both organizations focus, *inter alia*, on the management of water security which has recently emerged as a serious problem for Vietnam. In November the country saw the worst flooding in decades. Torrential rain and floods in 20 northern Vietnamese provinces claimed the lives of at least 85 people, damaged 180,000 houses, and devastated about 265,000 hectares of rice and vegetable fields. Total losses are estimated at over U\$440 million.[50]

Conclusion

The impact of the *doi moi* on Vietnam's international relations is an often underestimated effect of the reform process. In 1989 Vietnam had diplomatic relations with just 23 non-communist states and was internationally isolated. Two decades later Vietnam has established diplomatic relations with 172 nations and signed trade agreements with 76 countries and Most Favoured Nation status with 72 countries and territories, according to the Ministry of Foreign Affairs which stresses that "for the first time in history, Vietnam is now entertaining normal relations with all major powers and UN Security Council's Permanent Members".[51] As a non-permanent member of the UN Security Council (for the 2008–09 period) and one of the most influential members of ASEAN and sub-regional cooperation schemes, Vietnam has further strengthened its influence on the international stage. In 2008 Hanoi's bilateral relations with Washington and Brussels reached new heights with the start of talks on a bilateral investment treaty (BIT) and the commencement of a formal security dialogue in the case of the U.S. and negotiations for a Partnership and Cooperation Agreement as far as the EU is concerned. Sino-Vietnamese relations recovered from the diplomatic low point in the wake of the anti-China demonstrations in Hanoi and Ho Chi Minh City in December 2007 but remain troubled over conflicting sovereignty claims in the South China Sea.

The successes in the conduct of foreign relations, however, cannot hide the fact that Vietnam is still haunted by an international image problem — a message that the country's donors clearly drove home at the Consultative Group Meeting with the government in December — whose underlying causes, such as human rights issues and high levels of corruption, no longer escape the attention of domestic groups either. The conviction of two reporters who had covered one of the biggest corruption scandals in recent years was a stark reminder that the pace of political reforms is lagging a long way behind economic liberalization. Not least did the trial indicate the intensity of the growing conflict between the conservatives and reformist groups in the VCP. The economic turbulence of the past months has played to the advantage of the party's old guards, senior leaders from North and Central Vietnam who are associated with the armed forces and the VCP's security wing and preach the primacy of national stability. Seen through the conservative lens, any far-reaching economic reforms and even modest alterations to political decision-making pose a threat not only to the party's monopoly on power but its very survival. While the position of the Prime Minister appears not to have been openly challenged, Dung faces an uphill battle. At the economic front he must balance the reformists' calls for more growth with the conservatives' focus on economic stability while at the same time demonstrating that the government is capable of implementing effective measures to reduce corruption and increase government transparency, the main challenges to the VCP's legitimacy.

Notes

[1] Frank Zeller, "Vietnam jails reporter who wrote about state corruption", Agence France-Presse, 15 October 2008.

[2] David Koh, "Leadership Changes at the 10th Congress of the Vietnamese Communist Party", *Asian Survey*, vol. 48, issue 4 (2008): 650–72.

[3] Gareth Porter, *Vietnam: The Politics of Bureaucratic Socialism* (Ithaca, NY: Cornell University Press, 1993).

[4] Xuan Toan, "Gov't seeks Hanoi expansion nod despite lawmakers' reservation", *Thanh Nien*, 20 May 2008 <http://www.thanhniennews.com/politics/?catid=1&newsid =38673>.

[5] Agence France-Presse, "Vietnam halts planned local election project", 15 November 2008.

[6] Tin Que Huong, "Hundreds attend funeral of Vietnam pro-democracy activist Hoang", 18 Febuary 2008 <http://tinquehuong.wordpress.com/2008/02/18/hundreds-attend-funeral-of-vietnam-pro-democracy-activist-hoang/>.

[7] Agence France-Presse, "Dissidents condemn arrests in Vietnam land protests", 11 September 2008; Agence France-Presse, "Catholic protesters face court in Vietnam", 8 December 2008; Catholic News Agency, "Tens of thousands of Catholics protest land seizure in Vietnam", 2 December 2008.

[8] Economist Intelligence Unit, "Vietnam politics: How long can the party last?", EIU ViewsWire, New York, 25 April 2008.

[9] Mark E. Manyin, "U.S.-Vietnam Relations: Background and Issues for Congress", Congressional Research Service (CRS) Report for Congress, updated version, 31 October 2008, p. 16.

10   Vietnamese News Agency, "EU ambassadors delegation visit Dak Lak", 22 November 2008.

11   Ibid.

12   Agence France-Presse, "Western donors urge Vietnam to respect human rights", 2 December 2008.

13   See <www.bilaterals.org>.

14   Claire Innes, "Inflation Moderates in Vietnam", World Markets Research Center, Global Insight, 25 November 2008.

15   James Hookway, "World News: Inflation Fuels Vietnam Strikes; Workers Demand Hefty Pay Increases From Foreign Firms", *Wall Street Journal* (Eastern Edition), New York, 3 June 2008, p. A12.

16   Long S. Le, "Vietnam in Denial Over Economic Woes", *Far Eastern Economic Review*, vol. 171, issue 8 (October 2008): 45.

17   Ibid.

18   Shawn W. Crispin, "Vietnam's reforms on the line", *Asia Times*, 28 June 2008; Nga Pham, "Obituary: Vo Van Kiet", *BBC News*, 11 June 2008 <http://news.bbc.co.uk/1/hi/world/asia-pacific/7449094.stm>; Economist Intelligence Unit, "Vietnam politics: Conservatives in the ascendant", EIU ViewsWire, New York, 18 August 2008; Economist Intelligence Unit, "Vietnam: Country forecast summary", EIU ViewsWire, New York, 18 November 2008.

19   Carlyle Thayer as quoted in Olszewski, Peter, "Media is key battleground between Vietnam's Conservative and Progressive Factions", Media Blab News Bites, 30 June 2008.

20   *The Economist*, "Shooting the messenger", 22 May 2008.

21   Economist Intelligence Unit, "Vietnam politics: Journalists arrested", EIU ViewsWire, New York, 17 June 2008.

22   Freedom House, "Freedom in the World: Vietnam 2008" <http://www.vietnamhumanrights.net/english/documents/FH_rp2008.pdf>.

23   Asia Intelligence, "Reporters with Borders", *AsiaInt Weekly Alert*, 17 October 2008; Thah Nien, "Ex-journalists' trial opens in Hanoi, verdict expected today", 15 October 2008 <http://www.thanhniennews.com/society/?catid=3&newsid=42868>.

24   Vietnamese News Agency, "Vietnam rejects 'wrong opinions' on ex-journalists' trial", 24 October 2007.

25   Catherine McKinley, "Can a State Owned Media effectively monitor corruption? A study of Vietnam's printed press", *Asian Journal of Public Affairs*, vol. 2, issue 1 (Summer 2008): 12–38.

26   Economist Intelligence Unit, "Vietnam politics: Anti-graft campaign yielding mixed results", EIU ViewsWire, New York, 18 August 2008.

27   Freedom House (EN 20).

28   Economist Intelligence Unit, "Vietnam politics: Anti-graft campaign yielding mixed results", EIU ViewsWire, New York, 18 August 2008.

[29]   Transparency International, Corruption Perception Index 2008 <http://www.transparency.org/news_room/in_focus/2008/cpi2008/cpi_2008_table>.

[30]   As quoted in VietNamNet, "Chief gov't inspector discusses new anti-corruption strategy", 19 November 2008 <http://english.vietnamnet.vn/politics/2008/11/814363/>.

[31]   Thanh Nien Daily, "Vietnam still slack on anti-graft: int'l donors", 29 November 2008 <http://www.thanhniennews.com/politics/?catid=1&newsid=44149>.

[32]   Vietnam News Agency, "EC: Vietnam needs to maintain its international image", 4 December 2008. At the general diplomatic level relations between the EU and Vietnam further strengthened in 2008. In June, the first round of negotiations for a Partnership and Cooperation Agreement (PCA) between Vietnam and the EU took place in Brussels. The PCA, which builds on the 1995 Framework Cooperation Agreement, is a comprehensive agreement covering a broad range of subjects for dialogue and cooperation in the political, economic, development cooperation, social and cultural fields.

[33]   Vietnam News Agency, "Donors' commitments surpass 5 billion USD", 5 December 2008.

[34]   European Union, Delegation of the European Commission to Vietnam, EU Statement at the Consultative Group Meeting, 4–5 December 2008 < http://www.delvnm.ec.europa.eu/news/vn_news/vn_news60.html>; Agence France-Presse, "Western donors urge Vietnam to respect human rights", 4 December 2008.

[35]   Interestingly, however, at the time of writing in early December 2008 Vietnam was still listed on the State Department's official "Country of Particular Concern" website <http://www.state.gov/g/drl/irf/c13281.htm>.

[36]   H.R. 3096: Vietnam Human Rights Act of 2007.

[37]   S.3678, Vietnam Human Rights Act of 2008, Sec 2 (7).

[38]   Vietnam Country Reports on Human Rights Practices — 2007, released by the Bureau of Democracy, Human Rights, and Labor, 11 March 2008 <http://www.state.gov/g/drl/rls/hrrpt/2007/100543.htm>.

[39]   VietNamNet, "Vietnam reacts to U.S. Human Rights Report", 14 March 2008 <http://english.vietnamnet.vn/politics/2008/03/773345/>.

[40]   Joern Dosch, "The US and Southeast Asia", in *Contemporary Southeast Asia*, edited by Mark Beeson (New York: Palgrave Macmillan, 2009), pp. 220–33.

[41]   Mark E. Manyin, "U.S.-Vietnam Relations: Background and Issues for Congress", Congressional Research Service (CRS) Report for Congress, updated version, 31 October 2008, pp. 1–2.

[42]   Mark Beeson, "The USA's Relations with the Asia-Pacific Region", in *The Far East and Australasia*, 39th ed. (London and New York: Routledge, 2008), pp. 3–8.

[43]   Alexander L. Vuving, "Vietnam: Arriving in the World — and at a Crossroads", *Southeast Asian Affairs 2008* (Singapore: Institute of Southeast Asian Studies, 2008), pp. 375–93.

44   Robert Sutter and Chin-Hao Huang, "China-Southeast Asia Relations: Cyclone, Earthquake Put Spotlight on China", *Comparative Connections: A Quarterly E-Journal on East Asian Bilateral Relations*, vol. 10, no. 2 (July 2008).

45   Clara Tan, "China Bids to Resolve Long-Running Border Disputes With Vietnam", *International Oil Daily*, 29 October 2008.

46   Vietnam News Agency, "Vietnam asserts sovereignty rights over islands", 28 November 2008.

47   Joern Dosch and Alexander L. Vuving, *The impact of China on governance structures in Vietnam* (Bonn: German Development Institute, 2008), p. 10.

48   Carlyle A. Thayer, "The Structure of Vietnam-China Relations, 1991–2008", Paper for the 3rd International Conference on Vietnamese Studies, Hanoi, Vietnam, 4–7 December 2008 <http://ykienblog.wordpress.com/2008/11/23/the-structure-of-vietnam-china-relations-1991-2008/>.

49   Mary Vallis, "UN Urged to Bypass Burmese Junta", *National Post*, 13 May 2008.

50   US Aid, United States Provides Assistance to Vietnam Flood Victims, 21 November 2008.

51   Ministry of Foreign Affairs website <http://www.mofa.gov.vn/en/cn_vakv/>.

VIETNAM'S ECONOMIC CRISIS
Policy Follies and the Role of
State-Owned Conglomerates

Vu Quang Viet

Introduction

The year 2007 left an an important mark on the economic history of Vietnam. The country became the 150th member of the World Trade Organization (WTO) on 11 January 2007 after its accession package was approved by the General Council of the WTO on 7 November 2006. For Vietnamese political leaders and the population as a whole, WTO membership was the last hurdle to cross to make Vietnam fully integrated with the rest of the world, particularly in view of the perceived ability of the United States to block Vietnam's WTO membership and thus its path to economic development in order to extract political acquiescence from Vietnam. The admission to the WTO was therefore treated by the leaders of the Communist Party of Vietnam (CPV) as a major victory, and like any victory in the past, be it over France, or the U.S., they became consumed with the elixir of triumph and embraced grandiose plans in disregard of reality.

This time, Prime Minister Nguyễn Tấn Dũng's government came to believe that a quick catch-up with other countries in the region was within grasp. The plan for 2008 was set in terms of achieving a high rate of growth in GDP, in the range of 8.5–9 per cent, by focusing externally on attracting capital inflows

VŨ QUANG VIỆT, a former Chief of National Accounts Section at the United Nations Statistical Division (2003–08, New York), served as a member of the Advisory Group on Economic and Administrative Reforms to former Vietnamese Prime Minister Võ Văn Kiệt (1992–95). Recently he served as a consultant to the USAID to assist the ASEAN Secretariat in a project to improve national accounts statistics in the ASEAN community (2008).

through foreign direct and portfolio investment, and internally on expanding the state-owned conglomerates and their subsidiaries with easy credit, public land and public money. Politically, the economic plan was expected to win the support of the party's rank and file and the provincial governments throughout the country as it would provide benefits to them from the growth of the state-owned conglomerates and general corporations in terms of seed money, land-use rights, and shares in hundreds of semi-private enterprises spun out by the conglomerates and general corporations. This plan demised rather quickly in 2008 as inflation jumped, the stock market crashed and the economy was threatened by an imminent balance of payment crisis. It has cost the Prime Minister his credibility and his probable ambition to centralize the government economic power to himself, though not yet his position. In November 2008, the government reduced its expectation of the GDP annual growth rate to 6.7 per cent.[1] The actual GDP growth rate for 2008 turned out to be only 6.2 per cent.

The first part of this article attempts to review some important features of Vietnam's economic performance. This will serve as background for the second part which dwells on the political implications.

PERFORMANCE OF THE ECONOMY

Economic Growth

In terms of gross domestic product (GDP) growth rate, Vietnam's economy has performed quite well since 2002. The average annual growth rate between 2002 and 2007 was 8.1 per cent. Though it was not much lower than the 8.8 per cent of China, it was higher than the 6.8 per cent of India in the same period. It was, however, higher than the growth rates of most countries in the Southeast Asia (see Table 1).

Other indicators also showed that the economy was generally in good shape, at least up to the end of 2006, even though some disturbing signs had already appeared since 2004, indicating the need for some adjustment in monetary and related policies. Disturbing signs included inflation and a balance of trade that began to veer off from sustainable levels due to the expansion of money supply and credit. Inflation jumped from below 4 per cent before 2004 to 7–8 per cent in 2005 to 2006 and then accelerated. The balance of trade also turned negative at a rather higher percentage of GDP (almost 5 per cent and above). During the same period, fortunately, foreign debt was at a reasonbly low level of GDP, and debt service was also low, all due to the cancelling of foreign debts by foreign partners. The international reserves increased to US$20.7 billion as of June 2008

TABLE 1
GDP Rate of Growth and Inflation in ASEAN Countries, China and India 2002–07

Country	GDP 2007 (US$ billion)	Per capita income in 2007 (US$)	GDP rate of growth Average of 2002–07	Inflation rate, year-on-year change					
				2002	2003	2004	2005	2006	2007
Brunei	12	31,759	1.7	-2.3	0.3	0.9	1.2	0.1	0.3
Cambodia	9	598	11.4	3.2	0.3	3.9	5.8	4.7	—
Indonesia	433	1,869	5.5	-11.9	6.8	6.1	10.5	13.1	6.4
Lao	4	711	6.9	10.2	16.0	10.8	6.8	7.3	—
Malaysia	187	7,027	6.0	1.8	1.1	1.4	3.1	3.6	2.0
Myanmar	19	379	5.4	57.1	36.6	4.5	10.5	18.9	34.6
Philippines	144	1,639	5.5	3.0	3.5	6.0	7.6	6.3	2.8
Singapore	161	36,370	7.1	-0.4	0.5	1.7	0.5	1.0	2.1
Thailand	245	3,841	5.6	0.6	1.8	2.8	4.5	4.6	2.2
Vietnam	71	815	8.1	3.9	3.2	7.8	8.4	7.4	8.3
India	1,141	2,604	6.8	4.3	3.8	3.8	4.2	6.2	6.3
China	3,400	976	8.8	-0.8	1.2	3.9	1.8	1.5	4.8

Sources: Data of GDP growth rates and CPI for ASEAN countries are from ASEAN Secretariat, but CPI (Consumer Price Index) of Vietnam, which has been replaced by the revised data from the General Statistical Office of Vietnam (GSO). Data on per capita income, GDP in US$ are from UN Statistical Division. CPI for China and India come from Asian Development Bank (ADB).

though, at three months of imports,[2] they were still low. What seemed to be the most important achievement was the drastic reduction of the poverty rate from 37 per cent of the population in 2000 to 19.5 per cent in 2004.[3] A recent study showed that the poverty rate was 14.6 per cent in 2007 and increased to 17 per cent in 2008, when the individual income threshold was adjusted for inflation.[4] This of course means that inflation has partly wiped out the improvement in poverty rate since 2004.

With a good record of economic growth and admission to the WTO, Vietnam seemed on the threshold of increased investment from abroad and the press in Vietnam hailed the golden opportunity for the country. FDI (implemented) almost tripled in one year, from US$2.3 billion in 2006 to US$6.6 billion in 2007 (see Table 2). The stock market index jumped over 300 per cent from 300 in early 2006 to 1,150 in early 2007 when Vietnam officially joined the WTO (see Figure 1). However, the golden opportunity seemed to be wasted by an erroneous policy of Prime Minister Nguyen Tan Dung that led to serious inflation and the imminent threat of a balance of payment crisis, which will be analysed below. The stock market crashed, with the index falling back to 345 on 24 October 2008.

FIGURE 1
Vietnam's Stock Market Index

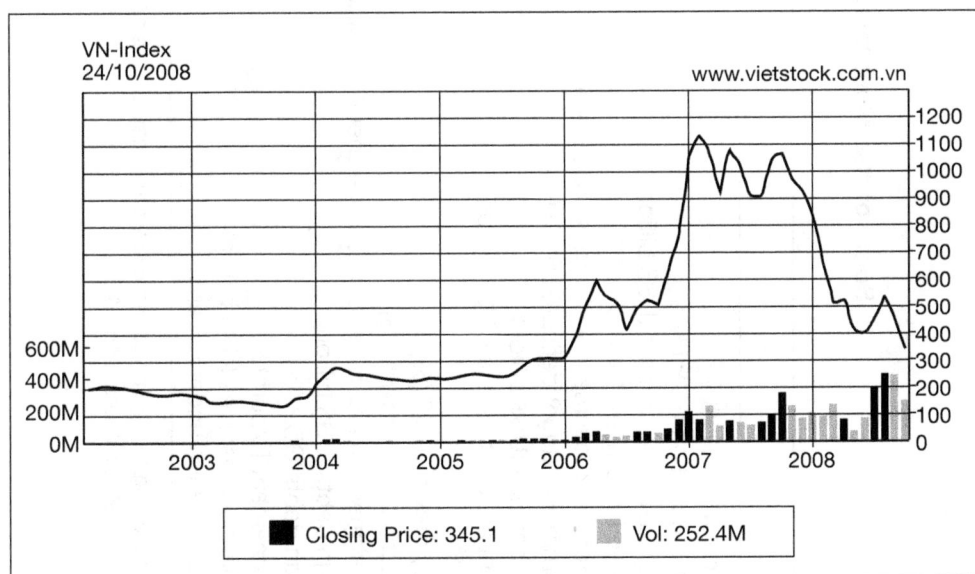

Source: Vietstock.

TABLE 2
Some of the Most Important Indicators of the Vietnam Economy, 2000–06

	2000	2001	2002	2003	2004	2005	2006	2007
GDP growth rate (%)	6.8	6.9	7.1	7.3	7.8	8.4	8.2	8.3
Capital formation/GDP (%)	29.6	31.2	33.2	35.4	35.5	35.6	36.8	41.7
Foreign direct investment (US$ billion)	1.1	1.3	1.4	1.4	1.6	1.9	2.3	6.6
Portfolio investment (US$ billion)*	0	0	0	0	0	0.9	1.3	6.2
Transfers from overseas Vietnamese (US$ billion)	1.6	1.1	1.8	2.1	2.9	3.2	3.8	6.2
Government budget deficit/GDP (%)	-4.3	-3.5	-2.3	-2.2	0.2	-1.1	-1.8	-5.4
Trade balance (US$ billion)	1.2	1.5	-3.0	-6.5	-8.5	-4.6	-4.6	-14.6
Current account balance (US$ billion)	3.6	2.1	-1.7	-4.9	-3.5	-1.1	-0.3	-9.8
CPI (%)	-1.6	-0.04	3.9	3.2	7.8	8.4	7.4	8.3
Money growth – M2 (%)	39.0	25.5	17.6	24.9	29.5	29.7	33.6	46.0
Domestic credit growth (%)	73.3	23.2	25.5	32.1	37.1	34.7	24.7	50.2
Foreign medium and long-term loans — net (US$ billion)	—	0.1	0.5	1.2	0.9	1.0	2.0	
Foreign debts (US$ billion)	12.8	12.6	13.3	16.0	18.0	19.2	20.2	
Foreign debts/GDP (%)	41.7	40.5	38.7	41.0	40.5	37.7	33.2	
Debt payment/Export (%)	8.9	7.8	6.7	3.6	2.7	2.8	2.2	2.4
International reserves (US$ billion)	3.4	34	4.1	6.2	7.0	9.0	13.3	
% of population under poverty	37	32	28.9	...	19.5			14.6

Note: Including foreign investment in Vietnamese shares and bonds (for example US$750 million of sovereign bonds issued in 2005.
Sources: GSO of Vietnam and ADB.

Inflation

Infation rates in most countries in the world are generally higher than before, but still at managable levels, in contrast to what has happened in Vietnam. In major advanced economies, CPI increased from 2.2 per cent in 2006 to 3.5 per cent in 2007, while in other emerging Asian countries in the same period inflation rates increased from 2.2 per cent to 4.8 per cent.[5] However in Vietnam, overall CPI was 8.3 per cent in 2007 and jumped to 23.15 per cent in the first 10 months of 2008 as compared to the same period of 2007 (see Figure 2). In May 2008, inflation was at the highest level since 2000 — at 3.9 per cent compared to the previous month and at an annualized rate of 60 per cent. Inflation was obviously due to the substantial rate of growth in money supply and domestic credit during 2007, which was 48 per cent and 50 per cent respectively as compared to the year earlier (see Figure 3).

Inflation subsided in September and October of 2008 due to a dracronian reduction of credit growth — an increase of 18 per cent as compared to 30 per cent in the same period in 2007.[6]

In fact, inflation has been a threat to Vietnam since 2004, reaching quite a high level: 9.7 per cent in 2004, 8.8 per cent in 2005 and 7.5 per cent in 2006, all well above the rates prevailing in Vietnam's major trading partners, whether in Asia or in other regions, and became severe after Nguyễn Tấn Dũng became Prime Minister on 26 June 2006 with his policy of high growth. The recent runaway inflation was due to many factors: the policy to pump credit to the state-owned enterprises, the flood of capital inflows because of the exuberant whipping up of Vietnam's prospects by the world financial press, the grandiose economic plans of the people in power and the people with connections to seize the opportunity to make money without any restraint, and of course the incompetence and/or unwillingness of the Vietnamese authorities to deal with the problems in a timely manner. These issues are outside the scope of this article but it is necessary to draw attention to them as possible subjects for future research; they also serve as a background to discussion on the politics of these issues later in this essay.

Balance of Foreign Trade and Balance of Payments Problems Resulting from Inefficiency and Obsession with Growth

The problems of inflation and balance of payments seem to be the result of an obsession with achieving high rates of growth of GDP by building up state-owned general corporations and conglomerates. In order to achieve such GDP growth rates, capital investment (i.e. gross capital formation) reached an extremely high level.

FIGURE 2
Monthly Inflation Rates in Vietnam in 2007 and 2008
(January 2007 to October 2008)

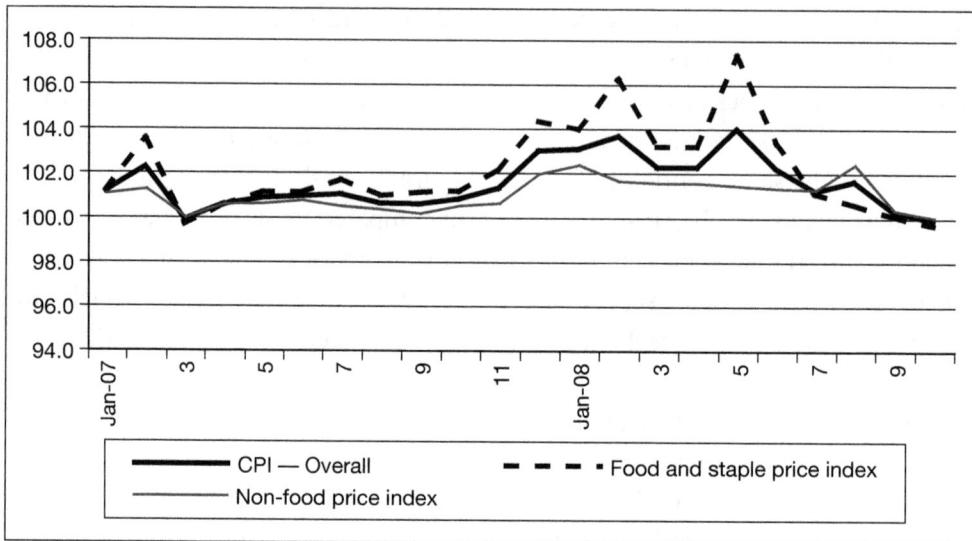

Source: GSO of Vietnam.

FIGURE 3
**Annual Rates of Increase in Money Supply (M2) and Domestic Credit
from 1993 to 2007**

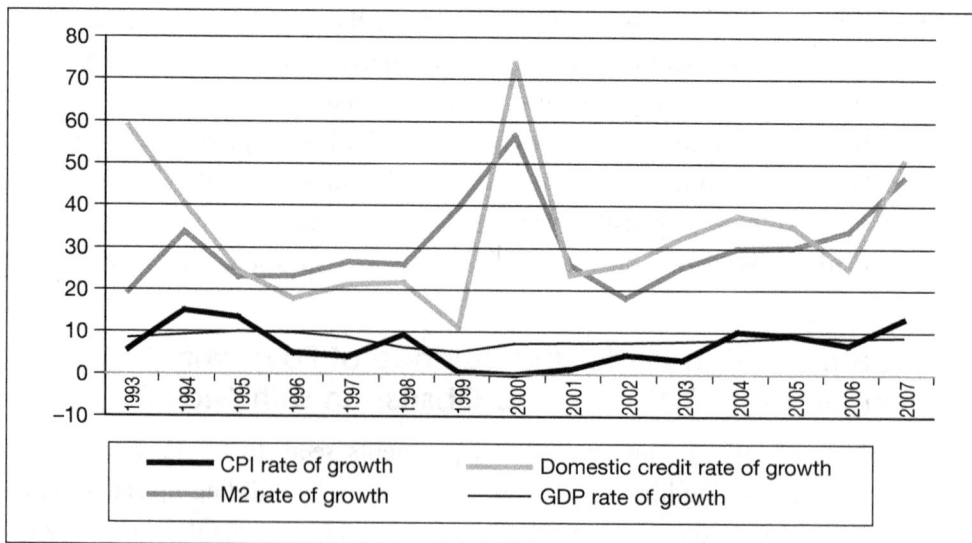

Sources: ADB and GSO of Vietnam.

It increased year by year from 29.6 per cent of GDP in 2000 to 41.7 per cent of GDP in 2007, a high rate rarely seen in the history of world economic development (see Table 2). However, unlike China and India which have similar high ratios of investment over GDP, Vietnam achieved lower GDP growth rates. Inefficiency is the natural explanation. The Incremental Capital Output (ICOR) ratio[7] of Vietnam was extremley high, on average at 5.2 (see Table 3) but with an average annual GDP growth of 7.7 per cent during the 2000–07 period. The ICOR ratio of China between 2001–06 was 3.9 with an average rate of GDP growth of 9.7 per cent. South Korea, with ICOR of 3.0, achieved an average annual rate of growth of 7.9 per cent during the 1961–80 period, which was a transition period to the status of a high income country. Thailand between 1981–95 achieved an average growth of 8.1 per cent with an ICOR of 4.1. Malaysia had a ICOR of 4.6 and average rate of growth of 7.1 per cent during the 1981–95 period.[8]

The trade balance reached a crisis point in late 2007 as a result of the high growth policy and inefficiency of state-owned enterprises in Vietnam. The trade deficit in 2007 was US$14 billion, making up 19.8 per cent of GDP (see Figure 4), more than triple the rate three years before. Without changes to government policy made in April by the Political Bureau of the Communist Party of Vietnam (PB CPV), which will be analysed later, the trade deficit could have reached US$30 billion at the end of 2008 and led to a balance of payment crisis, as the international reserves of Vietnam amounted to only US$22.0 billion, and especially when portfolio capital stopped flowing in because of the crash of the stock market. The statistics for the first nine months of 2008 show a sharp reduction of the trade deficit from over US$3 billion a month to below US$1 billion, probably through both a bureacratic imposition of restraints on imports of state-owned enterprises and a cut in credit growth. Even with the change in course, the trade deficit reached US$15 billion in the first nine months of 2008, and probably will reach at least US$18 billion at the end of the year, which is still a very high deficit. Table 4 gives more detailed information. It also shows that for many years, trade deficit has been incurred mainly by Vietnamese domestic producers because of the over-emphasis of growth by the government and over-investment by state-owned

TABLE 3
ICOR Ratios of Vietnam, 2001–07

	2001	2002	2003	2004	2005	2006	2007
ICOR ratios	5.14	5.28	5.31	5.22	4.85	5.04	5.38

Source: Data for calculation are from GSO of Vietnam.

FIGURE 4
Trade Balance 2000–08[9]

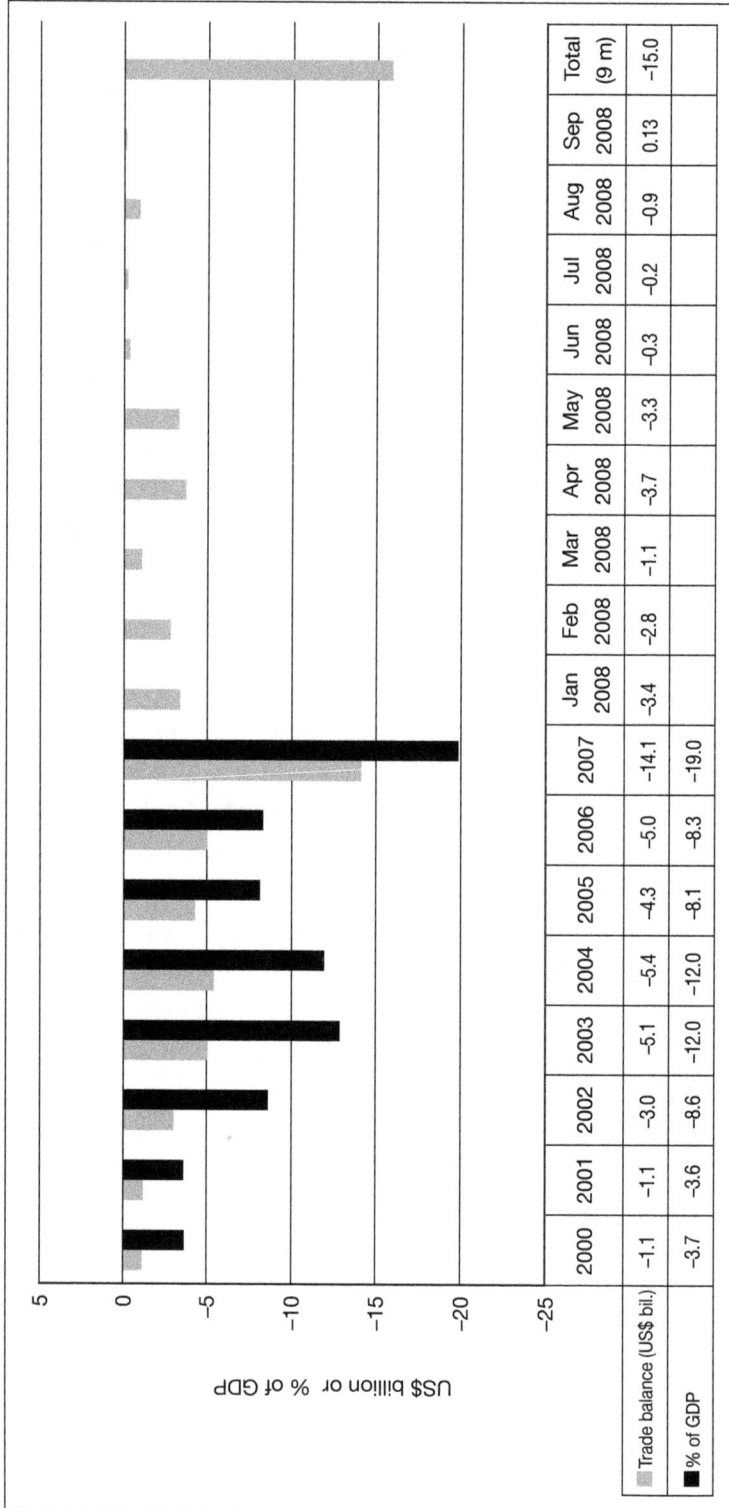

	2000	2001	2002	2003	2004	2005	2006	2007	Jan 2008	Feb 2008	Mar 2008	Apr 2008	May 2008	Jun 2008	Jul 2008	Aug 2008	Sep 2008	Total (9 m)
Trade balance (US$ bil.)	-1.1	-1.1	-3.0	-5.1	-5.4	-4.3	-5.0	-14.1	-3.4	-2.8	-1.1	-3.7	-3.3	-0.3	-0.2	-0.9	0.13	-15.0
% of GDP	-3.7	-3.6	-8.6	-12.0	-12.0	-8.1	-8.3	-19.0										

Sources: GSO for annual data. Ministry of Industry and Trade for monthly statistics.

TABLE 4
Exports and Imports of Merchandise in the First Ten Months of 2008

2008	Total merchandise exports	Exports of FDI	Total merchandise imports	Imports of FDI	Total trade balance	Trade balance of FDI
January	4,500	2,500	7,939	2.743	–3,439	2,497
February	2,243	2,617	5,059	4,006	–2,816	–1,389
March	6,283	2,441	7,394	2,102	–1,111	339
April	5,235	3,030	8,968	2,644	–3,733	386
May	5,137	2,852	8,457	3,472	–3,320	–620
June	6,297	3,480	6,653	2,366	–356	1,114
July	7,181	3,484	7,417	1,877	–236	1,607
August	6,445	3,241	7,399	2,753	–954	488
September	5,254	2,992	5,117	2,214	137	778
October	5,199	–8	5,662	2,787	–463	–2,795
Total for ten months	53,774	26,629	70,065	24,224	–16,291	2,405

Source: Ministry of Industry and Trade.

enterprises, not by FDI investors who have had a positive trade balance, even during the first nine months of 2008.

Foreign Direct investment (FDI)

FDI has in fact cushioned the impact of the recent crisis, and at one point it was used as a reason by the government to argue that there was no need to fear a balance of payment crisis as FDI would continue to pour in.

The government's Bureau of FDI reported that FDI capital approved in the first ten months of 2008 reached US$59.3 billion, six times higher than the figure reached in 2007. This seems to be unprecedented anywhere in the world, but a closer look shows that most projects are in real estate, high-class resorts, steel making and petroleum refining which add up to US$45 billion (see Table 5).[10] Many of these projects will certainly be postponed or cancelled due to the current international demand crisis and credit crunch.

The value of FDI implemented in the first ten months of 2008 was estimated to be US$7.1 billion.[11] It will probably reach at most US$10 billion for the year 2008.

For the year 2008 as a whole, assuming a trade deficit of US$18 billion, deficit for trade in services at US$3.0 billion and net payment of debt of US$2 billion,

TABLE 5
Analysis of Major FDI Projects Approved in 2008
(in US$ billion)

Project	Country	Approved Investment
A complex of steel mill, power plan and port in Ninh Thuan (Central Vietnam)	Malaysia	9.79
Port and steel mill in Ha Tinh (North Vietnam)	Taiwan	7.9
Petroleum refinery in Thanh Hoa (North Vietnam)	Japan and Netherlands	6.2
High class resort centre in Phu Yen (Central Vietnam)	Brunei	4.3
High lass resort centre in Vung Tau (South Vietnam)	Canada	4.23
Petroleum refinery in Vung Tau (South Vietnam)	Thailand	4
A complex of housing and international university centre in Ho Chi Minh City	Malaysia	3.5
Resort centre and golf course in Phu Quoc (South Vietnam)	British Virgin Island	1.6
Hotels and entertainment in Vung Tau (South Vietnam)	USA	1.3
Complex of hotels, high rises and software production in Ho Chi Minh City	Singapore	1.2
Financial centre in Ho Chi Minh City	Malaysia	0.93
Total		**44.95**

the total outflow will be US$23 billion. The inflow may include US$10 billion of FDI, US$6 billion of current transfers by overseas Vietnamese (estimated to remain the same as in 2007) and some uncertain but small amount of portfolio investment (since the stock market had crashed in early 2008), making a possible total inflow of US$16 billion. Thus the net capital outflow might be US$7 billion, which will cut down the international reserves of Vietnam by the end of 2008. It is clear that 2009 would require more cut back in capital investment to avoid a balance of payment problem.

Political Economy in Action

A Debate on Inflation

Vietnam suffered an extremely high rate of inflation in 2008, which is expected to reach 25 per cent. However, inflation had already been creeping up since the beginning of 2007 and became very serious from November of 2007 onward. It accelerated quickly and in December of 2007 and early 2008 reached monthly annualized rates of over 50 per cent. This was the time when Nguyễn Tấn Dũng, who became Prime Minister on 27 June 2006, could have demonstrated his economic expertise, instead of pushing on with his high growth strategy. At the November 2007 meeting of the National Assembly when some representatives expressed their concern about inflation while discussing the economic plan for 2008, the government insisted that the National Assembly approve the plan to attain 8.5–9 per cent rate of GDP growth in 2008 and not to set a ceiling for inflation at 7 per cent. Võ Hồng Phúc, Minister for Planning and Investment, argued on behalf of the Prime Minister that "high rate of growth always necessitates high inflation in any country" and that "if inflation was kept lower than 7 per cent the government would not be able to achieve high rate of GDP growth and would have to increase subsidies".[12] It is clear that the government was obsessed with high rate of GDP growth and was planning to allow state-owned enterprises to jack up prices to make profit or at least to reduce subsidies. No one in the government expressed any concern about the impact of inflation on the life of the working men and women during the National Assembly meeting. This was strange in the face of a growing number of labour strikes which increased from 71 in 2000 to 193 in the first 3 months of 2006, demanding higher wages to compensate for inflation.[13]

The inflation problem was flagged by this author in a 2004 paper,[14] analysing the reason why inflation was low during 2000–01 even with high growth in money supply and why that would not continue thereafter. The reason for low inflation was the reduction in money velocity due to a sharp jump in public confidence in money after the reform that put a stop to runaway inflation and led to wider use of money (monetarization). That effect would die down and lead to high inflation if high growth of money supply continued, and this was observed to begin in 2004. The IMF in a study in 2006[15] also concluded that "the main results [of the study] suggest that monetary developments have exerted an increasing influence on inflation in Vietnam over the last few years and that inflationary inertia plays a larger role in Vietnam than in other countries in the region". The influence of international food prices, especially rice, of which Vietnam is the world's second largest exporter, was undoubtedly a major factor in the double digit staple price index and food price index in 2004, but the fiscal policy also played up the demand side of the equation. Minimum wage was successively raised by 38 per cent in January 2003 and 20.7 per cent in October 2005, and another 28.6 per cent in October 2006, but it would affect only employees who have wages lower than the minimum wage. However, an increase in average civil service wages by an additional 30 per cent in October 2004 might have had stronger effect on inflation. Petroleum price was raised only in 2006, but the effect on Consumer Price Index (CPI) is small as it makes up only round 3 per cent of the CPI consumer basket. According to the same IMF paper referred to above, the correlation between inflation and monetary expansion seemed to be more prominent after the economic reform at the end of 1989, that liberated the economy from the rigid planned economy, took full effect. The major problem that needs further analysis and that distorted the relationship between prices and money happened between 1999 and 2000: a substantial increase of M2 as a percentage of GDP from 28.4 per cent in 1998 to 35.7 per cent in 1999 to 50 per cent in 2000, and as a result a significant increase in money supply of 35.7 per cent in 1999 and 50.5 per cent in 2000 did not increase CPI significantly. Leaving out these two years, the data from 2002 on shows that the correlation between M2 and CPI and particularly between credit growth and CPI was significantly higher, demonstrating the effect of monetary policy on inflation.[16]

Even with an acceleration of inflation to a very high level at the end of 2007 and through early 2008, policy-makers, continued to dismiss it — at first, as though it was a methodological error commited by the General Statistical Office of Vietnam, and later arguing that high inflation was induced by the increasingly higher prices of imported petroleum and major agricultural products such as rice.

Thus on 30 November 2007, Prime Minister Nguyễn Tấn Dũng issued Announcement 252/TB-VPCP[17] which contained instructions to various agencies to take action to combat inflation. The instructions included calls for more earnest efforts to achieve greater efficiency and higher output and more press relations activity to support government policies and avoid release of inaccurate information to the media that could affect popular psychology. These instructions were quite peculiar from the economic point of view. But worse, the announcement also included an order to the Ministry of Economics and Planning which supervises the General Statistical Office to "speedily revise the method of consumer price index in our country to be in line with international standards, especially with the structure of the basket of goods and services". This order was silently ignored after being questionned by critics.[18]

Prime Minister Nguyễn Tấn Dũng and his staff, however, continued to argue that his economic policy was on the right track. In an interview with the *Financial Times* correspondent Amy Kazmin before his trip to England on 2 March 2008, when questioned about his perceived overconfidence about the overall state of the economy in the face of a U.S. slowdown and the high inflation rate in Vietnam, he still strongly asserted that the economy would reach a growth of 8 to 9 per cent through his policy of expanding exports and increasing investment.[19] On 28 March 2008, the Minister for Finance Vũ Văn Ninh, in response to questions raised on the floor of the National Ambly on the causes of inflation said that inflation was inevitable in the context of world price increases, that "high inflation was not due to the government's bad management" but "was in fact due to our unrealistc forecast". This was obviously a misleading response. When prodded by a representative on why other countries in the region facing the same condition of commodity price increases did not suffer as high a rate of inflation as Vietnam, the Minister said "the situation is getting better due to our sound management".[20] After his testimony, inflation jumped from the annualized rate of 30 per cent in March and April to 60 per cent in May.

Prime Minister Nguyễn Tấn Dũng's economic policy was soon reversed by the Political Bureau of the CPV which issued on 4 April 2008 its conclusions on inflation (Conclusions 22/KL/TW).[21] [22] The document cited a number of objective causes of inflation, but concluded that the direct immediate cause was lax monetary and fiscal policy which had been tolerated for too many years, and had been particularly lax in 2007. The demand stimulation policy implemented in the face of deflation in the past had not been appropriately changed when facing inflation. According to the document "the top priority right now is to restrain inflation, restore macro-economic stability, keep economc growth at reasonable rate and in particular pay attention to social security, provide support and assistance to the poor and wage-earners suffering from inflation".[23] At least the Politburo took appropriate and timely action and the Prime Minister had no other choice but to go along. It is not clear who in the Politburo was the architect of that economic decision. Nevertheless, it is interesting to observe that even though the Politburo document was approved well in advance, its conclusions were made public only after the announcement on 17 April 2008 of government decision 10/2008/NQ-CP enumerating measures to combat inflation that was signed by the Prime Minister. The timing probably served as a face-saving device for the embattled Prime Minister. Central to the new policy is the restriction of credit and money supply, increase in the base interest rates and reduction of government capital expenses. After its first Conclusions, the Politburo has issued two more decisions to guide the government on economic policy. The second one was issued on 5 August 2008 (Decisions 25-KL/TW), and was followed by the decision of the government on measures to implement it on 29 August 2008 (Decision 20/2008/NQ-CP).[24] The third was issued after the meeting of the Central Committee of the CPV that took place from 2 to 4 October 2008.[25] The role of the Politburo of the CPV in economic policy was prominently mentioned in the statement of the October 2008 meeting of the Central Committee that also revealed the links between the dates of its instructions and those of the consequent decisions of the government to implement them.

During the 2008 mid-year meeting of the National Assembly, the target of GDP growth was officially reduced to 7.0 per cent at the request of the government but even that is not expected to be met. Thus, in the November 2008 Meeting, the target for 2009 had to be lowered to 6.5 per cent. The actions by the Politburo as discussed above have brought down inflation for now, as shown in the very low to negative month-to-month inflation in September and October 2008, and pulled back the balance of payments from the brink of crisis. Still more needs to be done to restore stability, particularly in restraining the flow of credit and government revenues to state-owned corporations and conglomerates so that their enormous but wasteful capital expenses can be cut down. This issue is discussed below.

A Debate on State-Owned Enterprises and Conglomerates[26]

The public sector as defined in Vietnam includes all activities of the government, from the state-owned corporations to all governmental institutions that provide public services such as social, education and health services, as well as police and defence services.

Since 2000 the public sector has generated in total around 4 million jobs, making up 9–10 per cent jobs in the economy. Within the public sector, the state-owned corporations employed 1.9 million employees in 2006, making up 4 per cent of the total employment in the country and 28.4 per cent of the corporate sector that also includes the domestic private and FDI corporations. The share of employment generated by the state-owned corporations is however declining not only in relative terms but also in absolute terms (see Table 6).

Although generating very little employment, the public sector has been allocated an inordinate share of investment funds by the government. The funds channelled to this sector have made up over 45 per cent of all investment in the economy, except for 2007 when the share was reduced unexpectedly to 40 per cent, due to the high inflow of foreign direct investment (see Figure 7). In 2007, with a GDP of US$71.5 billion, US$32.6 billion was earmarked for investment, out of which US$11.5 billion was for the non-state sector, and US$13 billion or 18 per cent of GDP for the public sector. Investment by state-owned corporations was not published, but given the estimate of government investment on infrastructure to be 7 per cent of GDP, the investment by state-owned corporations can be inferred to be 11 per cent of GDP.[28] Thus almost US$8.0 billion in 2007 was invested in the state-owned enterprises. This was an enormous amount compared to the investment amount of US$11.5 billion of the non-state domestic sector that encompasses all economic activities and all forms of organizations from corporations to household activities that are producing over 80 per cent employment for the economy.

As in the past, the state-owned enterprises continued to be a drag on the economy in 2008. Their performance has always been dismal when compared with non-state enterprises. Overall, the value of industrial production of all state enterprises, according to the Ministry of Planning and Investment, increased on a year-to-year basis only 6.4 per cent as compared to 29.5 per cent for the non-state domestic sector, and 17.9 per cent of the FDI sector during the first nine months of 2008.[29]

Most of the 5,970 state-owned enterprises are small or medium-sized. However, around 100 can be classified as general corporations and conglomerates and they have been showered with great favours by the government. Data on state-owned enterprises is still lacking, and when published by the General Statistical Office of Vietnam it is aggregated with government services. Thus any systematic research on state-owned enterprises will have to wait until statistics on them are made public. As a consequence of the lack of data, the analysis above and the analysis of state conglomerates below is based mainly on articles appearing in Vietnamese newspapers. Fortunately, data, though unsystematic, appeared recently in public as part of the criticism by National Assembly members of the failure of government economic policy and the defensive reactions of government officials.

TABLE 6

Employment in the Public Sector and State-Owned Enterprises

	2000	2003	2004	2005	2006	2007
Total employment (in thousands)	**37,610**	**40,574**	**41,586**	**42,527**	**43,339**	**44,172**
Employment in the public sector	9.3%	9.9%	9.9%	9.5%	9.1%	9.0%
Employment in private sector	89.7%	88.1%	87.8%	87.8%	87.8%	87.5%
Employment in incorporated enterprises (in thousands)	**3,538**	**3,933**	**5,770**	**6,238**	**6,722**	
State-owned enterprises (in thousands)	2,089	2,114	2,250	2,038	1,907	
State-owned enterprises	59.1%	53.8%	39.0%	32.7%	28.4%	
Domestic private enterprises	29.4%	33.8%	42.9%	47.8%	50.1%	
FDI enterprises	39.2%	36.8%	42.2%	41.0%	42.9%	
Change in employment in incorporated enterprises (in thousands)		**396**	**1,837**	**467**	**485**	
State-owned enterprises		26	136	-213	-131	
Domestic private enterprises		289	1,146	504	391	
FDI enterprises		82	556	176	225	

Sources: General Statistical Office and Central Institute for Economic Management, Vietnam.

TABLE 7

Share of Investment Funds and Gross Capital Formation by the Public Sector and the Economy[27]

	2001	2002	2003	2004	2005	2006	2007
Share of the public sector in national investment funds (%)	59.8	57.3	52.9	48.1	47.1	45.7	39.9
Share of investment funds in GDP (%)	35.4	37.4	39.0	40.7	40.9	41.5	45.9
Share of gross capital formation in GDP (%)	31.2	33.2	35.4	35.5	35.6	36.8	41.6

Source: General Statistical Office of Vietnam.

The role of state conglomerates in the current economic crisis in Vietnam is explored below.

It is easy to distinguish conglomerates and general corporations by the titles of "conglomerate" (tập đoàn) or "general corporations" (tổng công ty) added before the company names; but in reality they all act in a similar manner. By the end of 2007, according to a report of the Ministry of Finance, eight state-owned conglomerates (tập đoàn) and 70 state-owned general corporations (tổng công ty) together had an asset value of US$56 billion (almost 80 per cent of GDP), not including the value of land they are entitled to. Out of this asset value, the value of equity was US$25 billion (or VND 403 trillion); and the value of loans provided by state banks amounted to US$31 billion (or VND 500 trillion); the value of loans provided by international markets and the value of domestic bonds, however, is unknown. The conglomerates and the general corporations taken together have an average loans/equity ratio at two times which suggests that their business operations are risky. However, many companies among them are extremely risky, for example the loans/equity ratio is 42 for the General Corporation for Transport Construction No. 5 (Tổng Công ty Xây dựng Công trình Giao thông 5) and 22 for Vinashin.[30] [31]

So far there is no law to regulate the state-owned conglomerates nor is there a clear definition provided of a conglomerate, except that it is assumed to be a company that owns other legally independent companies. Although only eight companies are designated as conglomerates, the general corporations have been behaving as though they are conglomerates. They are establishing their own subsidiaries or associated companies. It was reported that these companies have already invested a total of US$7.3 billion (VND 117 trillion), 10 per cent of GDP, in fields that are not of their specialty, and in recent two quarters (the fourth quarter of 2007 and the first quarter of 2008), US$1.4 billion (VND23,000 billion) was invested in the stock market, real estate, financial services as well as for opening new associated commercial banks.[32]

The number of subsidiary enterprises proliferated immediately after the CPV agreed to allow their establishment on an experimental basis. Though the rates of return on these state-owned companies are not yet public information, a representative of the National Assembly in its recent meeting made a terse comment that "that money would have made a higher yield if deposited at a bank".[33]

It is easy to see that the main advantage of establishing such a conglomerate is to turn it into a pot of gold for all participants. A conglomerate can simply spin out numerous, in some cases a few hundred, subsidiary companies throughout the country, each of which gets the privilege, among others, of easy access to loans from state-owned banks and their own subsidiary banks, and more importantly, of obtaining the right to use public land at extremely low prices, most of the time at the expense of farmers whose lands under the right to use law are in the process taken back by the state. More importantly, the subsidiary company can then be "corporatized" (privatized but with a certain minimum share of the parent state enterprise), i.e. securitized and floated on the stock market. It is not rare that important share holders of the enterprises associated with the conglomerates are relatives of the managers of the conglomerates, loan providers and the local officials who may provide privileges. Conglomeration seems to be a legally recognized process to turn public property over to private hands.

A few examples reported in the Vietnamese press show how this has been done. The well-known high-tech zone in Ho Chi Minh City (Khu Công Nghệ Cao TPHCM) was set up in 2002, claiming 915 hectares between 2002 and 2004 from the farmers. Even before the project was approved by the Prime Minister in 2007, the then Chairman of the Board of Directors of the zone in 2006 leased 6,000 sq metres to a private company, Chip Sang, which turned out, when investigated by the National Deputy Chief Inspector on the basis of a report in the press, to be owned by the relatives (including wife, husband and sister) of the members of the Board of Directors of the zone, which is against the anti-corruption law.[34] (In general, the enterprise is set up in order to get a lease on an important piece of land from the state.) No legal action was taken against the Chairman as he was a former Deputy Mayor of Ho Chi Minh City. Other well known cases include an offspring of PetroVietnam (a conglomerate) which signed a US$17 million contract with an Ukrainian company which turned out to be fabricated without the knowledge of the Ukrainian company in order to pocket the money. The scheme was initiated by the Deputy Director General of PetroVietnam, with the involvement of the Chairman of the Board, who was later exempted from legal actions due to old age and other reasons.[35] A similar scheme was carried out by the Director of Ho Chi Minh City Power Company, a part of EVN (Vietnam Conglomerate of Electricity), who set up a private company that was supposed to provide high quality household electricity usage metres imported from Singapore, but were later found to be low grade locally-produced devices.[36]

Vinashin provides a rather typical example of conglomeration on which luckily more information is available than on other conglomerates due to the scrutiny of many national assemblymen during the November 2008 meeting of the National Assembly. Vinashin is a ship-building conglomerate, and known for the first successful issuance of sovereign bonds of US$750 million by the government in 2005. However, instead of focusing on what it might do best, and help build up the supporting industries for ship-building, Vinashin quickly spun out almost 100 associated companies all over the country, including a commercial bank and many financial, construction, trading and real estate companies.[37] When answering reporters' questions, Vinashin stated that its 2007 financial report audited by KPMG (which has not been made public), showed assets of VND 80,000 billion, roughly US$5.0 billion (not counting land rights), and an equity of VND 25,000 billion. The ratio of loans over equity was given as about two, which is much lower than the ratio of 22 reported by the Ministry of Finance.[38] This highlights the fact that no one seems to be on top of the financial situation of the conglomerates which have been put under the direct control of the Prime Minister (more on this point later). Also, according to Vinashin, it was a profit-making conglomerate, generating a profit of VND 700 billion in 2007. However, the rate of return was a mere 2.8 per cent. This rate of return was 50 per cent higher than that of 2006,[39] but would be much lower if the value of land provided by the state was also included.

Vinashin expected to reach sales of US$1.4 billion in 2008 of which US$400 million were already achieved with foreign customers during the first nine months of 2008.[40] The capital output ratio in this conglomerate based on this information seems to be very high and all the risks have been taken on by the Vietnamese government. Ship-building may be a good line of business for Vietnam to pursue, but its future prospects seem rather cloudy at best, judging from the information on management problems discussed above and the lack of technical skills discussed in a recent article in the *Peoples' Army Daily*.[41] According to this article, the ship-building industry produced under contract ships with tonnage capacity of 6,500 to 55,000 for a number of countries like Britain, South Korea and Japan, but unfortunately 90 per cent of inputs were provided by foreign suppliers. The same article noted that due to lack of engineers and skilled labour, ship repair services are almost non-existent; hence most of ships with 20,000 tonnes capacity or more have to be sent for repair abroad. From the information known to this author, in order to fulfill international contracts, Vinashin has to rely on foreign workers. To deliver on contracts already signed with foreign customers, the total capital of Vinashin will need to increase to at least US$6 billion which would require an additional loan of US$1.2 billion in 2008 during adverse market conditions because of the credit crunch.

Instead of focusing on improving its efficiency and profit rate Vinashin is planning to build a power plant and to enter into a US$10 billion joint venture with Lion Diversified Holding Behard of Malaysia to build a steel-making plant producing 10 million tonnes of steel a year, with most of the material inputs like low grade iron and coke imported. The steel-making plant should also be seen against the background that the demand for steel in Vietnam is now 6 million tonnes and is expected to reach 15 million tonnes in 2015, which can be easily satisfied by the four steel-making companies whose investment has already been approved.[42]

In response to the additional financial needs of Vinashin to fulfill the contracts with foreign customers, the Prime Minister's Office, on 22 September 2008, signed a public notice, No. 264/TB-VPCP, announcing the decision of Nguyễn Sinh Hùng, the Deputy Prime Minister, agreeing to a financial package of US$1.2 billion to Vinashin (which includes VND 3,000 billion in domestic bonds, VND 10,000 billion in domestic loans and US$400 million in foreign loans) and instructing the State Bank of Vietnam "to instruct the Bank for Construction and other commercial banks while implementing anti-inflation measures, must be flexible in providing credit to the ship-building industry". The public notice also announced that the Prime Minister will consider further the request of Vinashin to treat government foreign borrowing on behalf of Vinashin as state equity instead of government loans. This certainly would improve the dismal profit rate of Vinashin as interest and principal payment for loans would no longer be recorded as costs of doing business.[43]

The Vinashin example shows that Vietnam is eager to copy from South Korea the strategy to use conglomerates as the means to quicken economic development. However, there is an important difference between the Vietnamese copy and the South Korean original. The Korean one is fully private, while in the case of the Vietnamese one, the parent is public but the spun-out offspring are mostly joint stock corporations which, as analysed above, can easily be taken advantage of and in fact have already been manipulated by the people with political connections to enrich themselves. Not a few people have become extremely rich in the stock market and the real estate market using ill gotten money through their official connections, while the flare up of inflation due to the easy monetary policy of the government to the conglomerates has greatly impoverished the working people and thus outraged the public. It is an interesting topic for further study. But until now the blueprint for conglomerate development as well as the person or government agency accountable for it does not seem to be fully clear, which explains the anger of the representatives in the November 2008 meeting of the National Assembly[44] who demanded transparency in financial reporting of the conglomerates and general corporations, independent auditing and regular government reports on their activities.

What is known however is that the supervision is put directly under the Prime Minister himself. The demarcation of responsibilities between the Prime Minister and the Deputy Prime Ministers clearly points to this. Besides other responsibilities, the Prime Minister specifically assigned himself to be fully responsible for economic strategy and planning, government budget, monetary and credit policy which are normally expected, but also for strategic planning and development of the conglomerates and general corporations as shown in the Prime Minister's decision 1009/QĐ-TTg in 2006 and decision 1120/QĐ-TTg in 2007.[45] The allocation of responsibilities between the Prime Minister and the Deputy Prime Ministers was quite significant in the Vietnamese political context in the sense that not only no collective responsibility was mentioned but also the Deputy Prime Ministers "can in their assigned rights and responsibilities take initiative to decide; and inform promptly the Prime Minister with regards to significant, important and sensitive issues".

Interestingly, after the Political Bureau took over the economic decision-making, as discussed above, the role of supervising economic affairs was given to the Nguyễn Sinh Hùng, the Deputy Prime Minister responsible for economic affairs under the previous administration of Phan Văn Khải. This was done by Decision 1453/QĐ-TTg signed by the current Prime Minister on 8 October 2008. Without doubt, the role of the current Prime Minister has been declining because of the growing public discontent with the government's economic policies and its leaders' capability.[46] Criticism of the Prime Minister for his disregard for independent opinions and advice is shared widely by both foreign observers and Vietnamese. For instance, he disbanded for good the independent Advisory Group for Economic and Administrative Reforms to the Prime Minister set up long ago by his predecessors, apparently stating in private that it was unnecessary because he already had the Ministers and other government agencies as advisors. This was indirectly confirmed by his recent response to a representative at the November 2008 meeting of the National Assembly. When asked if the Prime Minister has any plan to have a dialogue with scientists and intellectuals, he responded that "I don't know what your definition of an intellectual is; I talk to them every day."[47] Jonathan Pincus of the United Nations Development Programme in Vietnam complained that "there is no shortage of people in Vietnam who understand the causes of the current economic instability and the steps needed to quell price inflation and restore stability to the markets" but "these people are not in a position to do much about it".[48]

At the November 2008 meeting of the National Assembly, many representatives demanded restrictions on the activities of the conglomerates, closer supervision of their investment decisions and regular government reports on their doings. Probably because of the success of anti-inflation measures issued by the Politburo of VCP and carried out by his government, the Prime Minister emphatically defended his policy of supporting the conglomerates at that meeting and stated that the policy was party policy which had been decided by the Party's Central Committee. His statement to the National Assembly needs to be quoted as it is important for understanding the current political economy of Vietnam. He stated that:

- "[We] need to be in unison in [our] understanding of the role of the state-owned enterprises in a socialist-oriented market economy, as affirmed by the resolution of the Central Committee of the [CPV] IX Congress";
- "The state economic sector must have a decisive role in maintaining socialism and stability in the economic, political and social development of the country";
- "… financial decision making of state-owned enterprises must be respected, … except in some activities where objective conditions demand monopoly; then a closely supervised mechanism is needed";
- "The efficiency of the state-owned enterprises must be judged comprehensively on all aspects: economic, political and social."

The only thing he seems to concede is that the conglomerates and general corporations may have to be restricted in their scope of activities and these activities must be supervised and made transparent — he therefore "welcomes the National Assembly to select the conglomerates and general corporations as a focus for general inspection in 2009".[49]

In a nutshell, the basic question is whether the focus on expanding the scope and the size of state enterprises would lead to a better managed economy and a more stable and just society. How valid is Nguyễn Tấn Dũng's theory that managers of state enterprises must be entrusted with independent authority in their investment and other business decision-making using taxpayers' money in order to maintain the socialist path of development? Or will the current policy simply allow the "organs of the Vietnamese state, political, administrative, and academic [to be] increasingly co-opted by interest groups who use them for self-enrichment and aggrandizement" as put by the Harvard Group report published in January 2008.[50] The removal of ministerial supervision of state-owned enterprises and the placement of the Prime Minister as the direct supervisor did not seem to work and instead created doubts about his leadership. Some foreign observers saw this as a conflict between the reform-minded Prime Minister and other conservative leaders,[51] but the analysis in this article does not lend support to that conclusion. In fact, his actions and his statements do not suggest that he is a man spearheading further economic reforms; rather they suggest personal concentration of power, at least through the building up of conglomerates. To be fair to the Prime Minister, this observation is still of a tentative nature and needs to be further verified.

Nevertheless, it is not possible to see any of his critics coming up with a better way of managing the state-owned conglomerates. Another option advocated by many is to expose all enterprises, either private or state-owned, to the same level competition, and take away all privileges given to state-owned enterprises. However, this option might be just wishful thinking in a country dominated by one political party.

Notes

[1]   Decisions of the regular meeting of the government on October 2008 (Nghị quyết phiên họp chính phủ thươwfng kỳ tháng 10 năm 2008), *Website of the Government of Vietnam.* <http://www.chinhphu.vn/portal/page?_pageid=33,167076&_dad=portal&_schema=PORTAL&pers_id=8093649&item_id=10795494&p_details=1>.

[2]   Minh Yến, "International reserve of Vietnam is US20.7 billion" (Dự trữ ngoại tệ của Việt Nam là 20,7 tỷ US), reporting the statement of Nguyễn Văn Giầu, Governor of the State Bank of Vietnam. 19 June 2008, *VTC* (Vietnam Television website) <http://www.vtc.vn/kinhdoanh/183352/index.htm>.

[3]   The GSO of Vietnam defined those under poverty as having an average monthly income in 2004 of 175,000 dong, which was only US$0.37 a day at the average exchange rate in 2004 (see *Vietnam Statistical Yearbook* 2006, table 303).

[4]   Lan Hương, "Inflation is distorting poverty criteria" (Lạm phát đang bóp méo chuẩn nghèo), *Dân Trí*, 11 September 2008. The article reported on a recent study by the Institute on Labor and Social Affairs of the Ministry of Labor, War Invalids and Social Affairs. The mentioned study is useful but not as reliable as those based on comprehensive surveys carried out by the General Statistical Office in 2000 and 2004. See <http://dantri.com.vn/kinhdoanh/Lam-phat-dang-bop-meo-chuan-ngheo/2008/9/250242.vip>.

[5]   IMF, *World Economic Outlook* (WEO), October 2008, Chapter 2.

[6]   Thanh Tuyền, "Money pumping to get the market recovered" (Bơm tiền vực dậy thị trường), *Tuổi trẻ*, 29 October 2008 <http://www.tuoitre.com.vn/Tianyon/Index.aspx?ArticleID=285359&Channel1ID=87>.

[7]   ICOR is capital/output ratio indirectly calculated by dividing change in capital over change in output, all in constant prices.

[8]   These ratios are calculated on the basis of data compiled by the UN Statistical Division <http://unstats.un.org/unsd/snaama/introduction.asp>.

9   Annual data published by the General Statistical Office of Vietnam (GSO) include trade in services, while monthly data reported by customs do not include trade in services and therefore these data are not fully compatible, but they are useful in showing the magnitude of the deficit in 2008. They also show that the threat of a full blown balance of payment crisis declined as the deficit decreased drastically during the last few months of the year 2008.

10 Lê Nguyên Minh, "Increasing FDI needs to focus on capital disbursement" (Thu vốn nước ngoài trọng tâm vẫn là giải ngân vốn), *Tuổi trẻ*, 5 November 2008 <http://www. tuoitre.com.vn/Tianyon/Index.aspx?ArticleID=286441&ChannelID=11>.

11 The value of implemented FDI reported by the GSO of Vietnam was US$9.1 billion, but on the basis of past experience, 30 per cent of this amount was contributed by Vietnamese partners; thus only US$7.1 billion is estimated to be FDI as internationally defined. See Tổng cục Thống kê, "Socio-economic situation in October 2008" (Tình hình kinh tế xã hội 10 tháng 2008) <http://www.chinhphu.vn/portal/page?_pageid=33,5913832&_dad=portal&_schema=PORTAL&item_id=10213067&thth_details=1>.

12 Vân Anh, "The National Assembly approved GDP growth target of 8.5–9%" (Quốc hội thông qua chỉ tiêu tăng trưởng 8,5 đến 9%), *Vietnamnet*, 12 November 2007 <http://vietnamnet.vn/chinhtri/2007/11/754394/>.

13 Vũ Quang Việt, "Labor-enterprises relationship after joining WTO" (Quan hệ lao động và doanh nghiệp thời mở cửa làm thành viên WTO), Diễn Đàn, 13 March 2007 <http://www.diendan.org/viet-nam/vqv_laodong/?searchterm=%22v%C5%A9%20quang%20vi%E1%BB%87t%22>.

14 Vũ Quang Việt, "Inflation in Vietnam nowadays and the need to re-examine the monetary theory" (Lạm phát ở Việt Nam hiện nay và sự cần nhìn lại lý thuyết tiền tệ). *Thời Đại Mới*, no. 3, November 2004 <http://www.tapchithoidai.org/>.

15 IMF, *Vietnam: Selected Issues, IMF Country Report* no. 06/422, November 2006, p. 5.

16 IMF, ibid, p. 19.

17 "The Prime Minister manages market and price at end of 2007" (Thủ tướng điều hành giá cả thị trường cuối năm 2007", *Vietnam News Agency*, reported on <http://vietnamnet.vn/xahoi/2007/11/757597/>.

18 Vietnam News Agency, "The Prime Minister gave orders on price management at end of 2007" (Thông tấn xã Việt Nam, "Thủ tướng chỉ đạo điều hành giá cả thị trường cuối năm 2007"). *Vietnamnet* <http://vietnamnet.vn/xahoi/2007/11/757597/>. Of course, there is nothing wrong with the method of calculating consumer price index (CPI) as practiced in Vietnam. In response to the Prime Minister's order, the author has written an article to analyse the method used in Vietnam and confirmed that there was nothing wrong with the method or with the basket of goods and services used. Somehow, the Prime Minister was misinformed that CPI issued by the General Statistical Office of Vietnam (GSO) had increased much faster than it should have

because the share of food and staples consumed in Vietnam and used by the GSO in its calculation was considered to be erroneously high and therefore exaggerated the increase in overall CPI when food prices increased faster than other products. The author confirmed that the share of food and staples in Vietnam at 42 per cent was quite likely at par with those of other countries like India (48.5 per cent), the Philippines (46.6 per cent) and Thailand (36 per cent), and more importantly, the food share in Vietnam was based on very detailed and costly surveys taking place every five years. Another interference with statistics was the announcement of the Ministry of Finance of a new index that reduced price increases by 2 per cent when compared with the old method of calculation. This new index is based on average CPI index for the period (namely, 11 months of 2007 as compared to the same period of 2006). This method is in reality not new as the GSO has regularly used it to compile the price index for the purpose of deflating current consumption (part of GDP) that is spread out throughout the year but is totalled up at the end of the year. It is important to point out that in order to monitor inflation, it is necessary to monitor monthly changes in commodity prices by comparing prices of a given month to a previous month and/or to the same month of the previous year, which is the essence of the old method. See Vũ Quang Việt, "Is Vietnamese statistics being de-professionalized?" (Phải chăng thống kê Việt Nam đang bị phi chuyên môn hóa?), *Diễn Đàn*, 2 December 2008 <http://www.diendan.org/viet-nam/phai-chang-thong-ke-viet-nam-111ang-bi-phi-chuyen-mon-hoa/>. This article was also published in *Lao Dong*, a Vietnam daily.

[19] Amy Kazmin, FT interviews: Nguyen Tan Dung, *Financial Times*, 2 March 2008 <http://us.ft.com/ftgateway/superpage.ft?news_id=fto030220081747550984>.

[20] Hồng Khánh, "High inflation is not due to government poor management" (Lạm phát cao không phải do chính phủ điều hành kém), *VNexpress*, 27 March 2008 <http://vnexpress.net/Vietnam/Xa-hoi/2008/03/3BA00BBC/?q=1>.

[21] Sài Gòn Giải phóng, 5 March 2008 <http://www.sggp.org.vn/kinhte/2008/4/148112/> or Ministry of Foreign Affairs <http://www.mofa.gov.vn/vi/nr040807104143/nr040807105039/ns080407130819?b_start:int=30>.

[22] The implied criticism of Nguyễn Tấn Dũng policy by the Political Bureau of the Communist Party of Vietnam was first raised in an overseas Vietnamese website by Âu Dương Thệ, "Political Bureau criticized Nguyễn Tấn Dũng for his anti-price policies" (Bộ chính trị chỉ trích Nguyễn Tấn Dũng trong việc chống lạm phát), *Đàn Chim Việt*, 15 April 2008, reposted on <http://www.viet-studies.info/kinhte/BoChinhTri_ChiTrich.htm>.

[23] Sài Gòn Giải phóng, 5 March 2008, ibid.

[24] Government Decision, Nghị quyết số 20/2008/NQ-CP ngày 29 tháng 8 năm 2008, *The Electronic Journal of the Communist Party of Vietnam* <http://www.cpv.org.vn/tiengviet/kinhte/details.asp?topic=5&subtopic=410&leader_topic=965&id=BT890851128>.

25 Communiqué on the 8th Meeting of the Central committee of the X Congress, by the Vietnam News Agency TTXVN as reprinted in *Nông thôn Việt Nam* <http://www. kinhtenongthon.com.vn/Story/thoisuchinhtri/tintuc/2008/10/15098.html>.

26 The issue has been partly discussed in Vũ Quang Việt, "Conglomerates: economic implications and danger ahead" (Tập đoàn tài chính: ý nghĩa kinh tế và nguy hiểm trước mắt), *Kinh tế Sài Gòn*, 31 August 2008 <http://www.thesaigontimes.vn/Home/ thoisu/sukien/9208/>.

27 Investment fund in the Vietnamese concept is not the same as the internationally accepted concept of gross capital formation. Investment fund also includes expenses that do not increase the volume of fixed assets and therefore are excluded from gross capital formation by the General Statistical Office of Vietnam. Thus Table 7 shows both values.

28 From Table 15, IMF, *Vietnam Statistical Appendix*, December 2007, capital expense of the government in 2007 was 8 per cent of GDP. Government capital funding for state-owned enterprises from the 2007 government budget was planned at VND 10,905 billion or at 1 per cent of GDP. Thus investment on infrastructure was 7 per cent of GDP. As public sector investment totalled 18 per cent of GDP, investment by the state-owned enterprises would be 11 per cent of GDP.

29 Government website <http://www.chinhphu.vn/portal/page?_pageid=33,5913832&_ dad=portal&_schema=PORTAL&item_id=8969663&thth_details=1>.

30 Nguyễn Quang A, "Listening to the conglomerates" (Nghe các tập đoàn lớn nói), *Lao Động*, 4 May 2008 <http://www.laodong.com.vn/Home/Nghe-cac-tap-doan-lon- noi/20084/86666.laodong>.

31 <http://www.na.gov.vn/htx/Vietnamese/?Newid=23769> website of the Vietnam National Assembly reporting on discussion on economic and social affairs.

32 Nguyễn Trung, "Reform the conglomerates: Dare to?" (Cải cách tập đoàn nhà nước và một chữ dám), *Vietnamnet*, 10 September 2008 <http://www.tuanvietnam.net/vn/ sukiennonghomnay/4757/index.aspx>.

33 Nguyễn Linh, "National Assembly has plans to regulate the conglomerates" (Quốc hội có kế hoạch giám sát tập đoàn), an interview with Nguyễn Đức Kiên, Vice Chairman of the National Assembly and Member of its Economic Committee, *Vietnamnet*, 29 October 2008 <http://vietnamnet.vn/chinhtri/2008/10/810727/>.

34 "Multiple wrong-doings at the High Tech Zone of Hochiminh City" (Nhiều sai phạm tại khu Công nghệ cao TP.HCM), *Vietnamnet*, 2 April 2008 <http://vietnamnet.vn/ cntt/2008/04/776399/>.

35 "Uncovering the scheme of corruption at the Petroleum General Corporation" (Bóc trần đường dây tham nhũng lớn ở Tổng công ty Dầu khí), *Việt Báo*, 3 June 2004 <http://vietbao.vn/An-ninh-Phap-luat/Boc-tran-duong-day-tham-nhung-lon-o-Tong-cong- ty-Dau-khi/10865005/218/>.

36 Phạm Điền, "Director of Electricity Company of Hochiminh City suspended" (Giám đốc công ty điện lực TP. HCM bị tạm đình chỉ công tác), *radio rfa*, 19 July 2005

<http://www.rfa.org/vietnamese/in_depth/DirectorLeMinhHoangSuspended_PDien-20050719.html>.

37   It is interesting to observe that the website of Vinashin in English lists only a very few associated companies, but the Vietnamese version lists almost a hundred associated companies, including many with titles linked to ship-building industry, but many are not, like Habubank (a joint stock commercial bank) and other financial, construction, high tech companies, etc. website of Vinashin, see <http://www.vinashin.com.vn/members.aspx>.

38   Nguyễn Quang A, *Lao Động*, 4 May 2008 <http://www.laodong.com.vn/Home/Nghe-cac-tap-doan-lon-noi/20084/86666.laodong>, ibid.

39   Anh Quân, "Government does not force bank lending to Vinashin" (Chính phủ không buộc ngân hàng cho Vinashin vay), *Kinh tế Việt Nam,* 21 October 20008, interview with the Chairman of Vinashin, Phạm Thanh Bình <http://www.vneconomy.vn/20081021090134203P0C5/chinh-phu-khong-buoc-ngan-hang-cho-vinashin-vay!.htm>.

40   This is based on a fax response to Port News Information, see <http://crewing.biz.ua/modules.php?op=modload&name=News&file=article&sid=20238>. In the same interview with the chairmen of Vinashin mentioned above, a higher values of sales, at US$2.5 billion and an export of US$532 were given to the Vietnamese press, see *Kinh tế Việt Nam* (21 October 20008), interview with the chairman of Vinashin above.

41   Vũ Văn Đức, "Vietnam's Ship-building industry: first success, difficulties ahead", (Công nghiệp đóng tầu Việt Nam: thành công bước đầu, khó khăn trong tương lai), *Quân Đội Nhân dân*, 15 November 2008 <http://www.qdnd.vn/qdnd/baongay.kinhte.chinhsachkinhte.46672.qdnd>.

42   Trần Thủy "Ship-building conglomerate asks for investments in electricity and steel production again" (Tập đoàn tầu thủy lại xin đầu tư vào điện, thép), *Vietnamnet*, 9 September 2008 <http://vietnamnet.vn/kinhte/2008/09/802793/>.

43   The same analysis has been mentioned in Vũ Quang Việt, "Different circumstances different solutions" (Tinh hình khác giải pháp khác), *Kinh tế Sàigòn*, 6 November 2008 <http://www.thesaigontimes.vn/epaper/TB-KTSG/So46-2008(934)/20855/>.

44   Typical was the statements of the Deputy Chairman of the Economic Committee Lê Quốc Dung, such as "conglomerates establishment are spreading without any restraint and invest all over the places"; "[we need] to rectify the conglomerates by both economic and administrative measures"; "First, limit their opening of more business, second examine the soundness of their ventures [resorts and banks], and stop them if unsound, even if these actions are painful." See "No support of VND4,100 billion for Petroleum Conglomerate" (Không hỗ trợ cho tập đoàn dầu khí 4,100 tỷ đồng", *Vienamnet*, 8 November 2008 <http://vietnamnet.vn/chinhtri/2008/11/812591/>.

[45]   The title in Vietnamese, "Quyết định về phân công của Thủ tướng và Phó Thủ tướng" signed respectively on 28 July 2006 and 24 August 2007.

[46]   See the reactions of the public in Vietnam in Long S. Le, "Vietnam in denial over economic woos", *Far Eastern Economic Review*, October 2008.

[47]   "No need to advertise when having dialogue with intellectuals" (Đối thoại với trí thức không cần treo bảng, Dân trí, 13 November 2008 <http://dantri.com.vn/Sukien/Doi-thoai-voi-tri-thuc-khong-can-treo-bang/2008/11/259891.vip>.

[48]   See previous reference.

[49]   Toàn văn báo cáo của Thủ tướng Nguyễn Tấn Dũng (the full speech of the Prime Minister), *Lao Động*, 13 November 2008.

[50]   See Long S. Le, "Vietnam in denial over economic woos", *Far Eastern Economic Review*, October 2008.

[51]   Roger Mitton, "Vietnam: Behind the Journalists' Jailins", *Asia Sentinel*, 24 October 2008 <http://www.asiasentinel.com/index.php?option=com_content&task=view&id=1 500&Itemid=188>.

www.ingramcontent.com/pod-product-compliance
Lightning Source LLC
Chambersburg PA
CBHW061831260326
41914CB00005B/955